THE PRACTICE OF CREATIVE WRITING

A GUIDE FOR STUDENTS

Nonfiction

Drama

Comics

THE PRACTICE OF CREATIVE WRITING

A GUIDE FOR STUDENTS

HEATHER SELLERS

Hope College

Bedford/St. Martin's

Boston ◆ New York

For Bedford/St. Martin's

Executive Editor: Leasa Burton
Senior Developmental Editor: Ellen Darion
Senior Production Editor: Deborah Baker
Production Supervisor: Andrew Ensor
Marketing Manager: Adrienne Petsick
Editorial Assistant: Melissa L. Cook
Copyeditor: Adam Groff
Text Design: Nesbitt Graphics
Cover Design: Kim Cevoli
Cover Art: Spare Parts #2 (casein on wood) 2003 by Bill Mead. Photo by Ben Caswell.
Composition: Stratford/TexTech
Printing and Binding: R. R. Donnelley & Sons Company

President: Joan E. Feinberg
Editorial Director: Denise B. Wydra
Editor in Chief: Karen S. Henry
Director of Marketing: Karen Melton Soeltz
Director of Editing, Design, and Production: Marcia Cohen
Managing Editor: Elizabeth M. Schaaf

Library of Congress Control Number: 2007922531

2   1   0   9   8   7
f   e   d   c   b   a

For information, write: Bedford/St. Martin's, 75 Arlington Street, Boston, MA 02116
(617-399-4000)

ISBN-10: 0-312-43647-5
ISBN-13: 978-0-312-43647-6

Acknowledgments

Brian Arundel. "The Things I've Lost." Reprinted with permission of the author.
Beth Bachmann. "Colorization." Reprinted with permission of the author. www.blackbird.vcu.edu/v4m1/poetry
Marianne Boruch. "Bad Cello." From *Poems: New and Selected* by Marianne Boruch. Copyright © 2004. Reprinted by permission of Oberlin College Press.

Acknowledgments and copyrights are continued at the back of the book on pages 402–04, which constitute an extension of the copyright page. It is a violation of the law to reproduce these selections by any means whatsoever without the written permission of the copyright holder.

PREFACE
FOR INSTRUCTORS

Any student can learn to write by going straight for the good stuff: the stuff that really matters, the stuff that captures the reader's attention and imagination. *The Practice of Creative Writing* helps students develop the habits and skills that real writers use—the strategies that produce good writing in any genre and that make it possible for students to focus and generate lots of material and discover what they really want to say.

For years, I taught creative writing the way it had been taught to me, taking my students through all the prescribed lessons on character, voice, point of view, theme, line breaks, meter, and symbol. But after a while, I felt like a fraud in the classroom; I didn't work this way myself. The fiction and poetry and essays I published I created by a very different process: I always started with *an image*, exploring a specific, grounded moment in time on a very physical level. I devoted a lot of energy to what is called "creative concentration." Also, I didn't ever think consciously about point of view or symbol and theme as I did when teaching in the literature classroom—writing poetry and plays and narrative was a lot more like going for a long run, dreaming, watching a movie, or the kind of focused imaginative play we entered into as kids. I have always found my way as I work, concentrating inside of an image. In interviews with artists and writers, I see this very same sort of method described again and again.

When we make something, whether it's a three-point shot from outside or a poem, we have to figure out what to do with our heads, where to put our doubts, our analytical minds, our fears. We have to get out of our own way. One of my students, both a writer and a runner, describes it this way. "You don't really *want* to go for a run or start writing. You have to kind of trick yourself," Bethany Katerberg says. "But then you start, and after a while this thing kicks in. By the time you are done, you feel great, inside and out. You can't imagine *not* having done this. I think it's mostly a head game."

In writing this textbook, I paid close attention to this state of mind. I researched creativity, play, and the "zone" athletes talk about when every shot swishes, when the goal just vacuums up the ball. At the outset of any writing class, teaching students how to *focus*, how to work while distracted, what to concentrate on (sensory visual images—the lifeblood of creative writing), seems more important and more helpful than anything else. Next, instead of separating the genres and learning their conventions, we bring to the forefront the strategies and techniques common to all good creative writing. Once the student is hooked into the writer's world and habits, she concerns herself with what makes a poem a poem, a story a story. Images, intensity, wisdom, and energy first, and genre conventions follow.

But first, in this book, students teach themselves how to play. They warm up. They work out. They learn how to locate their weak areas, and practice a little every day. Wind sprints. Scales. Exercises. And as students practice, they get better at what they're good at, and grow a capacity for awareness based on a habit of *looking more closely*. They build skills that help them become fearless observers of the world and people around them, all in the service of the reader's experience—they learn how to take readers, with words, through emotions and feelings that really matter. This approach to the creative writing classroom privileges the writer's way of knowing, the writer's way of seeing, and makes it possible for a wide range of students to come into the room and play.

The Practice of Creative Writing helps students move from writing "to express feelings" to writing to shape and reflect meaningful human experience. This book is for all students: the general education student in need of an arts class, a writing-intensive course, or both; the education/language arts student who needs a writing class for his major in elementary or secondary education; and the student who loves writing, is good at it and always has been, and who will go on to take more writing workshops, delving into specific genres. This book addresses all three types of students by immersing them in the writing process and showing them that the move from personal expression to powerful creative writing is thrilling and vigorous and rewarding. The book assures students: *Of course it takes time to learn to write well, but you can do this, and it's worth the trouble to try.*

AN ACCESSIBLE, SUPPORTIVE APPROACH FOR BEGINNING WRITERS

The Practice of Creative Writing shows students that things they already know how to do—observe, concentrate, practice—are the very skills they can use to become better writers. Throughout the book, students produce generative seed material and learn how to mine that material for images that will live and breathe.

In Part One, students begin to look at the world as subject matter, to see on the sensory, visual, imagistic level. Chapter 1, Finding Focus, introduces students to the work that practicing, published writers do—attending to focus and concentration, using daily practice and rituals, and learning to manage doubt, fear, distraction, and procrastination. All writers have to deal with these psychological aspects of the writing process, and *The Practice of Creative Writing* provides practical advice for handling challenges to creative concentration.

Chapter 2, Writing and Reading, shows students the moves writers make to draw readers in, hold their attention, and transport them to another world. Student writers have to learn to shift from focusing on the *self* to focusing on the *reader.* The reader's experience of the text is what counts. Creative writing isn't "personal expression." It's *for* the reader, and it exists to activate *her* feelings, her emotions. As students read published authors and their own peers, they develop a vocabulary that lets them talk about technique. As they become more articulate about what creative writing can do, how it works, and why, their own writing ability improves. Throughout the text, guided examples show students exactly how writers accomplish their goals; students then apply this instruction to the reading selections, paying close attention to how language works in multiple genres.

A FOCUS ON SIX STRATEGIES COMMON TO ALL GOOD WRITING

Part Two of *The Practice of Creative Writing* teaches students to focus on the essentials—vigor, depth, freshness, language, movement, the revelation of something interesting and important, sharp clear observations, and a good ear. The six strategies addressed in Part Two are the nuts and bolts of all good writing, regardless of genre. Successful creative writing always has energy, tension, and structure; it is always grounded in images; and it always creates patterns and suggests insight. These central chapters show how the strategies work individually and together to produce good creative writing: writing that is rewarding to create and rewarding to read and reread. Strategies are presented in order of difficulty, so students can build facility with them and layer the techniques to produce more sophisticated pieces as the course progresses. In each strategy chapter, a concept essential to good creative writing is introduced, and specific examples of what to do and what *not* to do are provided.

Then, the student reads—a poem, a short story, part of a screenplay, a short nonfiction piece—in order to increase awareness of how the strategy functions, what technique a writer uses in order to deepen the power of the work. For example, in Chapter 3, the student learns that creating work that has energy requires attention to time, language, leaps and gaps, and the shape of actual experience (rather than rendering thoughts and passive observations). In the chapter on tension, the student learns how to manipulate the elements of writing to intensify their power; in the pattern chapter, the student practices layering techniques used by professionals as she works with more sophisticated subject matter. Structure is another critical strategy writers use. This important topic is divided into two chapters, the first focusing on the "bits" that make up writing—words, sentences, lines—and the second focusing on how some fun and challenging "recipes"—pantoums, sestinas, three-act narratives—help students discover they have more to say than they thought.

Revision is another way to improve writing, and *The Practice of Creative Writing* presents revision as something writers do throughout the writing process, not an activity they quickly tack on at the end. Revision *is* writing. In order to give students more of a stake in this process, revision is presented as a stepping stone to bringing their best work to a larger community, whether that community is their class, the neighborhood coffeehouse, or a school or local publication. Revision is a skill built on close reading, so students are referred back to the early chapters on reading as writers as they learn to assess their own work and that of their peers by way of taking pieces further. Practical prompts and checklists aid students in differentiating revising and editing and encourage higher levels of reader awareness.

IMAGINATIVE WRITING ACTIVITIES

Practice activities throughout the book—suitable for in-class writing, small groups, journaling, or homework assignments, helping students try a wide range of approaches and building new skills—can also be a source for rough drafts for pieces that will be developed and extended. Practices build on each other, and the student is encouraged to work as professional writers do, returning to practices from previous weeks, combining and layering. Students learn to use image-listing as a way to generate their own writing prompts; other practices give direction for writing better dialogue, increasing the tension in lines of poetry, and using the senses to create depth in nonfiction. Longer, classroom-tested Projects—suitable for workshops, portfolios, larger assignments—ask students to relate and link what they have learned in previous chapters and guide them through full-length pieces. Workshop sections in each strategy chapter provide guidance for peer response and take students through the revision process, step by step. Writers' Tips and checklists also help students revise their own work and make constructive suggestions to peers. Thus, practices can become projects, which can ultimately be revised to create a portfolio, a chapbook, or a live reading at the end of the course.

In sum, Practices, Projects, Workshops, Writers' Tips, and checklists all provide opportunities for writing at every stage in the process. They help students develop productive writing habits and work with the strategies. They also give students the experience and confidence to build up to finished pieces for publication or public reading.

COMPELLING CONTEMPORARY READINGS IN ALL GENRES

The readings in the book are vibrant, lively, and popular among students, and include works by contemporary authors such as Ethan Canin, Rick Moody, Jamaica Kincaid, Michael Chabon, Richard Rodriguez, Art Spiegelman, Rita Dove, Lorraine López, Akhil Sharma, Michael Cunningham, Lorrie Moore, and Raymond Carver. A wonderfully wide range of work is presented, including short stories, flash fiction, essays, memoir, poems, prose poems, comics, monologues, and drama. Most importantly, every piece included represents aspects of the six strategies; each piece can be used to illustrate energy, image, tension, pattern, insight, and structure, and each chapter automatically encourages review of previously introduced concepts. Always, the focus in *The Practice of Creative Writing* is on helping students focus tightly on what makes good writing good, no matter what form the writer chooses.

In the introductory course, students benefit from seeing a wide range of voices, possibilities, themes, and styles. And, for many students, a concept is made clear only when presented in several forms — after reading for images or tension or energy in a play, a poem, and a story, suddenly the technique is crystal clear. Cross-training works, and students like it. Studying formal poetry strengthens the fiction writer's ear for rhythm; reading a monologue or a play teaches dialogue for prose writers; and, a nonfiction writer's use of insight helps student writers see the world more astutely.

ADDITIONAL SUPPORT FOR TEACHERS AND STUDENTS

The Web site for *The Practice of Creative Writing* includes additional Practices and Projects, suggestions for further reading, and downloadable Writers' Tips and checklists for students to use in peer response groups and for self-guided revising and editing. The book's Web site also links to LitGloss and LitLinks, convenient online reference tools featuring definitions of more than 200 literary terms and information about many authors who appear in this book, including Gwendolyn Brooks, Raymond Carver, Billy Collins, Timothy Liu, Lorrie Moore,

Katherine Norris, Naomi Shihab Nye, Sharon Olds, Gary Soto, James Tate, and Dylan Thomas.

For instructors, the Web site also offers sample syllabi and advice on using the Practices and Projects. Students and teachers are encouraged to contact me at sellers@hope.edu, with additional assignments, teaching ideas, and samples of their own work. My personal Web site is www.heathersellers.com. I look forward to hearing from you and your students.

ACKNOWLEDGMENTS

First and foremost, I am indebted to David Myers for his unflagging support from the outset. His confidence in my work and his mentoring have been invaluable to me. This book exists because of him. It is dedicated to Janet Burroway, who taught me how writing and teaching work together, why each matters, how to think about their sources, and what feeds both the classroom and the page.

Without my students, I would be lost. I am most grateful to the following Hope College student research assistants, who helped improve this book immensely all along the way: the delightful Chantelle Kramer, Anne Hoekstra, and Lauren Ericks—thank you! Outstanding student writers who assisted me as I worked on this textbook are Christian Piers, Bethany Katerberg, Kristin Olson, Matthew Baker, Elena Valle, Katherine Yanney, Nicole Brace, Laura Woltag, Katy Bray, Sarah Wright, Audrey Young, Dana Lamers, Krista Mehari, Jordan Wolfson, Katelyn Konyndyk, and Jennifer Stults. You are more junior colleagues than students; I am so grateful for your work. Lisa Lampen and Myra Kohsel provided office support—thank you for the extra help, your patience, and all the tape and #56 cartridges.

I am indebted to colleagues Deb Sturtevant, Jackie Bartley, Jack Ridl, Alfredo Gonzales, David Klooster, Susanna Childress, Beth Trembley, Barbara Mezeske, Bill Kooistra, and Jenny Krasner. Thank you for encouraging me in all kinds of helpful ways. Ann Turkle, Jesse Lee Kercheval, Lorraine López, Dinty Moore, Gingah Knuth, Robert Olen Butler, Mark Jarman, Michael Martone, Judith Ortiz Cofer, and Debra Wierenga—you are colleagues and teachers who show me what is possible and I am always grateful for your work.

At Bedford/St. Martin's, Leasa Burton and Ellen Darion have given this project extensive, excellent attention, and I am deeply indebted to them for all their efforts. Joan Feinberg, Denise Wydra, Karen Henry, and Steve Scipione all provided guidance and encouragement early on, and Deborah Baker, Elizabeth Schaaf, Anna Palchik, and Jerilyn Bockorick skillfully handled production and design. Joanna Lee and Melissa Cook helped with countless details, Adrienne Petsick and Amanda Byrnes coordinated marketing efforts, and Sandy Schechter and Warren Drabek managed permissions. I also want to thank Bill Mead for letting us use his painting, and Kim Cevoli and Donna Dennison, who designed the cover.

Many thanks to the following reviewers, who helped shape *The Practice of Creative Writing* with their excellent feedback and suggestions:

Rebecca Balcaral, Tarrant County Community College; Kim Blaeser, University of Wisconsin, Milwaukee; Gregory Byrd, St. Petersburg College; Dan Crocker, Kirkland Community College; Jeanne DeQuine, Miami Dade College; Nancy Edwards, Bakersfield College; Heid Erdrich, University of St. Thomas; Timothy Geiger, University of Toledo; Pamela Gemin, University of Wisconsin; Nancy Gorrell, Morristown High School; Barbara Griest-Devora, Northwest Vista College; Kurt Gutjahr, University of Iowa; Honoree Fannone Jeffers, University of Oklahoma; Lynn Kilpatrick, Salt Lake Community College; Michael Minassian, Broward Community College; Rebecca Mooney, Bakersfield College; Jeffrey Oaks, University of Pittsburgh; Randy Phillis, Mesa State College; Christopher Ransick, Arapahoe Community College; Vincent J. Reusch, University of Michigan; Gabrielle Stauf, Georgia Southwestern; Isaac Sullivan, University of Iowa; Stephanie Swartwout, Southeast Missouri State; Peter Telep, University of Central Florida; Michael Theune, Illinois Wesleyan; and John Walser, Marion College of Fond du Lac.

Heather Sellers
Holland, Michigan

BRIEF CONTENTS

CONTENTS

PART TWO

STRATEGIES   *67*

3 ENERGY   *69*

PART THREE

WRITING IN THE WORLD   *365*

INTRODUCTION: HOW CREATIVE WRITING WORKS

Creative writing—like sports, music, or dance—makes life more interesting. For both the creator—you, the writer—and the reader. When you make creative writing and reading a habit, a real part of your life, you increase your ability to observe, intuit, empathize, impose structure on chaos, read closely, and understand nuance. These skills will serve you well not just in your writing life but also in college and in every job you will ever have.

Creative writers in composing their work combine elements of architecture, psychology, philosophy, language, and scientific observation. In their attention to detail, every creative writer and every scientist shares a similar approach to the world. In designing and sustaining a creative writing life, writers have a lot in common with athletes and musicians, who know how to spend large blocks of time focused on one activity. Creative writing practice helps you become more thoughtful, discerning, and articulate.

WHAT CREATIVE WRITERS DO

We practice a process, a way of working with our intellect and our feelings to make art objects people learn from and enjoy. It's a mixture of individual hard work (focused time you spend at your desk, composing and shaping) and group work (interaction with other writers and their work, reading and listening).

Creative writing is like photography. As a photographer, you care about shape, emotion, pattern, human experience; all that meets the eye. It's not a hobby, it's a commitment to understanding all that is inside and outside oneself. Lots of people take snapshots—snapshots are wonderful for documenting the celebrations and daily moments of our lives. Photographers are artists. A snapshot, like the writing you do for yourself, is a picture of something. A good photograph is a composed image, which stops us, makes us enter a place and observe more closely. Good photographs and good writing have another key quality in common: They make the reader/viewer feel.

The practice of creative writing—like the practice of soccer, or piano, or kissing, or ballroom dancing—helps train our mind and enrich our soul. You become more able to concentrate, to sort and understand emotions and information, to read people more clearly, to take a broader view, to make finer distinctions. The practice of creative writing is useful in itself—you don't need to *do* anything with it—like publish it—to allow writing to enhance who you are, right now.

Creative writing is *not*:

- an easy way to get rich or famous
- a way to vent personal feelings
- for only a few talented geniuses
- rarefied, difficult, "artsy," special
- dark, creepy, "emo"
- just for English majors

Creative writers are everywhere. CEOs write stories about the life lessons they've learned. Stay-at-home dads keep journals about their days' pains, weirdnesses, and joys. Video game creators go to graduate school, writing new games. Students, travelers, novelists, grocery store clerks, and regular Joes create poetry, stories, graphic novels, and screenplays. Creative writing isn't for a chosen few. You don't have to be an English major to succeed at creative writing. You can take one course or a dozen. It helps if you read a lot, and you can learn to read like a writer, hungry for how-to.

Some writers publish. Some do not. Some have lifelong writing groups, meeting once a month, or online. This book introduces you to the range of experiences a successful creative writer needs to practice—generating material, conquering typical writing fears and blocks, entering the community of creative writers, productively revising work. Many people don't really know if they want to "be" creative writers or not. The purpose of this class is to offer you time to practice and to present some tools for making your creative writing more interesting to readers.

The study and practice called creative writing is:

- learning to pay closer attention to the world and human experience;
- practicing rendering, with words, those experiences, in a way that makes them alive in the reader's mind;

- using writing and words—both yours and others—to expand and extend who you are and what you can know.

QUESTIONS CREATIVE WRITERS ASK

The literary arts—those using words as their medium instead of paint or musical notes or movement or clay—take up the exact same questions studied in your philosophy, psychology, sociology, and communications classes.

- What is interesting about human nature?
- What is it like to be a particular human person, with a particular set of problems?
- What does it feel like and look like to attempt to be good, do the right thing, make a mistake, or utterly fail, given a person's set of circumstances?

Creative writing increases our ability to ask the questions that are important to us—hard, interesting questions—and come up with answers that both please us and inform others in a wholly original way.

Creative writers also wonder about process:

- Should I wait to write until I am inspired?
- Should I write my fantasy novel now or learn the short story form first?
- Do I want to be a writer?
- I hate sitting alone in a room. Can I really be a writer?
- What if someone criticizes my work, and I don't want to write at all?

This book helps you answer these questions, deal with doubts, work with other writers, get unstuck, and, most of all, write.

THE FOUR PARTS OF CREATIVE WRITING

Some people who have not written at all, or very much, mistakenly believe that creative writers disappear to the writing desk and come out some hours or days later with fabulous creative writing. While that magical kind of lucky break happens to some people, and only once in a while, nothing could be further from the reality of what it is like to be a creative writer, for real, over an extended period of time.

There are four different things you do with the time you devote to creative writing. Writing, of course, is the central part, but it is only a part. Creative writers also need to know how to read, work with other writers, and take their work to the next level by reading it aloud to an audience or submitting it to a literary publication.

Writing: Your Audience and Your Tools

Writing for Yourself. You may have written poems to express certain personal feelings. Maybe the poem was for one other person, but mostly it was written just for you. Some writing you do for yourself—venting, journaling, freewriting, IM-ing, keeping a diary, composing stories in your notebook—just for fun or practice, not necessarily to share with anyone else, or maybe to share with a trusted friend. The writing you do in order to seduce, please, or impress a lover is similarly private. Writing for yourself is an important part of your training as a creative writer. Writing for yourself or to another individual has as its purpose self-expression—love, angst, musing, stress relief. Writing you do for pleasure or necessity doesn't need to be "good" or "artistic." You do it for a lot of reasons: to express emotion, note something so you will remember it later, try to get someone to fall in love with you as much as you are in love with her. Another purpose of writing you do for yourself is practice. This book includes a number of opportunities for you to practice a specific writing technique or form—and while your teacher may collect or even grade this work, it's really for you and not for other readers. You're practicing. You'll probably want to keep limber by focusing some of the writing you do for yourself in a writer's notebook. Many working writers keep track of their thought processes and growth in a journal, through discussions with other writers, and by consciously attending to the process of writing.

Writing for Others. But some writing you do expressly for other people to read. Poems, stories, plays—these pieces of writing aren't about the expression of your personal feelings. They are pieces of writing designed to create an experience in your reader. They are *for* the reader. They may have lots of your own feelings in them, but pieces of creative writing we will work on this semester are designed not to express your experience but to create an experience in the reader. It's about him more than you.

The writing you do for your reader is very different from the writing you do just for yourself, for your own writing development. When you write for an audience, your goals as a writer are different, as are the techniques you employ. Creative writing isn't about *you* (the writer) having an emotion or an experience. It's about crafting language—words on a page—so that a reader (a stranger!) will have a specific kind of emotional experience. *Design* is the key word. Creative writing is essentially a service industry. We use our emotions, but expression of them isn't the goal. We use our emotions—along with craft, distance, insight, technical skill—to create a response in the reader.

Writing for others is a lot harder than writing for yourself. Writing for yourself is often pleasurable, fun, therapeutic. Instant results. You gain insight and reflection into who you are and what you are doing. Writing for others involves delayed gratification. You have to be patient. It takes a lot longer to transform your raw emotions, the stuff of life, into a piece of art. If we look at great creative writing from other centuries, other cultures, if we look at everything from Shakespeare to Aristotle to Amy Tan to J.R.R. Tolkien to Dan Brown to Stephen King to Jane Austen, from Robert Frost to Sylvia Plath, from the creators of great screenplays and comics and memoirs, we can identify six elements or qualities that great creative writing always shares. Six tools you can use, in other words, to make sure your creative writing is effective when you are writing for others.

These six tools are energy, images, tension, pattern, insight, and structure. As you learn, focus on each of these qualities, practicing them in poems, plays, stories, or creative essays and memoirs. As a beginner, the "cross-training" you receive by practicing in several genres serves to strengthen your abilities as you move, perhaps, toward a focus in one genre, like poetry or fiction.

Energy. Energy is the spark that makes a reader pay attention. Hemingway's taut, terse sentences emit a lot of energy. John Grisham's plots are packed with movement. James Joyce's inventive prose style is infused with life. Good creative writers pay attention to words that are energetic (compound abstractions like "ponderous sensation" or "evocative impediment" absorb rather than reflect energy), sentences and lines that are energetic (placing the strongest words at the beginning and end), and paragraphs and stanzas that are strung together so the reader feels momentum, pleasing leaps, interesting gaps and pauses. Energy is rhythm, excitement, and interest.

Images. Images are the living pictures, the "movie in the reader's mind," that your writing creates on the mental screen of the reader. Images are real. When you dream, you "see" things. The same with reading: When you are reading a great piece of writing, your imagination (notice that "image" is the root of the word) is activated; you can see, and smell, and hear, and touch.

Tension. Tension is the underlying push-pull, conflict, juxtaposition, or *what will happen next?* in all good creative writing. The reader has to have something to wonder about, though you should remember that while mystery is good, confusion isn't. To create tension, you push energy in two different directions. Readers *want* to figure things out, to feel smart, but they also want to be intrigued. They don't want you as writer to show off, overexplain, perform, or have more fun than they are having. Tension is like the bass line in a song—it's something you modulate as a writer, turning the volume up and down. To create energy, you vary the levels of tension.

Pattern. Pattern attracts the human eye, and repetition pleases us. From babyhood, you liked games that repeated: patty-cake, peek-a-boo, jump rope.

Creative writing is a sensory art form, and pattern is part of how creative writing makes its meanings. Pattern is a terrific way to subtly layer in your insights. Through repetition of images, words, or sounds, readers will pay attention to whatever you want them to notice—and they will feel like *they* are figuring it out. In fashion, design, computer programming, football strategies, cooking, love—and creative writing—pattern is how you give form to meaning.

Insight. We read to be entertained but also to learn, to see the world from the perspective of others. One of the reasons we read is to learn, and one of the reasons we read creative writing is to learn in a pleasurable way. We don't want our creative writing to lecture us or sermonize; but we want our art forms to indicate wisdom, to outline insights, so that we can come to our own conclusions. We want our writing to explain, through that transporting experience, what is messy, beautiful, and difficult in human experience. Good creative writing asks questions and provides insights through careful attention to human experience— wisdom is *in specific moments, actions, and objects.* Readers reject Big Conclusions laid on top of a piece of writing. In sum, with insight gained via the writing itself (not from thinking out an idea ahead of time), wisdom is threaded throughout a piece (not part of The Conclusive Ending or Grand Idea).

Structure. All good creative writing has a structure, whether a formal structure, like a sonnet or a three-act play, or informal, like a braided essay or a collection of images. We want to avoid venting or rambling. Early drafts usually lack cohesive structure; structure is the shape we develop to organize our material. Structure is like the recipe for your work. It's a blueprint, a map, a format. In composition, you may have learned the five-paragraph essay. There's also a structure to a business letter, a love letter, an official complaint, a divorce decree. Structure is how the building blocks—the smaller components—fit together. Messing around with structure can feel intimidating at first—you take apart all your hard work! But putting things back together in interesting ways is at the heart of creative writing. This book will provide numerous structures for you to practice in—and you'll likely invent your own.

Reading

Many students say they learn valuable reading skills from taking a writing class. Creative writers read closely, to see how effects are created, what the choices are, what can be done with little black marks on a white piece of paper, how to make fireworks go off in readers' brains. You read to learn what kind of energy drives good writing, and what kinds of shapes readers are hungry for. In creative writing classrooms, the work we read is alive to us, and we are interested in keeping it alive as we talk about it. Our analysis is invigorating: What's this writer doing, and how can I pick up some of his or her technique to make my own work stronger? We're a little greedy, we creative writers. Reading is usually pleasurable and instructive for writers, so we don't have to spend much time on learning to love reading.

Most writers are voracious readers—they read widely, they attend live readings, they surround themselves with words. We will consider some of the vocabulary associated with the writing process and responding to writing; these are concepts you need to know in order to create steadily over the course of a semester (not an easy thing to do) and in order to be a welcome participant in a writing workshop.

Writers read three kinds of work: stories, poems, drama, and creative nonfiction by published, expert writers; the writing-on-writing (just like your own writer's notebook) that guides us and provides insight into the craft of creative writing; and work by fellow students in the class.

Your instructor may share the published, professional readings that guided his or her own introduction into the world of creative writing, or your class may just stick to the excerpts and works in this textbook. You may be reading a book on the writing life alongside this text; there are excerpts and essays from the rich body of literature, interviews, and writers' journals included in this book, too. You may want to read more writing-on-writing on your own. There are so many delicious choices. See Chapter 12 for specific suggestions.

Working with Other Writers

Some of your focus this semester will be on how to read work written by other beginners and how to learn the same kinds of things from early triumphs and failures that you do from polished, published texts. Learning how to make meaningful, helpful observations is an art in itself. How to form bonds with members of the writing community, how to create a writing community where there isn't one, and how to nurture supportive writing relationships are essential to your sustained growth as a writer. Most writers have a writing group. Most successful writers support other writers by reading their work and talking about it, writing reviews, and going to readings.

Publication

Working with other writers naturally leads to that next step: taking your writing to the next level by testing it out in front of an audience. Most creative writers focus on practice—writing for oneself, writing for others, working with other writers, reading—for 90 percent of their writing time. But then, it's game day. Time to show what you know how to do. The audience might be a trusted friend, a teacher, a supportive reader, a small critique group. It might be your friends at a coffee shop. The audience grows as your confidence grows. Focusing on publication—whether that's reading a few poems out loud to your class or submitting work to your school's literary magazine—helps you learn to revise skillfully and efficiently. You can *hear* how the work will go over by gauging your listeners' reactions.

In your other classes this semester you will likely operate under the same principles. You learn by seeing how other people do it successfully (reading), by practicing (writing), and then by demonstrating (turning in a polished piece, reading to the class, sharing your work in a critique group). The creative writer, too, has these two modes—hours spent honing skills in practice, then performing. We make lots of mistakes in practice mode. The best creative writers develop a healthy detachment from their work at this stage. They *know* they're going to miss the mark lots of the time. It's *doing* the work, the training, every day, with a nonjudging beginner's mind ("of course I'm going to fail, that's part of writing!"). That's what counts.

A WRITING LIFE

PART ONE

Close the door. Write with no one looking over your shoulder. Don't try to figure out what other people want to hear from you; figure out what you have to say. It's the one and only thing you have to offer.

BARBARA KINGSOLVER

I think the most important part of the writing process is the creation of the first draft, wherein one is playacting in much the same way a kid does when in the sandbox with dolls or army men. You're lost in that miniature world, moving those toys around, speaking in their voices as though you, the player, don't really exist.

REGINALD McKNIGHT

Of course Nebraska is a storehouse of literary material. Everywhere is a storehouse of literary material. If a true artist were born in a pigpen and raised in a sty, he would still find plenty of inspiration for his work. The only need is the eye to see.

WILLA CATHER

CHAPTER ONE

FINDING FOCUS

You are reading a wonderful book. Time drops away, you forget where you are sitting, you no longer hear the sounds around you. When you are totally absorbed in a great piece of writing, you are *transported* to another time and place—the words create a new reality and you, the reader, inhabit another world. You not only see a kind of movie play out in your head as you read, but you also experience, with all your senses, another world. And that world is just as real and fully formed as this one.

THE MIND'S EYE

When you read creative writing, the kind of writing we will attempt in this course, you are meant to experience this very specific mental state, marked by visual images, sounds, and sensory experience—you can feel, taste, touch, and move around in this world. It's not fake. It's real.

In Shakespeare's play, when Hamlet says he is seeing his father "in my mind's eye," Hamlet's friend Horatio worries he is going mad. Horatio tells Hamlet his father is dead, he isn't seeing him. But Hamlet insists, and he is right. He *is* seeing his father. (If you close your eyes now and imagine your father, do you see an actual person? Try it. What do you see?)

The image Hamlet sees in his mind is *just as real* as breakfast, his girlfriend, the castle walls. It talks. It moves. The primary goal of creative writing is to create and link images—real, live moving images—in your reader's "mind's eye."

Art is a sensory experience, and creative writing—the making of art objects using language—appeals first to that sensory experience. We don't read creative writing to be told about other worlds. Learning about other worlds through the knowing, thinking brain is important, and it's the vital work of historians, philosophers, and scientists. In creative writing, in literature, we read in order to have an experience, to actually feel for real what it is like to be in another world, another body, another soul, another point of view. When it comes to creative writing readers want to forget they are reading. Take me somewhere, the reader says. Anywhere. But don't remind me—with too much description or analysis or thinking or interruptions—that I'm reading.

Think about how you tell the story of something that happened to you on a bad day when you tell it well versus when you tell it poorly. When you retell how hard it was for you to find a parking space this morning, if you are fully involved in your storytelling, some part of you is still sitting behind the steering wheel, trolling around, stressed out. Notice how we all do that: We relive the experience—in order to tell it well. Your stories and your jokes come out best when you *reexperience the original sensations* as you retell. You transport yourself into the scene you are trying to recreate. And, thus, you create it for your listener or reader. Weak writers, like weak storytellers, don't transport themselves back into the moment. They tell *about* the experience. And it's usually boring. "I looked all over for a parking space," they report, generalizing, distancing. "I can never find a place to park. It took like forever."

> *Get out of the blocks, run your race, stay relaxed. If you run your race, you'll win. Channel your energy. Focus.*
> — CARL LEWIS

Notice the difference in the good teller's rendition: "I was creeping down that back lane of Siberia, you know, by those bashed-in dumpsters, heading into the sun, I look at my watch—it's 8:02, I have the 8:00 class, and all of a sudden I hear, I hear this hissing. I was banging on the steering wheel, and this guy was coming towards me, almost running, pointing at my front passenger-side tire."

In order to put you, the reader/listener in the scene, the writer must focus all mental attention inside the very scene or image, to tell it in a way that makes it real for the reader/listener.

Write What You See

Think for a moment of flipping through cable channels, and landing, on Saturday afternoon, on one of those programs with a title like *Learn to Paint Oceans!* or *Perfect Flowers in One Minute!* A guy in a windowless television studio with a canvas, a lot of blue paint, a lot of white paint—and no ocean, no flowers—explains to viewers how to rotate the brush for a wavelike swoop, how to dollop more white for crests of waves, and, Ta-da!—a very cool little wrist motion that will create the perfect expanse of sand. Use pink paint and the same exact wrist motion to do roses!

At no point is it suggested we look at an actual ocean, or wave, or beach, rose, pansy, or peony. At no point is the viewer's experience of the painting considered. This kind of approach to art is based on tricks instead of looking closely at the real world. Fooling the eye, these shortcuts usually produce bad paintings that look like everyone else's bad paintings.

Techniques for making fresh art of high quality involve the artist's experience and, more importantly, focusing on the viewer's experience. The bad paintings don't really create a world, they suggest a shorthand for The Beach, The Ocean, Nice Garden Scene, Floral Medley. When you look at a bad painting, you see the painting. When you look at a good painting, you not only see the painting, you are transported to your own childhood memories of sweet afternoons at the shore, Grandma's rose bed, the peonies you grew last summer.

You want to avoid the kind of "quick trick" techniques that keep you from *really looking closely at the real world* and focusing on the people in it. "How to Plot Your Novel in Thirty Days," "Create Fabulous Characters in an Hour!"—these shortcuts do not usually produce very good work. What produces good writing is accurately noticing specific real living individuals and instances. Focus on the things you notice, and focus on the very small things you notice—the things other people, nonwriters, pass right over.

Creative writers work from life. They improve by *noticing* the tiny movements and gestures and details—a torn sock, a hangnail, nervous hair-tugging, the titles of the CDs strewn across the back seat—and they build from the ground up using the true observed stuff of real life.

| PRACTICE |

Think of an "idea" for writing. The bigger and broader and the less firsthand experience you have with this idea the better. For example, write about life, love, death, homelessness, or illness *in general*. Write fast. Ramble. Think, *don't try to see any one thing in particular*. Put in lots of your feelings and ideas. Avoid images and specifics. Think out loud on the page. Don't focus your mind's eye on anything.

Moving Images

Imagine a child swinging on a swingset at a playground.

Okay, do you have in your mind a picture of a kid, in motion?

Did you invent a kid or is the image hovering in your mind's eye of a real kid, someone you know, perhaps yourself when you were six? Look closer. Can you see what your kid is wearing? Where the kid stands? His hair, his arms, his hands, his face?

Pause for a moment, and using the power of your mind's eye, look at this kid, noticing anything small, anything interesting. Notice how you can make him swing faster. Slower. Notice how you can make him jump off the swing—

seeing this in your mind's eye all the while—and make him run across the park, over to a dog.

The point of this example is that your mind can create all of these things—real, live, moving images. You don't need a lot of description in order to have this experience; your reader doesn't either. In fact, the more information you give the harder it is for the reader to see what you are talking about:

> The kid was born in Orlando in 1972, to very poor parents who had worried constantly about everything for years. The hospital was really run down and the kid was always worrying and whining. He suffered from hemachromatosis later in life and made straight As, but not without a struggle.

Notice what happened to the image of the kid in your mind's eye. In the wordy description, where as reader you are overloaded with information, you don't really get an image in your mind's eye. You see words, you think, you remember, you consider—all valuable activities. But art is about apprehending a *sensory emotional experience*. Very different.

Even if you could keep a strong visual image alive in your mind during the general description above, you were working hard. Too hard. Readers can't be expected to work that hard; they need clear images to focus on. The reader wants to see her own kid, her own banana, her own house. She is fully capable of doing so all on her own. That's the central lesson of this chapter: If you write from a focused place—seeing the exact kid you want the reader to picture, in Prospect Park on 24th Street—your reader will see. If you see, in your mind's eye, the fruit, the animal, the break-up scene—your reader will see it too.

Be specific ("banana," not "fruit," "kid," not "person"). Name what you see. But most important of all, as you write, keep part of your mind in focus on the live scene, the image.

Many writers mistakenly believe scene painting is good writing, and they include adjectives and adverbs to decorate and enrich the writing. In creative writing, don't spend lots of time "painting" the perfect fruit ("the glowing red orb pocked with holes made by denizens of the humble earth" is really hard to see). Just say "old apple."

In tennis, baseball, football, you are constantly reminded by the coaches to "keep your eye on the ball." Same for writers. Keep your eye on what you are writing.

| PRACTICE |

Create a movie in your reader's mind. Bring in one of your favorite pieces of creative writing—a poem, a few paragraphs of a short story, a part of a memoir. You might use something you loved from childhood or a published story or piece from another class.

Read aloud from your piece. After you are finished interview your listener. Did your partner "see" something on the "screen" in her brain? What? What parts of the piece did or
did not activate this moving picture or live image? Compare your favorite published
pieces to the purposely unfocused writing you created (for the practice on p. 13). What are
the differences? What launches a reader into the scene and what blocks a reader from a
sensory experience?

As you practice creative writing in this course notice when you are aware of
an image, a movie, in your head, when you read and when you write. When you
aren't transported into an alive, moving image, what *does* happen in your mind
when you read? Paying this kind of close attention is tricky, but you will get better at it as you practice. Not every sentence or line in a piece of creative writing
has to feed the moving picture, but most probably do. And, it's important to notice what *is* happening when you aren't "in the moment" as a reader.

Practice noticing what you like to read, what moves you, what affects you.
When are you "lost" in the reading, totally unaware of this world because you are
in the author's creation? Try to articulate to yourself what makes a piece memorable and powerful for you, and your own writing technique will improve.

PRACTICE

Create a list of moving images you can use to generate creative writing in this course.
Number from one to twenty-five. Play the story of your life, from about age five to now,
so that item number one is the first image you see. Don't strain too hard — you are just
practicing noticing how your image-making mind works. What's the first little movie of
yourself you can see? Climbing onto a tractor? Running to catch the school bus? Slugging
your brother? Write down a little mini title: Tractor. Bus. Joey. Move through your life,
naming the little movies that star you. Don't work from photographs or memories of
photographs and don't use the Official Frequently Told Stories. Capture real images that
show you in action. Swingset Heather. New Skateboard Day. Disney World with Mom.
If you think of something, but can't see it, you can't put it on your list. Insignificant little
flashes of image are what you are looking for: Only include mental movies. Reread your
list. Which entries seem the most interesting for writing? Which create an image in your
mind's eye? Place a star by those.

SUBJECT: FOCUS ON WHAT?

What do I look at? That's a question writers ask all throughout their writing
careers. "What makes a good subject for my creative writing?" "What should I
write about?"

> *A playwright knows that what*
> *is most private in her heart*
> *of hearts is also the most*
> *astonishing.*
> — TINA HOWE

You can write about anything you want as long as you 1, focus on what you see; and 2, write as truthfully and honestly and accurately as possible. There are two considerations to keep in mind as you look for good subjects (no matter how fantastical, made-up, or imagined your work is): 1, write about what you know; and 2, write about what defines us as human.

Write What You Know

Your job as a writer is to report from the world you know, to bring the news of that world to us. What is there, how do people act, what do people yearn for? What are the rules in that world? What happens when they are broken? How do people act? Why? Any worlds to which you have behind-the-scenes access are going to be excellent choices for writing topics this semester.

Remember, this "knowing" we are speaking of is a *visual sensory knowing*. Write what you see. Not what you know in your head.

"I have an idea for a poem," writers often say. It's better to have an *image* for a poem. And, instead of making up fanciful images or chasing ephemeral ideas, start with a concrete sensory detail from a world you have special access to. If you know a lot about the prep schedule at the Windmill Restaurant, how Terry likes the eggs to be set up, how the bread is made fresh, how the delivery guy spits outside the door every single morning, then start with those images, the specifics you know really well. If you haven't ever been in a war, but you want to write a war poem, you will need to get some specific insider images — things only someone who has seen combat would have visual access to.

For now, as a beginner, as you are training in this craft, write what only *you* can write. It's going to take some practice to get a feel for how that works. How can your boring apartment in Rockaway Beach, your boring parents, your boring little sister, be the stuff of art? How can your dumb wedding plans in your dumb small town make a novel? Your ridiculous middle-class life in your homogeneous suburb? The great American writers John Cheever, Mark Twain, Julia Alvarez, Gish Jen, Sandra Cisneros, James Baldwin, and Zora Neale Hurston knew how.

PRACTICE

You do not need to write autobiography, but you do need to choose topics on which you are an expert. Fortunately, you are an expert on many, many things. Hamster-owning, work, your great Aunt Madge who was a roller-skating star — you know *a lot*. Your passions, your hobbies, your work environments, and the interesting lives of those around you are probably the topics you will choose from for your creative writing assignments. Start four lists. Add to them over the next few weeks. Using each of these categories —

such as jobs, relatives and parents, summer, and sports/hobbies, trips and journeys—come up with fifteen items in each category:

> *Jobs:* McDonald's, babysitting, working in the lab, raking for Mrs. Jones
> *Relatives' jobs:* accountant, stay-at-home mom, homeschooler, Uncle Joe the mortician in Jersey, jobs they held before you were born
> *Summer activities:* camps, archery, fort-building, falling in love, dog, swimming, school, building a house for Habitat
> *Sports/hobbies:* knitting, Nintendo, roller derby, Pancake House at 2 a.m.
> *Trips/journeys:* confirmation, Jamaica, the mall with Darcy, the Grand Canyon

You now have an additional seventy-five potential writing topics. Next time you are stuck or blocked, force yourself to choose an item and use this list to spark new images.

PRACTICE

Make a list of ten secret worlds you have or have had access to. Places no one else in this class has ever been—ever. Except for you. Burger King, 24th Street, the kitchen, summer 2004, when Marcie was managing. Under your little sister's bed the year she had the secret illegal pet snake. Your mother's office on Division Avenue the afternoon you saw the boss kissing her. Your soccer team in the locker room after a loss. Keep your list with your other lists from this chapter—you are generating terrific writing images to feed your work.

Explore What Makes Us Human

There is a famous writer who says that when you have someone special over to your house, you break out the best whiskey, the stuff you keep in the back for special occasions. And, he says, when you have readers, they must be treated in the same way as that special visitor, the one for whom you break out the good stuff. Your subjects must not be bottom-shelf, generic, unimportant. They must come from the place where you keep your very best, most treasured items—dark, potent, intense. Stuff you've saved up.

How humans interact with each other, with human emotions—love, fear, hatred, lust, joy—in tiny, real moments—that's what art is made of. By focusing tightly on the seen, and your visual experience, the elements essential to our humanity will come forward.

> *Discipline in art is a fundamental struggle to understand oneself, as much as to understand what one is drawing.*
>
> — HENRY MOORE

When you compose creative writing, unlike in a sermon or a police report, focus on a mixture of qualities. Let your good guys be a little bad, and they will be more human to your reader. Give your villains some appealing qualities, and we feel more engaged with the writing, more distraught at the outcome. Creative writing is a lot like a psychology course in action: Writers are always asking, Why do people act like this? Why do we keep making the same mistakes? Why do we keep ourselves from getting what we want? How do we fall in love with who we fall in love with? Your list of questions can point you toward your best material. You can change the players and mix and match the histories and settings and motivations, but staying close to the essence of the questions that trouble, delight, intrigue, and keep you up late at night is part of the secret to focusing on good subjects.

PRACTICE

Make a list of twenty things that confuse or concern you about how people treat one another. The questions can be large (Why do women fall in love with men who treat them badly?), but it's better if you make them small, and specific. Why does Aunt Ruthie live with a man thirty years her junior, and why does the whole family get annoyed and judgmental and weird about it? Why does my roommate go home every single weekend, when she never has a good time and just complains about the town and her high school friends and how immature they are? Why did I break up with Lori?

PRACTICING FOCUS

Writing from this place of visual, mental focus is a skill, and as you practice it you get better at it. Sometimes, our old writing habits—writing *about* things in general, using "head" and "thought" words like "it seemed," or, "she remembered," or, "realizing . . ."—block the reader's experience of a real visual image. In addition to the technique of "being there" when you write, it's useful to look at several practical and physical ways to support and increase your ability to focus.

> *I practice everyday. You have to stay on good speaking terms with your piano. Or the piano will rebuff you.*
> — HANK JONES

The Writing Habit

Becoming a writer means being creative enough to find the time and the place in your life for writing. A physical place and a committed block of time become habits you can count on. To the basic platform you learned above (how to use your mind's eye to focus on mental pictures in order to do creative writing), we will add another mental state: the focus that comes from establishing and sustaining a writing habit. Most beginning writers work best if they do a little creative writing every day, at the same time of day, in the same place, for the same amount of time. Without a writing habit, something reassuring you can count on, it's asking too much of your imagination and your confidence to write fabulous stuff on demand, just because you feel like it. If you don't have a writing habit, you aren't being fair to yourself. You might even be setting yourself up for failure. If you write only when you are "in the mood," or when you "have some time," you will never be able to write enough material to see what you are good at, what needs work. Good writers write whether they are in the mood or not. They practice whether they feel like it or not. It's the only way. Everyday practice. That's how you get better.

> *I never could have done what I have done without the habits of punctuality, order, and diligence, without the determination to concentrate myself on one subject at a time.*
>
> — CHARLES DICKENS

Writers are simply people who have figured out how to spend enough time in the writing room every day in order to create enough work so that some of it is good.

Remember: You will want to *avoid* writing. All writers struggle with procrastination, writer's block, distraction, or laziness. All successful writers develop strategies to deal with these issues. Conquering not-writing is probably half the battle when you are taking a writing class. Everyone struggles with this.

One strategy for overcoming not-writing is to simply schedule your daily writing session for the same time and same place every day. Some writers write in bed, first thing in the morning, before they are awake enough to get too freaked out and intimidated by the writing process. Others go to the basement of the library after work every night. Others like the white noise of a crowded coffee shop or restaurant during lunch hour. That's when they focus best.

Another way to ease yourself into a productive daily writing habit, where you can focus your mind on practicing various writing skills and techniques, is to use rituals.

PRACTICE

In your day-planner or class schedule, block out a period of time for writing each day. Usually, writers hook their writing time onto another activity. It's very easy to do all your other homework first and save the writing for last (and then not get to it). Will you write when you first get up? During lunch? Try to make your writing slot the same time each day.

Writing Rituals

Rituals help us achieve and intensify focus.

Writing rituals are the key to keeping your writing habit in place. Most athletes warm up. They run a few slow laps, do push-ups, stretch hamstrings. Most people don't pull into the parking lot, leap out of the car, and start jogging around the track in their business suits. Think about the other activities in which you engage every day. Are there rituals that go along with those activities? Pre-study

> *The problem of creative writing is essentially one of concentration and the supposed eccentricities of poets are usually due to mechanical habits or rituals developed in order to concentrate.*
> — STEPHEN SPENDER

rituals? Pre-dinner rituals? Rituals guide our brains into successful practice. The more you repeat a ritual, the smoother your practice is. You know the athlete who can't compete without his lucky shirt, or race without a specific pair of sneakers? Writers aren't weird, they're just human. Rituals let your body and your creating mind know it's time to work. It's unrealistic to rush home, bang out a poem, and then revise it as you make dinner, get your chemistry lab under way, and talk on the phone to Joey. Create a regular time for your daily writing, a block in your schedule where you go to a certain place, with specific tools. One writer I know lights a candle when he starts, and blows it out when he is finished. Every time. It doesn't matter what your rituals are; what is important is that you pay attention to what you do right before your writing sessions — and repeat what works for you.

Rituals teach your creative brain how and when to focus. Rituals save you valuable time. If you are a busy student, you might not have time to *not* rely on rituals.

| PRACTICE |

Take a few minutes to write out what your dream writing life looks like. If you had all the time in the world, didn't have to work to pay for school, didn't have a car payment or any other classes, what would your writing days look like? Would you write in the morning? Night? Pretend you can shape your writing life to look like anything you want. The only catch: You have to do it every day. How long would you want to spend? What would be in your writing room? What would this room look like? What do you have on your desk, your mp3 player, your laptop? Include a sketch if you like, and a list of your prewriting routine — what do you do to get in the mood? Share in class, and on the board keep track of the rituals that show up most often in people's dream lives. Are there some things that writers really do need to do in order to get to — and stay at — the writing desk? Next, make a list of three to five writing rituals that you would like to use during this course in order to establish a healthy daily writing practice. An example list: Light a candle, set a timer, read a poem to warm up, tune my ear, and when finished, blow the candle out.

Flow

When you are "in the zone" on the basketball court, the basket looks huge. You can't hear the fans in the stands. Things take place almost as if in slow motion. When you are in the zone as a writer, you lose all sense of time, too. You are *in* the scene or moment you are writing — you aren't sitting in your writing room at all. You can't hear your roommate's conversation. You are in the writing zone.

Some researchers call this state of creative concentration *flow* — when you are involved in an activity and you go into a kind of focused trance. Susan Perry, a psychologist who studies creativity, describes it this way in her book *Writing in Flow*:

> Flow is a relatively new term for an essential and universal human experience. You know you've been in flow when time seems to have disappeared. When you're in flow, you become so deeply immersed in your writing, or whatever activity you're doing, that you forget yourself and your surroundings. You delight in continuing to write even if you get no reward for doing it — monetary or otherwise — and even if no one else cares whether you do it. You feel challenged, stimulated, definitely not bored. Writing in flow, you're often certain you're tapping into some creative part of yourself — or of the universe — that you don't have easy access to when you're not in this altered state. Sports figures call this desired condition being "in the zone."

> *Ninety percent of my game is mental. It's my concentration that has gotten me this far.*
> — CHRIS EVERT-LLOYD

Psychologists who study the creating brain identify the state where work happens, almost effortlessly, as "flow." You know flow. You play for hours at pastimes that absorb you — Nintendo, lacrosse, bike-riding, knitting, talking with friends — whatever your passion. You fall out of time and become lost in a narrative. You create and sustain another world because you do it all the time. When you're in chemistry class, dreaming about your weekend with your friends, you are *in* that world, and probably in flow, if you don't hear a single word your professor is saying.

Practice paying attention to when you are absorbed utterly by a task. How did you get into that state? What brought you out of it?

When you write creatively, your task is to get yourself into that state.

PRACTICE

When were you last in flow? How do you know when you are in it? Have you had a flow experience as a writer? In any other parts of your life?

LACK OF FOCUS

Every single writer faces difficulties with focus such as writer's block or procrastination. *Writer's block* can be best defined as the inability to focus, the loss of creative concentration. Often what gets labeled "writer's block" is actually distraction — external or internal distraction. You probably say you have a problem with procrastination, but actually, you may want to consider all of these issues — writer's block, distraction, and procrastination — as various manifestations of *the loss of focus*.

As a writer, you will need strategies for combating lack of focus. To develop such strategies, it may help to learn a bit more about the nature of writer's block, distraction, and procrastination. After all, the known enemy is easier to defeat than the unknown enemy.

> *Nothing interferes with my concentration. You could put on an orgy in my office and I wouldn't look up. Well, maybe once.*
> — ISAAC ASIMOV

Writer's Block

Writers sometimes say they are blocked when they cannot write. They feel disconnected from their own work. The blocked writer feels tapped out, completely devoid of imaginative energy. The blocked writer can't envision the scenes and moments and images that transport *the writer*, much less a reader!

In order to cure a block, most experts recommend you try a five-part approach:

- Begin at least five new pieces — just start things. Multiple things.
- Write for a set amount of time each day, say ten or fifteen minutes only.
- Allow yourself to write poorly without judging the writing.
- Study the psychology and process of writing (your teacher can recommend some books on blocks, or see Chapter 12).
- Have a friend call out a random number between one and ten. Using one of your lists from this chapter, force yourself to write for three minutes, using the list topic corresponding to that number.

Expect to get stuck at unpredictable times. Plan on getting stuck just when things are going well; that is very common. Good writers are good learners — they pay attention to what it is that led them to being stuck. They also pay attention to what exactly — mentally, physically, emotionally — preceded a great writing session. Good writers are self-aware. Like excellent scientists, beginning writers study their own processes in order to prepare for and work through blocks.

> *Writer's block is the greatest side effect of boredom.*
> — JASON ZEBEHAZY

Most writing blocks are actually manifestations of fear: fear of not being good enough, fear of being cheesy, fear of hurting someone with your words. Most writing fears are common, normal, and realistic: You probably *do* want to be a better writer than you are now. You might write some clichéd pieces, especially when you are just starting out. And, words are extraordinarily powerful: It's wise to be aware of your intentions and sensitive to how your work might affect others. Perhaps you will create a list of writing "rules" that work best for you.

WRITERS' TIPS: Getting Unstuck

Here's a checklist of methods for getting unstuck—some of the most popular tricks writers use to break through inevitable blocks.

1. Set the timer. Write for ten minutes at a time.

2. Stay in the moment. Stay present by focusing just on what you *see*.

3. Write a smaller chunk: Take something you already have and slow it down, move closer, really go blow-by-blow.

4. When voices of doubt plague you, write down what the voices are saying. Or, banish the judge/critic by swearing at it.

5. Write every day for at least ten minutes. Don't worry if today doesn't go well. There's always tomorrow. (If you miss a day, remember the next three will be harder than you think they ought to be.)

6. Write by hand when you are stuck. Slowing down often helps the mind focus. Try writing in all capital letters.

7. Go back to the last thing you wrote that you liked. Use it as a jumping-off point for new work.

8. Take another try at an assignment you liked, one that went well. Doing more of what you are good at is a great way to get unstuck.

9. Make your own list of "ways to get unstuck" based on what has worked in the past; notice what gets you stuck, and how you work through blocks.

10. Plan on getting stuck, and don't beat yourself up. Writers get stuck. It's part of writing. Stop, start up again later.

Distraction

There are two kinds of distraction. Internal—where the thoughts in your head keep you from staying focused—and external. External distractions include your roommate, your three-year-old, your dog, your boyfriend, your feelings about your boyfriend, the radio, the temperature of the room. Distraction destroys flow.

Writers are often distracted by external circumstances, and smart writers work hard to set up their writing life (using rituals!) so that they have uninterrupted time each day to work. Libraries, empty classrooms, and very early or very late hours are what writers gravitate toward. Trying to write ten minutes before dinner with a living room full of hungry friends and the television playing is unlikely to produce good writing or teach you much about focus.

When you do get interrupted, notice how you get back into your piece. Next time you are writing along happily about your sister and the way she was cutting the gum out of your hair and the phone rings—the real phone—what do you do? Take the call, talk, and get back to work. Notice what your mind does. When you come back to the piece, and you can't remember—Where was I going with this?—what do you usually do? Many writers reread their last few sentences, or start at the beginning, reading and fiddling with the words until they get caught back up in the piece. Notice how you get seduced back into your work, reoriented in the "moving picture," simply by *reading*.

External distractions are easy to manage when you believe your writing practice is important. You deserve a quiet, comfortable place to work, and the time to work. Make sure you set yourself up for success. You will be interrupted. Notice how you concentrate and recover.

Procrastination

Procrastination is simply internal distraction. You want to write, you intend to write, but some force inside you keeps you from doing it.

Many students say they procrastinate. They suspect they are lazy. They wrongly assume there are "real" writers out there, working around the clock, on schedule, happily scooting along, churning out poem after poem.

Psychological research on creativity proves that we work better when there is a limited amount of time—some time pressure—in which to complete a task. Many students, and many writers, constrict the amount of time they have so they can jump-start their ability to focus. T. S. Eliot once said that not having as much time for his writing as he would like allowed him to concentrate better. Perhaps this is why we procrastinate instead of doing the work for our classes.

> *Procrastination is fear of success. People procrastinate because they are afraid of the success that they know will result if they move ahead now. Because success is heavy, carries a responsibility with it, it is much easier to procrastinate and live on the "someday I'll" philosophy.*
> — DENNIS WAITLEY

Having a limited amount of time forces us to concentrate. In that state, where we are passionate about getting the project done, we concentrate with our full creative powers. You can use that human instinct to your advantage: Always set a time limit for your writing session (limit the time to ten or fifteen minutes at first), and set micro-deadlines for yourself. Use the compression and intensity of a deadline to jump-start flow.

When you catch yourself being distracted—unfocused on an image or scene or your writing topic, or avoiding the writing altogether—instead of beating yourself up as a lowly procrastinator, listen to what is going on. You are probably nervous about writing. Writing is hard, and scary, and daunting. That never really changes; expert and published writers describe this state as a daily part of the writing life.

You need strategies. You need ways to get your focus back on the *image*. You need to catapult yourself into the scene at hand. Find out what works for you by practicing. How do you get out of procrastinating and into work-flow mode? Run around the block? Draw a sketch of the scene at hand? Start a new, different piece? Start by copying over or revising what you worked on yesterday? Experiment. Repeat what works for you.

Procrastination is a lack of focus caused by internal distraction. Learning how your mind works and repeating productive behaviors is your best line of defense, and your best way back into focus. However, if you are using procrastination itself as a focusing tool, and it works for you, perhaps procrastination isn't the worst thing. If you have plenty of extra time in your life procrastination doesn't hurt anything. If you are pressed for time, you will need to develop more efficient strategies.

Often, the secret to breaking through a procrastination habit is to become more aware of the inner voices of judgment that are holding you back from working to your greatest potential.

Judgment

To avoid loss of focus, you need strategies for nipping it in the bud, when it first crops up. Psychologists who study creativity theorize that blocks, distractions, and procrastination—all the things we do to sabotage ourselves—are caused by judgment, that unhelpful critical voice.

Above, you tried to write down all the judging voices that crop up when you sit down to work—the parents, teachers, or friends who may have said negative things about your creative efforts, and the negative comments you've directed toward yourself.

But judgment doesn't have to be negative to be distracting. If you are thinking how great you are, how much money you will make, how profound you are, how beautiful the words will sound when you read them aloud at your Pulitzer acceptance, you are distracted. You aren't focused on the reader's experience. And, chances are, the writing won't be nearly as powerful as it could be.

If you go to your writing session to beat yourself up or to feel really brilliant and poetic, it's going to be hard to focus. When you write from your center self, and keep in mind that moving picture, you are focused, and there isn't room for judging the work: You *are* the work.

Your question isn't, "Is this going well?" or, "Is this bad?" because you can never really know that. When you are at work, your question is, "What else interesting do I see, do I experience, what interesting thing is my character about to do?" And you watch. And follow.

What a strange endeavor, this writing business. You don't know how it's going. Well, remember our main concept: It's not about you. It's about your reader. You are a sort of middle-person, a channel. Your job as a writer is to reach down and scoop up the stuff that is buried at the image level inside of you—in your body, not in your head. You bring it up to the light, trying not to over-analyze the emotions or explain what's going on to your reader—just show them the movie in your mind.

WRITING PROJECTS

1. Write a dialogue between you and the critical voice in your head. Give the voice a name. Discuss your writing life with the critical voice; argue with it. Format the piece like a play.

2. Write a poem or narrative piece about becoming a writer or being a writer-at-work, but use another activity (baseball, cooking, making your bed) that you know well to describe the steps, pitfalls, or processes. Use images. Don't write *about* what you see. Write the actions and images, experiencing them on the sensory level as you write.

3. Rewrite the Practice you did on page 13, translating the feelings and thoughts and ideas and analyses into images so that the reader sees people, action, and real objects.

CHAPTER TWO

WRITING AND READING

Writing and reading are, for creative writers, parallel acts of paying close attention. As we craft a piece, we read and reread, trying to get at the core experience our audience will have. As we read other people's work—stories, creative nonfiction, poems, and plays—we writers are constantly stimulated, our imaginations sparked, our own pieces germinating, coming to life. Many, many famous writers have said they learned to write creatively not by attending classes, but by *reading*. By exploring the tightly knit relationship between reading and writing, you will discover some practical strategies, and some time-saving tricks—techniques that will help your writing.

> *There is creative reading as well as creative writing.*
> — RALPH WALDO EMERSON

Writers approach reading as musicians do live shows. We check out a new band or book for similar reasons: to see how it's done, to pick up new moves, because we are curious, because it's how we get inspired. As a writer, you are looking for the moves the author of the piece has made. Whether you are reading Virginia Woolf or a poem written by your roommate, your goal is to figure out what the writer is doing in order to create the reader's imaginative experience, and how she is doing it.

READING WORK IN PROGRESS

A good rule of thumb: When you comment on other people's work, ask yourself, What am I learning about how the writer put this piece together that could be helpful to me as I work on my own creative writing? Learn from the successes and mistakes of others. Put another way, perhaps your mother's way: Talk about other people's work the same way you want yours talked about.

QUESTIONS TO ASK: Reading as a Writer

Focus on these aspects when examining work by peers or published writers.

1. What creates the energy in this piece of writing?
2. Why is the piece interesting? What exactly makes me read on?
3. If I want to stop reading, if I space out, why?
4. When am I transported, fully, and how does that happen?
5. How does the writer hook me?
6. What are the patterns?
7. What am I learning?
8. What am I paying attention to?
9. What am I seeing differently?
10. Where does the writer start the piece, end the piece? Why there?

Being a thoughtful reader of class work means paying attention to a few guidelines, all of which are common sense. Balance your praise comments with your questioning comments. Make your praise honest and specific. Earn the respect of your peers by reading carefully, asking questions, and trying to figure out what the writer is trying to do *before* suggesting changes. Even if a peer piece isn't on a topic you particularly enjoy, you must assume the role of the *ideal reader*. The ideal reader can't ever say, "I hate Barbies. So I hate all stories written about Barbies. I hated this." An ideal reader can't say, "I'm vegetarian. I don't do well with stories featuring meat products." In a writing class, all the members of the class try to be the best reader they can be for each piece. You're like an electrician looking inside a house—you don't care about the décor. You are there to see what's working, what's hooked up, what's not. Focus on the piece at hand, and the tools the writer is using to make the piece. Leave your own particular reading tastes out of the conversation. Likewise, leave your opinions about the author out of the conversation—this is about the writing, not the author. Whether you are reading a piece of writing for class that's written by a student or by a professional, published writer, it's good to talk about the nature of the piece itself before you begin your evaluation. This is called nonjudgmental response.

Taking the time to answer these questions (orally or in writing) before your class starts critiquing gives the writer essential information about his writing. A

QUESTIONS TO ASK: Reading Creative Writing for Discussion

Focus on these topics when talking about student or published work.

1. What is the piece about?
2. What effect is the writing trying to have on the reader?
3. How is the piece put together, what are its parts?
4. What kind of writing is this? What other writing/art forms does it remind you of?
5. What insights/conclusions does it make?
6. What questions does the piece want the reader to mull over, respond to?

writer can't see what it would be like to read his own piece. Slowing down at the outset of a feedback session so the author has time to see what it was like to have this piece in your mind's eye not only builds the author's trust in your insights and objections, but it also lets him see exactly what it is he has written. We aren't used to this kind of conversation, so expect this part of the workshop to be a bit of a challenge.

Workshop

Workshops are groups or whole classes; everyone brings copies of a piece in progress. The time is divided evenly between the participants, and your instructor may or may not give you guiding questions. Sometimes the work is submitted anonymously to the class, to make the writer and readers more comfortable, to keep the focus directly on the work. Usually the writer isn't allowed to talk (because it's natural for us to want to defend and explain our work in progress). The writer usually takes notes (encouraging people in the class to talk honestly and longer about the work).

Sometimes the comments are helpful; sometimes they aren't. You, as the writer, have to find your own way through the piece. Learn to take what is useful from the comments around you, manage your defenses, stay open to learning, and go home and work on the writing. You will get conflicting feedback—if you didn't, you might worry you enrolled in a school of robots! It's your job—and some of the pleasure of being the writer, the person in control—to sort out what you think the piece needs next.

In class, remember what kinds of comments are helpful to you as a writer, and model your own responses after those. You are often most helpful when you present your reactions to other works as those of a fellow beginner, another artist trying to do the same hard things. The goal is for the members of the class to always leave *wanting* to write more, not less.

Revision

Revision is part of the writing process, not a dreaded thing tacked on at the end. Most writers don't draft, then smoothly "revise," and then declare, "I'm done." They use their tools, getting the work as good as they can get it on all the different fronts. Real writing is a kind of circling around. Revision is truly re-seeing your work—it's stepping back, guessing where you might go next.

Revising involves picking up another technique or tool, and going in and fiddling around, seeing what you come up with. This messing around doesn't happen in a prescribed order. Sometimes, the second draft (and it's often hard to say when that draft starts—usually writing morphs) is worse than the first. That's just part of the process. Writing, like music-making and atomic physics, is about trial and error. What happens if Jane *doesn't* fall in love, if she goes on a road trip instead? (Turns out to be boring. Next draft: Send her on a trip to Nantucket with rich adoring boyfriend, who has another girlfriend there. . . .)

Workshops and teacher conferences can let you "re-see" pieces of the work, or the whole. Sometimes starting over is the quickest way to improve. Some pieces you write this semester you won't revise—they'll have come out right the

---

QUESTIONS TO ASK: Reading First Drafts of Creative Writing

Focus on these aspects of the piece to help the writer identify revision strategies.

1. What images are most transporting? Where did you "see"?
2. Are there sections where you were confused?
3. Where are the places of greatest energy? Least energy?
4. What is/are the essential tension(s) in the piece?
5. What additional examples of tension does the writer employ?
6. What oppositions could be made more tense?
7. Is the dialogue efficient, realistic, tense?
8. What small and large insights does the piece offer or imply?
9. What patterns can you find? Are there places pattern could be enhanced?
10. What structure does this piece use? Are there any structural weaknesses?

first time, or they'll just be so confounding and messy, you won't have the heart to go back in. Start lots of new pieces. Work in your own way, at your own pace.

See revision as a reading process. You spin the wheel, choose another tool, and apply that tool to your work: heightening tension, working on dialogue, intensifying patterns, sharpening your insights. Revision is not a dead end, not a looming chore or a deadline. The more tools and strategies you have, the more interesting and fun revision will be; the more productive will be your reading, too. As you learn more things to do with reading work in progress, you will—believe it or not—come to enjoy the fiddling and fixing that is revision.

Editing

Editing is reading with a fine-tooth comb. Only a few pieces make it this far. After honing your images, crafting your piece so that it has energy, images, tension, pattern, structure, and insight, edit before you bring a piece out into the world. Many times, we revise our work only to lose sight of its strengths, or we become overwhelmed by its weaknesses. While every single writer wishes it were otherwise, not every piece of writing we start gets finished. Only our very best work is deserving of the nit-picking that is editing.

For a formal class workshop, bring work that has been carefully edited, so your classmates don't have to be distracted (out of the dream, un-transported, remembering they are reading for homework) by typos. Before you submit for publication or in an end-of-semester portfolio, edit the work carefully. Like getting dressed for the most important date of your life, when you edit, you are motivated to check every single word, every space, every tiny detail.

Editing uses a completely different part of the brain than revising. Revising is a kind of re-dreaming; editing is more like paying your bills. You read through your piece from top to bottom, looking for anything that might distract the reader: grammar errors, typos, weird formatting. Then, read the piece from back to front (so you are less likely to get caught up in the narrative, or become impressed or horrified by the work itself). Then, trade with someone else—it is always, always harder to find your own mistakes—and, if you are prone to typos or are a poor speller, take the time to go through your piece for a third and final edit.

If you rely solely on your word processor to edit, you won't be reading your work carefully enough. Your computer is only one tool in your toolbox. A professional edit job requires the master tool: the human brain. There are many errors your computer will not catch (if you confuse "there" and "their," for instance), and there are passages or word choices your computer will tell you are wrong that are actually important aspects of the piece (repeating a word for emphasis, inverting a sentence). Use your computer, use your brain, and give your own eyes the final say.

READING FINISHED WORK

When you read published stories, essays, poems, or other material, you have the same goal as when reading work in progress: Figure out how the piece works. Learn something to help you with your own writing every single time you read, no matter what. At the end of this chapter, there are readings by student writers, alongside the work of professionals.

> *Reading is equivalent to thinking with someone else's head instead of with one's own.*
> — ARTHUR SCHOPENHAUER

As you read the selections in this chapter, what differences do you notice between the professional writers and the student writers? Do you tend to ask different questions of student work than published work?

This semester, your professor may have you keep a reading journal, where you will practice taking notes, reading actively, and learning all you can from other writers about the craft of creating writing. Whether or not you keep a reading journal, by all means read with a pen, write your questions and comments in the margins, take each piece apart, and turn the component parts over in your hands. Develop a reading plan, and allow yourself to try new styles, new authors, new countries, new periods, new genres.

TYPES OF CREATIVE WRITING

Genre refers to the various categories of creative writing. There are genres of form (poetry, fiction, plays) and genres of subject (fantasy, science fiction, romance). Your introductory class will likely focus on some of the following kinds of writing: creative nonfiction, fiction, poetry. In the beginning, stay open to experi-

QUESTIONS TO ASK: Reading Polished Creative Writing

Ask of published, finished work the same establishing, orienting questions you ask of a work in progress.

1. What is the piece about?
2. What effect is the writer trying to have on the reader?
3. How is the piece put together? What are its parts?
4. What kind of writing is this? What other writing/art forms does it remind you of?
5. What insights/conclusions does it present?
6. What patterns are used throughout the writing?
7. What questions does the piece want the reader to mull over, respond to?

mentation; don't pigeonhole yourself as Poet or Playwright too quickly. Who knows, you might be one of those people who letters in cross-country, basketball, and tennis, an all-star writer who excels in prose poetry, graphic novels, and screenplays. All of the following genres, when done well, use the same core strategies: images, energy, tension, insight, pattern, and structure.

> *The greatest part of a writer's time is spent in reading; in order to write, a man will turn over half a library to make one book.*
>
> — SAMUEL JOHNSON

Fiction

Narrative, or story, can take the form of short stories, short-shorts, novels, novellas. Usually, two characters are in a situation that forces one of them to undergo some kind of change or realization, and the secondary character serves as the catalyst for the primary character's change. For this reason, stories with just one character are very hard to pull off.

Additionally, contemporary narrative is built out of scenes, slices of real time, so the reader sees events play out on a kind of stage in the mind's eye. Fiction is like a play in the reader's head. It's not a report, or a summary of events — we experience the events as the characters do, in "real time." Short stories typically run from a couple of pages in length up to forty or so pages. A short-short is a very short story — a paragraph or a page in length. A novella is a short novel, and the length varies greatly, but 50 to 100 pages is typical. Novels are usually 200 to 600 pages long, and can focus on more characters and perhaps cover more time — years instead of moments — than we typically see in a short story.

QUESTIONS TO ASK: Responding to Fiction

Focus on these aspects when reading work in progress or published writing in this genre.

1. What do you see in your mind's eye when you read?
2. What is interesting? Visually? Emotionally?
3. Who is the story about?
4. Where does the story take place?
5. What is "versus" what in this story? What is the nature of the conflict?
6. What's different on the last page from the first page? What has changed? For a short-short, what's different in the last sentence from the first sentence? What has changed?
7. So what? What makes you care about what happens to these characters?

Creative writing classes often use the short story as the training ground for writers learning to write fiction because it can be read in one sitting, is complete in and of itself, and provides many challenges—you have to do everything quickly.

Many writers practice short stories first, to get comfortable with how narrative works, honing their skills in the shorter form. And, they read. Reading widely—all kinds of fiction, long, short, funny, serious, fantastic, realistic, etc.—is the fastest way to improve fiction-writing technique.

Fiction includes genres such as fantasy (George R. R. Martin and J. R. R. Tolkien) and science fiction (Robert Heinlein), horror (Stephen King), romance, western, detective, gay/lesbian, teen, and middle-grade (ages 9 through 12). These subcategories have very specific publishing conventions, and many students who are interested in gaining expertise in one of these categories turn to the books that lay out the conventions. Some writers have success tweaking these conventions, combining and reinventing the rules.

| PRACTICE |

Read the short-short story by Lorraine López, "The Night Aliens in a White Van Kidnapped My Teenage Son near the Baptist Church Parking Lot," on page 52. Answer the questions on the previous page.

Creative Nonfiction

It's always interesting—and somewhat annoying—when a vocabulary term is defining something it is *not*. Nonfiction is a broad category that includes history, guides on caring for your new pet kookaburra, sociology, books on wine-making and cycling and weather. All nonfiction. This kind of writing uses summarizing, instruction (like this book you are reading now), reporting, and telling to get its points across. Creative nonfiction is always about the real, true, known world. However, it specifically refers to a kind of creative writing that uses the conventions of fiction in order to tell a true story. Instead of reporting, analyzing, explaining, or describing, which is what you do in straight nonfiction or essay-writing, creative nonfiction relies heavily on the technique of scene-making—letting the reader *see* the story, instead of being *told* about it. In creative nonfiction, the reader is *transported* visually and emotionally—the reader is in the scene. The story plays out as a movie in the reader's mind's eye, instead of appealing to the reader's intellect alone.

There are two subcategories within creative nonfiction: memoir and researched creative nonfiction. In both forms the writer uses images, scenes, metaphors, dialogue, and pattern. Creative nonfiction shows a writer expanding and questioning perceptions, learning more about the world and the self. In memoir,

QUESTIONS TO ASK: Responding to Creative Nonfiction

Focus on these aspects when reading work in progress or published writing in this genre.

1. What do you see in your mind's eye when you read?
2. What is interesting? Visually? Emotionally?
3. Who is the story about? How do you come to know the people in the piece?
4. Where does the story take place?
5. What is the conflict in this story?
6. What information do you learn? What insights do you gain?
7. What's different on the last page from the first page? What has changed?
8. So what? What makes you care about what happens?

you tell a story from your own life in order to help the reader see his or her own life in a new, richer way. Researched work (sometimes called *new journalism*) combines facts and imagination in order to create scenes. Robert Kurson, for example, in *Shadow Divers* (2004), leads you through a deep-sea shipwreck with professional scuba divers; when they enter the wreck of a German submarine, you feel like you are right there, gasping for air (see excerpt on p. 153). Kurson's research (reading and extensive interviews with professional wreck divers) allowed him to create scenes so real, when you read them it feels as though you are having the experience.

As with fiction, creative nonfiction can be almost any length, from a paragraph-long micro-essay to book length.

PRACTICE

Read the creative nonfiction piece by Kathleen Norris, "Rain," on page 53. Answer the questions above.

Poetry

Poetry could be defined as creative writing where the lines don't go all the way to the right side of the page. But that doesn't *really* get at the nature and range of poetry. A poem is compressed. Poems are short and also rich with language and emotion. Readers are expected to read a poem several times, allowing the nuances to unfurl. There are two basic kinds of poetry: narrative and lyric. You will study these subcategories in depth in the chapter titled "Structure." Narrative poetry uses some of the same tools stories use: character, conflict, story. Lyric poetry doesn't tell a story, necessarily; instead, it presents a brief (sixty lines or fewer) concentrated feeling or emotion.

PRACTICE

Read Sebastian Matthews's poem "Buying Wine" on page 53, and also read "The Question Mark," by Gevorg Emin, on page 54. Which one tells more of a story? Which one focuses more on evoking a single emotion in the reader, concentrating on a very specific effect? Support your answer with specific references to each of the poems.

Prose Poems

Prose poems are poems in blocks of type, usually one paragraph or sometimes two. The prose poem looks like prose (prose is fiction and creative nonfiction, work that is formatted in traditional paragraphs). Sometimes there are characters, but not always; a prose poem can be all description. It has to be read with the same amount of concentration as a poem, because the stage setup we are comfortable with in fiction — scenes, characters, images playing out in our mind's eye in real time — may not exist. There may be strange, surprising, or surreal situations. The prose poem may not be a story at all; it might be pure emotion and feeling and description. A prose poem usually employs the heightened language of poetry: images, sounds, and feelings, with more overt rhythm to the words.

QUESTIONS TO ASK: Responding to Poetry and Prose Poems

Focus on these aspects when reading work in progress or published work in these genres.

1. Who is speaking?
2. Where is the poem taking place?
3. What are the images?
4. What is the structure of this poem?
5. What happens in the poem? What's the "story"?
6. What do you see in your mind's eye?
7. What feelings are evoked?
8. What sounds in the poem emphasize the visuals, the feelings?
9. What gives the poem its energy?
10. What makes you, the reader, interested in the poem?

PRACTICE

Read A. Van Jordan's "af•ter•glow," on page 55, and Jamaica Kincaid's "Girl," on page 55. Which one is more like poetry, and therefore more readily classified as a prose poem? Which one focuses more on story, presenting a sequence of events? Would you consider either of these a short-short story? Use examples from the works to support your answers.

Plays and Screenplays

Plays and screenplays are works designed to be performed or filmed. They exist on the page in two forms: One form, which you will practice this semester, is formatted for readers. The second is formatted for an entire theater company or movie production. If you are interested in writing for stage or screen, there are numerous books available on the specific conventions for formatting and submitting your work. In this course, we will focus primarily on how to write strong basic conflicts and fresh, energetic dialogue. Later, you may choose to take a more in-depth course focused exclusively on scriptwriting.

Playwriting is storytelling in images. Too many hopeful screenwriters get distracted by the cool things they can do with cameras that they forget about what the writer must still do: Create a story, with images, that moves reader-viewers. Like fiction and creative nonfiction, plays (in all their forms) must always be about people in specific places with specific problems. Obviously, writing in this genre helps your dialogue skills if you are a fiction or creative nonfiction writer. But a play also uses sound, music, and rhythm, just as a poem does.

Like a poem, a play is short, focused, and intense. Instead of images, however, the play relies on dialogue to tell the story and illustrate the conflict. Reading aloud takes much longer than reading to yourself, but you will be amazed at how fast a few pages of dialogue are used up. Drama is intensely concentrated, with the dialogue hyper-focused, fast-moving, and multilayered. Conflict (as in fiction) is the mother of drama, and the challenge for the author of a play is to make sure the words the character or characters are speaking reveal conflicts, layers, tension, and action. In poetry, the author has to play with sound and meaning; in a play, several things have to be going on simultaneously on the visual and verbal levels, even in monologues, where only one person is talking.

> *Without tradition, art is a flock of sheep without a shepherd. Without innovation, it is a corpse.*
>
> — WINSTON CHURCHILL

PRACTICE

Read Anna Deavere Smith's "I Was Scared," an excerpt from her play *Twilight: Los Angeles 1992*, on page 56. Then answer the questions on the next page.

QUESTIONS TO ASK: Responding to Plays and Screenplays

Focus on these aspects when reading work in progress or published writing in these genres.

1. What is the story of the scene, act, or play?
2. Who talks?
3. What is the psychology of the person or people in the play?
4. What are the conflicts that come through in the dialogue?
5. What conflicts come through in the action?
6. What conflicts come through via the setting?
7. What changes over the course of the play?
8. What images do you see in your mind as you listen to the dialogue?

Graphic Novels, Comics, and Experimental Pieces

Creative writing is not limited to the four genres discussed above (fiction, creative nonfiction, poetry, and drama). Creative writers have for centuries resisted rules and boxes, consistently reinventing and redefining what can be done with black marks on white sheets of paper. A particularly fertile genre for new writers, the graphic novel has a long and sturdy history. A graphic novel is a comic that works like a prose novel or novella, and while some are as short as fifty pages, others are long enough to take up multivolume sets!

Comics and graphic novels have always attracted some of the world's wisest and most adventurous artists; you may know Art Spiegelman's *Maus* or the work of Matt Groening (creator of *The Simpsons*, who originally wrote a comic strip appearing in college and alternative newspapers). Cartoons and comics are terrific training in the essentials of storytelling, because the author has to construct a clear, compelling narrative that proceeds step by step. Because the artwork carries a lot of the information, the writing itself is often pared down and simplified, making the form fascinating and rewarding to study. You can literally see everything that is going on. Like a play, graphic literature uses words to render dialogue, and images to render action and setting. Just as the playwright has to coordinate the visual line with the aural (spoken) line, the graphic artist works the visual and verbal in tandem. The graphic writer, then, has to be expert at every single genre, every single technique available to creative writers. Graphic novels are currently experiencing a surge in popularity, just as they did in the nineteenth century, the 1930s, and the 1960s.

PRACTICE

Read the excerpt from Art Spiegelman's *Maus* (p. 59), his powerful book-length comic about the Holocaust. Answer the questions below.

Experimental creative writing is also fertile ground for new writers. Realize that the more difficult your work is to read, and the more off-putting your subject matter, the fewer readers you will have. One rule to consider (and possibly break): The author should never have more fun than the reader. The more you stray, as a writer, from a strong, clear narrative story line, the harder your reader has to work to understand what is going on and stay involved in the piece. If there is a great payoff—in terms of humor or insight—the reader may rise to the occasion. Think about what you love to read, and try to give your readers the same kinds of pleasure. The longer your experiment the harder it is to sustain. Ultimately, creative writers *are* lovers of experiment and play. Try new things. Risk failing. Read work you wouldn't normally be drawn to. If you are working at the edge of what is comfortable for you, you are very likely growing as a writer.

> *Everything has been said before but since nobody listens, we have to keep going back and beginning all over again.*
> — ANDRÉ GIDE

QUESTIONS TO ASK: Responding to Graphic Novels, Comics, and Experimental Pieces

Focus on these aspects when reading work in progress or published writing in these genres.

1. What is the work about?
2. What's the story the piece is telling?
3. What emotions are covered in this piece?
4. Is the dialogue accurate, lively, and interesting?
5. What does each panel/section/line do that is different from the other panels, sections, or lines?
6. What keeps you interested in reading this work?
7. How does the artwork (if included) amplify the power of the story?
8. What does the experiment (if included) ask the reader to do? Is it worth it?

PRACTICE

Write an informal response reflecting on the various genres you have just read and practiced writing—fiction, creative nonfiction, poetry, drama, comics, and experiments. Which genre did you think you would like the best? Which one ended up being the most fun for you to read? Any surprises? Rank the six genres in order of your favorite to least favorite. What affected your choices? Do you think by practicing in your least favorite genre, you will develop writing "muscles" that will help your chosen genre? Do you like reading the same ones you like writing? Which do you like reading least?

READING TO WRITE: THE ART OF IMITATION

When you were tiny, you learned to walk, talk, and make friends by watching other people do these things and copying them. You copied, you learned; life was good.

Imitation is a time-honored way to understand more deeply and to get more proficient at any art or skill, whether it's writing, cooking, painting, dancing, composing, acting, or designing clothes, furniture, or houses. Beginning chefs at first copy the recipe closely, getting their techniques down. Then, they start to add more and more of their own special touches, finally inventing not just recipes, but techniques and concepts of their own (which are then imitated, taught in culinary school, etc.).

> *Stevie Wonder told me that he heard me coming in on the radio from Windsor [Ontario], that I had influenced some of his pieces. It wasn't like he copped the lick or anything like that, but basically he went in a more adventurous chordal direction than he would have had I not existed. That's the kind of influence that I like. It is not copying.*
>
> — JONI MITCHELL

It works similarly in writing. By carefully examining, from the inside out, how other writers work—by copying, in essence—you become a better writer. And nothing forces you to read more closely, more carefully than imitation.

Most writers find they have to practice every day, just like athletes and musicians and painters. The imitation practices in this chapter are useful for writers who need a jump start, who want to have "something to do" for their daily practice, or for stuck writers who want to limber up, stretch old muscles, and strengthen new ones. The imitation process is flexible, and you can bend it to fit your needs. You can imitate an *aspect* of a piece, or a whole piece—there are many options for ripping off the greats, so to speak.

Imitation is a great way to hone your creative thinking skills, to increase your confidence, and to help you find your way to your own best material. It's like dancing on someone else's feet. It might feel awkward, but it's a quick, fabulous path to body-memory, internalizing the basic moves that separate amateur from pro.

Imitation: Guided Practice

Some students feel weird about imitation at first. They feel like they are stealing. Or they fear people will think they are too dim to come up with their own ideas. Most writers want to be original. But when you hear a great new band cover a classic song, you don't think to yourself: Gosh, the White Stripes can't come up with anything new. They've turned into mindless copiers! No. You think: Cool version. You think: I didn't ever hear it that way before. Interesting. To cover a song, to imitate a published piece of creative writing, is to pay homage.

The writer Voltaire put it this way: "Originality is nothing but judicious imitation. The most original writers borrowed from one another. The instruction we find in books is like fire. We fetch it from our neighbors, kindle it at home, communicate it to others, and it becomes the property of all."

When you imitate, you aren't copying or stealing. You're performing a training exercise, one that has a long and respected tradition in the arts. You of course always acknowledge the imitation. It's against the law to take someone else's words or ideas and pass them off as your own, and it's embarrassing to pretend your work is original when clearly it is not. That's not what you are doing. Here, in this class, you are not going to try to publish your imitations, or pass them off as your own totally inspired personal invention. You're practicing. Imitation is training, development. You are trying to block out your normal thinking habits and force yourself into some new patterns and new moves. Imitation works.

You are imitating whenever you write, unconsciously. All writers are influenced by the works they have read, what they watch, what they know about literature. Stories you learned as a child are stuck in your head. Phrases and rhythms of works you read last semester lodge in your writing mind, and come out in your work. This is a good thing! Successful writers enjoy embedding subtle references to other pieces of literature in their works. We pass on, translate, adore, and keep alive the writers who influence us, consciously and unconsciously. We're all imitating to some extent, every time we sit down to write. The more widely you read, the more texture your own writing has—artist as melting pot. If you slavishly read only one or two writers, your work may suffer from a poverty of influence.

Some students worry that if they imitate, they will lose their own personal stamp. To *truly* imitate another writer is nearly as impossible as imitating another person. When you do impressions of your roommate, her accent and mannerisms, everyone knows it's you, not her. You can get close to taking on someone else's voice and tone; maybe over the telephone you can fool people. You heighten some aspects of her personality and leave out other ones entirely. But we know it's *you*—it's *you* being *her*. That's what intentional literary imitation is, too. It's you, but dressed in the clothes of someone else—someone who has really learned how to shop! Someone with style that's better than or different from your own. Imitation doesn't decrease creativity. It strengthens and feeds creativity.

Young musicians usually have extensive collections of music by other young musicians. They attend performances in weird warehouses and in the garages of friends of friends. Up-and-coming musicians know enormous amounts about who is playing what, with whom, and how well. Do musicians immerse themselves in the music scene in order to steal ideas, chord combinations, clever lyrics? No. They do it because they know that surrounding yourself with other practitioners of your chosen art *feeds your work*. When you are a working artist, you can't *not* be obsessed with what everyone else is doing. It's how you learn how to do what you do better.

Writers are the same way. Our garage bands are often little magazines, zines, and blogs. Our shows are live readings. We follow poets to community centers, colleges, parks, and theaters to see what they have. In the same way we go to see our favorite live bands again and again, we drive hours to see our favorite fiction writer for the fifth time. Our favorite writers are those who have something to teach us. We learn by following them, sometimes word by word.

When you imitate, remember, you are experimenting. It's just for practice. Stay loose, stay open. When you go back to your own ways of writing, you'll be a better writer. You'll have new tools, new approaches, a whole new range. Imitation is a way to practice writing.

Types of Imitation

There are two basic types of imitation writers use for their experiments: scaffolding (writing between the lines) and fill-in-the-blank (a form of Mad Libs). Each one allows your front brain, your thinking/planning/knowing mind, to step aside so that the back of your mind, the creative part, dormant for much of daily life, can come forward and *play*. Gaps, leaps, nonsense, surprise, discomfort, weirdness—all these are welcome aspects of imitation. Remember, this is for practice, not necessarily for publication. You are learning new dance steps to increase the range of what you can do.

Scaffolding: Writing between the Lines. Scaffolding is when you use another writer's text, line by line, to create your own piece. Call to mind a building under construction. You know the system of platforms constructed *around* the building site, as the new floors are built? That's scaffolding, and that's the function of the text we use to launch our imitations. Then, when the new piece is completed, the scaffolding is removed. The building stands. We forget all about the scaffolds. The original text provides the inspiration and supports the new work.

When you imitate in this way, don't worry about fitting everything together, or making absolute sense. You are after a sense of play. It might feel awkward, silly, tipsy, or fun — like when you were a kid, and you danced, standing on someone else's feet.

Scaffolding a Poem. Choose a poem you enjoy, but perhaps do not completely "get." Copy the poem over on a sheet of paper, skipping three lines in between each line of the poem. That's your scaffold. You build your own poem in between the existing lines, the supports. Here's an example of how the technique works, using a poem by James Tate, "Consolations After an Affair," as the scaffold. (The poem appears in its original form at the end of the chapter, on p. 51.)

James Tate
Consolations After an Affair

[*You put your title, based on this one, here—perhaps "consolations" after something else?*]

My plants are whispering to one another:

[*Your first line is written here, inspired by Tate's line. Consider focusing on some physical element interacting with itself or something else.*]

they are planning a little party

[*Here is your second line—you write a subject, verb, and object just as Tate did.*]

later on in the week about watering time.

[*In this line, you are making your comment, perhaps about what is happening later on in your week, finishing the sentence you started as Tate does.*]

I have quilts on beds and walls

[*Here, you notice, with your own eyes, a visual image, a specific.*]

that think it is still the 19th century.

[*In this line, you make a wild leap into the imagination of something inanimate.*]

They know nothing of automobiles and jet planes.

[*Continue musing about what your object might know/not know.*]

For them a wheat field in January

[*In the same vein, you continue to "think like a quilt"—give the objects in your poem an interior life and let them speak about something in nature, in winter.*]

is their mother and enough.

[*Continue the image.*]

I've discovered that I don't need

[*Move to a statement of discovery—what do you not need?*]

a retirement plan, a plan to succeed.

A snow leopard sleeps behind me

[*Move next to an image—an animal or something alive.*]

like a slow, warm breeze.

[*Use a simile to make the reader feel the image.*]

And I can hear the inner birds singing

[*Use one of the senses you haven't used yet—touch, taste, sound?*]

alone in this house I love.

[*End up, with the same number of lines as Tate, concluding with a statement about what specific element of this place it is you love.*]

After you write lines of your own *inspired by or built from Tate's lines*, copy out just your poem, on a new sheet of paper. As you copy, tinker with your lines. Delete and add words to make them connect to each other. If there is a line that really interferes with your new poem, leave it out; or add lines as you need to.

Read the poems out loud to the class. Do you notice the scaffolding? Are the poems alike or different? Did you make any new moves that you would not have thought of without Tate as the trigger?

If you decide to submit the piece to a literary magazine or class anthology, you can simply put "After James Tate's 'Consolations After an Affair'" under the title, if you feel it is still very closely related to the original. Poets and writers often talk to each other in this complimentary fashion; it's not unusual at all. Imitation is, after all, the highest form of flattery.

| PRACTICE |

Try the above experiment again, on your own. Choose one of the poems in this book, such as "Buying Wine" by Sebastian Matthews on page 53 or "The Question Mark" by Gevorg Emin on page 54. Another poem in this book that works well for the scaffolding practice is "Squirt Gun" by Robert Morgan on page 98. Your teacher may provide alternate examples for you to work from: Emily Dickinson, Tomas Tranströmer, Robert Hass, and Rumi work well—poets who are slightly opaque, surreal.

To begin, copy over the poem you will imitate, triple spaced. Cover up the lines with a second sheet of paper so you can only see one at a time. Then, using each line, one at a time as a prompt and guide, write in your own lines.

Variation 1: Scaffold off a classmate's imitation of Tate, using the student's new poem as your prompt poem.

Variation 2: Use one of the poems a classmate wrote for this course. Copy over the student's lines, triple spacing, and write in your own lines.

Variation 3: Your teacher or a partner gives you the lines from a poem you have never read before, one at a time. You write your own line in response to each line.

Narrative Scaffolding. Creative nonfiction and fiction—the narrative genres—provide excellent opportunities for increasing your creative techniques by imitation. In order to practice, we will work with an excerpt from writer Amy Fusselman's memoir. In Fusselman's *The Pharmacist's Mate*, she writes about herself and her family. The book's arc traces her unique journey: As she mourns the death of her father, she is also on a quest to have a child. Because she writes in short, deft sections, she provides a good model for creating a prose piece of your own using the scaffolding method. Instead of relying on (perhaps clichéd) random ideas, or spending hours staring off into space hoping for a good idea, you work the muscles of inspiration by paying close attention to how writers like Fusselman work, what they write about, and how they braid and relate disparate topics to generate more interest and create fresh meanings. This is how imitation helps us be less predictable and more bold and original.

> *Imitation gave me room to operate with my own scalpel in someone else's scrubs. To use a style that I wasn't used to connected some circuits in my head, and I felt more freedom to explore different directions with the tools I already had. I could discover rhythm and ride the wave all the way to shore.*
> — STUDENT WRITER CHRISTIAN PIERS, ON IMITATING AMY FUSSELMAN

PRACTICE

On page 60 you will find the excerpt from the opening portion of Amy Fusselman's memoir, *The Pharmacist's Mate*. Read the selection, and answer the questions for creative nonfiction on page 35.

When you imitate someone or something, you study it closely. You learn how it moves. What its habits are. To get ready to write, reread the Amy Fusselman selection. Examine it closely. Notice the different layers of her text. Fusselman braids together three kinds of information. What are the categories of information in her various sections?

stories about her body, trying to get pregnant
excerpts from her father's journals, kept when he was young
stories about her father, her brother, family

What order does she put the sections in? Can you detect a pattern? Reread her work. How does she start her sections? End them? Why are they numbered? As we closely read, we find the ultimate subject of her book—youth, family, and parenting—becoming a mom, reinventing herself as a sister, and learning how to be a daughter, in the wake of her father's death. The three subjects intertwine in a pattern that adds up to more than the sum of its parts. Reading a piece in order to imitate it encourages you to identify its parts. It's like inventing a recipe from a cooked dish that you really like. What's in it? How might the cook/author have assembled the parts? In what order?

> *Nothing is new except arrangement.*
> — WILL DURANT

Imitating is a lot like reading through a microscope. Look more closely. What makes a section a section in Fusselman? What kind of unit does she use? Are these sections mini stories? Does each one have a particular insight? Or is there something else that all these units have in common? Are there several types of units?

When you scaffold off a piece of prose, think of the sections as stanzas in a poem, and the paragraphs—the groups of sentences separated by white space within her numbered sections—as lines.

You will do the same thing we did for "Consolations After an Affair" by James Tate above: Launch your own "lines" based on Fusselman's.

Also, before you begin, you want to be oriented in time and space on the image level. In order to orient yourself, choose your three braids, or *types* of information to include in your personal memoir, your rendition of *The Pharmacist's Mate*.

Filling in the Blanks. Imitation exercises are like weight lifting or strength training. They build new muscles. Scaffolding is one way to use close reading and imitation to get out of a writing rut and increase your creative abilities. Imitation via "filling in the blanks" is another. Fill-in-the-blank exercises may remind you of Mad Libs. In the original Mad Libs game, a player is given a story or poem or passage, with key words left out. The left-out words are presented as blanks, with a clue indicating what part of speech (adjective, place name, etc.) belongs there. For creative writers, fill-in-the-blank is a kind of imitation that lets the beginning or blocked writer practice moving the mind in new directions. It's a kind of stretching, a yoga for the creative brain, if you will.

Do not read the poem "Winter Field" by Ellen Bryant Voigt on p. 51. In order to experience the greatest effect of fill-in-the-blank, you are *not* to read the poem in its entirety. You have to work "blind" in a way, and try hard not to think, but to put down the first flash in your mind. Whatever you see first. Writing out your "answers" by hand works best. In some classes, your teacher may want to set up the poem so that you have read to you or are handed only one line at a time, so you *can't* glance ahead.

With imitation, you want randomness, surprise, awkwardness. That's how the best lines are won: accidentally. To work with less control will often make you feel a bit unsettled, but that's okay. It's likely that this will feel uncomfortable, especially at first. It's always weird to walk in someone else's shoes.

In order to imitate successfully, orient yourself in the physical climate of the poem (or piece). Evoke images in your mind's eye. It doesn't matter if they are real or imagined, from your life, or made-up — it only matters that you *see*.

To prepare, draw an X on a sheet of blank, unlined paper. That X is you. Imagine you are in a winter field near where you live. Jot down what's on the ground, what's over your head, what's way above your head, way below the ground (forty feet). How do you know it's winter? Look around, use your eyes. What are you wearing? Use your eyes, look at your body. Don't make it up. What's on your feet? Is anyone else there? What do you smell? What's the light like? What time of day is it?

Jot the answers to these questions around your X. Just a word or two to anchor the image — don't write away all the energy, just jot down a word or three, just up to the point where you are strongly situated in the image.

Next, use a card or a piece of paper to cover the poem exercise below, so you only see the line you are working on. Read the poem line to yourself, then fill in the blank, using the cues provided.

Try filling in the blanks with the poem "Winter Field" as your guide.

Ellen Bryant Voigt
Winter Field

The winter field is not _____

[*Write what you see the winter field not being/doing/knowing/understanding — use your eyes and write what you see.*]

the field of summer lost in snow: it is _____

[*Write whatever pops into your mind here — it's okay if it doesn't fit, but try to flow from "it is."*]

another thing, a different thing. _____

[*Write a short sentence that flows from this.*]

"We shouted, we shook you," you tell me, / but there was no _____

[*Write what you can see or imagine missing, absent, don't read ahead and don't worry about making sense.*]

only _____

[*Write what there was, or could be.*]

After they'd pierced a _____ and fished me up, _____

[*Fill in the blanks. Work quickly—don't think and don't try to make sense.*]

after they'd reeled me back they packed me under _____

[*Write what you are packed under, what it looks like, and how you felt—you can still be in the winter field if you like.*]

The summer field, _____

[*Describe the same place in summer—use your eyes and write what you see.*]

has its many tasks; _____

[*Connect this line to the summer field line above.*]

the winter field _____

[*Fill in the blank; let yourself be surprised, you don't have to make sense. It's okay if you repeat things from earlier in your writing, but don't look back, or ahead.*]

For those hours / I was _____

and my body _____

which you have long loved well _____

did not love you. _____

Fill in the final four blanks as quickly and intuitively as you can. This may feel very uncomfortable and forced—you are improvising. Write one last line, sparked by "Did not love you."

Your instructor may have you read these aloud in class, reading the original lines and the lines with the fill-ins each time. Then, someone else may read the original poem, in its untampered-with state. Where are the new lines successful? Do you like any of your classmates' poems better than the original?

PRACTICE

Try this exercise again with the same poem. Imagine the same field, but you are a different age, or in a very different mood. Do you come up with different "answers"?

WRITING PROJECTS

1. Write a short-short story. Limit yourself to one page (about 250 words). Working from the lists you created in Chapter 1, choose a slice of time and write a fictional story—perhaps simply one complete scene—in which the characters are struggling against something difficult or surprising.

2. Compose a short essay (250–1000 words). Focus your mind's eye on an important feature of the landscape or city where you live. You could look at a specific aspect of the weather, architecture, plant life, or noise. Choose a topic that you can present in images—actual experiences you've had with this thing. Make your images as vivid as possible. End with a line of dialogue.

3. What kind of poetry do you prefer to write, lyric or narrative? Do you focus tightly on one image or topic, or are you more of a storyteller? Write a poem, just for practice, in the mode you like best, lyric or narrative. Feel free to write without punctuation. Consider, if you are writing a narrative poem, choosing to present a moment when you realized something interesting but confusing about a parent or caregiver.

4. Try writing one of each of the poem types: prose, narrative (in which you tell a story), or lyric (in which you focus on emotion and feeling). Feel free to use published authors as models. For example, you could create a poem as a dictionary definition or encyclopedia entry.

5. Think of a friend who talks in stories—maybe telling two or three stories at once, going off on tangents readily. Write a short monologue (one to three pages) in which your friend talks about two or three things (a dramatic incident from his or her life, what's going on in the room right now) as a way of avoiding talking about something more important. How can you indicate to your readers/listeners what he or she is avoiding mentioning through your dialogue?

6. Write a short dialogue scene in which two characters in a busy location (designated clearly by you) are talking. Each character wants something but doesn't want to say so. For example, Person A wants to buy herself an engagement ring (she has no fiancé) and the clerk, Person B, wants to ask her out.

7. Take one of the pieces you have written this semester and recast it in play form. Do you need to change the location to make it more visually interesting? Write the dialogue, seeing your characters' actions as you write. For example, if you wrote a narrative poem about a tricky parental conflict, after Sebastian Matthews's "Buying Wine" on page 53, you could recast that piece as a micro-play, focusing on the dialogue from that scene.

8. Rewrite any of the pieces you drafted from the scaffolding assignments, growing, stretching, honing your lines, cutting out what you don't like and adding more of what you do like. Keep the best lines, while elaborating, clarifying, and cutting. Bring your piece to class, and with a partner or in a group, discuss the questions for responding to a piece of poetry on page 36. Are there further changes you will make after the discussion?

9. Try building a prose poem or a short story using the scaffolding technique. Use the story by Lorraine López on page 52 or the piece "Girl," by Jamaica Kincaid on page 55. Or choose another short-short story that you like or as assigned by your teacher. Set up the physical page or pages of the story, covering it with a piece of blank paper so you only see one line at a time. Write your own sentences, inspired by the one you are reading, and, working one step at a time, slowly slide your cover sheet down the page. Read your story aloud to a partner. Does anything in it surprise you? Were you prompted to come up with things you wouldn't have come up with otherwise?

10. Bring one of the prose scaffold projects, the Fusselman or another piece, to class. Give copies to your class, partner, or group. Using the questions for responding to creative nonfiction on page 35, discuss each participant's work. Does scaffolding limit you or free you to come up with interesting material?

11. Choose three parts of your life to work from. If you can use another person's texts for one of your sections, as Fusselman uses her father's journal entries, your work will be even easier. Students have used emails from old friends, parents' letters, family histories, Xanga, Facebook, and their own high school diaries. The other two parts of your life are inspired by Fusselman's work: Choose wisely. You might use as one of your topics the struggle to make a team, fight an illness, begin a relationship, or conquer a difficult project. The third topic, Fusselman's dealing with the death of her father, might be for you the fallout after a death in your own family, the loss of a friendship, a grandparent's illness, or a sibling's trouble. Working one section at a time, tell your three stories, piece by piece, sticking closely to the Fusselman model. When she writes dialogue, you write dialogue. When she writes what "the big problem" is, you state your big problem. When she has a theory, you write a theory of your own. And so on, until you have twelve short sections.

READINGS

James Tate
Consolations After an Affair

My plants are whispering to one another:
they are planning a little party
later on in the week about watering time.
I have quilts on beds and walls
that think it is still the 19th century.
They know nothing of automobiles and jet planes.
For them a wheat field in January
is their mother and enough.
I've discovered that I don't need
a retirement plan, a plan to succeed.
A snow leopard sleeps beside me
like a slow, warm breeze.
And I can hear the inner birds singing
alone in this house I love.

Ellen Bryant Voigt
Winter Field

The winter field is not
the field of summer lost in snow: it is
another thing, a different thing.

"We shouted, we shook you," you tell me,
but there was no sound, no face, no fear, only
oblivion—why shouldn't it be so?

After they'd pierced a vein and fished me up,
after they'd reeled me back they packed me under
blanket on top of blanket, I trembled so.

The summer field, sun-fed, mutable,
has its many tasks; the winter field
becomes its adjective.
                    For those hours
I was some other thing, and my body,
which you have long loved well,
did not love you.

Lorraine López

The Night Aliens in a White Van Kidnapped My Teenage Son near the Baptist Church Parking Lot

He admits being peeved, my boy does. Not allowed to sleep over with a shady friend with no phone, only a beeper, my son settles enough to go to bed, earlier than usual even. But he tosses, twists—then pops the screen and leaps out, scrambling for the damp lap of grass near the Baptist church parking lot across the street. In the muzzy mosquito haze funneling from the street light, he considers *in-* words, like "injustice" and "inalienable rights," when extraterrestrials— two or twenty, he can't be sure—careen in a white Dodge van—brakes shrieking, tires thumping speed bumps—onto the church lot.

Laughing and scratching like their skins don't fit, they ask for directions to Peanut's Red Neck Bar-be-cue, and my boy, ever helpful, starts to explain as they hurtle from the van, rushing him. They snatch him with long, spongy arms and slam him into the back. Then, tires wailing, they haul out to the street. Cramped between crates, he's still keen to idea. When the aliens brake for a red light, he yanks the latch, spills out the rear door, runs like fire for the back streets. In an alley, he pulls a mangled girl's bike from a trash heap and wobbles home.

Because I'd locked his window after finding his bed empty, the buzzing doorbell jolts me alert. Shaken, he can barely speak. Says if I call the police, they'll *never* believe it. Shush, I say, hush. I run him a bubbling tub, press two baby aspirin into his palm, and finally tuck him to sleep. Now *I* twist and toss, pull the curtains apart to check for white vans, listen for the squeal of brakes, the awful laughter, *something* alien out there ready to wrench my boy from me.

Kathleen Norris
Rain

> Above all, it is a land in serious need of rain.
> — WILLIAM C. SHARMAN, *Plains Folk*

Until I moved to western South Dakota, I did not know about rain, that it could come too hard, too soft, too hot, too cold, too early, too late. That there could be too little at the right time, too much at the wrong time, and vice versa.

I did not know that a light rain coming at the end of a hot afternoon, with the temperature at 100 degrees or more, can literally burn wheat, steaming it on the stalk so it's not worth harvesting.

I had not seen a long, slow rain come at harvest, making grain lying in the swath begin to sprout again, ruining it as a cash crop.

Until I had seen a few violent hailstorms and replaced the shingles on our roof twice in five years, I had forgotten why my grandmother had screens made of chicken wire for all the windows on the west side of her house.

I had not seen the whimsy of wind, rain, and hail; a path in a wheatfield as if a drunken giant had stumbled through, leaving footprints here and there. I had not seen hail fall from a clear blue sky. I had not tasted horizontal rain, flung by powerful winds.

I had not realized that a long soaking rain in spring or fall, a straight-down-falling rain, a gentle, splashing rain is more than a blessing. It's a miracle.

An old farmer once asked my husband and me how long we'd been in the country. "Five years," we answered. "Well, then," he said, "you've seen rain."

Sebastian Matthews
Buying Wine

When we were boys, we had a choice: stay in the car or else
follow him into Wine Mart, that cavernous retail barn,

down aisle after aisle — California reds to Australian blends
to French dessert wines — past bins loaded like bat racks

with bottles, each with its own heraldic tag, its licked coat
of arms, trailing after our father as he pushed the ever-filling cart,

bent forward in concentration, one hand in mouth stroking
his unkempt mustache, the other lofting up bottles like fruit

then setting them down, weighing the store of data in his brain
against the cost, the year, the cut of meat he'd select at the butcher's:

a lamb chop, say, if this Umbrian red had enough body to marry,
to dance on its legs in the bell of the night; or some scallops maybe,

those languid hearts of the sea, a poet's dozen in a baggy,
and a Pinot Grigio light enough not to disturb their salty murmur.

Often, we'd stay in the car until we'd used up the radio
and our dwindling capacity to believe our father

might actually "Just be back," then break free, releasing
our seatbelts, drifting to the edges of the parking lot like horses

loosed in a field following the sun's endgame of shade; sometimes
I'd peer into the front window, breath fogging the sale signs,

catching snippets of my father's profile appearing and disappearing
behind the tall cardboard stacks. Once I slipped back into the store,

wandering the aisles, master of my own cart, loading it to bursting
for the dream party I was going to throw. But mostly, like now,

as I search for the perfect $12 bottle, I'd shuffle along, dancing bear
behind circus master, and wait for my father to pronounce, tall

in his basketball body, wine bottles like babies in his hands, "Aha!"

Gevorg Emin
The Question Mark

Translated by Diana der Hovanessian

Poor thing. Poor crippled measure
of punctuation. Who would know,
who could imagine you used to be
an exclamation point?
What force bent you over?
Age, time and the vices
of this century?
Did you not once evoke,
call out and stress?
But you got weary of it all,
got wise, and turned like this.

A. Van Jordan

af • ter • glow \≈\ *n.* **1.** The light esp. in the Ohio sky after sunset: as in the look of the mother-of-pearl air during the morning's afterglow. **2.** The glow continuing after the disappearance of a flame, as of a match or a lover, and sometimes regarded as a type of phosphorescent ghost: This balm, this bath of light / This cocktail of lust and sorrow, / This rumor of faithless love on a neighbor's lips, / This Monday morning, this Friday night, / This pendulum of my heart, / This salve for my soul, / This tremble from your body / This breast aflame, this bed ablaze / Where you rub oil on my feet, / Where we spoon and, before sunrise, turn away / And I dream, eyes open, / swimming / In this room's pitch-dark landscape.

Jamaica Kincaid
Girl

Wash the white clothes on Monday and put them on the stone heap; wash the color clothes on Tuesday and put them on the clothesline to dry; don't walk barehead in the hot sun; cook pumpkin fritters in very hot sweet oil; soak your little cloths right after you take them off; when buying cotton to make yourself a nice blouse, be sure that it doesn't have gum on it, because that way it won't hold up well after a wash; soak salt fish overnight before you cook it; is it true that you sing benna[1] in Sunday school?; always eat your food in such a way that it won't turn someone else's stomach; on Sundays try to walk like a lady and not like the slut you are so bent on becoming; don't sing benna in Sunday school; you mustn't speak to wharf-rat boys, not even to give directions; don't eat fruits on the street — flies will follow you; *but I don't sing benna on Sundays at all and never in Sunday school;* this is how to sew on a button; this is how to make a buttonhole for the button you have just sewed on; this is how to hem a dress when you see the hem coming down and so to prevent yourself from looking like the slut I know you are so bent on becoming; this is how you iron your father's khaki shirt so that it doesn't have a crease; this is how you iron your father's khaki pants so that they don't have a crease; this is how you grow okra — far from the house, because okra tree harbors red ants; when you are growing dasheen, make sure it gets plenty of water or else it makes your throat itch when you are eating it; this is how you sweep a corner; this is how you sweep a whole house; this is how you

---

[1]Calypso music.

sweep a yard; this is how you smile to someone you don't like too much; this is how you smile to someone you don't like at all; this is how you smile to someone you like completely; this is how you set a table for tea; this is how you set a table for dinner; this is how you set a table for dinner with an important guest; this is how you set a table for lunch; this is how you set a table for breakfast; this is how to behave in the presence of men who don't know you very well, and this way they won't recognize immediately the slut I have warned you against becoming; be sure to wash every day, even if it is with your own spit; don't squat down to play marbles — you are not a boy, you know; don't pick people's flowers — you might catch something; don't throw stones at blackbirds, because it might not be a blackbird at all; this is how to make a bread pudding; this is how to make doukona;[2] this is how to make pepper pot; this is how to make a good medicine for a cold; this is how to make a good medicine to throw away a child before it even becomes a child; this is how to catch a fish; this is how to throw back a fish you don't like, and that way something bad won't fall on you; this is how to bully a man; this is how a man bullies you; this is how to love a man, and if this doesn't work there are other ways, and if they don't work don't feel too bad about giving up; this is how to spit up in the air if you feel like it, and this is how to move quick so that it doesn't fall on you; this is how to make ends meet; always squeeze bread to make sure it's fresh; *but what if the baker won't let me feel the bread?;* you mean to say that after all you are really going to be the kind of woman who the baker won't let near the bread?

---

[2]A spicy plantain pudding.

Anna Deavere Smith
From *Twilight: Los Angeles 1992*

I WAS SCARED

Anonymous young woman: student, University of Southern California

February. A rainstorm. Late afternoon, early evening. Dark out. Just before dinner. A sorority house at the University of Southern California, which is a very affluent university in the middle of South Central. We are in a small room with Laura Ashley furnishings. Lamplight. While we are talking, someone comes by ringing a dinner bell which is a xylophone.

I was scared to death.
I've never felt as scared, as frightened, in my life.
Um,

and it was a different fear than I've ever felt.
I mean, I was really afraid.
At a certain point
it dawned on us that they might try to attack the row,
the sororities and the fraternities.
Because they did do that during the Watts riots.
And, um, they . . .
they went
into the house,
where they smashed the windows.
I don't know how we got this information but somebody knew that,
so that
spread in the house real fast,
and once we realized that,
we started packing.
We all packed a bag and we all had put on our tennis shoes.
This was late in the evening, and we all sat in our hallways upstairs,
very small hallways,
and we all said,
"Oh, if they come to the front door, this is what we're gonna do."
Many things I can tell you.
First of all, my parents were on their way,
to drive to California,
to take part in a caravan
in which they bring old cars,
old forties cars,
and a whole bunch of 'em, all their friends, a huge club.
They all drive their cars around the country.
My dad has an old car.
It's a '41 Cadillac.
I told 'em, to turn around, go home.
I said, "Go home, Mom."
All I can think of . . . one bottle.
One shear from one bottle in my father's car,
he will die!
He will die.
He collects many cars,
he has about fifteen different kinds of cars.
This is his thing, this is what he does.
He's got Lincoln
Continentals

and different Town and Countries.
All forties.
His favorite is a '41 Cadillac.
And, um, so . . . he keeps them from five to ten years,
you know.
Depending on whether you can get a good value for 'em.
It's a business
as well as a hobby.
And so I don't specifically know what he came out in.
But one of 'em.
And those are his pride
and joys.
They are perfect.
They are polished.
They are run perfect.
They are perfect.
All I can think of is a bottle gettin' anywhere near it.

Art Spiegelman

From _Maus_

Amy Fusselman
From *The Pharmacist's Mate*

1.

Don't have sex on a boat unless you want to get pregnant. That's what my friend Mendi's sailor ex-boyfriend used to tell her.

I want to get pregnant. Or maybe more accurately, I don't want to die without having had children.

I was a child once, with a dad. My dad is dead now. He died two weeks ago. I have never had anyone so close to me die. I am trying to pay attention to what it feels like.

I know it's early, but I keep thinking he's still here. Well, not here, I know he's not here, but on his way here. On his way back here from somewhere. Coming here.

Of course, I don't think it's my old dad in his old body coming here. It's my old dad, in a new form.

Thinking your dad might be coming in a new form is not so bad. It's like you're always excited, and getting ready, and listening for the door.

2.

The big problem I have had in trying to get pregnant is that I don't ovulate. Thus, I don't get my period. I mean, I can go six months.

I don't know why this is. And after a million tests at the gyno, they don't seem to know why either. Everything looks OK.

My theory is that I am stopping myself from having my period. I am doing this with my brain. I don't know how I am doing it, but I am doing it. And I am doing it because as much as I want to get pregnant, I am also very afraid.

3.

Before my dad was a dad, he was a guy on a boat in a war. This was World War II.

My dad had been studying pre-med at Virginia Military Institute. He had enlisted in the Army in 1944, but after a few months they discharged him because, my dad told me, "They didn't know what they were doing with medical students." So my dad went back to school for a while, until my grandfather called him up from Ohio and said people at home were starting to talk, and they were saying my dad was studying pre-med just to get out of serving. My dad told me that's when he said the hell with it, and signed up for the Merchant Marine. This was in the fall of 1945. He was twenty-one.

My dad was the Purser-Pharmacist's Mate on the Liberty Ship *George E. Pickett.* He kept a log from his first eight months at sea. He wrote a lot about his work.

Sample:

> Chief Steward came to me today with a possible case of gonorrhea. I'm going to wait until tomorrow to see how things turn out. Had him quit handling the food, at least.

It's funny to read things like that, because my dad never became a doctor. After the war, he went back to school and got his MBA.

4.

Sometimes I think this problem with children is something that runs in my family. My brother, who lives in Houston and is ten years older than me, had a problem with children fifteen years ago. He was in Ohio visiting my parents (I was away at school), when all of a sudden the phone rang. It was his live-in girlfriend, telling him she had just had two babies, a boy and a girl. Twins.

My parents didn't even know she was pregnant. My brother flew back to Houston. The next thing my parents heard, they had given the infants up for adoption.

The whole thing was so shrouded in weirdness and secrecy that several years after it happened I called my brother just to make sure that it was true. Because all I knew was what I had heard from my parents.

And my brother had said yes, it was true. He sounded pained. My brother and I are not very close. I didn't ask him more than that.

Another thing: my brother has a job selling high-tech sonar equipment to clients like the Navy, equipment they use to do things like search for John F. Kennedy Jr.'s plane.

And another: I have always wondered if someday these kids might show up on our doorstep.

5.

I am trying to get pregnant with Frank. Frank is my husband. He is 6'4". My dad was 5'7". Frank and my dad got along. Even though Frank's full name is Frank, my dad always gave his name two extra syllables, and said it sing-song, "Frank-a-lin."

Frank and my dad were both born and raised in Youngstown, Ohio. When they got together they liked to talk about the town landmarks, Market Street and Mill Creek Park, places I didn't know because I grew up around Cleveland.

And it never came up in conversation, but long ago, even before I was born, my dad had made arrangements to be buried in the cemetery at the end of Frank's street: Forest Lawn.

6.

I want to talk to my dad, but my dad is dead now. I know we can't have a regular conversation so I am trying to stay open to alternatives. I am trying to figure out other ways we can communicate.

Right after my dad's funeral, I came back to New York for a week of visits to the high-end fertility doctor. I had just started with the high-end fertility doctor, after nine months of getting nowhere with the low-end one.

I needed a week of visits to have my follicles monitored. I had just taken five days' worth of clomiphene citrate, a drug that tricks your pituitary gland into producing extra FSH (follicle stimulating hormone) and LH (luteinizing hormone), two natural gonadotropins that encourage follicle growth.

A follicle-monitoring appointment at the high-end fertility doctor involves the following: getting there between seven and nine a.m.; putting your name on a list; waiting until the nurse calls your name; going and getting your blood taken; returning to the waiting room with your arm bent around a cotton ball; waiting for the nurse to call your name again; and when she does, going to the examination room to lie on the table with your pants off so one of the ever-changing array of attractive, resident physicians can stick the ultrasound probe in your vagina to measure how big the follicle is. You need a follicle to get to eighteen millimeters before they will give you the shot of hCG (human chorionic gonadotropin) to make the follicle burst and release the egg.

After four mornings of this, a resident told me that one follicle, on my left side, had hit eighteen. So they gave me the shot, and then the next day, I was inseminated.

And I was sure when it was over that I was pregnant, because unlike all the other times I had taken clomiphene citrate, and been shot with hCG, and been inseminated, this time I was doing it with my dad being dead. And I was sure my dad would be trying to help me out.

But the morning I was supposed to take my pregnancy test, I got my period.

7.

1/31/46: Eight days have now been spent in port at Pier 15 Hoboken, NJ. Ship still remains unassigned and unloaded. Vessel is of the Liberty type and called the *George E. Pickett*. It is manned and operated by the Waterman SS

Co AT 0625. On 1/26 an adjoining vessel struck us and wrecked the No. 4 lifeboat davit. Hell of a racket. The crew is not a bad lot, but always clamoring for advances on their wages. The "Old Man," A. C. Klop, a Hollander by birth, is as tight with money as they come. There are many bets being made among the crew as to our port of destination, but it still remains a secret.

The ship is undergoing repair now, which it badly needs. Has been dry-docked, scraped and painted. All guns and mountings have been removed.

The previous voyage was to Yokohama, Japan, and lasted seven months. Some of the original crew remained for this voyage, but very few.

I am determined to learn to navigate, and study a little geography. Knowledge of both these subjects very poor.

8.

Before my dad died I saw the world as a place. By place I mean space. Fixed. Space did not move, but people moved in space. People and space could touch each other, but not very deeply.

After he died, I saw that people and space are permeable to each other in a way that people and people are not. I saw that space is like water. People can go inside it.

9.

My dad loved guns, loved them. My mom told me that when she and my dad were dating, he drove with a Luger lying in the space between their seats. Part of me chalks this up to the fact that my dad went to military school, then war. Part of me thinks he was living in a different time. Part of me isn't sure.

My father was in the hospital for six weeks before he died. When it became clear that his condition was really serious, my brother came home. One of the first things my brother did was roam around the house, searching for the guns. My mother had never wanted anything to do with them, and didn't even know where they all were stored.

My brother found three automatics, a revolver, and two rifles. He couldn't find the old Luger, though he said he knew my dad still had it.

He unloaded the guns. Then he laid them all out in a long row, on my dad's dresser:
    one stainless steel Walther PPK .380 caliber automatic
    one stainless steel Seacamp .32 caliber automatic
    one blued steel Colt .380 caliber automatic
    one titanium Smith & Wesson .22 caliber revolver with laser target
    one Armalite .22 caliber survival rifle
    one .30 caliber M-1 carbine

When I saw all the guns like that, rounded up from their hiding places and dis-assembled, the semi-automatics and rifles separated from their clips, the revolver emptied of its bullets, that's when I started to know that my dad wasn't going to live much longer.

10.

2/16/46: Well, I'm as salty a sailor as they come now. We have had the worst possible weather these last three days. It can't get any worse. As far as seasick-ness, I guess I'm immune to it. My stomach felt a little squeamish the first two days but it is all over now. I can eat just as regularly as on land. It is good to feel the roll of the ship under your feet, and these Liberties roll more than any cargo ship afloat, since they are almost flat on the bottom. We were hav-ing a 36° roll last night.

Had a fellow receive two nail punctures in his foot in the steering engine room. Couldn't do much about it. Opened it up and put sulfathiazole creme in it, and gave him a tetanus shot. I couldn't remember whether to give it sub-cutaneous or intravenous. Gave it sub-q and hoped for the best. At least I got it in. Looked it up in *Christopher's Minor Surgery* later and found out I gave it right. It's just an accident that I happened to have the antitoxin with me. I was so darn busy in port that I was going to let it go and take a chance by not having it. I just happened to be down near the WSA warehouse so I took the time to pick it up. It's a good thing.

11.

What is it about my dad being dead that I can't say it enough? That I feel like My Dad Is Dead would be a good name for my son?

That I can picture myself saying, "I can't talk right now, I have to pick My Dad Is Dead up from hockey?"

Singing, "Happy birthday to you, happy birthday to you, happy birthday dear My Dad Is Dead"?

I look My Dad Is Dead up on Yahoo! and discover that there is a band with that name. And they're from Ohio, like my dad, like me. And I can listen to their song right now, a noisy, static-y MP3 called "Don't Look Now."

12.

My dad is invisible. Everything invisible is interesting to me now. Like when I sit in the apartment we just moved into, and play guitar. When I sit here and am aware, as I play and sing, that the music is invisible. And I imagine what I would look like to a deaf person. That I would look like someone opening and closing her mouth and sliding one hand along some wood and using the other to touch some strings. And how that doesn't look like much. Just someone sitting, making little movements. Little patterns with the mouth, open close, open close, little patterns with the hand, up and down, up and down. And how the only way a deaf person would know what I was doing is because the movements are creating vibrations. And how even though the vibrations are invisible, I can feel them in the air. I can feel them, they are there, they are as there as I am.

I have always thought that seeing a band play in a bar is more interesting theater than most plays in theaters. The guitarist standing there, wiggling the fingers, and making the giant vibrations, is about hundred times more poetic and mysterious than someone in a costume saying words they memorized, words that are supposed to be About Something.

But I say that and then I also have to admit that when I am at home playing guitar and singing, I am playing and singing a song I wrote when I was in college, in a band that played in bars. And the song is called "I Love My Mom," and we played it loud and fast:

> *I love my mom*
> *I love my mom*
> *She's no sex bomb*
> *But she's my mom*
> *She sends me food*
> *When I am gone*
> *She's old, she's cool, my mom rules*

> *I love my dad*
> *I love my dad*
> *I am so glad*
> *That he's my dad*
> *He sends me money*
> *Even though I'm bad*
> *He's old, he's cool, my dad rules*

And on one level the song was supposed to be funny, because even though it had sweet lyrics, we played it like a rant. But on another level it wasn't funny at all, because at the time I wrote it I was mad as hell at my mom and dad, and the song was like an imitation of how I was loving them then, through clenched teeth.

And now, when I sing the song, I remember specifically how I held my dad's hand and sang it to him in the hospital, two days before he died.

STRATEGIES

PART TWO

*Wisdom consists of rising superior both to madness
and to common sense.*

HENRI-FRÉDÉRIC AMIEL

*The beginning of human knowledge is through the senses,
and the fiction writer begins where human perception begins.
He appeals through the senses, and you cannot appeal to the
senses with abstractions.*

FLANNERY O'CONNOR

*Like an ability or a muscle, hearing your inner wisdom
is strengthened by doing it.*

ROBBIE GASS

CHAPTER THREE

ENERGY

Are you creating work readers are excited about reading? Or are you writing stuff people read only because they are in class, polite, or for some other reason (like they are in love with you)?

As readers, we may get bored easily. Competing for our attention are great writing and many responsibilities, distractions, and endeavors. As writers, we have to be creative to capture and keep our readers. You can make *everything* you write more interesting and attractive to readers by paying attention to a single concept: energy.

> *Think of the fierce energy concentrated in an acorn! You bury it in the ground, and it explodes into an oak! Bury a sheep and nothing happens but decay.*
> — GEORGE BERNARD SHAW

THE PRINCIPLES OF ENERGY

There are three principles writers work with in order to increase the energy and interest level in all types of creative writing.

1. *Subjects.* A good writer can make any topic interesting. Deadly boring subjects are usually those everyone knows a little about. Subjects that will lead to energetic writing are those which you a, experience firsthand, b, wonder about passionately, and c, have strongly mixed feelings about. If you are into it, your reader will follow.
2. *Leaps.* Writers leave gaps on purpose, so that the reader has the pleasure of filling in pieces of the picture on his or her own. Leaping is one of the most effective energizing techniques available, and one of the simplest to master. Visual artists use negative space to add drama to their work, and so do writers.

3. *Words.* Some words spark and sizzle and pop. Others (think of a legal brief, anything boring you have read lately) make the reader's eyes glaze over. Words in unexpected places create energy, too.

Subject: Focus on What's Fascinating

As humans, as readers, we're automatically drawn to the new. If you write about something you alone on the planet and no one else are able to write about, your writing is going to be interesting and energized.

What to choose for a subject? What you alone know. Everyone knows what it is like to grow up, turn seven years old, struggle with your mother's rules. But no one knows what it was like to turn seven inside Apartment B10 on Prospect Avenue, where a kid sat on a cake, and the mother drank three martinis, and all this happened before noon. And your Superman underwear was really, really itchy.

> *I merely took the energy it takes to pout and wrote some blues.*
> — DUKE ELLINGTON

Most people know high school graduation, loneliness, flat tires. But no one knows *your* specific experience. It doesn't matter if you are writing poetry, fantasy fiction, love letters, short stories, or screenplays. It's your specific repertoire of emotions and details that make good writing good. The American playwright Edward Albee is gay, but he writes male-female marital discord better than anyone else. Writers use their own firsthand emotional experience—with their parents, friends, coworkers—to create an energetic backdrop, landscape, and engine for original creative writing.

If you can *put* yourself there, using only the power of your mind, you can write it. You can tell you have chosen a good, alive subject if it gives you energy to work on it. A good creative writing topic unnerves you a little. When a subject in this class is alive, it's going to shift as you work, too. You'll start out writing about your relationship with a lover, and realize you are also writing about your parents! You'll start out writing about how ridiculous your relationship was, and realize, by the end of your piece, how complex two people really are. Some students feel uncomfortable with that fact—subjects shift and drift. But good subjects *are* alive. Good subjects aren't static (if they are, they are B-O-R-I-N-G). If you are already know what you are going to say about your subject, you're going to struggle to keep the writing energized.

Good writers choose a topic they know a lot about—relationships, travel, growing up, bedrooms, hotels, restaurants, the synagogue on 42nd Street—and they trust (this is the hard part) that they will discover things about the topic as they work.

> *There is a vitality, a life force, an energy, a quickening, that is translated through you into action, and because there is only one of you in all time, this expression is unique.*
>
> — MARTHA GRAHAM

Guidelines for Increasing Energy Using Subject

Provide interesting information. See the Fennelly poem where she presents three ways to say, "I'm hungover." Provide information—specific insider details and expert vocabulary. This is a valuable way to keep your reader interested in your work. We read for many reasons, but one is to learn. Smart writers include interesting facts and weave in startling, unusual, and specific details.

Avoid the general, which always lacks energy: "Hangover is a word in some languages and not in others, but I'm not really sure what ones." Strive for the specifics in your subject: "In Arabic, there is no word for 'hungover.'" We read that line in Fennelly's poem and many of us learn something new, something interesting. Good writers always get the real name, the actual address, the specific phrase, the right translation, because the power in writing lies in that exactness.

Write about lively, particular subjects you know intimately. Some topics are hard to make interesting, though clever writers always find a way. Homeless people you know nothing about, historical figures you're mildly familiar with, general types, indistinct locations—these are all energy black holes. Subjects that force you to write about passive conditions—dreaming, falling asleep, driving—are all hard to infuse with energy. Conversely, you can write energetically when your focus is last night's brawl at the Dirty Parrot. Your rich aunt's summer visit to your trailer park. A pack of high school punks wreaking havoc, Robin-Hood style, in the Sunset Heights subdivision at the edge of Detroit—that's the kind of subject that is already infused with energy.

In sum, you don't need to reveal your deepest darkest secrets, but you do need to make readers feel you are giving them your best stuff. What's juicy? What do you know about that is strange, interesting, unusual? What kinds of things have you seen that are outside normal day-to-day experience? Use a microscope to view your life, the lives of people you know, your past. If you observe normal day-to-day experience closely enough, you will create energy.

PRACTICE

Make two two-column lists. First, list all the places you have lived (include summer camps, extended vacations, weekend stayovers). In the second column, list the most dramatic thing that occurred at each location. Next, make another list, of the outdoor settings of your life from ages five to eighteen. Start with your backyard on Jenson Street. Pan your mind's movie camera (you have to "flash" or see the location in order to put it on your list) across the kindergarten playground, the big plastic slide. Then, slowly panning the exterior shots of your life, to the grocery store parking lot, then the sandlot where you played baseball, then fifth grade's creek where you went every day. Your secret woods spot in middle school. The train tracks where you kissed. In the second column for this list, write down the name of one or two other people who were also there.

You now have subjects. Mine these lists for the rest of the semester, for fiction, poetry, nonfiction, or plays. You can invent situations, but they will always be based in a real, energized scene. That's the secret of subject: grounding in the real.

Leaps: The Power of Gaps

Remember Amy Fusselman's memoir (p. 60) of her father, her pregnancy, and her daily life as an itinerant musician? In those short sections, Fusselman *leapt* from topic to topic. She kept cycling through key moments in the three braids, those three stories. The short sections create energy. When you look at the page, your eye leaps around, as with a poem. The interplay among the white space, the numbered sections, and the tinier sections within the numbered parts invites the reader to leap.

Readers like short sections.

Readers are attracted to *movement*. Fiction writers, essayists, and poets employ the method of leaping in order to leave plenty of room for the reader to engage with the material.

> *The artist never entirely knows.*
> *We guess. We may be wrong, but*
> *we take leap after leap in the dark.*
> — AGNES DE MILLE

Spelling everything out, providing detailed transitions, explaining and reviewing and going over it again: That may be effective for your chemistry textbook, but it's death to art. Art is more like a game, a pleasing game, one that's got a bit of a challenge in it.

The reader *wants* to figure things out. The reader wants to play. So creative writers leap, because leaping creates energy.

PRACTICE

Read Brian Arundel's "The Things I've Lost" on page 99. Make a list of the leaps, and analyze how leaps energize this piece.

When you employ leaps in your work, you are comprehensible and interesting on the first reading, but the aware reader knows there's more there. The reader gets a full, confusion-free experience the first read. On a second and third reading, the piece reveals more information, more connections. Leaps leave room for that dynamic between a reader and a work.

Read the following excerpt, from "The Impossibility of Language," by Beth Ann Fennelly (see p. 94).

When in doubt, make a fool of yourself. There is a microscopically thin line between being brilliantly creative and acting like the most gigantic idiot on earth. So what the hell, leap.

— CYNTHIA HEIMEL

Try a simple sentence: "I am hungover."
For Japanese, "I suffer the two-day dizzies."
In Czech, "The monkeys swing inside my head."
Italians say, "Today, I'm out of tune."
Languages aren't codes that correspond —
in Arabic, there is no word for "hungover."

Compare the writing above to this prose excerpt from another writer.

When the alarm clock went off, I woke up and I reached over and turned it off and got out of bed. I walked across the room and I went to the bathroom which was close by and when I went in, I turned on the light so I could see. I was wondering what I was going to do today. I was just waking up.

Which piece has more energy? Why? Notice how in the first example the poet leaps from country to country, language to language, phrase to phrase, from one specific example to another, and just when the reader gets used to that pattern (she gives three examples), Fennelly changes strategies, leaping to a statement about language itself. If she kept listing hangover examples from twenty languages, can you see how you might at some point have grown bored? Leaps make your work lively. Notice, too, the small hop at the end of the poem—a statement about a language where the speakers do not have or, perhaps, desire a word for the results of alcoholic excess.

In the second excerpt, we find a blow-by-blow description of a fairly typical morning. This example shows the opposite of leaping. Here, things are filled in completely, with no surprises. Everything is predictable, and explained. The reader may read along, but what is the point of this piece? Would you read it again? Does it have any energy?

Don't explain. Leap—from bathroom to office, from something interesting to the next interesting thing. Leaps are the places where the writer purposely leaves something out, skips ahead, or changes topic. Leaps, like dotted lines, trace complete thoughts, but *gaps* allow the reader to actively participate in creating the image, thought, or meaning.

We readers like to be set up for success. We want to feel smart when we read, not clueless, and we want to make sure you the author know what you are doing. We don't want to be set up for a fall (there's no pattern, there's no point, or you don't really let us see). To follow the random associations of someone thinking out loud can be confusing, boring, or pointless. To be provided with planned surprises — that's energy.

Adjust your focus: Write what you see; leap, leave out filler sections (or simply take them out before sharing your work with others). Once you start using the leaping technique, you will be amazed at how much explanation you can leave out. Readers are pretty savvy — they figure out a lot from just a few hints.

By writing what you see, you allow the reader to form an image and *draw his or her own conclusions.*

One of the most important places this principle occurs is in dialogue. Good dialogue leaps. Nothing is deadlier to creative writing energy than dialogue that explains and tells.

> JOEY: What's wrong, Emily? You look really sad. Are you blue because you got a D– on your history test this morning in first period? It seemed like you were really struggling with that test.
> EMILY: Thanks for noticing, Joey. That test was so hard. I'm really feeling bad about this.
> JOEY: This is terrible. Is it going to kill your average?
> EMILY: It may cause me to fail the class.
> JOEY: What can you do?
> EMILY: I don't know.

Here, one character is being used by the author to get information out of the other character. In good creative writing, dialogue bristles with energy when each character has his or her own agenda, and the agendas conflict, causing gaps, leaps. Good dialogue (as you know from being in great conversations) is like a tennis match. The energy moves back and forth, with equal force on both sides. Each person is trying to win. Here, no one is even in the game! Emily did poorly on a test. Okay. Why should I care? Unless she cares passionately, I'm not going to. And what's Joey's angle? Does he want to sell her an answer key? Drugs? Get a date? Unless he wants something that directly conflicts with what Emily wants, leaping is going to be really hard. Both characters are on the same topic, plodding along. Explaining. Carefully, slowly, boringly, filling in all the gaps.

In dialogue, you'll be able to leap if your characters are at cross purposes. They'll each be going in a different direction. Your reader will have to move quickly to keep up — that's what you want.

Compare this example of crisp, energetic dialogue from *The Sopranos* by James Manos Jr. and David Chase. Tony and his daughter Meadow are visiting colleges. Meadow comes out of the admissions office, and her father asks her how it went.

MEADOW: They've got a 48 to 52 male-female ratio which is great—strong liberal arts program, and this cool Olin Arts Center for music. Usual programs abroad—China, India—

TONY: You're just applying here and you're already leaving?

Notice the energy. Meadow is specific. She broadcasts her agenda. She leaps from social benefits to infrastructure to study abroad. Tony's agenda probably isn't for his daughter to enjoy the benefits of an equal male-female ratio. When he asks her for more information, the reader *leaps*: We know he doesn't care how she answers the question. He is not asking her *for more information*. There's a gap in what he says—on the surface—and in what he intends. Meadow lists what she likes about the college. She doesn't really care what her father thinks at this point. Tony doesn't want her to go away, to be too far out of his control. No filler. No explanation. The leaps and gaps leave plenty of room for the reader to figure things out—that's the pleasure of energy. We readers are set up by the author to know *more* than the characters themselves. The dialogue leaps, and we scoot along to keep up.

> *We must walk consciously only part way toward our goal, and then leap in the dark to our success.*
>
> — HENRY DAVID THOREAU

The Tony-Meadow conversation continues like this as they stroll across campus:

MEADOW: It's an option, Dad. Junior year.

TONY: What do you study in India? How to avoid diarrhea?

MEADOW: They don't require SAT scores but mine'll help 'cause they're high. Socially—I don't know. This one girl told me there's this saying, "Bates is the world's most expensive form of contraception."

TONY: What the hell kind of talk is that? You mean the girls at the other colleges we been to just put out?

MEADOW: Oh, my God.

TONY: And another thing—every school we visit there's the gay/lesbian this and that—the teachers know this is going on?

MEADOW: Oh, my God. [Stops, admires campus.] Pretty, huh?

TONY: [Agrees, then—] Two to go. Colby up. [They walk through the leafiness.]

MEADOW: Dad . . . how come you didn't finish college?

TONY: I had that semester and a half at Seton Hall.

MEADOW: Yeah? And?

This dialogue emits a high level of energy because the characters leap just as we do in real life conversations. Meadow is simultaneously thinking out loud, signaling her father to stop being an idiot, and admiring the college. Tony leaps from social criticism, to fatherly overprotectiveness, to homophobia, to the next college on the list.

Notice what isn't here, what isn't explained. By leaping a writer generates reader involvement. Information about conflict, values, and character comes out between the lines. We readers (or viewers) know, without it being said—this information comes through in the gaps, called the *subtext*—that Tony wants his daughter to have a good education and a conventional life. We know he is embarrassed by his lack of formal education. We know he is afraid of her leaving home. We know Meadow isn't afraid of her father. She's curious about him, and she doesn't know a lot about his history. She's mostly concerned with her ability to enjoy the social benefits of her educational experience. Is Meadow in some ways more worldly than her father? Is she embarrassed by him? Does Tony feel in over his head, is he giving up fighting with her when he says, "Two to go. Colby up"?

Just when the reader has gotten the pace, the thread, the track, the good writer switches up again. Tony landed someplace different in that line, didn't he? Not where we expected (Meadow's interrogative). The leaps vary in length and pace.

Consider again Joey and Emily: We know so very little about their values, backgrounds, and conflicts. Their dialogue lacks energy—of subject, of gap (they mean exactly what they say). The dialogue is used to interview one character for one reason alone: to give information to the reader. Creative writing is alive only when all the component parts are activated.

Which brings us to words. Contrast the word choices in the Joey-Emily and Tony-Meadow examples. As we see next, words are a powerful way to energize your work.

Words

Words are what creative writers use to make their art forms. It's worth taking a closer look at these building blocks.

All the words in everything you write are important. You might have a great subject and leap like Michael Jordan, but if the words you are using are dead, flat, or abstract, energy will leak out of your piece with a slow steady *woosh*.

Writers are people for whom words are *interesting*. Writers like messing around with words, adjusting, fussing, trying out different words. Use language like painters use their tools. Make a mess. Play around. See what combinations flicker with energy, see which ones beam.

Most creative writers find it easier to fine-tune, adjust, mess with writing as they are doing it. Few writers feel their first drafts are ready to show. Experimenting with different words—*word by word*—is part of the pleasure, and the challenge, of creative writing. Notice how you work best. Do you fiddle around with sentences, lines, dialogue, testing different word choices as you go? Or do you work better when you write a whole draft and then go back and look for flat, ineffective, vague word choices?

Specificity. Words that generate energy create a spark in the reader's brain. These are fresh, lively, simple, clear, or unexpected words that capture our attention while aiding our apprehension of the image. *Word packages* are overly familiar phrases in which perfectly fine words lose energy because they are constantly yoked together: "beautiful blue eyes"; "red rose"; "gaping hole"; "awkward moment." Good writers enjoy busting up word packages and recombining their elements to create original effects: "gaping moment"; "awkward rose." See the difference? Avoid your thesaurus, and focus on moving words around into interesting, unusual combinations, and you will instantly energize your work.

PRACTICE

Rank the following words, using a scale of 0–10. A 10 is high octane, a 0 is very low pulse rate. Do you notice anything about what the 5+ words have in common?

Frisky	Blue
Surge	Beautiful
Important	Wondering
Prick	Apartment
Understanding	Number 10
Very	

Abstract words (think SAT vocab words!) clot your writing with low-energy spots. When the reader has to *think*, she's not in your piece of writing. She's working. Readers want to enjoy the reading experience, and you the writer need to do the work to make that happen. Fiddle around, don't write from habit: Choose words that are surprising, fresh, interesting, unexpected, different (but not distracting). Simple one-syllable words are going to make your writing pulse.

Consider the differences between the two words in each of the following pairs:

road	avenue
jerk	unpleasant person
party	reception
fun	enjoyable
tunes	aural interlude

Many writers, when they are starting out, feel obligated to sound "writerly." They choose words that sound bookish and important. Their poor readers! Some overly writerly words include many adverbs (suddenly, finally, interestingly, absolutely) and clichéd shortcuts to rendering emotions: "she furrowed her brow," "he raised an eyebrow," "her mouth dropped open." Use what you learned in Part One, and write what you see. What does your character *really* do when he or she is frustrated, skeptical, or shocked? Use the words that describe your actual scene, not the general population's explanatory shorthand.

Every word counts.

Good writers choose a straightforward, fresh, simple, lively vocabulary. Crisp nouns, simple adjectives, used sparingly are energetic and produce a picture, like a movie or a dream, in the reader's mind. In one of the examples below are words trying too hard to sound "literary," and abstractions that short-circuit energy instead of creating it.

Consider the following paragraph by Rick Moody, from his short story "Boys" on p. 94.

> Boys enter the house, boys enter the house. Boys, and with them the ideas of boys (ideas leaden, reductive, inflexible), enter the house. Boys, two of them, wound into hospital packaging, boys with infant pattern baldness, slung in the arms of parents, boys dreaming of breasts, enter the house. Twin boys, kettles on the boil, boys in hideous vinyl knapsacks that young couples from Edison, NJ, wear on their shirt fronts, knapsacks coated with baby saliva and staphylococcus and milk vomit, enter the house.

Compare this to the following paragraph. What do you notice about the differences in language choices?

> They were just typical kids. You know kids. The normal American kind. The boy was thinking about how he just wanted the day to end so he could get out of school and get to the project. He had been dreaming about this project for years. It was so great to finally be so close. So close. And yet so far, too. It seemed as though he and his buddy would never be able to really get there. Those afternoons were slow.

PRACTICE

For the examples above, underline each word that has some spark, some specificity—some energy. Which words are vivid, energetic? Circle all the words in each passage that are deadweight, predictable, blocking energy rather than creating it. Which passage has higher octane? Reflect on where you "see" the writing, intuitively, versus where you use your intellect to make a picture. Does the higher-energy passage "pop" images into your mind's eye?

PRACTICE

Reread Amy Fusselman's memoir excerpt from *The Pharmacist's Mate* on page 60, and Rick Moody's story "Boys," which appears in full on page 94. In each piece, locate at least six phrases that do not usually occur in that combination. "Wild horses" and "thin man" are word packages. You are looking for fresh, unusual combinations (and energy), such as "elephant pants," "Sleeping Tubby and Snow Weight," "shirtsleeves aglow with torchlight." You will end up with a list of twelve phrases. Number your pairs, with 1 being the most energetic, high-wattage combination, and 12 being sparkly, but not as much as the others.

Verbs. The most energetic word—the pulse point in any sentence—is the verb. Verbs must be strong, vivid, clear, and simple in order for the reader to stay interested in your writing. When you describe actions, the verbs, crisp action verbs—*run, fling, pour, pinch*—are the muscles of your sentences. Readers move through your sentence or line hungry for action, for movement, and when they get to the verb, something needs to happen.

> *Drama is life with the dull parts left out.*
> — ALFRED HITCHCOCK

When you describe *thinking* (I wondered, I reflected, I worried, I thought, He reminded me of, He was brooding, I concluded), the energy decreases, sharply. These *filters*—words that refer to mental activity—are flabby, and can be deadly to strong, energetic writing.

Muscles. Let's say you are writing a story about a college freshman's visit to his physics professor's office. The purpose of the visit is to go over a flunked test. As he waits for his prof to call him into the office, the student thinks to himself, I don't like this guy, I don't like the way he lectures, the textbook is confusing, and my roommate, who put the exact same thing for the essay question as I did, got a B–.

No action. No muscle. A guy, in a chair, *thinking*. There aren't any action verbs—any muscles—any vehicles for energy. It's all taking place in a human head. Good writers don't do this. They find ways to set up situations where they can show off their facility with *verbs*.

PRACTICE

Go through Rick Moody's "Boys" on page 94 with a highlighter (or make a list). Locate every single verb: *enter, wound, slung, wear, coated, dreaming, striking, speaking,* etc. What *kinds* of verbs does Moody choose? What verbs does he avoid using? Of his verb choices, the ones on your list, which are the most energetic, the strongest? Are there a few verbs you would like to incorporate into your own writing?

As you scan back over the work you have read so far this semester, you may notice that the published writers choose their verbs very carefully. Authors like verbs that pack a punch, avoiding the forms of the verb "to be" and reflective, passive verbs.

In our student-professor tale, if we apply muscles to our sentences, as Moody does, what happens? What if instead of having him *think* this in the department foyer, you had him *say* this to the department secretary, another student, or the professor himself? Could your student boil over, cross, shimmy, shoot? What would be interesting? Notice that all the aspects of energy—subject, leaps, and words—interrelate and overlap.

PRACTICE

List three activities you are *very* familiar with: soccer, cooking, sailing, tae kwon do, sewing, baby-sitting. Make three columns, with your topics at the top. Fill each column with the verbs associated with that activity: flying could lead to *fuel, pitch, roll, yaw, soar, dive, crash, loft, jet*. Running might give you: *sprint, pace, bolt, trudge, fly, race*. Return to your lists often, to replace the verbs you circle as weak in your writing with these more energetic words. Add to your lists when you think of new verbs; when you are reading, note verbs that are interesting, ones you could use yourself: *remove, leap, drop, cover, smell, swoop, fry, angle*.

Filters. We call thought words like "seemed," "felt," "wondered," and "realized" *filters*. They describe mental activity, and weaken your writing by drawing attention to the writer's thought process instead of the scene at hand.

In first-year composition, where students are taught to write expository essays, a list of commonly used verbs is often distributed.

acknowledges	claims
advises	concludes
agrees	declares
allows	disputes
answers	remarks
asserts	thinks
believes	

These words, while useful for writing essays for academic classes, are the *opposite* of the words creative writers use. Expository essays appeal to the intellect. Creative writing, and all the other arts—dance, painting, sculpture, music, drama—appeal to the senses, to the feelings and emotions, the eyes, the heart. Our words must be, therefore, visual and anchored in human *physical* responses. Art gets to the brain through the body. The brain filters information. It's like a police officer up there deciding who can get through. Avoid the filtering agent. Let your creative writing appeal, unfettered, to the heart and the eyes of your reader. You are trying to create a movie in the mind of your reader. Imagine how irritating it would be to have an official at the front of the local Star Theatre movie screen, explaining the import and meaning of each scene. "Here, Tom Cruise believes . . . ," "We can now conclude Natalie Portman realizes. . . ." The reader can figure out what's going on, as long as your images are clear. Don't explain.

The best way to avoid filters is to avoid writing about trite situations where the character will be left alone with his thoughts, prone to brooding: solo car trips, waking up, airplane travel, staring out windows. In poetry, start somewhere specific. Orient us in time and place—make those images captivating by using strong verbs, and you buy yourself a little platform of time to talk, muse, or think aloud. When writing prose, you can avoid much filtering by simply always having two or three characters on stage at once, never one character *alone with his or her thoughts*.

Remember, we read in order to be *transported*, to experience, as you learned in the first two chapters of this book, a world for ourselves. We don't read to get the writer's feelings and opinions, we read in order to form and extend and see our own feelings and opinions. We read to *have* an experience, not hear about one. The stronger your verbs, the more clear your images, and the less you are proselytizing, sermonizing, musing, or rambling around; the more we see.

| PRACTICE |

Divide a sheet of paper into three columns. Label the columns Kincaid, Morgan, Self. Reread Kincaid's piece "Girl" on page 55. List the words in her piece that give off the most energy. Do the same with Morgan's "Squirt Gun" on page 98. Lastly, choose a poem or very short prose piece of your own, and make a list of the words that give off energy. Now, go over the three pieces one more time. Do you find any filters? Skip down a few lines in each column, and label this part of the list "Filters," making note of each filtering word you find.

One of the most common mistakes writers make is to unintentionally distance the reader. Because writers tend to be fairly observant, thoughtful, introspective people, it's natural for them to record the fact that they are thinking, observing, watching, musing. This is a mistake. Readers don't want a filter, a block, an *entity* processing information for them. It's like prechewed food. We want to chew for ourselves. We want it to feel like *we are seeing* this, that it's happening before our eyes.

Filtering is using words that describe *how* the speaker or a character is experiencing something, instead of letting the reader experience it him- or herself, firsthand. Words that filter your writing for the reader deaden the reader's ability to experience the energy in your work. Filter words include: *felt, thought, realized, assumed, intended, knew, wondered*—anything that describes the thought process rather than letting the reader *experience the sensory nature of the topic at hand.* Weak "thinking" verbs (filters) yank us from the poem or story into the mind of its creator, leaving the reader stuck outside looking in. *Appears* and *seem* soften focus and diffuse energy. After joining three lifeless verbs, *seemed to have been*, the energy is just about all gone.

In fiction, passive verbs like *was* and *were* drain energy. In poetry, watch for *-ing* words and in both prose and poetry, check for passive constructions that use *should, could, would, might*, and *may*. Helping verbs like *had* (as in *had seen*) and *had been* reveal a sloppy relationship to time.

PRACTICE

Experienced writers use this energy-increasing exercise, checking everything they write. Trade one of your recent pieces of writing with a partner. Circle all the verbs. Now, working from your lists created earlier in this chapter, substitute new verbs for every single verb in your partner's piece. Don't worry about making sense or messing up the piece. This is just an exercise. You want to spark surprising combinations, new energy. Read the new pieces aloud. Now, looking over your piece, which has been revised by your partner, decide which substitutions you will keep. Can you find at least one place where a verb that seemingly does not fit actually ends up making *more* sense than the expected verb?

MANIPULATING ENERGY

Choosing energetic subjects, setting up your writing so that it invites the reader to make his or her own connections (to leap), and paying close attention to every single word: Whether you are a minimalist poet or a lush, expansive novelist, these are the basic principles that form the foundation for everything creative writers do.

As you practice these principles, notice two other tools for increasing and intentionally modulating energy in your work: pace and point of view.

Pace: Choose When to "Go for It"

By increasing the pace you increase the energy, of course. However, once your reader adjusts to the speed, the energy flattens out again. Varying pace is a key to sustaining energy. After about three beats, three "points," the reader is adjusted.

It's time to change things up again. That's one reason the waking-up paragraph example earlier in this chapter falls flat. Everything is at the same pitch, the same pace.

Pacing means being attentive to how much time passes through your paragraphs or stanzas. In Rick Moody's story "Boys," the author presents the intense, fast coming-of-age arc of boys' lives. Moody speeds time up and then slows it down, varying the pace. As the writer, use pace to create the effect you want on your reader. What you don't want to do is *just write*, laying down sentences or lines of poetry block by block like so much cord wood, oblivious to pace.

Good writers, the ones we read again and again, use the full continuum of pace, the full range, just like good musicians do. Practice moving from slow to fast, and to medium. Change how far, how close you are when you are looking at the scene before you. Take a step back. What do you see now? Move closer than is polite. What senses are engaged now? Practice getting fluid with your camera, and watch what happens to the pace of your writing.

> *Vary the pace—one of the foundations of all good acting.*
> — ELLEN TERRY

As the writer, you calibrate pace based on the effects you want to achieve. Ignore pace, and you risk letting all the excitement evaporate. Most writers intuitively know that when you want to increase the energy of your writing, you use short sentences to describe a lot of action:

> The man took the knife. He held it over her throat. There was a loud noise. Her eyes flashed in terror. Suddenly . . .

But what truly effective writers do is more subtle and more interesting. First of all, if you are moving fast—lots of action, lots of images per second—you have to be headed somewhere slow; the pace has to change in order for the effect to work. Writing everything at breakneck speed is just as boring as slow writing that drags on and on. It's *variety* of pace—slowing down, speeding up, slowing way down—that keeps the human mind intrigued, on point. Think about how a roller coaster works. It's not all whooshing downhill at 150 miles an hour. There's the slow climb. A little short fast dip. A quicker climb. A pause at the top—then, the giant fall. Think about driving at exactly seventy-five miles an hour on the highway, your engine set on cruise. After a while, have you noticed how that speed feels almost slow? Compare the experience of idling along at six miles an hour, and then suddenly peeling out, getting to sixty in six seconds. You're going slower than seventy-five, but which feels faster? Which is more exciting? The energy is in acceleration, not in top speed.

Rick Moody is a master of pace. Watch how he speeds up time in this passage from the story "Boys." (Moody is also a musician.)

Boys enter the house carrying their father, slumped. Happens so fast. Boys rush into the house leading EMTs to the couch in the living room where the body lies, boys enter the house, boys enter the house, boys enter the house.

Moody puts single-word phrases at the ends of his sentences ("slumped") and uses sentences with missing pieces ("Happens so fast"). Those techniques add speed to the story, which is one long paragraph, isn't it? He repeats the word *boys*—a lot—and lists make his sentences jolt, surge, and compress. In his paragraph, he covers a whole childhood, which ends with the death of a father. That's a large scope for a short-short story! Moody packs in the detail. He uses pace to force the reader through the story, headlong.

Notice how much detail he includes. Edison, N.J., balsamic vinegar, the Elys' yard. Pump action BB gun, Stilton cheese, mismatched tube socks. When you cover a lot of time in a short space, you create energy. Bind the reader to your words by making every single one bristle with specificity. In fast-paced writing, you can't afford to be general. We have to grasp, fully, each thing you name, completely, before you rush us on to the next thing. A common mistake, easy to avoid and easy to fix, is to write fast and without detail. Overwrite the detail your first year as a writer. You can pull back on it later, if you need to.

PRACTICE

Find three other examples of fast pace followed by a closeup, a slowing down, in Moody's story "Boys," on page 94.

Slow Down to Increase Energy. There's a whole movement afoot in the world—you may have heard of it, the Slow Movement. It started with slow food, in Italy, to counter the encroachment of fast food. It has spread to involve conferences and books and Web sites devoted to slow sex, slow driving, slow living, even whole Slow Cities.

There is power in Slow. You notice a lot more. You remember a lot more.

Remember, pace doesn't have to be breakneck to be classified as energetic. Pace doesn't mean *fast*. It means paying attention to the flow, the *intensity*. Pace means focusing on what's most interesting—and the easiest way to make things more interesting for your reader is to give the reader more information. Information, by its very nature, is definition. Taking giant steps closer to your subjects, so you can see their pores, smell their breath, feel their heartbeats— that's a powerful place to write from. Many beginning writers work in the same way amateur videographers do. They film everything from the same distance, move the camera around at the same rate (if at all), never getting close enough to the interesting thing going on in the corner. Slowing down, moving in for a super-closeup, and spending a lot of time on one interaction provides writing with an energy boost.

Practice increasing the energy of your writing by slowing time down.

PRACTICE

Choose as your subject something fast that you are very familiar with. Your sister's driving. Shivering Timbers Roller Coaster rides. NASCAR. Flying down Suicide Hill on your Trek. Use the slow motion techniques to cover a few minutes of time in several pages of writing.

Something very simple and plain can be made riotously funny by slowing down and spending a great deal of time on the topic. Think of the *Seinfeld* episodes where George deliberates over taking the éclair out of the wastebasket, or where the entire cast is lost in a parking garage. Take a little thing—a common misunderstanding—and make a big deal out of it. That's pacing.

Writing that flies—short sentences, quick winks, strong verbs, lists, breaks, dashes—can be so purely pleasurable to read, it's as much fun as roaring down a waterslide.

PRACTICE

Make a sketch of the room you woke up in this morning. Who/what is there? Notice the little things around you. When you have completed your sketch, fill three pages with a blow-by-blow description of five minutes—only five!—from your early-morning waking routine. Include what you said, what you did, what you saw. While you are working, select verbs that have energy and avoid filters. Read your piece to a partner or group. Where does slowing down increase the energy? Where does slowing down deaden, kill the energy? What's interesting slow and close up? What's more interesting told at breakneck speed? Discuss.

Vary Pace to Sustain Energy. The quality of pace that is most important to practice is this: variety.

Some writers rush the reader pell-mell through a poem or story—gobs of action, flying snakes, car wrecks, superheroes, mayhem, and then alligators! They believe they have created something with a lot of energy. Actually, because of the way the human brain is wired—we quickly adjust to whatever the pace—it's *change* that fuels our interest. If you *unexpectedly change pace*—fast, slow, slow, fast, slow, fast—we'll stay interested. Good writers keep their writing energized by varying the pace. They know we adjust quickly and use as our new default setting whatever you put in front of us.

Camera Work

As a writer, you are always looking at something interesting—your subject—through a kind of lens: your mind's eye. Often, creative writers take on viewing the subject through *someone else's eyes*: a character or a speaker does the seeing, recording, remembering; it's a specific person, not the writer, to whom everything interesting in the piece happens. The location of the writer's camera—in the brain/mind/eye of Joey, or on the ceiling, or in the collective head of the Student Body at Poindexter U—is called the point of view. Point of view simply refers to where you set your camera in order to transmit the scene being viewed by your reader. Paying attention to point of view—camera work, like human activity, rarely stays fixed or static—is an important way to increase and control the energy in your work.

Already you can probably see that if point of view deals with the vantage point of the writer, in whatever guise he or she has taken on for the particular story or poem, it's going to also deal with the relationships that speaker/character has with the other people in the piece. Usually, writers pick one head to be inside of, and they look out at the world with that person's eyes. But you don't have to limit yourself in that way. Pay attention to the camera work when you read. Where is the camera? What is being recorded? Where is the author, what is the reader directed to focus on? Does the camera move? Does the viewer of the scene change?

As always with creative writing, your job as writer is to pay attention to the experience your reader will be having when he or she reads your work. If you jerk the camera around a lot, it's probably going to be kind of interesting at first, and then maybe mostly annoying, like amateur video, or a movie filmed by a clueless three-year-old.

There are endless variables to point of view. For now, there are two aspects to point of view—two settings on your camera—to consider as you play with various energy effects.

Proximity: What are we looking out at? How close are we?
Intimacy: Whose head are we in? How deep inside that head are we?

The more proximity and the more intimacy, the more energy you create. As with pace, movement and change support energy. Control is key. Think of a child with a video camera, wildly flailing the lens around—not very interesting filmmaking. Think of the great film directors you love, Tarantino, Scott, Scorsese. A shot of the party, from overhead. A closeup on the heroine. A middle-distance shot of the villain and his evil henchman. A carefully planned-out pace. A sequence, with variety. Writers use their knowledge of movies to enhance their ability to play with point of view. Watching film with the sound off or the commentary on is great practice for writers studying energy and the effects artists use to increase energy in their work.

You can do whatever you want with point of view, but traditionally, there are three categories for "viewing" in creative writing.

First Person:	"I sent for the chief of staff." (Camera planted in the brain of "I.")
Second Person:	"You send for the chief of staff." (Camera planted in the brain of "you," with remote viewing additional simulcast watching You from the outside, close up.)
Third Person:	"The man sent for the chief of staff."

In general, it's best to limit your point of view to one consciousness, one person's viewpoint. You increase energy by going deep into that one consciousness (be aware that withholding vital information—he really is the murderer!—can be considered cheating at worst, manipulative at best).

In each example, the author chooses how much information to reveal. We readers can be told everything by "I," or nothing at all. "I" can be lying about the whole chief of staff sending issue, and the author can indicate to us, or not indicate, the real truth. Point of view is all about intimacy—how far in do we go?

In second person, the "you" can function as an "I" or a "he," depending on how much information the author gives us about the interior life—the thoughts, dreams, fears, insights—of the "you." In third person, we can be really far back as viewers, seeing the "man" from across the city, from an airplane, or from a camera implanted in his brain. If we learn that "the man felt terrible that he had just taken a sip of the chief's coffee," it's as if we are *inside* him.

Instead of worrying too much about point of view, writers are well served by consistently asking one question: What point of view supports the energy of this piece of writing?

Poetry tends to use the term *speaker* to identify who talks in a poem (the speaker may or may not be the poet). In screenplays and drama, the characters talk and we experience the play from their points of view in a general way—they may tell us what they are thinking deep inside, but we don't see things through their eyes. In graphic novels and comics, examine point of view by looking at where the "camera" is positioned. The closeup, the long shot, the dream sequence, the cityscape are all different points of view. Changing point of view in graphic forms adds energy.

Unlike in film and cartoons, however, in forms using purely words—novels, stories, memoir, creative nonfiction—sudden movements of the camera angle tend to suck energy out of a piece. The reader has to scramble to reorient; the movie in the reader's mind is fractured whenever he or she has to *think*. We read to get lost in a world, not see the hand of the writer.

As you study and practice creative writing, you may hear terminology familiar to you from your literature courses. To review:

First person means you are writing "I," as in, "I came in and sat down."

Second person means you are writing "you," as in, "You came in. You sat. You wondered where the heck Judy was."

Third person means you are writing "she" or "he" or "they," as in, "Judy left the apartment and went to the store. She was exhausted."

Omniscience means the point of view knows all—he or she can go inside any head, any time, as superficially or deeply as he or she chooses.

Objective describes an approach in which the point of view reports everything that happens as though we readers are perched on the shoulders of the characters—not inside their heads, but very close. We readers can smell them. We can guess at their interior lives.

| PRACTICE |

Review three pieces of writing and determine the point of view: What is the point of view in Kincaid's "Girl" on page 55? What about Moody's "Boys" on page 94? López's story on page 52? In order to figure out the point of view, answer the following questions for each story: Who talks? And to what or whom? Are we, as readers, living inside that person, or being shown that person from the outside? Do we have access to everything the point-of-view character thinks and feels, or is our access as readers limited? Does the author talk? Write out the answers to these questions for each of the three stories. Which point of view allows the author to generate the most energy?

You've watched amateur video—maybe your dad's proud footage of all your Micro-League Baby Soccer Games? Amateur videographers tend to stand in one place, without moving the camera. They are too far back from the action. Avoid those mistakes in your writing: pan slowly (you won't run into a pole or a soccer mom—you're in your chair!), vary your distance, and shoot much, much closer than you think you need to be.

Pay attention to where your camera is, who is operating it, and move closer—most beginning writers "film" from too far back. By moving your camera closer to your subject and limiting shifts in point of view, you increase and sustain energy in creative writing. To act as though you are deep inside someone's head, seeing the world from behind their eyes, means you must stay limited to just what they could know, see, feel, understand. Whatever your character/speaker knows, the reader knows; they are sharing a brain. Looking through someone else's eyes—that's part of the power and drama of literature, or the reading experience.

Point of view changes come at an energy cost. If Amy Fusselman had told her memoir from the points of view of her husband, unborn child, mother, brother, *and* herself, we would learn interesting perspectives, but we would miss out on the development and depth of her own perspective. Usually, shorter works (poems, short-short stories, songs) are from a single person's (or, sometimes, an animal's or a piece of furniture's) point of view — one brain, one set of eyes, one recording consciousness that we readers adopt for the duration of the reading. Longer works (novels, sagas, ballads, television series) may allow us to live through multiple characters. Usually, the writer focuses on a few "leads" — heads we go into. Minor characters add energy in other ways: comic relief, plot information, setting, or thematic detail.

In movies and plays, how do you address point of view? As you watch these forms this semester, pay attention to the role of energy and point of view. Whose mind — whose deepest thoughts, desires, reactions, dreams — do we audience members have the most access to? When the camera pans across the town or over New York City from a bird's-eye view, what's the effect on point of view? Are there equivalents in novels and poems and plays?

Some authors like to play with point of view. You may write a story or a poem from a collective point of view — the "we" that comprises a group of waiters or office workers or moms. If part of the premise of your piece is that these souls have so much in common that their perspective is "one," your point of view will have energy; just be consistent.

Point of view is a continuum. Choosing one point on the continuum and staying there with intense focus is an important way to keep your creative writing on track.

Too Much Energy?

Energy is about focus, and it's about control. It's about paying super-close attention to what will happen in your reader's brain when you use a technique, turn up the volume, withhold information, leap ahead.

Think about some of the ways you use energy already. In a conversation, when things flag, get boring, or there's a long silence, you keep the energy going by asking more questions or introducing a more exciting topic. But if you keep all your conversations going all the time by just talking, yourself, nonstop, if you suck up all the air in the room, your interlocutors grow tired, disinterested.

Conversation, like good writing, is a kind of game. It's a passing back and forth. Too much revelation at the wrong time is misplaced energy. Yelling when whispering would be appropriate is too much energy.

It's the same in writing. Modulation is what calibrates the amount of electricity in your work. You want the sparks to fly, but only when you have your readers exactly where you want them. As a good writer, control the energy flow.

As you may have already noticed, there is such a thing as too much energy: too many words, too many images, too much information, too many full-throttle, high-pitched events, too much action, too many disturbing revelations. When readers get overwhelmed, they tune out. Manic, wild, out-of-control passages can be really fun to write, and a little fun to read—but probably not for hundreds of pages.

Tell your stories and write your poems with simplicity and clarity. Don't try to be too creative. Some beginning writers mistakenly believe good writing is dense, incomprehensible, and obscure. Other writers rely on adjectives and adverbs, the stimulants and crack cocaine of writing, in order to pep up their paragraphs. Strong verbs and clearly seen scenes will always do more to transport your reader than flash and verbiage.

Some writers resort to excessive embellishment—too many words per square inch. Writing in this hyperactive mode is like turning on all the lights in your house: It misses the point. Focus, highlight, and *modulate* the energy. Slowly dim the lights in the most special room in your house, and boom, you have our attention.

Sometimes, using all your energy tools at once, at full volume, is a way of avoiding the truth of what you have to say, a way of putting off real writing. It's sometimes more fun to show off than show up, unadorned, saying what's true, small, tender, and difficult.

TROUBLESHOOTING ENERGY

The troubleshooting chart below will help you evaluate and control the level of energy in your creative writing as you work on various pieces in various genres.

	Increases Energy	**Decreases Energy**	**Depletes Energy**
Subjects	Subjects known intimately from real life.	Subjects known secondhand from friends, family members.	Subjects informed by television-viewing, movies, general assumptions and impressions.
Leaps	Leaps from one juicy piece of information to another.	Answers that fit the questions.	Explanation.
Word Choice	Specific, sharp, concrete nouns and action verbs.	General words, filler words. Adjectives, adverbs.	Abstract words, filtering verbs.

Conflict	Conflicting agendas.	Long answers. Agreement.	One person alone with thoughts.
Pace	Varied pace.	Even pace.	Lack of attention to pace.
Distance	Close-up camera work.	Long shots, pulling back, writing from far away.	Camera in one spot.
Point of View	Tiny details observed from a single point of view.	Multiple points of view.	Author talking, author reporting (point of view not a character or speaker).
Sentence Variation	Variety in sentence length, word choice.	Lack of variety in constructions.	Lack of attention to length and shape of sentences, sections.

If you choose all the tools from the "Decreases Energy" column, you might still write a great piece, but it might be harder to make that piece realistic for your reader. If you write about your sister's cancer, for example, write about your experience of living with someone very ill. If you focus on your sister's experiences, then you will want to choose from the "Increases Energy" column for your other tools, so that you write from her point of view, close up, and with words only she uses, focusing on the tense, leaping scenes that reveal the most intimate aspects of her story. You won't be able to include much explanation and still sustain your readers' interest. If you are the main character in that story, though, there will instantly be more energy, so the reader will go with you to the doctor's office, learn with you as you comprehend the details of the illness—just as long as you leap!

WRITING PROJECTS

1. Write a prose poem, a short-short, or a very brief play (dialogue or monologue) using every word or phrase (in any order, any combination, repeating words as needed) from your practice with fresh word combinations on page 79. Use all the words from your list! Is the piece more energetic and lively than a typical piece of writing? Do you have a favorite line or combination?

2. Make a list of everything that kills energy. Then write a piece in which you commit every crime on your list. Read your new version aloud. Is there any remaining energy?

3. Pull out a piece of writing you did for an assignment in Chapter 2. Using your list from the practice on page 80, where you developed a list of strong verbs, replace every single verb in your piece of writing. It's okay if the meaning changes a little or a lot. Read the two pieces aloud, and notice which one has more energy.

4. Take any one of your pieces from this semester, and change the point of view. If it's a poem, have someone else speak. For example, if you wrote your "Winter Field" exercise from the point of view of yourself, change the point of view to that of a parent or sibling or animal. When you are finished, write a short paragraph about what the piece gained and what it lost with the new point of view. What's *different* now in terms of the energy level? Are there places the energy is increased with the new point of view? Are there places where the original has more energy?

5. Using your lists of topics, choose one and write a story, poem, or memoir—anything you like—in short sections. Pay special attention in this piece to filters: Watch for filters and avoid using verbs that relate to thought. Make the sections fragments—leave out information. When you read the piece aloud, do your readers tell you they can fill in the gaps?

6. Write a piece with a very fast opening, a slow middle section, and a speedy end. Don't use the passive voice in any sections, or filters—check back over the piece before you turn it in and substitute filters with verbs from your lists.

7. Write a piece that imitates Rick Moody or Jamaica Kincaid, using your own life experiences. Trade pieces with a partner from your class. Where does your piece have the most energy?

8. Write a very short piece about an incident that occurred at a secret place you favored as a child. Now, rewrite the piece from another kid's point of view—choose a kid who was very different from you. Use the first person, or "I," for your first and second versions. In a third version, write in the third person ("he" or "she"), from the point of view of your mother, who stumbles upon the scene. Don't use filters.

ENERGY WORKSHOP

The prompts below will help you constructively discuss your classmates' work.

1. Identify an example of each of the principles of energy — subject, leaps, word choices — in the student piece you are reading. Highlight or underline at least one good example of each principle.

2. Identify a place in the student piece where the energy could be increased by moving the camera closer in on the people/place in the piece. Circle this moment and label it "close up."

3. Identify a place in the student piece where the pace changes throughout a paragraph or stanza. Underline this section, this series of sentences, and label it "good pace."

4. Identify a passage in the student piece where the pace stays at about the same level for longer than it probably should. A place where the writer has clearly established the emotional climate, and there aren't any accelerations or decelerations. Circle and label "pace?"

Beth Ann Fennelly

From "The Impossibility of Language"

THE MYTH OF TRANSLATION

Try a simple sentence: "I am hungover."
For Japanese, "I suffer the two-day dizzies."
In Czech, "The monkeys swing inside my head."
Italians say, "Today, I'm out of tune."
Languages aren't codes that correspond—
in Arabic, there is no word for "hungover."

Does the Innuit wife, kept on ice all winter,
sucking fat from ducks for her hunter's leggings,
not divine the boredom her language doesn't name?
Or would the word's birth crack the ice for miles,
drowning the hunter who crouches with a spear
beside the ice hole for the bearded seal? She sucks
the fat slowly, careful not to quill her throat
with feathers. She grows heavy. It is, as it was
from the beginning, a question of knowledge.
If she bites into the word, she'll be alonesome.

Rick Moody

Boys

Boys enter the house, boys enter the house. Boys, and with them the ideas of boys (ideas leaden, reductive, inflexible), enter the house. Boys, two of them, wound into hospital packaging, boys with infant pattern baldness, slung in the arms of parents, boys dreaming of breasts, enter the house. Twin boys, kettles on the boil, boys in hideous vinyl knapsacks that young couples from Edison, NJ, wear on their shirt fronts, knapsacks coated with baby saliva and staphylococcus and milk vomit, enter the house. Two boys, one striking the other with a rubberized hot dog, enter the house. Two boys, one of them striking the other with a willow switch about the head and shoulders, the other crying, enter the house. Boys enter the house, speaking nonsense. Boys enter the house, calling for Mother. On a Sunday, in May, a day one might nearly describe as *perfect*, an ice cream truck comes slowly down the lane, chimes inducing salivation, and children run after it, not long after which boys dig a hole in the backyard and bury their younger sister's dolls *two feet down*, so that she will never find these dolls and these dolls will *rot in hell*, after which boys enter the house. Boys, trailing after their father like he is the Second Goddamned Coming of Christ Goddamned Almighty, enter the house, repair to the basement to watch baseball. Boys enter the house, site of devastation, and repair immediately to the kitchen, where they mix lighter fluid, vanilla pudding, drain-opening lye, balsamic vinegar, blue food coloring, calamine lotion, cottage cheese, ants, a plastic lizard that one of them received in his Xmas stocking, tacks, leftover mashed potatoes, Spam, frozen lima beans, and chocolate syrup in a medium-sized saucepan and heat over a low flame until thick, afterwards transferring the contents of this saucepan into a Pyrex lasagna dish, baking the Pyrex lasagna dish in the oven for nineteen minutes before attempting to persuade their sister that she should *eat the mixture*; later they smash three family heirlooms (the last, a glass egg, *intentionally*) in a two-and-a-half hour stretch, whereupon they are sent to their bedroom, until freed, in each case thirteen minutes after. Boys enter the house, starchy in pressed shirts and flannel pants that *itch so bad*, fresh from Sunday School instruction, blond and brown locks (respectively) plastered down, but even so with a number of cowlicks protruding at odd angles, disconsolate and humbled, uncertain if boyish things—such as shooting at the neighbor's dog with a pump action bb gun and gagging the fat boy up the street with a bandanna and showing their shriveled boy-penises to their younger sister—are exempted from the commandment to *Love the Lord thy God with all thy heart and with all thy soul, and with all thy might, and thy neighbor as thyself.* Boys enter the house in baseball gear (only one of the boys can hit): in their spikes, in mismatched tube socks that smell like Stilton cheese. Boys enter the house in soccer gear. Boys enter the house carrying skates. Boys enter the house with lacrosse sticks, and, soon after, tossing a lacrosse ball lightly in the living room they destroy a lamp. One boy enters the house sporting basketball clothes, the other wearing jeans and a sweatshirt. One boy enters the house bleeding profusely and is taken out to get stitches, the other watches. Boys enter the house at the end of term carrying report cards, sneak around the house like spies of foreign nationality, looking for a place to hide the report cards for the time being (under the toaster? in a medicine cabinet?). One boy with a black eye enters the house, one boy without. Boys with acne enter the house and squeeze and prod large skin blemishes in front of their sister. Boys with acne treatment products hidden about their persons enter the house. Boys, standing just up the street, sneak cigarettes behind a willow in the Elys' yard, wave smoke away from their natural fibers, hack terribly, experience nausea, then enter the house. Boys call each other *retard, homo, geek,* and, later, *Neckless Thug, Theater Fag,* and enter the house exchanging further epithets. Boys enter the house with nose hair clippers, chase sister around the house threatening to depilate her eyebrows. She cries. Boys attempt to induce girls to whom they would not have spoken only six or eight months prior to enter the house with them. Boys enter the house with girls efflorescent and homely, and attempt to induce girls to sneak into their bedroom, as they still share a single bedroom; girls refuse. Boys enter the house, go to separate bedrooms. Boys, with their father (an arm around each of them), enter the house, but of the monologue preceding and succeeding this entrance, not a syllable is preserved. Boys enter the house having masturbated in a variety of locales. Boys enter the house having masturbated in train station bathrooms, in forests, in beach houses, in football bleachers at night under the stars, in cars (under a blanket), in the shower, backstage, on a plane, the boys masturbate constantly, identically, three times a day in some cases, desire like a madness upon them, at the mere sound of certain words, words that sound like other words, *interrogative* reminding them of *intercourse, beast* reminding them of *breast, sects* reminding them of *sex,* and so forth, the boys are not very smart yet, and, as they enter the house, they feel, as always, immense shame at the scale of this *self-abusive cogitation,* seeing a classmate, seeing a billboard, seeing a fire hydrant, seeing things that should not induce thoughts of masturbation (their sister, e.g.) and then thinking of masturbation anyway. Boys enter the house, go to their rooms, remove sexually explicit magazines from hidden stashes, put on loud music, feel despair. Boys enter the house worried; they argue. The boys are ugly, they are failures, they will never be loved, they enter the house. Boys enter the house and kiss their mother, who feels differently, now they have outgrown her. Boys enter the house, kiss their mother, she explains the seriousness of their sister's difficulty, *her diagnosis.* Boys enter the house, having attempted to locate the spot in their yard where the dolls were buried, eight or nine years prior, without success; they go to their sister's room, sit by her bed. Boys enter the house and tell their completely bald sister jokes about baldness. Boys hold either hand of their sister, laying aside differences, having trudged grimly into the house. Boys skip school, enter house, hold vigil. Boys enter the house after their parents have both gone off to work, sit with their sister and with their sister's nurse. Boys enter the house carrying cases of beer. Boys enter the house, very worried now, didn't know more worry was possible. Boys enter the house carrying controlled substances, neither having told the other that he is carrying a controlled substance, though an intoxicated posture seems appropriate under the circumstances. Boys enter the house *weeping* and hear weeping around them. Boys enter the house, embarrassed, silent, anguished, keening, afflicted, angry, woeful, *griefstricken*. Boys enter the house on vacation, each clasps the hand of the other with genuine warmth, the one wearing dark colors and having shaved a portion of his head, the other having grown his hair out longish and wearing, uncharacteristically, a tie-dyed shirt. Boys enter the house on vacation and argue bitterly about politics (other subjects are no longer discussed), one boy supporting the Maoist insurgency in a certain Southeast Asian country, one believing that *to change the system you need to work inside it*; one boy threatens to *beat the living shit out of the other*, refuses crème brûlée, though it is created by his mother in order to keep the peace. One boy writes home and thereby enters the house only through a mail slot: he argues that the other boy is *crypto-fascist*, believing that *the market can seek its own level on questions of ethics and morals*; boys enter the house on vacation and announce future professions; boys enter the house on vacation and change their minds about professions; boys enter the house on vacation and one boy brings home a *sweetheart*, but throws a tantrum when it is suggested that the *sweetheart* will have to retire on the folding bed in the basement; the other boy, having no *sweetheart*, is distant and withdrawn, preferring to talk late into the night about family members gone from this world. Boys enter the house several weeks apart. Boys enter the house on days of heavy rain. Boys enter the house, in different calendar years, and upon entering, the boys seem to do nothing but compose manifestos, for the benefit of parents; they follow their mother around the place, having fashioned their manifestos in celebration of brand-new independence: *Mom, I like to lie in bed late into the morning watching game shows*, or, *I'm never going to date anyone but artists from now on, mad girls, dreamers, practicers of black magic*, or *A man should eat bologna, sliced meats are important*, or, *An American should bowl at least once a year*, but these manifestos apply only for brief spells, after which they are reversed or discarded. Boys don't enter the house, at all, except as ghostly afterimages of younger selves, fleeting images of sneakers dashing up a staircase; soggy towels on the floor of the bathroom; blue jeans coiled like asps in the basin of the washing machine; boys as an absence of boys, blissful at first, you put a thing down on a spot, put this book down, come back later, *it's still there*; you buy a box of cookies, eat three, later three are missing. Nevertheless, when boys next enter the house, which they ultimately must do, it's a relief, even if it's only in preparation for weddings of acquaintances from boyhood, one boy has a beard, neatly trimmed, the other has rakish sideburns, one boy wears a hat, the other boy thinks hats are ridiculous, one boy wears khakis pleated at the waist, the other wears denim, but each changes into his suit (one suit fits well, one is a little tight), as though suits are *the* liminary marker of adulthood. Boys enter the house after the wedding and they are slapping each other on the back and yelling at anyone who will listen, *It's a party!* One boy enters the house, carried by friends, having been arrested (after the wedding) for driving while intoxicated, complexion ashen; the other boy tries to keep his mouth shut: the car is on its side in a ditch, the car has the top half of a tree broken over its bonnet, the car has struck another car which has in turn struck a third, *Everyone will have seen.* One boy misses his brother horribly, misses the past, misses a time worth being nostalgic over, *a time that never existed,* back when they set their sister's playhouse on fire; the other boy avoids all mention of that time; each of them is once the boy who enters the house alone, missing the other, each is devoted and each callous, and each plays his part on the telephone, over the course of months. Boys enter the house with fishing gear, according to prearranged date and time, arguing about whether to use *lures* or *live bait,* in order to meet their father for the *fishing adventure,* after which boys enter the house again, almost immediately, with live bait, having settled the question; boys boast of having caught fish in the past, though no fish has ever been caught: *Remember when the blues were biting?* Boys enter the house carrying their father, slumped. Happens so fast. Boys rush into the house leading EMTs to the couch in the living room where the body lies, boys enter the house, boys enter the house, boys enter the house. Boys hold open the threshold, awesome threshold that has welcomed them when they haven't even been able to welcome themselves, that threshold which welcomed them when they *had* to be taken in, here is its tarnished knocker, here is its euphonious bell, here's where the boys had to sand the door down because it never would hang right in the frame, here are the scuffmarks from when boys were on the wrong side of the door *demanding,* here's where there were once milk bottles for the milkman, here's where the newspaper always landed, here's the mail slot, here's the light on the front step, illuminated, here's where the boys are standing, as that beloved man is carried out. Boys, no longer boys, exit.

Robert Morgan
Squirt Gun

The orange see-through plastic makes
the gun at first appear red-hot.
But water in the grip is cool
and sloshes when you raise to aim.
The trigger slides the cylinder
and shoots a needle clear as light
across the porch to break as mist.
The gun is fun because it shoots
clear piss. You point and pee on leaves,

on ants, on flowers yards away.
You spray the sun and make rainbows
that melt away in instant rain.
You sprinkle dust along a step
and scare the cat again and hit
a June bug like a Messerschmidt.
And when the gun is almost dry
you place the barrel between your lips
and close your eyes and fire a sip.

Brian Arundel
The Things I've Lost

Fleece hat and gloves: in the backseat of a Boston cab in 2002, before driving back to Maine. Round, purple sunglasses: in an Atlanta pool hall over drinks with Ashy, whose wife was determined to save their marriage by having a baby. A measurable dose of self-skepticism: at about 14, when I realized I was very good at both playing violin and baseball, while not necessarily everyone else was. A school-wide presidential election in sixth grade, after I was drafted to run by Mrs. Sticoiu, the most frightening teacher in the school, while I was out of town. A copy of *The Little Prince*, in Mrs. Sticoiu's class the previous year. A floppy disk that contained my paper on ideological subversion in Wendell Berry, the first essay I'd written after returning to graduate school following a four-year respite. A black scarf from Pigalle: somewhere in Maine before moving west.

The chance to kiss Leslie Wertmann, and, later, that redhead in seventh grade with a smile that could buckle steel—Kim, Christine, or Kathleen maybe—and the blonde at the freshman dance because I couldn't recognize flirtations, even when told that I looked like Bruce Springsteen. My virginity: in 1980, a couple weeks short of 16, in a ritual so brief, awkward and forgettable that I have, in fact, forgotten it. My heart, or so I thought, in 1985, when Susie dumped me; my naivete, three months later, when I learned that she'd slept with at least three other guys I knew while we'd been dating.

Belief that my mother was somehow more than human: in 1972, the first time I saw her fall down after getting drunk. Belief that my father was more than human: a few months beforehand, after learning that he'd had an affair and was being thrown out of the house. The belief that my sister was stable: 1976, when she began pointing at random objects and saying their names, a few months before getting arrested, the first of many times, for disturbing the peace by refusing to leave a Western Union office until they gave her a job. A ten-dollar bill on a

DC subway in 1985, on my way home to my friend Tommy's, where I was staying after leaving my father's house—after he'd moved back in, once my mother remarried and moved south.

The chance, in 1986, to meet Raymond Carver: the only person invited to sit in on an interview, I instead drank all night with friends and overslept. A quarter-inch off the tip of my left thumb, in 1987, while slicing Muenster cheese on an electric Hobart slicer. My shit, figuratively, that same summer when Bob Weir sang "Looks Like Rain" just as my acid trip was peaking at a two-night Dead stand in Roanoke, Va. The Buick a friend had given me as a tax write-off in 1996, which I let someone take for a test drive without holding collateral.

The thought that officials were somehow more evolved than those who elect them: in 1972, listening to my father explain the Watergate burglary. Faith in politics—particularly a two-party system relegated to fundraising contests perpetuated by shallow sound bites, mudslinging and outright lies for the Mindless American Voter so that each party can pursue a majority with which to repress the other, with complete disregard for actually trying to improve the lives of citizens: gradually over time, culminating in 2000. Fundamental hope that Americans really would overcome their vacuity, fear and greed to evolve beyond sheep determined to re-elect George W. Bush: 2004.

The ability to drink until late at night and go to work the next day without feeling like I need to be zipped inside a body bag: sometime in my early thirties. General insecurity and inadequacy: during the past seven years, as I've tried to allow myself to be loved without guilt or judgment. Self-pity and -importance, at least most days, while striving to look beyond the borders of my own desires in a steady ascent that some might refer to as maturation. The desire to remain in this country: since 2004. A black beret: in a Minneapolis bar, just a few days before relocating to Georgia in 1993. A taste for soy sausage patties: inexplicably, sometime in the past six months, leading up to a Saturday brunch three weeks ago.

CHAPTER FOUR

IMAGES

Creative writing relies on images: three-dimensional mental pictures that inspire thoughts and feelings. Like painting or sculpture, creative writing is an art form that works through the five senses. We want the reader engaged with a picture that has physicality, emotion, action, meaning, color. That's what we are trying to make happen in our reader's brain—a sustained *moving picture* that's real, alive. Like a dream or a movie.

THE PRINCIPLES OF IMAGES

We all access this creative space—the image—when we read, write creatively, or dream. When children play, they are hooked into a live image. They are not pretending they are riding a sea horse. They *are* riding a sea horse, they can feel its reins, hear it whinny. The story as it plays out on your mental movie screen is entirely real.

Thus, images *activate* the five senses. If asked, you could tell me what the desk chair you are sitting in right now feels like, what it smells like, what sound it makes when you drag it across a tile floor. You could taste the sea horse if you wanted to (you probably do not care to).

> *The book is a thing in itself, and it is not me. There is no ego in it. I am glad that you sense that while I am in it and of it, I am not the book. It is much more than I am. The pictures have come to me out of some hugeness and sometimes they have startled me. But I am glad of them.*
>
> — JOHN STEINBECK

Images Are Active

Within this image—this moving picture made in your head by *reading words on a page*—you have all your senses available to you. Your feelings, memories, and ideas are stimulated by something from the concrete, visible world. Images—bundle memory, smell, vision, action for the reader: Everything happens at once, providing a rich, seamless experience. The reader is *there*. Not being told something, but experiencing, firsthand, for him- or herself. That's the essential difference between what we call "creative" writing and other kinds of writing. Not showy, wordy emotion-fests. But works that trigger this live moving picture in our audience's brain.

> *My task is to make you hear,*
> *feel and see. That and no*
> *more, and that is everything.*
> — JOSEPH CONRAD

When we read creative writing we expect a visual, sensory experience. A sensual, physical experience. We rely on images to make our way through a play, a story, a poem. When we read history or criticism or a book on how to rebuild our engine block we respond with very different mental imaging strategies. It's intellectual work: abstract, analytical, and thought-based. Pleasure in art is based in the sensory, moving, living image. Art makes meaning not with ideas and concepts, but with pictures.

Reading Is Image Viewing

Read the following excerpts, or, if you can, have someone read them aloud to you while you close your eyes. As you read, concentrate on the picture in your head. What do you see? When there isn't a picture in your head, what *is* happening? Can you break down the different ways in which parts of your mind are activated? Can you isolate the "thinking" mind versus the "seeing" mind versus the "experiencing" mind?

Go slowly. Reading this way takes a lot of focus and a little practice. You are trying to watch what happens in your mind as you read.

1

I've never met, or personally known, anyone who was blind. This blind man was late forties, a heavy-set, balding man with stooped shoulders, as if he carried a great weight there. He wore brown slacks, brown shoes, a light-brown shirt, a tie, a sports coat. Spiffy. He also had this full beard. But he didn't use a cane and he didn't wear dark glasses. I'd always thought dark glasses a must for the blind. Fact was, I wished he had a pair. At first glance, his eyes looked like anyone else's eyes. But if you looked close, there was something different about them. Too much white in the iris, for one thing, and the pupils seemed to move around in the sockets without his knowing it or being able to stop it. Creepy.

— RAYMOND CARVER, "Cathedral"

2

The orange see-through plastic makes
the gun at first appear red-hot.
But water in the grip is cool

and sloshes when you raise to aim.
The trigger slides the cylinder
and shoots a needle clear as light
across the porch to break as mist.
— ROBERT MORGAN, "Squirt Gun"

3

BUDDY: Good?
SAM: Uh huh.
BUDDY: They look good.
SAM: (His mouth full.) They are good. (Silence.)
BUDDY: Make 'em from scratch?
SAM: (Mouth still full.) Bisquick.
BUDDY: Bisquick is good.
SAM: I like Bisquick.
BUDDY: Makes a lotta pancakes.
— PETER MORRIS, "Pancakes"

4

On the first Friday afternoon, I took the red cones he had asked for and arranged them carefully on our chosen field, at the corner of Fifth Avenue and Seventy-ninth Street. I looked over my shoulder at the pseudo-Renaissance mansion that houses N.Y.U.'s Institute of Fine Arts, right across the street. We had met there, twenty-three years earlier, his first year at the Institute of Fine Arts, and mine, too. . . . He would come into the lecture room, in turtleneck and sports jacket, professor-wear, and, staring at his shoes, and without any preliminaries, wait for the lights to dim, demand, "First slide, please," and, pacing back and forth, look up at the image.
— ADAM GOPNIK, "Last of the Metrozoids"

Which samples from the above created the most vivid moving picture in your mind? What or who do you remember "seeing"? Did you see a classroom, a teacher? Were you transported to a breakfast scene of two men discussing Bisquick? Could you see those men, that kitchen? What *did* you see as you read?

Read again. Read the four passages a second or third or fourth time. Watch, again, for any images to flash in your mind's eye. Practice reading with an awareness of what it is you are "flashing on" as you read. This takes concentration.

> *Draw what you see, not what you know.*
> — GWEN DIEHN

Practice reading to try to notice the difference between *knowing* and *seeing*. They are two different ways for the mind to apprehend information. Regular essays explain: "My mother confronted me about the drinking." Or, "My kid's coach was this amazing lecturer." Regular writing tells, reports information.

Nothing wrong with that at all! It's just very different from what we do. We create images, and creative writing shows. A mother walks her daughter down to the pond. It's a beautiful day. The daughter has a hangover. She is tiptoeing, practically. The mother brings up the forbidden topic; this is the day she says out loud what no one has said out loud: You have a drinking problem. Boom. There's an image, and it's alive, moving. Creative writing works—and powerfully—in images.

PRACTICE

Try tracking images. Write out what you see in your mind's eye when you read the four excerpts above. Be as careful and specific as you can—jot down what you flash on as you read. Either in class or at home, compare responses with a partner. If there is a lot of variety in what's seen in these images by other readers, discuss why.

Notice that in each of the above image examples, there are a few ingredients in common. All images have:

- Two people or a person versus a thing (a man meeting a blind man, a kid and a squirt gun, Sam and Buddy, a dad and his teacher).
- People (entities) doing things, active things. If they are thinking, the thoughts are active, rich, specific, detailed, and action-oriented.
- A specific moment in time that bounds, or frames, the image—a living room, a kitchen, a back porch or backyard, an urban football field.

Every mind is different. Each person's set of experiences is different, so the picture you see will vary from your teacher's, your friend's, the author's. Reading is viewing, but every viewer is a little bit different; we all come from different backgrounds, different cultures, different experiences. If you grew up in New York City, and you know Seventy-ninth Street, or if you have visited that part of the country, you are going to have a flood of images when you read Adam Gopnik's creative nonfiction essay. If you have messed around with squirt guns, your image-firing mechanisms in the brain are going to light up when you read Robert Morgan's poem. If you have never seen a blind man, or thought much about blindness, you may not "see" clear-cut images when you read Raymond Carver's passage. You may have a general sense of what he is talking about. Try to notice this—when you are skimming over a passage, and when your brain is working in image mode. You want to notice the writing techniques that make you *see in images as you read*.

The more you read, though, the more wide-ranging your transporting experiences will be. If you don't see a lot right away, keep practicing. The more images you expose your brain to, the more perceptive you will become. A side benefit of this practice: You will see more nuances in real-life situations, too. Dating, job interviews, interactions with teachers and parents—you'll be reading them all like a writer does, alert and attentive to the little gestures and actions and specifics that reveal the secrets you need.

| PRACTICE |

Read or listen to the poem "Driving Through" by Rita Dove on page 124. List the images you *see*. Distinguish, if you can, between what your mind *knows* (thoughts, not images) and what it knows by *seeing* (images). List what you see. Next, elaborate on what it is you can conjure in your mind's eye, based on the prompts the poem offers up. What do you flash on, offstage, around the edges of the pure descriptions? What does your mind see?

The Opposite of Thought

Let's define *thought* as any nonpictorial mental activity. Images are the *opposite* of thought.

Most beginning writers *overwrite* the thoughts and *underwrite* the images. Not surprising. Writing instruction is usually limited to a focus on essays—thinking pieces. Many of us haven't had encouragement or support or training in trusting our eyes, and writing what is seen, *not* what is thought or felt. Many new writers don't trust their eyes to get the job done; they forget how potent reading is, and how creative the human brain is—your reader *is* going to see it, and get it, and understand many layers of feeling and thought, without your interrupting the flow to explain.

You might try to exaggerate in the opposite direction. Try to *overwrite* the images. Try to be too visual, too sensory. Get your audience to say to you: I can see this too clearly! This is too vivid!

You are likely very, very good at writing thoughts; most anyone who survived high school has been trained to write this way. It might even feel uncomfortable to *not* write thoughts. Creative writers constantly have to work against that comfort zone. In all your other classes this year you should be *thinking*. But not when you sit down to write creatively. In this class, in this kind of writing, you work with your eyes. Here, you are practicing *transporting yourself to another place and seeing*. Thoughts suck the drama and the richness out of your writing. They keep everything juicy and hot offstage. Thoughts are filters, middlemen. The writer's job is to make it easy for the reader to see.

> *Nothing exists in the intellect that has not first gone through the senses.*
>
> — PLUTARCH

There is an enormous difference between thinking, "My mother is sitting," and seeing your mom, plunked down in the old red chair. Practice now. Do it as a thought. Mother in chair. Pure intellect, just the concept—do not let your mind see a picture. Then, do it as an image. See: your mother in a specific chair, in a room, with light coming in the window, right in her eyes . . . see the difference? We are trying to avoid the first mental action and focus our attention and energy on the second. The second practice, that's the real thing.

The basic unit for creative writing is this image, this alive word picture. The ability you have as a writer to create these living word pictures in your reader's head is where the magic and transformative power of our craft resides. Creative writers don't want their readers to think. We want them to see and feel. If your work comes from thoughts, it might be great writing, but it won't be what we call creative writing. For example, in an essay (writing that may well be creative, but isn't what we are doing in this course), you might write, "The Pueblo method of divorce can be as simple as this: A woman leaves her husband's moccasins on the doorstep. And it's over." In creative writing, using images, you want your reader to have the weight of those shoes, to be able to imagine the house, the marriage, the sky, the pain of the divorce for both parties — all that. And more. Images let you trigger whole worlds of consciousness in your reader.

> *It is not sufficient that what one paints should be made visible. It must be made tangible.*
> — GEORGES BRAQUE

When you write, put yourself there physically. Don't think, Okay, Pueblo stuff, what do I know about that? *See something:* "She brushed her skirt and sat on the bed with his shoes next to her. His toes seemed to be always in these shoes, in all his shoes — there were five dimples at the tops of each shoe, shiny, where the suede was worn away. She picked one of the moccasins up. They were always heavier than they appeared to be. She threw the shoe at the door."

Your images shouldn't be about describing, they shouldn't be *about* anything at all; they should *be the thing.* Experience the musty leather as you write; if you experience, your reader will too. When you fully imagine that house, that marriage, the bedspread, the smells of the field, all you have to do as a writer is paint some deft strokes, outline a few items, an emotion, the palm of a hand — and your reader will fill in the entire town. Eventually, as you gain practice using images, you can make your images so powerful that by describing a front porch, your reader will see the whole county, and feel like he or she has been there before.

So. Don't write what you think. Write what you see. If you can't see it, you can't write it. If you rely on explanation, prefacing, concluding, analyzing, musing, reflecting, thinking — you deny your reader a large part of the pleasure and impact of creative writing, of what we do.

Instead, give yourself over to the experience of image. Go where it goes. Don't think it out.

Determine if the following is an image or a thought:

I was really into boys. All I thought about was boys, boys, boys.

Thought. Essentially, this writer is thinking out loud on the page, an approach we might use for writing essays, journals, letters, notes to the self. It's perfectly fine writing, but it's not exactly creative writing. The writer/speaker is looking back at her life, making a conclusion. It's a thought about a thought—and that kind of approach to creative writing is dangerous. Your reader is basically on pause here. No mental image occurs. The disk spins, but the reader, like the writer, is not engaged. The two sentences above are not alive. They're fine, they're not wrong, they're just not *doing* anything.

You, as writer, have wasted an opportunity to make something happen in your reader's brain. You must use that opportunity; you cannot waste it. Creative writing isn't about simply knowing. It's about knowing *through seeing and experiencing something alive.* Thoughts kill that process. They pierce the experience, like light coming into a darkened movie theater.

Thoughts ruin the image. *Thoughts* include:

CONCLUSIONS	"Ultimately, I really did love him."
	"Class wasn't so bad."
	"I ended up in the emergency room."
	"The summer I turned 8 my mom decided I was spending too much time in front of the television and ruining my eyes."
EMOTION DESCRIPTIONS	"Hannah hated hearing her brother Brian complain about Mrs. Danch when he was in seventh grade."
	"She was speechless."
	"I wished I hadn't quit."
THOUGHT REPORTS	"I figured it was a good way to get out of karate."
	"I knew she was an idiot."
EXPLANATIONS	"To be clear, my mother was mad. Real mad."
	"Once I am out of a relationship I am really ready to get back in one."

Most thought sentences are actually images waiting to be born. Your writing will be instantly and dramatically better as you translate thoughts into images.

PRACTICE

Read the short story by Akhil Sharma, "Surrounded by Sleep," on page 125. With a highlighter (or by taking notes and making a list), mark every passage that is an image (where you see, or could see, a scene play out in your mind). Focus on where you see people in action. What percentage of the story is images?

Generating Images

In order to create a live image to work from as a writer, you answer a set of questions. Ground yourself in space and time in order to generate images.

Grounded in images, your work will be instantly alive. Oriented in place and time, you hit the ground running. Trust your reader and trust the power of images—they will provide the second half of the equation. Write from this deeply experiential point of view. Instead of doing a rough draft, practice anchoring yourself in time and space before you write. You will save *hours* of revision time.

Instead of writing, "Hannah hated hearing her brother Brian complain . . . ," which is a conclusion about a memory—all thought, no action, no image—translate the thought into an image.

PRACTICE

Read Anne Panning's "Candy Cigarettes" on page 139. Make note of every image based on people in action.

QUESTIONS TO ASK: Orienting Yourself in Images before Writing

Always, before you write, locate yourself with an image. Use these questions to locate yourself, your writing eye, deeply within the image before you start writing. *Answer the orienting questions before beginning any piece of creative writing.*

1. Where are we? What room, neighborhood, town, county, place?
2. What time is it? What minute, hour, day, month, year?
3. What is the weather outside like? What's the atmosphere inside like? (Lighting, hot/cold, smoky, comfortable, etc.)
4. Who is there, "onstage"? Who just left? Who is nearby?
5. Who is expected?
6. What just happened?
7. How old is each person "onstage"?
8. What are people wearing? What do they have in their hands?
9. What is in the room/location? What "stuff" is around?
10. What is the dominant smell?
11. What is/are the dominant sound/s?
12. As you gaze around the image, what else do you notice?

Before you write, every single time, be securely in the moment you are writing. It doesn't matter if it's poetry, fiction, nonfiction, or a play. Know exactly where your character/self is in time and space. It doesn't matter if your work is based on your life or completely fantasy, totally made up. Become the person you are writing and jot down: Where are you? Where is Brian? Where is Mrs. Danch? Where is Hannah? Are *you* Hannah? What sounds do you hear? What meal was just eaten? What clothes are you (as your person) wearing? Get in the habit of writing anchored. When you slip out of the image, practice translating your thoughts back into pictures. Full-blown images.

> *I want to reach that state of condensation of sensations which constitutes a picture.*
> — HENRI MATISSE

PRACTICE

In order to prepare to write an image, draw a sketch that answers the orienting questions above, or make a list of your answers (or your character's answers) to those orienting questions. Let the answers launch you into an image—write a paragraph, a few lines of dialogue, a few lines of poetry, about the same length as the excerpts above (pp. 102–103). Stay in the image. Follow the action/speech, don't scene-set.

CREATING WITH IMAGES

Focus on People in Action

Now that you know how to launch an image, begin working with images by focusing on two essential components of the image: people (or beings of some kind) and action (meaningful movement by the beings).

Few creative works are purely abstract—no people, no action, nothing we can see. Even poems about beautiful sunsets or perfect, still fields often *imply* people and action.

Noncreative writing begins with ideas, principles, or theories. Creative writing begins with Joe, in a tree, watching his grandmother's front yard, where a fight is breaking out.

Creative writing is rooted in individuals, struggling and interacting with the physical world, and others in that world. It's easiest to create pictures your reader can see when you have two or more entities. People alone are often thinking. Thoughts aren't usually interesting enough on their own to sustain creative writing. But two or more people—that attracts the eye. These ingredients—two people, something happening—give you the spark you need to ignite images.

> *Seeing is polysensory, combining the visual, tactile, and kinesthetic senses.*
> — ROBERT McKIM

Choose six of the thought examples on page 107 to translate into images. Take each thought and translate it into an image, a moving picture, that will create something alive in the reader's head. Do the anchoring activity each time, using your sketch or floor plan, so you are firmly in the room, in the image, before you start to write. Read a few of these short passages out loud either in class or on your own. Ask your group to tell you what else they can see in your picture. Do they guess any of the items from your jotted list correctly? Things you didn't even mention in your writing, but had in mind when you wrote? In your group, rank your most successfully vivid images in order of best to least effective.

Collect your creative writing pieces—all your drafts—from the course so far. Take a highlighter, and, go through your writing and underline and label as many conclusions, emotion descriptions, thought reports, and explanations as you can. Do you tend to rely on one of these four image-killers more than others? Write a brief analysis of your particular image-killing habits, and list a few of your strongest images.

> *Merely to see is not enough. It is necessary to have a fresh, vivid, physical contact with the object you draw through as many of the senses as possible—and especially through the sense of touch.*
> — KIMON NICOLAIDES

Think from Within Images

How do writers use thoughts, then, in their work? Sparingly. And only when firmly, deeply anchored in the image. Make sure you have an image up and running, with action and moving pictures, *before* you offer the reader a thought, insight, conclusion, or comment.

Read the following passages. Which ones are more grounded, providing a flash or a moving picture in your mind? Which rely on reporting or present generalized thought and not images?

1

I love my freedom. My relationships, especially the one with Dana, were always really strained, especially after the deadly three-month period. There is no reason for people to try to control each other so totally.

2

I am mad at you
But you make me laugh
I'm still mad at you
But now I'm laughing
We are the same.
Our hair, our eyes, our interests.

3

BOB: This party sucks.
JEN: I know. It is so ridiculous.
BOB: Why did we even come?
JEN: You wanted to talk to you know.
BOB: I just can't stop thinking about it, you know?
JEN: I know.

4

There she is, standing next to her own mother, behind the symmetrical and somewhat religious arrangement of two Coca-Cola bottles flanking a birthday cake on a small table.

— ALEIDA RODRÍGUEZ, "My Mother in
Two Photographs, among Other Things"

5

I'd peer into the front window, breath fogging the sale signs,

catching snippets of my father's profile appearing and disappearing behind the tall cardboard stacks. Once I slipped back into the store,

wandering the aisles, master of my own cart, loading it to bursting
— SEBASTIAN MATTHEWS, "Buying Wine"

Which of the above engages you most fully, really makes something happen for you in your mind's eye? What *causes the image to pop into your head*?

PRACTICE

Place the samples of writing, above, numbered one through five, in order (example 1) from most thought-oriented (you process the writing through the analytical part of your brain) to most imagistic—you see a picture of something in your mind's eye (example 5).

Remember that different readers experience images differently. You may not "see" the same images as your classmates. It depends on your life experiences and how experienced a reader you are. It's useful for you to practice sensitizing yourself to the experiential qualities of creative writing. As you do so, always keep this in mind: Thoughts distance us from images. Thoughts are like the voice-over in a movie, or playing a DVD with the commentary on. In creative writing, in art, be careful with thoughts. Be generous with images. The thoughts will take care of themselves; readers are more interested in their *own* thoughts and conclusions, not yours. Trust your reader; trust your material. If you are faithful to the image, the truth—and better ideas than you could ever "think" of—will come out!

PRACTICE

Take your answer for examples 1 and 5 above and translate them into their opposite. For example, if one of your answers for those two questions involved Dana and a relationship, do a sketch, answer the orienting questions on page 108, and write a scene containing a moment you show to the reader as an image, completely free of any telling or explaining or thinking. Then do the reverse, taking the most imagistic of the quotes above, and summarizing it into a thought. Keep the reader from seeing anything.

If there is a picture in your reader's brain—blue ocean, hot white sand, your old worn flip-flops—you have an activated image. If your reader is *thinking about* what it would be like to be at the beach, but not *picturing it in real time*, you have created a thought; that's not exactly what creative writing is trying to accomplish. You do not have complete control—literature isn't brainwashing material. Some of your readers will be distracted. Some won't have strong muscles of concentration. Others will have had so many similar experiences, images flood in as they read. Finally, the stock-in-trade of creative writing is creating images—that's what we do. We try to put on paper words that will create a vivid, continuous sensory dream in our readers' brains. If the dream is really compelling, we may stop the film, talk briefly, explain something. But that is dangerous. When the film isn't running, the reader is likely to stop reading. We don't want that. If that happens, we are out of a job. Our goal is to keep readers from thinking and force them to experience the image as a moving, real-time film, running in his or her brain. Created by us.

Use Specifics

Specific words—concrete nouns, place names, proper nouns, active verbs—are the fuel that feeds the image, keeping it alive and sparkly.

It's not enough for writers to "be descriptive." In fact, you have probably heard readers say, "The description goes on too long; you can skip it." It's very likely you have done some skipping or skimming yourself; most of us have.

Sentences that billow with very formal language and flowery word choices might seem specific. These kinds of sentences may draw praise from some teachers, friends, or parents not trained as creative writers. Actually, lots of *words* may block your reader's engagement with the piece:

The pulsating rivers plunged towards their ultimate and terrible death!

This is the story of heartache and heartbreak, of tumultuousness and terror and I want you to always remember, this is true, and real!

The joy of holding hands,
You are in my mind always

My heart beating and yours
Beating beating as one heart.

It's unlikely you really see any specific images in the above quotes. What's blocking the image? Not thoughts this time, but language. General or overblown language is as ineffective as thinking when you are trying to get your reader fully absorbed in your writing.

In fact, usually more simple writing activates the brain's image-making machine. Instead of worrying about adjectives and beautiful word-picture-painting — "writerly things" — concentrate on where *you* are, in your mind's eye, when you write. Creative writing isn't about the writer. It's about the reader, having an experience, being somewhere, seeing through someone else. You don't report your emotions and thoughts, you activate your reader's. Creative writing serves readers. It's not a stage for show-offs.

When writing in images, name the simple, actual things in the world. Instead of writing "missing you," you place your lover and yourself in your car, your last Friday night together, ever. Instead of "car," you write, "Angel's old Cadillac," or, "the sedan with the human teeth marks." Instead of writing "fruit," write "five strawberries." See the difference for the reader? See how "fruit" makes you think; you may or may not picture a fruit—you think *fruit* as a concept. That's absolutely contrary to the goals and pleasures of creative writing. "Five strawberries," and you've got them. Your mouth might even water. When you are in the image, writing what you see, write really, truly, what you see. Be specific by looking carefully, naming the small parts, and keeping it simple.

PRACTICE

Catalog the specific words in the two poems at the end of this chapter (Rita Dove's "Driving Through" on page 124, and Gary Soto's "Everything Twice" on page 136) by making a list of every single specific word choice. Of the number of words in the two poems, what's the percentage of specific words in each? Apply the same process and do the math on two of your own poems. What do you notice?

When a photograph is out of focus, we adjust the lens to sharpen the image. Sharpening the focus of your written image means choosing more specific words. Specific concrete nouns and clear action verbs *intensify* images. Professional, published writers go over their work many, many times, to sharpen every single word choice, to make sure every single syllable is contributing to, not distracting from, the moving live picture in the reader's head. Poets do this, of course, but so do narrative writers in their creative nonfiction and fiction.

PRACTICE

Reread the short story on page 125, Akhil Sharma's "Surrounded by Sleep." Scan back through the story using your highlighter (or making a list) to capture every single specific in the story. This is going to be a long list! *Isocal, Hindi women's magazine*, It's a Wonderful Life, chaplain, Clark Kent, Three Musketeers, Harlem Globetrotters, Budweiser, dark dress pants, mouth, lungs, stomach, mini-mall, pizzeria, Reese's Peanut Butter Cups, 7 train, fat as a heel, etc. Estimate what percentage of the story is made up of specifics.

Move around in Images

Images are alive, which means that things move in that picture inside the reader's head. Action takes place. Whether it's a poem, play, nonfiction piece, or story, the image has movement in it.

Amateur videographers tend to make one common mistake. They stand in one place when they shoot Freddy's soccer game or Bitsy's first Christmas. No matter what is happening—a great attack resulting in a point scored, or Bitsy biting the dog—we the viewers watch the action but are forced to remain in a fixed location. Amateur videographers have a hard time following the image to where it is most alive. *America's Funniest Home Videos* is a collection of amateurs who happened to get lucky—something amazing happens to be caught. Most of the time, hours of footage are shot and nothing happens. The photographer holds the camera at eye level, pointing it straight ahead. The real action, the lively images, take place off-camera, somewhere else.

We tend not to watch other people's Freddy and Bitsy videos, because *nothing very interesting happens*. The image is moving, but we aren't moving anywhere interesting as we watch. When you create an image (using your checklist from p. 108), you create a solid starting point. Once you have the image launched, the good creative writer *moves*.

Move to where, to look at what? What's interesting. It will feel funny at first, just as it does to walk around with a video camera, filming *but not looking through the camera*. Keep your eye on what's interesting, what's dramatic, what tiny specifics you can see that will reveal so much more about this person than words ever could.

If you started your image in the living room, where your mom is sitting in her favorite chair, but she is just sleeping, you need to move your camera. You need to get really, really close up, so we can see the pores of her skin, *or* you need to let your camera-eye capture something that is *more interesting*. Leave the room. No need to write boring. Film your way into the kitchen. Your dad fighting with your obnoxious older brother who refuses to lift a finger around the house? That could be good. Move in close. Really close. Recall the story "Boys" by Rick Moody on page 94. Notice how there is always action, always lots of movement—the boys run around, in and out of the house, year after year, shooting a dog, itching and scratching, breaking out into pimples, calling names, torturing their sister. Notice where the camera is in each of these image flashes: positioned over the neighborhood, then, *whoosh*, down into a backyard, then in a church pew, right over the shoulder of one of the boys, then at the bathroom mirror, close up on a boy's face, then the camera, *whoosh*, is on a dolly, tracking down the upstairs hallway as the boys chase the sister. The camera is *always moving. The distance between the camera and the subject is constantly changing.*

At first, it feels awkward to walk around and film simultaneously. As you practice writing this way, focused on the moving image, you will feel more comfortable.

PRACTICE

Examine "Surrounded by Sleep" on page 125. Make a list of at least ten moving images. Where are you transported (where do you see the full image play out on the movie screen in your head)? Notice where the camera is positioned, and how close the writer is to the image. How much movement is there? Which images are closeups, which are filmed from further back?

Amateurs tend to stay back. It's weird and intrusive and uncomfortable to get in people's faces. But that is what artists do. The amateur stands stock still, and everything is filmed from the same distance. Excellent filmmakers vary the distance. They open with a long shot, we see the whole world. Then, for high impact, they close in. Then, they pull out a little. Then we zoom in, and all we can see is part of a face. Part of a life. A secret inside view. Keep moving. Keep changing your angles. That's how you get the good stuff, the alive parts of your image.

One Sentence, One Action

Action feeds the image. Action keeps it alive. But often, while tracking actions and gestures we get all tangled up.

> Nancy was rushing to get to the class on time and she stumbled and fell while picking up her books from the sofa to get out the door on time.

What's wrong here is that the author thinks she is writing in the image, using action, nouns, and verbs. But she isn't. Because the human brain reads English sentences in a linear fashion, from left to right, we take in the order of events sequentially. If your image sequence is off, if your sentences try to handle too many actions, the reader won't be transported. He or she may be able to muscle

> *We live on the leash of our senses.*
> — DIANE ACKERMAN

through, and *think* out what is happening, but that isn't what you want as a writer. You want the reader *not working too hard*. The reader wants to just see what's happening. The reader doesn't want to have to sort out all the stage directions. That involves thinking, heavy lifting. Creative writing is all about *seeing*.

So, an important aspect of manipulating images is remembering the limitations of the sentence. Do only one thing at a time.

Harry grabbed the gin and tonic. He rushed down the driveway, spilling.

As opposed to:

Harry, coming in the door, grabbed his drink and got undressed and changed into his soccer shorts.

It's physically impossible to come in a door and grab a drink *and* get undressed. This is summary. It's not a real image. It's a list of events. Good writers break down what they see and render what's important for the reader to notice.

Notice how in the readings in this chapter, most of the sentences are devoted to one action, one thing. Readers are reading lines, in a linear fashion, from left to right. Sentences that try to do two things — "She walked in and put down her coat and he read the comic book to his brother" — are not as effective as sentences that are allowed to devote themselves to a single action, a single concept. Simplify your sentences and make them into straight lines, simple, sharp, clearly aimed at their target. You can still write complex sentences and complex actions. It's just a matter of tightly focusing your logic and lining it up with your tightly focused camera work. Isolate the action one thing at a time, and the sentence breaks the action down into bite-sized pieces.

Rita Dove's poem illustrates this point perfectly.

I turn toward her, meaning to confess
my wild affliction, my art. Instead
I hiss gibberish; she panics,
slams the door handle down

A complex argument, a lot going on in this moment. But Rita Dove lets her sentences do one thing at a time. I was going to do X. Instead I did Y, which caused Z.

Compare to a typical non-image sentence:

All the girls fluttered their eyelashes and giggled when he walked by.

Wait. One sentence. Do it right. One thing at a time. What happens first here? The male walks by. That's the event that triggers the flirting behaviors. So set up your image so that the *reader* sees the male walking by. Make that happen, first. Then what happens? The girls react. What do you see? Do they really flutter their eyelashes? Or is that a shorthand, a made-up summary of what really happens? Can you see, if you are the author of this piece, what these girls look like, where they are? Often, sentences like this, that don't really transport a reader into an image, are written when a writer is not grounded in this image, not really seeing anything, just making it up. So to rewrite get grounded. Answer those questions on page 108. What does each girl look like? How does she stand? When is this? Where, exactly? Who giggles first? Do it as an image, and let your sentences work hard but don't send them careening in two directions at once. Don't give us the first information last.

New writers often make mistakes relating to image focus in transitions. For some reason, we get all hung up in transitions, when people move from house to car, or driveway to party. Try to just take out awkward transitions—getting people into and out of cars, leaving rooms, saying goodbye—and use white space instead, skipping two double lines.

His father said, "One minute," and they climbed out of the car.

They went up the wooden steps into the bar. Inside it was dark and smelled of cigarette smoke and something stale and sweet.

Look again at the way Sharma keeps his images moving, alive, thrumming. He uses physicality, action, gesture, movement. He describes actions—what his characters are doing, how they are moving, what tasks they are involved in; emotions and statements are used sparingly, and only when the image is very strong, very alive, so its momentum will keep playing out in the reader's mind while he pauses to give you information, say something he just really wants to say. When writing a transition simplify the image. Write what you see. Stay focused on what's alive and practice cutting out unnecessary logistical explanations.

Summary Images

In a short piece—a poem, or a short-short, for example—you can sustain an image and that can be your entire piece. In a longer work, a more complex short story—say, Akhil Sharma's "Surrounded by Sleep," for example—you have to build bridges between the images. There are two kinds of bridges. One is quick and slides the reader from one place and time to another in a single sentence, a transition from image to image. We'll look at *slides* in a moment. The second type of bridge, or transition, is a *summary image*.

Summary passages are just as important as image-based sections in creative writing. Summary provides the connective tissue so that the images work together. Summary also lets you cover a lot of time deftly and vividly. And, summary highlights images so that they show up, framed, emphasized. The difference between a summary and a slide is that the summary is bigger, fuller, richer. It's like grout. It fills in the spaces between the image tiles with information, drama, backstory.

Summary images help the reader understand the relationship of the parts to each other and to the larger themes of the piece. "However, on the other hand," and "Following up on that point," are the essay-writer's cues that we are adding more information to counter or develop a previous point. In creative writing, all this work is done with the mental movie intact. A summary image gives a sweeping overview, a look at the big picture. The camera is much further back. It may present snapshots of numerous typical moments, skidding over time to get to the next important point in the piece, which of course will be presented in a full-blown image.

In Sharma's story, to show the entire life of Ajay's family after the accident *in images* would fill many volumes! Sharma has to pick: Some things will be shown in full-blown images—the key moments. Other moments are shown to the reader in a different way—summary images.

Summary images have to be interesting, active, and vibrant, but presented in less detail. Signal phrases that announce we are in a summary image often have to do with time. "That summer," or, "For five weeks it went on," are the kinds of cues that let the read know, "Here's how things generally went over the next chunk of time."

Notice in paragraph two of "Surrounded by Sleep," Sharma gives a summary, the backstory, an overview of how Ajay's family arrived at the pool that August afternoon. During this summary, what happens in your mind's eye? Does the screen go blank? Do you reason your way through this passage, as in a chemistry textbook? Do you *see* as you learn more information about the family?

A period of weeks is covered, and in the reader's mind these weeks probably play out in a series of brief flashes, glimpses—the mother's attempt to manipulate the doctors, the call from the insurance company, the father's visits to the hospital. You imagine, just below the level of "movie," what this *felt like, looked like*. It's different from a police report. It's different from reading sociology. Art appeals to our emotions and the physical senses, and so does summary—we are aware of these actual people moving through their real lives. We keep hold of the image in summary as we get more necessary information. We don't leave the playing field. The writer doesn't break the movie-dream.

The same rules apply to summary images as regular images: Make sure, as you write, that you *experience* the moment, not just write about it. Stay close up, use concrete nouns and action verbs. And, keep your focus on the actions.

Sliding

To move from summary to real-time image and back again, or to move from place to place, image to image, in your poem or story or play, you learn to slide. Sliding is like smooth camera work, when you gently shift the image focus, moving your reader's attention slowly from the park swingset, where two kids are playing, gently over to the mall parking lot across the street. Moving the "camera" is called sliding. You slide in fiction, poetry, nonfiction, and plays.

Writers who don't learn sliding frequently commit two writing sins. If you whip the camera around, you make your reader sick or dizzy or, worse, confused. (Your point might be that these characters are sick, crazy, unfocused. Then, you might *choose* to jump from one thing to the next.) Too many locations, not enough depth, and no transitions might result in this type of scattershot, slideless writing:

> Joey ate his sandwich. The diner was crazy. When he was talking to Clara later at her house he picked yet another fight with the girl. On the dance floor she wouldn't talk to him.

The other problem resulting from not using the slide is boring writing. Many writers, unsure of how or when to move the camera, the focus, the action, simply keep writing. They have something going, and because so much can go wrong, they just stay with it. There will be a long paragraph, maybe the whole first page of a story, about waking up. Turning off the alarm. Getting ready. Next page, leaving the apartment, driving to work. There's no slide—*everything is explained*. This approach is difficult for the reader. Everything is presented at exactly the same level of intensity. It's like a security camera. Lots and lots of hours of footage. Very rarely something interesting to look at.

Not using the slide will prevent your reader from entering the image and moving around in your piece.

Marisa Silver, author of "What I Saw from Where I Stood" (p. 167) is a master of the slide. Examine this short excerpt from her story, which you will read in full later, and simply notice the sliding action:

> I drove Dulcie's car to work the next day. When I got home that night, Dulcie had moved our mattress from our bed into the living room, where it lay in the middle of the floor, the sheets spilling over onto the carpet.

Silver slides from the narrator's workday into the scene that follows, where the couple discovers, and argues over, the rat. The reader doesn't need the workday, the car ride, the character's entrance into the apartment:

> "It's the rat," she said. "He's back."

The reader knows we have slid into the apartment scene. The reader has space in the image to move the narrator from his car up into the apartment—no need to spell that out in a full-blown scene. The slide is an efficient summary that uses action, location, and an anchored image to slide over time, covering a large amount quickly. A slide is a bridge, different from pure summary, in that the slide moves us scenically to a new location and time. The reader needs these slides—and the spaces between them—in order to engage actively with the piece.

PRACTICE

Sliding and summary in Soto's poem: Read Gary Soto's poem on page 136, "Everything Twice." How do images in the opening two lines connect to the images in the last two lines? Is this poem written in images? Are there summary images? Slides?

Examine the following passage (p. 129) from Sharma's story, and notice where the slide from summary to scene occurs:

> Sometimes when Ajay arrived his mother was on the phone, telling his father that she missed him and was expecting to see him. . . . Ajay had thought of his parents as the same person: MummyDaddy. Now . . . Ajay sensed that his mother and father were quite different people. After his mother got off the phone, she always went to the cafeteria to get coffee for herself and Jell-O or cookies for him. He knew that if she took her coat with her, it meant that she was especially sad. . . .
>
> That day, while she was gone, Ajay stood beside the hospital bed and balanced a comic book on Aman's chest. He read to him very slowly. Before turning each page, he said, "Okay, Aman?"

Sharma uses *image* summary to make us experience how it is when someone is in the hospital. A bunch of days are all alike. These days blur together. Sharma, in summary-image mode, can stop and tell us Ajay's new insights into his parents, how he is seeing them as people, as more than just entities designed to meet his needs. Sharma doesn't stop and lecture to us though. He stays deep in the moment by calling out the four main physical images from those days: coffee, Jell-O, cookies, and his mother and her coat. That's the key: Anchor summary in specific images—moving ones. When you have your specific images in place, you can hang insights, conclusions, etc., on them. Without the images, the summary becomes too heavy, it ceases to be art, and it becomes an essay. Nothing wrong with essays. It's just not what we are doing here as

Every picture I paint is a three-way struggle between what I know, what I see and what I want.
— THOMAS BUECHNER

creative writers. When we read creative writing, *imaginative* writing, we expect to have pictures play out in our minds. That's part of the deal.

So, with the summary passage engaged, alive, and made out of the stuff that transports a reader to a time, mood, and place simultaneously, notice how Sharma slides from the generalized summary image to the full-blown "this is happening right now" image. The change happens so smoothly. Sharma freezes the frame on one day. In summary-time, the mother walks outside. "That day, while she was gone . . ." is the line where Sharma hits the pause button. See how he does that? We've been seeing her come and go, do her coffee-and-coat routine, and one day, while she is out, Sharma anchors us firmly in real time, in an image we are going to be in for a while. We're going in for a closer look. And, voilà — she goes out, and we are given Ajay. Real time.

We are in a full-blown scene, an image with a floor, a ceiling, walls — it's not a blur. We're going to stay here. Something is going to happen. Time slows down, the comic's pages are turned slowly, and we are up against Aman's chest — see how much closer we are? Notice where the camera is, and what happens in your mind as you read. Sharma writes this by imagining what it's like to see through Ajay's eyes. He doesn't write about the boy, he writes from the boy. And so we follow this image-moment, the reading of the comic, with an extended closeup focusing on Aman's physicality, his equipment, his injuries. Notice how this description is never laid on top of the skin of the story, it's part of the story. We are in Ajay's body. We see how he sees. His brother reminds him of that terrible melted bowl. The images aren't decorative. The images are how a character sees, feels, exists, moves in the world.

PRACTICE

Highlight with one color all the present-time images from "My Mother in Two Photographs, among Other Things" on page 137. Now, highlight the summary images. Do the same for one of your stories or creative nonfiction pieces. Compare. Do you use summary or real-time images more? Does Rodríguez use real time or summary time more?

A WORD ON IDEAS

Ideas are giant super-thoughts. A lot of nonwriters think that what writers do is Have Great Ideas. Nothing could be further from the truth. Writers See Great Images. In fact, ideas can be potentially bad for writers.

Many writers have ideas for writing. When the idea is a *picture in the brain*, when the idea isn't in words yet, it is viable. But many "ideas" for writing are dead on arrival — the thought demons have already fed, and all you really have is a carcass. For example, you have an idea for a poem about your grandmother. Often, starting from the thought—grandma was beautiful, even in old age—is more difficult, more distancing. Better to start with a description of you and her, in a room, on a particular day, what her toes looked like, what she said. Get in the habit of working from images. The ideas will take care of themselves, and your writing will be fresher, richer, more original. And smarter.

> *People have to go out of their minds before they can come to their senses.*
> — TIMOTHY LEARY

Don't think. Write. Don't make this work cerebral, keep it sensory (and sensual). Don't save up ideas. Instead of thinking in ideas for stories and poems and plays, collect images, details, specifics, and overhead bits of real-world dialogue. Jot those things down in your journal, and avoid ideas, such as "homeless man" or "war story." Get in the habit of writing in images instead of putting down all your thoughts, hoping to translate them into images later. Try to have the experience while writing—even when you are at the very very earliest note-taking stage—that you want your reader to have while reading.

WRITING PROJECTS

1. Break the rules. Write a piece that is all thoughts, commentary, no images. How do you engage, transport the reader?

2. Write a piece that is completely creating images in the reader's mind, no thoughts or commentary allowed.

3. Take an image from any previous piece of writing and extend it, moving in closer with your camera, and slowing time down, so that you expand this single moment, this glimpse, into five pages of prose or twenty lines of poetry.

4. Use an image from Akhil Sharma's short story "Surrounded by Sleep" to serve as a launching point, and write an imitation, using a similar scene from your own life—a sibling accident, a hospital scene, an outing with a parent, etc. Use at least three of the same techniques for achieving presentness that Sharma does. Your piece may take the form of a play, short story, or memoir.

5. Write a piece that involves a slide from summary image into full-blown scene, and a slide from full-blown scene into summary image. Avoid clichés: waking up, falling asleep, drifting into reflection.

6. Write a piece of creative nonfiction in the same form as "My Mother in Two Photographs, among Other Things" by Aleida Rodríguez on page 137.

Choose, from your own collection of photographs, a few photos of the same person, someone you are close to, at different points in life. Write paragraph sections inspired by the images in the photographs, very directly, as well as images from your life with this person. Avoid thoughts! You can make each section a photograph section if you have enough photos. Make your essay four to seven sections in length.

IMAGES WORKSHOP

The prompts below will guide your discussion of your classmates' work.

1. In the student piece you are reading, highlight the places you truly see as "moving images," the alive parts of the piece, where you aren't reading words on a page as much as experiencing something, seeing.

2. Identify three to five places in the student piece where an image could be made more powerful, alive, and focused. Look for passages that rely on thoughts, feelings, explanations, description. Circle these.

3. Identify a place in the piece where the student writer uses summary images effectively. Label it "good summary."

4. Find a passage in the student piece where there is a transition from one real-time image to another, a slide. Box it. Label it by naming the locations: "kitchen to bedroom," or, "parking lot to lobby." Find another section in the piece where the transition from one moment to another is rough, not an image, or confusing. Box it. Make a suggestion for improving the flow so that the reader stays focused on the moving image, and is never jolted out of the present.

5. Identify your favorite image in this piece.

Rita Dove
Driving Through

I know this scene: There's an engine
idling, without keys, just outside Mr. Nehi's
algebra class. I escape without notice,
past the frosted glass of the wood shop
and the ironclad lockers with their inscrutable hasps
that never shut clean. I know
the sweet hum of tires over asphalt,
green tunnels trickling sun,
proud elmfire before Dutch blight
vacuumed the corridors bare. And the rowdy kids
cluttering the curb, nappy heads bobbing,
squirrel blood streaking their sharpened sticks—
I know them, too. After all, this is the past
I'm driving through, and I know I'll end up
where I started, stiff-necked and dull-hearted,
cursing last night's red wine. So when

this girl, this woman-of-a-child
with her cheap hoops and barnyard breasts
snatches the door and flops onto the vinyl shouting
Let's ride!, I nod and head straight for
the police, although I can't quite recall
where the station is, law enforcement
not being part of my past.
Run me home first, she barks,
smiling, enjoying the bluff:
I need my good earrings.
I tell her we're almost there, which
we aren't, not by half, and how would I know
where she lives, anyway? We're both smiling
now; but only when we're good and lost,
traffic thinned to no more than

a mirage of flayed brick and scorched cement,
does she blurt out: *You're lying.*
True, I think; but lying is what I do best.
I turn toward her, meaning to confess
my wild affliction, my art. Instead
I hiss gibberish; she panics,
slams the door handle down and hurls
her ripe body into the street where
no one will ever remember seeing her
again.
     What was that?
My husband bolts up from his pillow.
Just a dream, I stammer, head pounding
as I try to fall asleep again—
even though I knew that girl was lost
long before I went back to find her.

Akhil Sharma
Surrounded by Sleep

One August afternoon, when Ajay was ten years old, his elder brother, Aman, dove into a pool and struck his head on the cement bottom. For three minutes, he lay there unconscious. Two boys continued to swim, kicking and splashing, until finally Aman was spotted below them. Water had entered through his nose and mouth. It had filled his stomach. His lungs collapsed. By the time he was pulled out, he could no longer think, talk, chew, or roll over in his sleep.

Ajay's family had moved from India to Queens, New York, two years earlier. The accident occurred during the boys' summer vacation, on a visit with their aunt and uncle in Arlington, Virginia. After the accident, Ajay's mother came to Arlington, where she waited to see if Aman would recover. At the hospital, she told the doctors and nurses that her son had been accepted into the Bronx High School of Science, in the hope that by highlighting his intelligence she would move them to make a greater effort on his behalf. Within a few weeks of the accident, the insurance company said that Aman should be transferred to a less expensive care facility, a long-term one. But only a few of these were any good, and those were full, and Ajay's mother refused to move Aman until a space opened in one of them. So she remained in Arlington, and Ajay stayed too, and his father visited from Queens on the weekends when he wasn't working. Ajay was enrolled at the local public school and in September he started fifth grade.

Before the accident, Ajay had never prayed much. In India, he and his brother used to go with their mother to the temple every Tuesday night, but that was mostly because there was a good *dosa* restaurant nearby. In America, his family went to a temple only on important holy days and birthdays. But shortly after Ajay's mother came to Arlington, she moved into the room that he and his brother had shared during the summer and made an altar in a corner. She threw an old flowered sheet over a cardboard box that had once held a television. On top she put a clay lamp, an incense-stick holder, and postcards depicting various gods. There was also a postcard of Mahatma Gandhi. She explained to Ajay that God could take any form; the picture of Mahatma Gandhi was there because he had appeared to her in a dream after the accident and told her that Aman would recover and become a surgeon. Now she and Ajay prayed for at least half an hour before the altar every morning and night.

At first she prayed with absolute humility. "Whatever you do will be good because you are doing it," she murmured to the postcards of Ram and Shivaji, daubing their lips with water and rice. Mahatma Gandhi got only water, because he did not like to eat. As weeks passed and Aman did not recover in time to return to the Bronx High School of Science for the first day of classes, his mother began doing things that called attention to her piety. She sometimes held the prayer lamp until it blistered her palms. Instead of kneeling before the altar, she lay face down. She fasted twice a week. Her attempts to sway God were not so different from Ajay's performing somersaults to amuse his aunt, and they made God seem human to Ajay.

One morning as Ajay knelt before the altar, he traced an Om, a crucifix, and a Star of David into the pile of the carpet. Beneath these he traced an *S*, for Superman, inside an upside-down triangle. His mother came up beside him.

"What are you praying for?" she asked. She had her hat on, a thick gray knitted one that a man might wear. The tracings went against the weave of the carpet and were darker than the surrounding nap. Pretending to examine them, Ajay leaned forward and put his hand over the *S*. His mother did not mind the Christian and Jewish symbols—they were for commonly recognized gods, after all—but she could not tolerate his praying to Superman. She'd caught him doing so once several weeks earlier and had become very angry, as if Ajay's faith in Superman made her faith in Ram ridiculous. "Right in front of God," she had said several times.

Ajay, in his nervousness, spoke the truth. "I'm asking God to give me a hundred percent on the math test."

His mother was silent for a moment. "What if God says you can have the math grade but then Aman will have to be sick a little while longer?" she asked.

Ajay kept quiet. He could hear cars on the road outside. He knew that his mother wanted to bewail her misfortune before God so that God would feel guilty. He looked at the postcard of Mahatma Gandhi. It was a black-and-white photo of him walking down a city street with an enormous crowd trailing behind him. Ajay thought of how, before the accident, Aman had been so modest that he would not leave the bathroom until he was fully dressed. Now he had rashes on his penis from the catheter that drew his urine into a translucent bag hanging from the guardrail of his bed.

His mother asked again, "Would you say, 'Let him be sick a little while longer'?"

"Are you going to tell me the story about Uncle Naveen again?" he asked.

"Why shouldn't I? When I was sick, as a girl, your uncle walked seven times around the temple and asked God to let him fail his exams just as long as I got better."

"If I failed the math test and told you that story, you'd slap me and ask what one has to do with the other."

His mother turned to the altar. "What sort of sons did you give me, God?" she asked. "One you drown, the other is this selfish fool."

"I will fast today so that God puts some sense in me," Ajay said, glancing away from the altar and up at his mother. He liked the drama of fasting.

"No, you are a growing boy." His mother knelt down beside him and said to the altar, "He is stupid, but he has a good heart."

Prayer, Ajay thought, should appeal with humility and an open heart to some greater force. But the praying that he and his mother did felt sly and confused. By treating God as someone to bargain with, it seemed to him, they prayed as if they were casting a spell.

This meant that it was possible to do away with the presence of God entirely. For example, Ajay's mother had recently asked a relative in India to drive a nail into a holy tree and tie a saffron thread to the nail on Aman's behalf. Ajay invented his own ritual. On his way to school each morning, he passed a thick tree rooted half on the sidewalk and half on the road. One day Ajay got the idea that if he circled the tree seven times, touching the north side every other time, he would have a lucky day. From then on he did it every morning, although he felt embarrassed and always looked around beforehand to make sure no one was watching.

One night Ajay asked God whether he minded being prayed to only in need.

"You think of your toe only when you stub it," God replied. God looked like Clark Kent. He wore a gray cardigan, slacks, and thick glasses, and had a forelock that curled just as Ajay's did.

God and Ajay had begun talking occasionally after Aman drowned. Now they talked most nights while Ajay lay in bed and waited for sleep. God sat at the foot of Ajay's mattress. His mother's mattress lay parallel to his, a few feet away. Originally God had appeared to Ajay as Krishna, but Ajay had felt foolish discussing brain damage with a blue god who held a flute and wore a dhoti.

"You're not angry with me for touching the tree and all that?"

"No. I'm flexible."

"I respect you. The tree is just a way of praying to you," Ajay assured God.

God laughed. "I am not too caught up in formalities."

Ajay was quiet. He was convinced that he had been marked as special by Aman's accident. The beginnings of all heroes are distinguished by misfortune. Superman and Batman were both orphans. Krishna was separated from his parents at birth. The god Ram had to spend fourteen years in a forest. Ajay waited to speak until it would not appear improper to begin talking about himself.

"How famous will I be?" he asked finally.

"I can't tell you the future," God answered.

Ajay asked, "Why not?"

"Even if I told you something, later I might change my mind."

"But it might be harder to change your mind after you have said something will happen."

God laughed again. "You'll be so famous that fame will be a problem."

Ajay sighed. His mother snorted and rolled over.

"I want Aman's drowning to lead to something," he said to God.

"He won't be forgotten."

"I can't just be famous, though. I need to be rich too, to take care of Mummy and Daddy and pay Aman's hospital bills."

"You are always practical." God had a soulful and pitying voice, and God's sympathy made Ajay imagine himself as a truly tragic figure, like Amitabh Bachchan in the movie *Trishul.*

"I have responsibilities," Ajay said. He was so excited at the thought of his possible greatness that he knew he would have difficulty sleeping. Perhaps he would have to go read in the bathroom.

"You can hardly imagine the life ahead," God said.

Even though God's tone promised greatness, the idea of the future frightened Ajay. He opened his eyes. There was light coming from the street. The room was cold and had a smell of must and incense. His aunt and uncle's house was a narrow two-story home next to a four-lane road. The apartment building with the pool where Aman had drowned was a few blocks up the road, one in a cluster of tall brick buildings with stucco fronts. Ajay pulled the blanket tighter around him. In India, he could not have imagined the reality of his life in America: the thick smell of meat in the school cafeteria, the many television channels. And, of course, he could not have imagined Aman's accident, or the hospital where he spent so much time.

The hospital was boring. Vinod, Ajay's cousin, picked him up after school and dropped him off there almost every day. Vinod was twenty-two. In addition to attending county college and studying computer programming, he worked at a 7-Eleven near Ajay's school. He often brought Ajay hot chocolate and a comic from the store, which had to be returned, so Ajay was not allowed to open it until he had wiped his hands.

Vinod usually asked him a riddle on the way to the hospital. "Why are man-hole covers round?" It took Ajay half the ride to admit that he did not know. He was having difficulty talking. He didn't know why. The only time he could talk easily was when he was with God. The explanation he gave himself for this was that just as he couldn't chew when there was too much in his mouth, he couldn't talk when there were too many thoughts in his head.

When Ajay got to Aman's room, he greeted him as if he were all right. "Hello, lazy. How much longer are you going to sleep?" His mother was always there. She got up and hugged Ajay. She asked how school had been, and he didn't know what to say. In music class, the teacher sang a song about a sailor who had bared his breast before jumping into the sea. This had caused the other students to giggle. But Ajay could not say the word *breast* to his mother without blushing. He had also cried. He'd been thinking of how Aman's accident had made his own life mysterious and confused. What would happen next? Would Aman die or would he go on as he was? Where would they live? Usually when Ajay cried in school, he was told to go outside. But it had been raining, and the teacher had sent him into the hallway. He sat on the floor and wept. Any mention of this would upset his mother. And so he said nothing had happened that day.

Sometimes when Ajay arrived his mother was on the phone, telling his father that she missed him and was expecting to see him on Friday. His father took a Greyhound bus most Fridays from Queens to Arlington, returning on Sunday night in time to work the next day. He was a bookkeeper for a department store. Before the accident, Ajay had thought of his parents as the same person: MummyDaddy. Now, when he saw his father praying stiffly or when his father failed to say hello to Aman in his hospital bed, Ajay sensed that his mother and father were quite different people. After his mother got off the phone, she always went to the cafeteria to get coffee for herself and Jell-O or cookies for him. He knew that if she took her coat with her, it meant that she was especially sad. Instead of going directly to the cafeteria, she was going to go outside and walk around the hospital parking lot.

That day, while she was gone, Ajay stood beside the hospital bed and balanced a comic book on Aman's chest. He read to him very slowly. Before turning each page, he said, "Okay, Aman?"

Aman was fourteen. He was thin and had curly hair. Immediately after the accident, there had been so many machines around his bed that only one person could stand beside him at a time. Now there was just a single waxy yellow tube. One end of this went into his abdomen; the other, blocked by a green bullet-shaped plug, was what his Isocal milk was poured through. When not being used, the tube was rolled up and bound by a rubber band and tucked beneath Aman's hospital gown. But even with the tube hidden, it was obvious that there was something wrong with Aman. It was in his stillness and his open eyes. Once, in their house in Queens, Ajay had left a plastic bowl on a radiator overnight and the sides had drooped and sagged so that the bowl looked a little like an eye. Aman reminded Ajay of that bowl.

Ajay had not gone with his brother to the swimming pool on the day of the accident, because he had been reading a book and wanted to finish it. But he heard the ambulance siren from his aunt and uncle's house. The pool was only a few minutes away, and when he got there a crowd had gathered around the ambulance. Ajay saw his uncle first, in shorts and an undershirt, talking to a man inside the ambulance. His aunt was standing beside him. Then Ajay saw Aman on a stretcher, in blue shorts with a plastic mask over his nose and mouth. His aunt hurried over to take Ajay home. He cried as they walked, although he had been certain that Aman would be fine in a few days: in a Spider-Man comic he had just read, Aunt May had fallen into a coma and she had woken up perfectly fine. Ajay had cried simply because he felt crying was called for by the seriousness of the occasion. Perhaps this moment would mark the beginning of his future greatness. From that day on, Ajay found it hard to cry in front of his family. Whenever tears started coming, he felt like a liar. If he loved his brother, he knew, he would not have thought about himself as the ambulance had pulled away, nor would he talk with God at night about becoming famous.

When Ajay's mother returned to Aman's room with coffee and cookies, she sometimes talked to Ajay about Aman. She told him that when Aman was six he had seen a children's television show that had a character named Chunu, which was Aman's nickname, and he had thought the show was based on his own life. But most days Ajay went into the lounge to read. There was a TV in the corner and a lamp near a window that looked out over a parking lot. It was the perfect place to read. Ajay liked fantasy novels where the hero, who was preferably under the age of twenty-five, had an undiscovered talent that made him famous when it was revealed. He could read for hours without interruption, and sometimes when Vinod came to drive Ajay and his mother home from the hospital it was hard for him to remember the details of the real day that had passed.

One evening when he was in the lounge, he saw a rock star being interviewed on *Entertainment Tonight*. The musician, dressed in a sleeveless undershirt that revealed a swarm of tattoos on his arms and shoulders, had begun to shout at the audience, over his interviewer, "Don't watch me! Live your life! I'm not you!" Filled with a sudden desire to do something, Ajay hurried out of the television lounge and stood on the sidewalk in front of the hospital entrance. But he did not know what to do. It was cold and dark and there was an enormous moon. Cars leaving the parking lot stopped one by one at the edge of the road.

Ajay watched as they waited for an opening in the traffic, their brake lights glowing.

"Are things getting worse?" Ajay asked God. The weekend before had been Thanksgiving. Christmas soon would come, and a new year would start, a year during which Aman would not have talked or walked. Suddenly Ajay understood hopelessness. Hopelessness felt very much like fear. It involved a clutching in the stomach and a numbness in the arms and legs.

"What do you think?" God answered.

"They seem to be."

"At least Aman's hospital hasn't forced him out."

"At least Aman isn't dead. At least Daddy's Greyhound bus has never skidded off a bridge." Lately Ajay had begun talking much more quickly to God than he used to. Before, when he had talked to God, Ajay would think of what God would say in response before he said anything. Now Ajay spoke without knowing how God might respond.

"You shouldn't be angry at me." God sighed. God was wearing his usual cardigan. "You can't understand why I do what I do."

"You should explain better, then."

"Christ was my son. I loved Job. How long did Ram have to live in a forest?"

"What does that have to do with me?" This was usually the cue for discussing Ajay's prospects. But hopelessness made the future feel even more frightening than the present.

"I can't tell you what the connection is, but you'll be proud of yourself."

They were silent for a while.

"Do you love me truly?" Ajay asked.

"Yes."

"Will you make Aman normal?" As soon as Ajay asked the question, God ceased to be real. Ajay knew then that he was alone, lying under his blankets, his face exposed to the cold dark.

"I can't tell you the future," God said softly. These were words that Ajay already knew.

"Just get rid of the minutes when Aman lay on the bottom of the pool. What are three minutes to you?"

"Presidents die in less time than that. Planes crash in less time than that."

Ajay opened his eyes. His mother was on her side and she had a blanket pulled up to her neck. She looked like an ordinary woman. It surprised him that you couldn't tell, looking at her, that she had a son who was brain-dead.

In fact, things were getting worse. Putting away his mother's mattress and his own in a closet in the morning, getting up very early so he could use the bathroom before his aunt or uncle did, spending so many hours in the hospital—all this had given Ajay the reassuring sense that real life was in abeyance, and that what was happening was unreal. He and his mother and brother were just waiting to make a long-delayed bus trip. The bus would come eventually to carry them to Queens, where he would return to school at P.S. 20 and to Sunday afternoons spent at the Hindi movie theater under the trestle for the 7 train. But now Ajay was starting to understand that the world was always real, whether you were reading a book or sleeping, and that it eroded you every day.

He saw the evidence of this erosion in his mother, who had grown severe and unforgiving. Usually when Vinod brought her and Ajay home from the hospital, she had dinner with the rest of the family. After his mother helped his aunt wash the dishes, the two women watched theological action movies. One night, in spite of a headache that had made her sit with her eyes closed all afternoon, she ate dinner, washed dishes, sat down in front of the TV. As soon as the movie was over, she went upstairs, vomited, and lay on her mattress with a wet towel over her forehead. She asked Ajay to massage her neck and shoulders. As he did so, Ajay noticed that she was crying. The tears frightened Ajay and made him angry. "You shouldn't have watched TV," he said accusingly.

"I have to," she said. "People will cry with you once, and they will cry with you a second time. But if you cry a third time, people will say you are boring and always crying."

Ajay did not want to believe what she had said, but her cynicism made him think that she must have had conversations with his aunt and uncle that he did not know about. "That's not true," he told her, massaging her scalp. "Uncle is kind. Auntie Aruna is always kind."

"What do you know?" She shook her head, freeing herself from Ajay's fingers. She stared at him. Upside down, her face looked unfamiliar and terrifying. "If God lets Aman live long enough, you will become a stranger too. You will say, 'I have been unhappy for so long because of Aman, now I don't want to talk about him or look at him.' Don't think I don't know you," she said.

Suddenly Ajay hated himself. To hate himself was to see himself as the opposite of everything he wanted to be: short instead of tall, fat instead of thin. When he brushed his teeth that night, he looked at his face: his chin was round and fat as a heel. His nose was so broad that he had once been able to fit a small rock in one nostril.

His father was also being eroded. Before the accident, Ajay's father loved jokes—he could do perfect imitations—and Ajay had felt lucky to have him as a father. (Once, Ajay's father had convinced his own mother that he was possessed by the ghost of a British man.) And even after the accident, his father had impressed Ajay with the patient loyalty of his weekly bus journeys. But now his father was different.

One Saturday afternoon, as Ajay and his father were returning from the hospital, his father slowed the car without warning and turned into the dirt parking lot of a bar that looked as though it had originally been a small house. It had a pitched roof with a black tarp. At the edge of the lot stood a tall neon sign of an orange hand lifting a mug of sudsy golden beer. Ajay had never seen anybody drink except in the movies. He wondered whether his father was going to ask for directions to somewhere, and if so, to where.

His father said, "One minute," and they climbed out of the car.

They went up wooden steps into the bar. Inside, it was dark and smelled of cigarette smoke and something stale and sweet. The floor was linoleum like the kitchen at his aunt and uncle's. There was a bar with stools around it, and a basketball game played on a television bolted against the ceiling, like the one in Aman's hospital room.

His father stood by the bar waiting for the bartender to notice him. His father had a round face and was wearing a white shirt and dark dress pants, as he often did on the weekend, since it was more economical to have the same clothes for the office and home.

The bartender came over. "How much for a Budweiser?" his father asked.

It was a dollar fifty. "Can I buy a single cigarette?" He did not have to buy; the bartender would just give him one. His father helped Ajay up onto a stool and sat down himself. Ajay looked around and wondered what would happen if somebody started a knife fight. When his father had drunk half his beer, he carefully lit the cigarette. The bartender was standing at the end of the bar. There were only two other men in the place. Ajay was disappointed that there were no women wearing dresses slit all the way up their thighs. Perhaps they came in the evenings.

His father asked him if he had ever watched a basketball game all the way through.

"I've seen the Harlem Globetrotters."

His father smiled and took a sip. "I've heard they don't play other teams, because they can defeat everyone else so easily."

"They only play against each other, unless there is an emergency—like in the cartoon, when they play against the aliens to save the Earth," Ajay said.

"Aliens?"

Ajay blushed as he realized his father was teasing him.

When they left, the light outside felt too bright. As his father opened the car door for Ajay, he said, "I'm sorry." That's when Ajay first felt that his father might have done something wrong. The thought made him worry. Once they were on the road, his father said gently, "Don't tell your mother."

Fear made Ajay feel cruel. He asked his father, "What do you think about when you think of Aman?"

Instead of becoming sad, Ajay's father smiled. "I am surprised by how strong he is. It's not easy for him to keep living. But even before, he was strong. When he was interviewing for high school scholarships, one interviewer asked him, 'Are you a thinker or a doer?' He laughed and said, 'That's like asking, "Are you an idiot or a moron?"'"

From then on they often stopped at the bar on the way back from the hospital. Ajay's father always asked the bartender for a cigarette before he sat down, and during the ride home he always reminded Ajay not to tell his mother.

Ajay found that he himself was changing. His superstitions were becoming extreme. Now when he walked around the good-luck tree he punched it, every other time, hard, so that his knuckles hurt. Afterward, he would hold his breath for a moment longer than he thought he could bear, and ask God to give the unused breaths to Aman.

In December, a place opened in one of the good long-term care facilities. It was in New Jersey. This meant that Ajay and his mother could move back to New York and live with his father again. This was the news Ajay's father brought when he arrived for a two-week holiday at Christmas.

Ajay felt the clarity of panic. Life would be the same as before the accident but also unimaginably different. He would return to P.S. 20, while Aman continued to be fed through a tube in his abdomen. Life would be Aman's getting older and growing taller than their parents but having less consciousness than even a dog, which can become excited or afraid.

Ajay decided to use his devotion to shame God into fixing Aman. The fact that two religions regarded the coming December days as holy ones suggested to Ajay that prayers during this time would be especially potent. So he prayed whenever he thought of it—at his locker, even in the middle of a quiz. His mother wouldn't let him fast, but he started throwing away the lunch he took to school. And when his mother prayed in the morning, Ajay watched to make sure that she bowed at least once toward each of the postcards of deities. If she did not, he bowed three times to the possibly offended god on the postcard. He had noticed that his father finished his prayers in less time than it took to brush his teeth. And so now, when his father began praying in the morning, Ajay immediately crouched down beside him, because he knew his father would be embarrassed to get up first. But Ajay found it harder and harder to drift in the rhythm of sung prayers or into his nightly conversations with God. How could chanting and burning incense undo three minutes of a sunny August afternoon? It was like trying to move a sheet of blank paper from one end of a table to the other by blinking so fast that you started a breeze.

On Christmas Eve his mother asked the hospital chaplain to come to Aman's room and pray with them. The family knelt together beside Aman's bed. Afterward the chaplain asked her whether she would be attending Christmas services. "Of course, Father," she said.

"I'm also coming," Ajay said.

The chaplain turned toward Ajay's father, who was sitting in a wheelchair because there was nowhere else to sit.

"I'll wait for God at home," he said.

That night, Ajay watched *It's a Wonderful Life* on television. To him, the movie meant that happiness arrived late, if ever. Later, when he got in bed and closed his eyes, God appeared. There was little to say.

"Will Aman be better in the morning?"

"No."

"Why not?"

"When you prayed for the math exam, you could have asked for Aman to get better, and instead of your getting an A, Aman would have woken."

This was so ridiculous that Ajay opened his eyes. His father was sleeping nearby on folded-up blankets. Ajay felt disappointed at not feeling guilt. Guilt might have contained some hope that God existed.

When Ajay arrived at the hospital with his father and mother the next morning, Aman was asleep, breathing through his mouth while a nurse poured a can of Isocal into his stomach through the yellow tube. Ajay had not expected that Aman would have recovered; nevertheless, seeing him that way put a weight in Ajay's chest.

The Christmas prayers were held in a large, mostly empty room: people in chairs sat next to people in wheelchairs. His father walked out in the middle of the service.

Later, Ajay sat in a corner of Aman's room and watched his parents. His mother was reading a Hindi women's magazine to Aman while she shelled peanuts into her lap. His father was reading a thick red book in preparation for a civil service exam. The day wore on. The sky outside grew dark. At some point Ajay began to cry. He tried to be quiet. He did not want his parents to notice his tears and think that he was crying for Aman, because in reality he was crying for how difficult his own life was.

His father noticed first. "What's the matter, hero?"

His mother shouted, "What happened?" and she sounded so alarmed it was as if Ajay were bleeding.

"I didn't get any Christmas presents. I need a Christmas present," Ajay shouted. "You didn't buy me a Christmas present." And then, because he had revealed his own selfishness, Ajay let himself sob. "You have to give me something. I should get something for all this." Ajay clenched his hands and wiped his face with his fists. "Each time I come here I should get something."

His mother pulled him up and pressed him into her stomach. His father came and stood beside them. "What do you want?" his father asked.

Ajay had no prepared answer for this.

"What do you want?" his mother repeated.

The only thing he could think was "I want to eat pizza and I want candy."

His mother stroked his hair and called him her little baby. She kept wiping his face with a fold of her sari. When at last he stopped crying, they decided that Ajay's father should take him back to his aunt and uncle's. On the way, they stopped at a mini-mall. It was a little after five, and the streetlights were on. Ajay and his father did not take off their winter coats as they ate, in a pizzeria staffed by Chinese people. While he chewed, Ajay closed his eyes and tried to imagine God looking like Clark Kent, wearing a cardigan and eyeglasses, but he could not. Afterward, Ajay and his father went next door to a magazine shop and Ajay got a bag of Three Musketeers bars and a bag of Reese's peanut butter cups, and then he was tired and ready for home.

He held the candy in his lap while his father drove in silence. Even through the plastic, he could smell the sugar and chocolate. Some of the houses outside were dark, and others were outlined in Christmas lights.

After a while Ajay rolled down the window slightly. The car filled with wind. They passed the building where Aman's accident had occurred. Ajay had not walked past it since the accident. When they drove by, he usually looked away. Now he tried to spot the fenced swimming pool at the building's side. He wondered whether the pool that had pressed itself into Aman's mouth and lungs and stomach had been drained, so that nobody would be touched by its unlucky waters. Probably it had not been emptied until fall. All summer long, people must have swum in the pool and sat on its sides, splashing their feet in the water, and not known that his brother had lain for three minutes on its concrete bottom one August afternoon.

Gary Soto
Everything Twice

Biology was a set of marble-colored tables
And gas spouts where we bloated up frogs.
Science scared me. But I knew
I had a chance if I bought the book
Early and read it with my lips moving,
Maybe twice, maybe with my roommate half-listening.
I tried chemistry. I tried astronomy,
Which was more like honest-to-goodness math
Than the star of Bethlehem shining down good news.
I was never good
At science. So at the beginning of spring
I leaned the elbows of my boredom

On a piss-colored desk.
But when our biology prof stumbled
Into the classroom wiping his mouth,
When he moved a chair out of the way
And still bumped into it, I knew I had a chance.
He was drunk. His bow-tie was a twisted-up
Twig and a nest of hair grew
From each ear. I looked to the skeleton
In the corner and smiled. A breeze stirred
The bones, which clacked on strings and wire.
With the classroom splayed with sunlight
And hope, the students sighed.
A few pencils rolled to the floor—
An easy grade for all. The prof slurred,
"Man was never created equal."
He fumbled for the chalk at the blackboard.
When he turned to us, chalk dust clung to his face.
For a moment, I don't think he knew where he was.
He touched his bowtie. He stuck a finger
Into a hairy ear
And repeated, "Man was never created equal,"
Took a step and stumbled into chairs. Right then
I knew I didn't even have to buy the book.
He was already repeating himself. Right there,
I looked out the window and sucked in
The spring air. Trees wagged blossoms
And the like. One petal would sway,
Then another, sway after slight sway,
A repetition that was endless
And beautiful in the uniquely scientific world.

Aleida Rodríguez
My Mother in Two Photographs, among Other Things

There she is, standing next to her own mother, behind the symmetrical and somewhat religious arrangement of two Coca-Cola bottles flanking a birthday cake on a small table. If you look closely, it's really the sewing machine shut down, the cake on the slightly raised platform in the center, where the machine part turns upside down into its cabinet: a little altar for an impromptu picture of "just the family."

It is December 1962, my cousin María's eighth birthday. My brother, my sister, and I were sent five months earlier to a foreign country, so we are not in the picture. In two days, my grandmother will die, and on the right side of the photograph, directly opposite her, forming a Rorschach double, lurks the dark figure of the guide who came to lead her away. The shadow's hand is on its hip, its face swirls in a smoke that obscures the features. My grandmother is the only one not looking—even the baby held up by Panchito is—into the camera, the eye of the future. She seems distracted, as though she's contemplating an answer. Two days after her party, María and Panchito wake up with our grandmother, who has wet the bed and will not rouse.

But what about my mother? Like opposite aspects of the same person: my mother, my grandmother's shadow. Here, she's smiling, though not broadly. Her children are gone, but her mother's there, telling her *aguántate, cálmate*, as they sit over *café*. Or maybe she's relieved. It is, after all, the first time since their marriage that she and my father are alone, like newlyweds. But suddenly a kitchen towel, embroidered with the day of the week, *martes*, and smeared with another woman's lipstick, flies from my mother's hand, lands like an open book by my father's mud-caked boots.

In this photograph, a coffee-dark V shows through the collar of her dress, evidence of the enforced labor in the cane fields since the revolution. Above her head is a wall vase filled with plastic flowers, hanging under the framed painting of a saint, who can't be seen above the melted-chocolate folds of a robe, and above that, perhaps, two hands are held palms up, checking the spiritual weather. But the hands are outside the photograph, just like my hands, which can't touch my mother at that brief oasis, or my grandmother, right before she turned and left with the shadow.

Grandmother left so abruptly, left my mother in mid-sentence, fingering the legendary length of fabric her mother had once transformed into the Miracle of the Three Dresses. Alone, she collapsed into her mother's absence like a slave into bed at the end of the day.

Then one afternoon two years later the air of her kitchen spun like someone whirling toward her, and she knew something had happened to her son: locked in a mental ward at sixteen after chasing his foster mother around the block with a kitchen knife. He had dropped out of high school, washed dishes for a living.

Sporting long sideburns, he rewarded himself first with a round-backed two-toned Chevy then a series of garish Mustangs. Married to his fate, he left a trail of cars, each wrapped like a wedding ring around a telephone pole.

A vision of her oldest daughter—forever regretting she hadn't been born into a TV family—flashed thin against the white walls of college, her body a blade sharpened to sever the question from the answer. Her face a glossy ad of the ideal American living room.

In the newspaper photo above the caption "Family of Cuban Expatriates Reunited Here," I am the only one gazing at the camera, my face twisted into a complex curiosity. Two years on my own among strangers had only taught me how to be one. I stood, my first tongue ripped out, with my mother's wet, round cheek pressed to the top of my head. The dark flag of her mustache. Their sour smell, like clothes trapped in a hamper. Emblems of the exile. While bureaucrats toyed with their time and their fate, my parents had waited, uncomplaining, afraid.

But I didn't know that back then. I placed myself instead in the camera lens, looking back at the spectacle we made in the bus station. Under my skin, the rice fields of my hometown were flooding the place of language. Though my mother pulled me toward her with one arm, she scooped up only watery absence; my body had long since drifted downriver. My mother's face in this photograph, captured by a stranger, betrays the weight of emptiness in her arms.

Anne Panning
Candy Cigarettes

While your parents drank in Schmidt's Bar, you and your cousins gathered under buggy streetlights. No one watched you. No one cared. You all ran down a big hill in the dark, holding hands. Then up again. Later, inside the bar, you begged for everything: cashews warmed in white waxed cups, giant pickles like dead babies in brine, Orange Crush in bumpy bottles, candy cigarettes: Marlboro, Winston, Lucky Strike. The cigarettes powdered your lips white. The tips brushed pink with false fire. All of you stood outside the bar, smoking. You knew the positioning well: one arm folded over the stomach. Your other elbow propped upon it: the cigarette swing arm. In. Out. Break to chew. Which always seemed like a failure of sorts: breaking the thing they taught you.

When you were fourteen, you found your mother gasping in bed, blue. I *have* to quit smoking, she said, but I *can't*. You stood there in your cheerleading uniform: twiggy legs, curling iron bangs, eyes squinting through smoke. You were on the edge of everything. You would succeed and supercede, or come down like the rest. You hid the cigarettes for her under the kitchen sink by the Comet. But your father continued, souring up the house. You could hear the grind of his old metal lighter first thing in the morning, last thing at night. He kept the lighter in his pocket, and sometimes, when he took it out, you held it, warm silver square, in your hand. Its heat leaked through. And into you. Your mother quit her two-pack-a-day habit. And lived.

Later, you married a two-pack-a-day smoker. But meeting in a foreign country made this okay. Even expected. Because he was tall and thin and smart—your requirements—you bummed a cigarette off him, though you didn't smoke. Two things made you fall in love. The way his long fingers curled around a coffee cup. The way he held his cigarette so tenderly to ash upon the floor. Unlike some, he was a beautiful smoker. Long-limbed. Dark-eyed. He blew smoke up, then ushered it away from you with cupped hands. He was eager to please. Which pleased you. Cold turkey is the only way, he said years later. And quit one weekend while overhauling the engine of the old Datsun. Sometimes, still, you miss that cloudy haze.

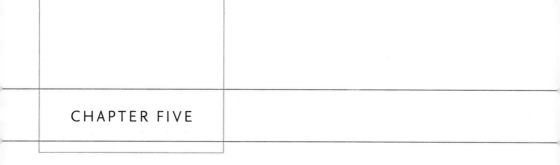

CHAPTER FIVE

TENSION

Writers use tension to make their work more readable, and more meaningful, and more interesting. Writers hook a reader into a piece by paying attention to energy and images. To keep this reader engaged, delighted, and connected to your writing, manipulate the level of tension.

Tension is defined as trouble on the page. Tension is conflict; it's a technique a writer uses to keep readers a bit off balance, making them guess, forcing them to wait, allowing them to worry, or to wonder, or to hope.

> *There are no dull subjects.*
> *There are only dull writers.*
> — H.L. MENCKEN

There is a lot of beautiful writing that simply does not hold the reader's interest. Tension allows you to make sure *everything* you write has enough pull to keep your reader with you for the whole ride.

THE PRINCIPLES OF TENSION

Desire + Danger = Tension

To make sure your writing has enough tension to keep a reader engaged, focus on your character/speaker's main desire: Keep every sentence, line, or stanza in the piece *closely* focused on what this person wants, and what forces are keeping her from getting it. Usually, the writer presents the desire both externally and internally. The character or speaker wants a ride to the concert, drugs for her sick child, or quieter kids. Externally, we see her trying to get the thing she wants by her actions. Internally, her thoughts reveal the significance and the conflicts her desire holds. She hopes to meet her ex-boyfriend at the concert, she hopes her child will grow up to be a doctor, she wants the children to spend more time with their father.

If there is no danger, if nothing *bad* will happen if she doesn't get what she wants, you have no tension. If the kid just has a mild case of the sniffles, the reader is going to wonder why you are making him read about this kid. If meeting the ex-boyfriend doesn't hold the promise of a life-altering interaction — she wants to go back to him and desert her husband (her desire + her danger) — why drag the reader along through a tedious explanation of who Ellen is, who Joey is, why set the scene in the restaurant, why bother at all?

When you combine desire (the thing a character or speaker wants — connection, money, to score points, to not be stupid) and danger (the potential harm that will come to the person — rejection, a scam, loss, shame), you automatically create tension.

Desire without danger is boring. Beautiful, perhaps. But boring.

Danger without an individual character's strong focused clear desire is perhaps exciting, but only for a short time.

Consider these situations.

1. It's the first day of the last semester of your college career. You are wait-listed for three classes: Math, Physics, and Biology. The registrar's office: inconveniently closed the entire break. You need all three of these classes in order to graduate. On your schedule, you have one class only, Tennis, and you do not need this elective, not at all. You can't afford a fifth year. When you arrive at the math and science building, there is a line of a hundred students, jamming the front doors, spilling out onto the lawn. Every single student has an add slip. Every student needs Math.

   Desire to Graduate + Horrendous Drop/Add = Drama
   Tension.

   A boy wakes up, wonders what he will do that day, eats a nice breakfast, strolls down the sidewalk to school. Gets there safely. Recess goes well.

   No Desire (mild wish to get to school) + Safe Arrival = Boring
   No tension.

2. You are dating two people. Both of them live in the same building, Joey on the floor above you, Carlo just underneath you. They don't know about each other. Both Joey and Carlo have declared themselves loyal to you, and you have promised each, in the heat of the moment, that he is The One. Every time you walk into that building, you feel it: tension. Tonight both Carlo and Joey meet you at the mailboxes. It's clear they have been talking. Joey has a knife in his hand. Carlo is holding a letter, thwapping it against his flat palm.

Desire for Joey + Desire for Carlo + Assurances That Are Lies ("You are the only one") + Human Propensity Toward Jealousy, Violence = Drama
Tension.

A man looks around his room, remembering all the pleasant moments of his life. The luxurious autos, the silk suits, the comfortable gardens. He realizes he has lived well. He has worked hard, and it has been worth it. He turns on the classical station, sits on a large leather sofa, stares out the window at a beautiful view. His nice wife brings him a gin and tonic. It tastes great.

Happy Man + All Desires Fulfilled = Boring
No tension.

3. You work twenty-nine hours a week. You despise this job, which a small child could do. You are behind in all your classes. You have nineteen cents in checking and your Visa is maxed out, and two payments behind—the account was frozen this morning. You are driving home—speeding—to spend Friday evening with your mother, who has a bad heart; your girlfriend is pissed you're missing her sorority social; you told her you bought her a corsage, and she can pick it up at the florists right about now, but your card was declined, of course—there is no corsage at Julie's Flowers for her. You race home to your mother worrying about your midterm grades; you need a *much* higher GPA to compete for a good job upon graduation. The cops pull you over. Seventy-five in a thirty.

Desire to Be a Good Son and Boyfriend + No Money, Bad Grades and Lack of Attention to Posted Speed Limits = Drama
Tension.

It's hard to create tension without focusing your reader's attention on *both* a strong unmet desire *and* risk factors—the *problems*—that will affect him adversely.

Your obstacles—the risk factors—needn't be murders, car chases, or battlefields. Often it is the subtle, tiny annoyances that actually create the most tension. The low-level constant needs children present, climaxing when they get tired, hungry, bored. The kind of day where you lose your keys, get a flat, are served with a speeding ticket, and your boss says, No, you can't have that extension on the Miller file. It's not life-or-death drama that truly feeds the pulse of tension.

It's the little stuff.

> *Art disturbs, science reassures.*
> — GEORGES BRAQUE

In this chapter, you'll learn to practice paying attention to what *increases* tension. And you will learn a few tricks for avoiding the things that kill tension (explanation, clichés, generalizing, distance).

PRACTICE

Desire + Danger = Drama. Write 5 to 10 tension "formulas," the essential conflicts for potential stories, poems, essays, or plays. Be radical, weird, wonderful, serious, or silly: You are just swinging your racket here, getting loose, getting a feel for the nature of tension. For example: Girl wants to be free of her mother and grow up and have fun + Mother is overbearing and whole town watches her every move = "Girl"—a mother versus daughter showdown: Will she rebel? Or obey?

PRACTICE

Read Ethan Canin's "Fly-Fishing for Doctors" on page 196. Try a few formulas where you spell out Desire + Danger = Drama for this creative nonfiction; what are the dangers, the desires, and the drama here? How is the drama made interesting to the reader?

Setting the Thermostat: The Four Elements of Tension

Read the following example, and rate the tension level on a scale of 1 to 5:

> I wake up when my alarm goes off and I get out of bed. It's 7:47 a.m. I can't believe I have to go to work. I get dressed, and drive—the traffic is terrible. I get out of my car and stand on the gravel. I see my aunt waiting for me. She is wearing tan clamdiggers and her black shirt complements her dark olive skin and her black hair. Her Teva-saddled feet are next to a white ball. Sneaky sees me, his stomach hanging down to his hind legs. When he reaches me I pick him up. Marilyn says hey I'm glad you made it. I'm just glad I am not late.

> *Sanity is madness put to good uses.*
> — GEORGE SANTAYANA

The piece seems fine, in many ways. It's showing action, describing people, including setting, staying in one point of view. The characters are doing things. But somehow, the piece falls flat. Not a lot is happening. The narrator is late, but what are the consequences? Will anything *result* from these events? Is there any danger, really? A true problem?

> A person wakes up, goes to work, finds her aunt, and collects a dog into her arms.

Readers say: So what? Why are you telling me this?

You don't ever want your reader saying "So what?" You always want your reader saying, "How is this going to turn out? What happens next?"

How do you move from "So what?" to "what's next"? Set the thermostat. One person wants something strongly *and is not able to get it*. Right away, and all through the piece. Then, immediately, you change the level of tension, increasing or decreasing it. You *change* the thermostat. And never let your reader go.

PRACTICE

Read the story "What I Saw from Where I Stood" by Marisa Silver on page 167. Make a list of the three most tense scenes or sections in the story. Then write a short comparison/contrast of the tension in the opening of this short story and Akhil Sharma's "Surrounded by Sleep" on page 125. Which is the more tension-filled opening? Why?

Compare the passage above, about the alarm clock going off, a first paragraph, to the first paragraph from Marisa Silver's story, "What I Saw from Where I Stood":

> Dulcie is afraid of freeways. She doesn't like not being able to get off whenever she wants, and sometimes I catch her holding her breath between exits, as if she's driving past a graveyard. So, even though the party we went to last week was miles from our apartment in Silver Lake, we drove home on the surface streets.

There is more tension here than in the first example. What contributes to the tension in this passage?

First of all, a woman named Dulcie (and just naming a character creates a little bit of tension — we will invest more in someone with a name than in "the girl" or "a man") is afraid. There is a *clear threat*. Weird, but clear: freeways.

Dulcie drives the other person in the story home the long way. She wants something. *To avoid something? To extend her time with the driver? To delay going home?*

The "I" (the narrator) catches Dulcie "holding her breath." Dulcie's tense. That makes us tense. Plus, we worry about the effect of all of Dulcie's desires on the narrator: the fear of freeways, the route demands, her anxiety. What is *up* with her?

Three simple sentences. Quite a bit of tension. How? The focus is on the character's desire, which is used to set the thermostat: create heat. Start your piece with a problem.

To establish the tension temperature we need: a person; the person wanting something rather strongly; and finally, something keeping that person from getting what she wants.

In chart form, it looks like this.

The Four Elements of Tension

Component	Considerations
1. PERSON: A person with a problem	Be specific. Provide age, station in life, situation, location, cultural/social information.
2. DESIRE: The person wants something specific—has a strong desire.	What the person wants drives the entire passage. Ideally, the character/speaker has an external, physical desire that parallels or contrasts with an interior, psychological need.
3. STAKES: What the person wants is very important—it has to matter to her, greatly.	What is at stake for this person? What if she doesn't get what she wants? How bad will it be? Whatever she wants, she needs to want it *a lot*, even (especially) if it is a little thing. If your character doesn't care about what happens, the reader won't.
4. OBSTACLES: The person has to be thwarted by obstacles that keep her from getting what she wants. Obstacles can be opponents (another person or people interfering with the goal), or forces (grief, fear, weather, etc.). Obstacles need to be realistic, meaningful, and have consequences.	When the person gets what she wants, the piece is over, the tension is resolved. During the piece, don't let the character get what she wants and/or keep creating new needs, new wants. Your job as a writer is to move her closer to her need and then either further way, or have the meeting of the need create a new desire.

| PRACTICE |

Find the four components of "setting the thermostat" in a section of the Marisa Silver story "What I Saw from Where I Stood" on page 167. What tension(s) are set in the section of the story? Use the chart above to create an analysis of the four elements of tension.

In Silver's story, "What I Saw from Where I Stood," Dulcie wants to manage her fears. She wants to be happy again (interior psychological wants). This is a high-value desire: She might ruin her relationships, asking too much of those who love her. She might never recover from grief. What she wants — the bad things to not have happened — is completely and utterly not-gettable. The force of despair is as strong as her desire to change her life situation.

> *One must still have chaos in oneself to be able to give birth to a dancing star.*
> — FRIEDRICH NIETZSCHE

Notice that in this short story, as in most, things start bad — fear of highways — and the writer keeps giving more information that *increases* the tension. Moving in closely again on that excerpted passage, above, notice that in addition to the highway fear, Dulcie holds her breath. The party is far away (higher stakes). Notice how Silver, the writer, is dialing up the tension one notch at a time, one sentence at a time.

Narrative poetry (poetry that tells a story, as opposed to lyric poetry, which expresses a single feeling or emotion) also uses the components of tension in order to set the thermostat, and keep reader interest high.

PRACTICE

Read Thomas Lux's poem, "The Man into Whose Yard You Should Not Hit Your Ball," on page 179 and consider how he balances the forces of tension. Does he use all four components from the chart on page 146? Find words or phrases that support each component.

In Thomas Lux's poem, "The Man into Whose Yard You Should Not Hit Your Ball," the battle is the kids' joy and sheer love for baseball versus a mean old man who lives to mow. That's a good battle: fun wild kids, grumpy guy. And the stakes are high (the kids could get in a lot of trouble, the guy has a daughter in jail). The balls keep going over there. Lux does a brilliant job sustaining, drawing out, the tension inherent in this battle. At the end of the poem, we learn that it's the old guy who *doesn't follow the rules*, doesn't read "the manual" for his lawn-mower. You aren't supposed to mow up balls and make them into "coleslaw." What are the real directions here? the poet asks. Who was really breaking the rules? In this poem, the kids win. Score one for youthful passion and freedom and baseball.

MAINTAINING TENSION

Work with Two or Three Characters

Never work with one character who is alone. Always work with two or three characters, so that you can have "sides." When you write just one person, you tend to rely on thoughts, because there can be nothing at stake. It's hard to create tension with a character alone onstage, lost in thought. There's not a lot to see there. There's not much we can really engage with as readers. Solo is boring. Two's a game. Three is always interesting—because there is so much more opportunity for *problems* to arise.

Match Your Opponents

When do you leave a game early, before the final score? When it's clear one side will win. Nothing is at stake in the fourth period when the score is 108–15. As a writer, the same rule applies. You will lose your reader unless you keep the stakes high.

The "sides," the power struggle—the thing the person wants and the thing keeping her from getting it—have to be equally matched.

Power shifts generate and sustain tension. Review our formula for creating tension:

> A person who wants something important badly, who is experiencing difficult obstacles that are keeping him/her from getting the things he/she wants.

Think of a sporting match. A good game. What do you notice? There are *two sides*. If your team goes out on the field to practice, the group doesn't pretend to have a game *against no one*. You divide up, shirts and skins. You *have to have sides*.

In a great game, a really tense match, the kind you stay into triple overtime in pouring rain to see finalized, the sides are evenly matched—it's not going to be a blowout.

Super close. Triple overtime. We in the stands are on the edges of our seats, worrying the whole time. *Who is going to win?* And, more importantly, *how are they going to get from where they are now to that win?* Each play is riveting. Every step, every pass, every glance matters.

> *Dimension means contradiction.*
> — ROBERT McKEE

If you are on the winning team, a blowout can be fun, but not for the spectators (i.e., the readers). For them, there is no tension. You don't want to be the writer having all the fun—the piece *has* to work for the readers.

In "What I Saw from Where I Stood," grief is a worthy opponent. Charles uses his love for Dulcie to combat Grief. For Dulcie, Grief keeps taking form: first the hoodlums, then the pestilence. We don't know if she—and she and her partner—will make it or not. That's the tension in the story. Dulcie and Charlie are good and young and strong. But they have been hit hard. Will they make it?

That's the tension. To find out the answer to that question, we track the battle that is the story. Even the title indicates this is a report from the frontlines, an eyewitness account.

PRACTICE

Read the play excerpt by Anna Deavere Smith on page 56. Find the four elements of tension in the monologue. What are the opposing forces? Remember, the "battle" can be between two people or two forces. Both of them, on some level, must be right.

Stay Specific

Generalizations kill tension. Another habit writers accidentally fall into is writing *general* instead of writing *specific*. "They fought" sums up what happened; no tension there. The summary gives a general impression, and will never be as tense and interesting as us getting to see the specifics of *how*. "Carlo sliced the letter across Joey's face, and the papercut beaded blood drops on Joey's pale cheek."

Compare "it was such a drag driving across town and always boring" to the paragraph detailing Dulcie's highway avoidance rituals. Detail—getting very specific—is actually a method you use to create and sustain tension.

> *The business of the novelist is not to chronicle great events, but to make small ones interesting.*
> — ARTHUR SCHOPENHAUER

Robert Kurson, author of *Shadow Divers*, employs this principle. He avoids the general and always names the specifics, which increases the tension in his award-winning writing. Notice how the visual details, the images, increase the tension in this piece.

A good diver reveals himself in the way he gears up. He is at one with his equipment. He knows where every piece goes; every strap is the perfect length, every tool expertly placed, and everything fits. He moves instinctively, his hands and stuff in a swoop-tug-and-click ballet until he is transformed into sea creature. He rarely needs help. If another diver moves to assist him, he will usually decline, saying, "No, thank you" or, more likely, "Don't touch my shit." He favors ten-dollar knives over the hundred-dollar versions because when he loses the cheaper ones, he does not feel obligated, under the pressure of narcosis, to risk his life searching the bottom to rescue them. He cares nothing for the prettiness of his gear, and often tattoos it with patches, stickers, and graffiti that testify to past dive exploits. Neon colors do not exist for him; greenhorns who choose those hues don't have to wait long before hearing the boat's opinion on such loudness. When he is fully geared up, a good wreck diver looks like a German car engine; more ordinary divers resemble the interior of a child's toy chest.

Kurson could simply say that professional wreck divers relate to their equipment differently than amateur divers. The "versus" is implied: good divers versus newbies. However, there's not a lot of tension there. The fight isn't really equal; of course the better divers are *better*. To keep the tension in this passage high, Kurson uses specifics. We see that the quirks of the great divers all have a reason, an important reason. The better divers are smart. They're odd, they're messy, they're arrogant ("Don't touch my shit"). They have to be, in order to survive. The same specific qualities that aid them in getting dressed, on land, Kurson shows us, are the very ones that let them live while others may die.

| PRACTICE |

Turn back to the memoir excerpt on page 60, from Amy Fusselman's *The Pharmacist's Mate*. How many specifics do you find? List each specific word or phrase. Then, write a brief response explaining how six of these specifics work to increase the tension. Lastly, identify places tension would be lost or decreased without the specifics.

Write from Close-Up

> He sat in the room for a long time.

What do you see in that sentence? What image appears in your mind's eye? What do you feel about the "he"? Anything at all?

The writer of this sentence has *generalized* time (it's a "long" time, but we have no idea *how* long and, more important, *when*.) The writer has also generalized *space*. It's just generally a room. There's no situation. There's not actual space we can touch and move around in.

There is no tension because *there's nothing there*.

Write from close-up. Be in the time — the exact moment — and the space — Apartment 4D, Sunset Heights, golden retriever and girlfriend on sofa — you are writing.

Distance kills tension. You want to avoid distance. Write from a close-up position, tight with your characters, the details, and the emotion; not from too far back. Your images training in the first unit has prepared you to write from *within* the experience, not hovering above, a reporter, or hiding behind the veil of time.

Many beginning writers write as though they are on a stage. The audience — the reader — is looking at the curtain, waiting for it to rise. But the beginning writer tends, often, to report to the audience — so that the play is going on behind the curtain. The writer sees it, and explains what is happening back there. This is not very pleasurable for the audience. We want the intermediary removed.

When you write, move closer, and you will increase the tension every time. Be in the room with the famous musician; be in the yard that is forbidden, looking for your lost baseball; be driving with your grieving girlfriend; clueless as to what to do next. Don't write *about* the experience, or you kill the tension. Don't look back, remember, think, or reflect: *Stay in the moment.* And stay close-in. Write from a few inches away from your subject.

MANIPULATING TENSION

A lot of what you are doing when you work to create or increase the tension in a piece of creative writing is *creating oppositions.* That is, you set qualities in the work against each other. A beautiful beach scene is the location for a woman telling her husband she wants a divorce. A boy tells a girl how much he hates his parents while carefully cleaning out the family garage, devoted to his task (his dialogue shows us he just wants to look cool in front of the girl).

In each of these cases, the setting and the action clash. Tension is created by working with exterior visual oppositions. But, oppositions also must be created within characters.

The good guy has to have some weaknesses. Seinfeld is a neat-freak and germophobe. The bad team has to have some good traits. Newman is a brilliant strategist and usually gets what he wants. Hamlet is kind and insightful but hesitates to make decisions. The Joker is evil, but very, very funny. Readers have to be able to connect with both "good" and "bad" characters in order for the piece to work on us.

Consider the power of juxtaposition. If the kittens are terribly cute, and you smile when you play with them, and their ribbons are pink, you are putting cuteness next to delight next to adorableness—there's not any surprise there. There's nothing for the reader to engage with. No tension.

You create tension when you put things that don't rest easily next to each other: adorable kittens, deep rejection, your angry mother. A broken barrette, a brother in trouble, a new car, the perfect pizza. A great date, a car accident.

Three useful strategies help you create and sustain tension in a piece of writing: the "thermostat"—the amount of tension in any given line or sentence; layers, which allow you to create and increase tension by moving your work from the simple to the complex (e.g., more than one thing is going on at once; you aren't stating the obvious); and, dialogue, used in special ways. All three strategies help create the oppositions and layers that make creative writing interesting to read.

Thermostat Control: Adjusting the Temperature

The secret to creating tension, in life and on the page, is to *vary the situation.* Ups and downs are much harder for us (and therefore much more successful in literature) than a steadily awful time. If things go from bad to worse, we can usually adapt. What drives us to the brink of madness is when the situation is bad (the line for Math Add is terrifically long), but it improves (Joe lets us cut ahead of him in line), and then gets worse (the Drop/Add people are leaving for lunch *just* when you get to the front of the line), and then much worse (your two boyfriends show up at the Drop/Add counter to confront you, loudly).

And then better.

Then worse.

In real life it's called "Being jerked around."

Tension is: ups and downs, back and forth, tension and the release of tension. This up-and-down is the rhythm of creative writing. Change appeals to our basic need for stimulation. Don't let your reader adapt. Once he gets the emotional tenor of one line, you have to change it up again. Be thoughtfully unpredictable. Don't let your piece remain at the same tension level for long.

Reread the poem "Buying Wine" by Sebastian Matthews (p. 53). Notice the tension level in the first stanza. A choice is always imbued with some tension; here the choice is backseat or Wine Mart. Each one has plusses and minuses. Arbitrarily, somewhat, we could assign a number to that level of tension, on a scale of 1 to 5. Let's say it's a 2. Because the speaker in the poem is a child, either choice is at least a little scary.

In the second stanza, the tension goes down — the boy is in the store, trailing Dad, and things look good, orderly, even familiar, "like bat racks." The tension is perhaps a 1. And not for long. In stanza three, the cart is "ever-filling" — and this is not good and it's getting worse because the father is "unkempt" and pretty much flinging liquor into the cart in the aisle. Tension in stanzas three through five could be said to dial up quickly; 2, 3, then 4. In stanza five, Matthews ratchets the tension meter back down — the speaker, a child, sees his father shopping here as he shops at the meat store. Things are okay, aren't they? We're just shopping for food. It's good to match wines and food, put a pinot grigio with scallops . . . right? The tension dances down to near 1.

Notice the leap that occurs between stanzas seven and eight. While the boy is adjusting to his father's wine-shopping ritual, he slips into a reverie, remembering other wine store trips where he made the other choice, and stayed in the car. Whenever a writer switches locations, pops into a flashback, moving back in time and space, the reader experiences a tension shift. "Often, we'd stay in the car" moves the tension from 1 back up to 2 or 3, and then in the second line of stanza eight — notice the tension shift in that "dwindling capacity to believe our father" comment. Boom. This isn't a kid who still worships his dad. This is a kid who has been disappointed by this dad many, many times. That statement charges the poem with energy, intensity.

That intensity is increased — to a 5, perhaps, on the tension meter — in the next stanza, where the kids in the back seat are imagined as free from the car,

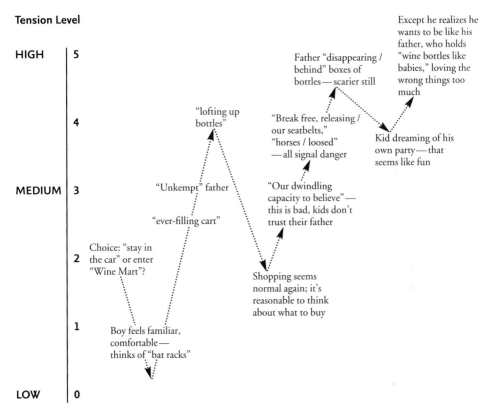

Map of tension in Sebastian Matthews's poem "Buying Wine" (p. 53). Tension level ranges from 1 to 5. The arrows represent the direction of the tension; the length of the arrows indicates how much the tension increases or decreases.

roaming. Unsupervised offspring of an alcoholic father, "like horses" for a moment, and anything could happen. Lots of tension here. Which drops back down when the boys are, sadly, drawn to the liquor store window, to peek in, glimpse "snippets of [the] father's profile." They want to be like him. They want to be with him. They want to be free. The tensions in the poem are further dialed up a notch in the line when he disappears "behind the tall cardboard stacks" as if he's being swallowed up by liquor, which, in fact, he is.

When the kid loads up his own cart in stanza twelve, do you see that as more or less drastic than the preceding stanza? Some readers will say it's just as tense: a 4 or a 5. Because the boy is hurt so deeply in the preceding stanza, seeing his dad disappear, other readers will see this stanza as less tense—a kid acting like a kid. Readers will react differently; what's important for you as the writer is to keep *changing* the intensity.

When the speaker is dreaming of parties, some readers may feel this is the most tense part of the poem, because it's so easy to imagine the speaker going down a bad path. Others will believe that the final image, of the father holding "wine bottles like babies in his hands," creates the deepest emotional impact of the entire poem, as we see the father being more careful with the wine than with his real children.

Remember, if everything is at the same high level of excitement, your reader will grow just as bored as if there is no tension at all. Scientists and psychologists have shown definitively that the human mind adjusts quickly; it is designed to *adapt*. It's part of the human genius. We get used to things very, very quickly—loud background noise disappears, our surroundings homogenize, we don't notice changes in family members we see every day. Give us a bad situation, and it's human nature to adapt. Just when the room is getting too hot, turn down the thermostat; make the reader cool off. Then, just as the reader is cooling, crank the heat back up. That's the oppositional nature of this strategy: When things get bad, they have to get worse. When they get worse, they then have to get better.

As you practice, you will find more ways to intensify and manipulate the temperature. Here is a chart listing various elements of a piece of writing, presenting ways for adjusting the thermostat and modulating tension.

Adjusting the Temperature: Ways to Decrease and Increase Tension

Decreases Tension	Increases Tension
Agreement	Disagreement
Safety	Danger
Things are okay	Things are not okay
Generalization	Specific information; intimate details
One thing is going on	Two or three things happening at once
Linear, chronological exposition	Leaps
Moving ahead as expected	Reversals
Having all needs met, ease, simplicity	Wanting something badly, needing, yearning
Overcoming obstacles easily	Thwarted again and again
Solution = resolution	Solution to problem creates new problem
Explanation, telling	Mystery, withholding
Static character, doing nothing	Character in action

Character alone with thoughts	Character in a triangle with two other characters
Speeches, interior dialogues	Crisp dialogue based on an argument
One technique used at length (all description, all dialogue, all interior thoughts . . .)	Variety of techniques (dialogue first, then description, then interior thoughts, then more dialogue . . .)
All long or all short sentences or lines	Short sentences or lines mixed up with longer ones
Seeing the big picture; long shots	Seeing things from *very* close-up

Layers: Adding Dimension

A stack of halved parsnips, looking like naked human limbs, maybe dead, in the fluorescent light of a refrigerator—not very interesting. Slightly creepy, perhaps, but what's the point? You have a pile of scary vegetables. So what? The image is two-dimensional.

Add a young woman with cancer, who has to cook these parsnips for a wealthy family, where there may be adultery, deceit, neglect—a family with emotional cancers—and you've got something. Layers infuse your images with meaning, interest, and excitement. Jessica Shattuck's "Bodies" is rich with layers.

PRACTICE

Read the short story "Bodies" by Jessica Shattuck on page 180, and as you read, see if you can notice the layers in the piece. When does one action or element of the story indicate or inform another action, character, or element?

Writers don't always plan and control the layers in the poems, plays, memoirs, and stories they craft. Often, getting two tracks going—a needy kid watching *Lion King* in the other room, a babysitter with cancer dabbing the parsnips with butter—results in the images talking to each other, and creating more than the sum of their parts. When Shattuck describes Annie's view of little Anthony, her charge, Annie sees the old man in the tiny five-year-old. "He is five years old, blond, and freckled, with close-set blue eyes. Something about his mouth and his stubby but prominent little nose hints already at the old man he will be—stubborn, soft-spoken, a little unforgiving." Annie is aware of death, even in a little kid. The themes of the story—who talks, who forgives, what gets passed on—are embedded in the description of a five-year-old. Images are layered, and themes come out for the reader. The writer stays close-up—close enough to see

> *Nothing is more odious than music without hidden meanings.*
> — FRÉDÉRIC CHOPIN

the mouth, the exact nature of the nose, close enough to count the freckles on a cheek—and writes what she sees. As she works on her story, she becomes aware of patterns, images that keep coming up, calling for attention.

Bottom line: If you provide only one layer in your writing, readers will not find the tension in your piece, and will grow bored at best, and stop reading at worst. Girl goes to party, has fun, meets great guy, parties all night, has to dash to work late the next day—that's one layer. You need more layers in order to transform this series of events into creative writing.

Layering Images. Earlier, we noted the energy a writer gains by juxtaposing images, layering a series of "health" images over a series of "illness" images. Look at how Jay's devotion to buffing his body contrasts with Annie's illness. She imagines Jay doing handsprings; she herself pretends to be woozy when she isn't. He gets more muscular; she gets sicker. "Bodies" is a good title for this story, which is about death, sex, passion, children—all the things that tie us irrevocably to the body.

One way to layer images in a poem or a narrative is to locate, in a draft already in progress, some oppositions or potential oppositions. Notice that when you are following images where they are alive—in a state of flux, moving, action-oriented, when things are changing—it will be easier to layer.

A moving image has traction—other images will stick to it. Layer the important stuff, not the background stuff. Layers not only create and increase tension, they tell the reader to pay attention—*this is important!* Layers make meaning.

PRACTICE

Find at least four examples of image layers in Marisa Silver's story "What I Saw from Where I Stood" on page 167. List the layers and write a brief explanation.

Layering with Triangles. Triangles are a simple strategy for creating complex tensions. Think about triangles when looking for ways to layer your work to increase complexity. "Bodies" and "What I Saw from Where I Stood" both use triangles in order to make the work tension-filled, and interesting. Unlike a beginning painter, who might stick a tree in the middle of the canvas and call it good, a skilled artist employs many triangles, laid over each other. In the popular sitcom *Friends*, as in most film and television, triangles form the architecture of the series and create almost all the opportunities the writers have to use tension. Consider the two triangles that every episode uses: Joey-Chandler-Ross and

Monica-Phoebe-Rachel. The setting is also a triangle: two apartments and the coffee shop. Can you think of others?

Triangles form the basic tensions in "Bodies." There's a Cleo-Annie-Jay triangle. Annie is drawn to Jay. Cleo is married to Jay. Jay is attracted to and repelled by Annie—she scares him, her illness scares him, she lives in his house, cares for his children (more attentively than Cleo, the mother of his children). Cleo loves Jay, relies on Annie. This is a love triangle, but it's also a triangle created by *complex* human relationships. Good creative writing relies on relationship triangles. Pieces with just one character, or two characters in a simple relationship, aren't going to hold reader interest as readily as triangle pieces.

Shattuck is a very skilled writer. She uses triangles to create friction in her main characters, and amplifies those tensions with yet another triangle, the Michele-Cleo-Jay triangle. The Michele-Cleo-Jay triangle provides the subplot, the undercurrent, and this triangle operates as the catalyst for the story. Michele, Cleo's niece, is in love with Jay, who maintains a secret relationship with the girl. Annie is stunned, as we are, by this secret triangle. Anthony is quite literally stuck in the middle of these adult relationships, which make a complex web around him. Good writers, just like visual artists, think in terms of threes, because groups of three add dimension, excitement, possibility, and interest. Threes always work.

Creative writers always avoid having one character alone with her thoughts. Basic tension is achieved when two people are in conflict with each other, presenting desires that are at odds. Better yet is creative writing that involves three

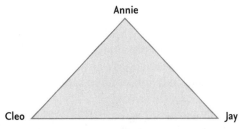

Tension triangle in Jessica Shattuck's story, "Bodies." Annie, Jay, and Cleo form a triangle. There will always be tension whenever these three are together at the same time.

points of conflict, three forces. In a sophisticated or longer piece, writers layer one triangle over another in order to create dimensions. This is how tension works in creative writing.

With triangles, you create a space for the reader to form conclusions and insights. As a writer, you can use triangles to guide and deepen your images, to keep you on track. You have a triangle whenever three people are involved, each of whom represents a different agenda.

Recall the scene where Jay enters the kitchen (Cleo's abandoned space) to pour vitamins "fat as roaches into his palm." Notice the specificity—all the vitamins are named, described. Annie thinks about Cleo—so Cleo is present, although not physically. Notice the triangulation. Jay asks Annie to touch him. The images are intensified because they come at an intersection—sickness, the mad pursuit of perfect strength, milk/mother/Cleo/kitchen. Shattuck stays a long time, makes a big deal out of Annie's fingers on Jay's "warm wrist." Notice how much more time—five paragraphs, a dialogue conversation—is spent here. We stay on these images because they are dramatic, intense, uncomfortable—skin on skin. The kitchen scene's images link up with the roof scene later—when Annie gets her strength back, Shattuck doesn't have to explain it to us—Annie feels "her own blood finally—she is aware of its quick rhythm in the channels of her veins." And, "It is as if some door had opened inside her and she could hear everything."

Layering Dialogue and Action.   Some beginning writers fill whole pages with direct dialogue, including long conversations that often don't create images in the reader's mind. No images: no tension. People yakking away mindlessly, or people stating the obvious in direct dialogue, is not good creative writing. Long speeches, monologues, and he said–she said predictable dialogues weaken good creative writing. Writer and teacher Robert Boswell explains that while we probably say 3,000 lines of dialogue out loud every day in our regular lives, perhaps twenty of those lines are worthy of including in a piece of literature. Like everything else in your poem, story, or play, dialogue has to have layers.

Here's an example of unlayered dialogue and action:

> "I love you," he said. He handed her the flowers and the card.
> "Thank you," she said. She opened the card. "It's so beautiful!"
> "Thanks," he said, and leaned over to give her a kiss.
> "I love you," she said, and she kissed him back, with pleasure.
> "We're so great together," he said.
> She said, "I totally and utterly agree."

There's no reason to use dialogue to render the happy moment. The skilled writer covers this scene in two words, "They kissed," and moves on to the next moment of tension. Save dialogue for the places in your story or poem or essay where the emotions are mixed, and tease out the tension by layering the dialogue and action.

Other beginning writers avoid dialogue altogether, relying too heavily on description and reflection.

Notice the poems in this book that you have read so far that use dialogue. How often do people speak? How often is their speech summarized for us, so we have a sense of exactly what is spoken? In the fiction we have been studying, how much dialogue is used? When? How do you blend the dialogue into a piece of creative writing so it doesn't stick out, so it flows?

Dialogue is always going to attract a lot of attention from your reader. It's close-up (someone is actually talking, the author is far back, summarizing a conversation). It's specific, by definition, and usually at least two characters are present, since it's a conversation.

PRACTICE

Read aloud just the dialogue—nothing else—from the short story by Jessica Shattuck on page 180. What do you notice about the dialogue? Now, go back through and highlight the actions that attend each spoken bit. How do the actions create oppositions? Tension? What is lost if we just hear the spoken parts? Which dialogue-action bits have the most tension? Rank them in order of most tense to least tense.

In order to sustain tension in dialogue, it's useful to remember that dialogue never occurs outside of human action. When we speak, we use our full body, our face moves around, and our arms and gestures and habits punctuate our phrases. We interrupt, we slam the book on the table, we cross our arms, we roll our eyes, scoot our chair back, stroke the arm of our partner—all that is part of the conversation. Dialogue can't be separated from action, and so action is automatically a crucial part of *what is said.*

Recall this scene from the short story "Bodies." A man walks into the kitchen; the image starts. A woman pours a glass of milk, asks about his resting pulse, feels his wrist, and he talks to her, revealing his fear. Everything that happens in those five minutes, in that little micro-movie, is the image, and dialogue is part of the soundtrack. You want, as a writer, to vary the way you represent direct speech—sometimes you start with an action, then use a direct quote. Then, you have someone look away—no direct speech. Next time, you have one person look, move, try to speak, but they can't. Person B starts to talk, Person A interrupts. You want to vary the position of your camera eye, the closeness, the angle, the length of time spent on a conversation.

Dialogue needs to be written so that the reader feels somehow present as a witness or eavesdropper.

Work with dialogue and action as units, as a single thing with the two layers: the speech *and* the motions. Try to avoid disembodied dialogue, which loses energy fast in the past.

When writing dialogue, it's vital you use your training with the image. Often, new writers can sound like television programs, because so much of the dialogue we hear comes from that source. Really focus on what your characters truly say, even—especially—if it surprises you. Don't make it up. Take dictation. Let them surprise you. Never force characters in your work to say things *just for the sake of the piece you are writing*.

Avoid using clichés—overly familiar dialogue expressions, things people never *really* say. And, avoid not just spoken clichés but also action clichés, called emotional shorthand: raised eyebrows, grimaces, smiles, winks, pounding fists. Those are all shortcuts, cartoon gestures for real emotions, and the sign of lazy writing. Stay focused on the image, and write what you truly see there. Action-dialogue units need to have freshness, and truth in them. Stay very real, very focused.

Write exactly the tiny things you see in the conversation. Does she stick her pen in her mouth after each sentence? Shift her weight so that her pant leg hikes up? Shoot her fingers at you like she thinks she is so cool? Click her tongue and spit with each sentence? The tiny things that give an individual away—the things Carlo does when he talks that Joey *never* does—let those movements become part of the dialogue itself.

Practice listening to your friends and coworkers. What lines do they say that are worthy of putting in a piece of creative writing? "Hey, how you doing?" probably isn't going to make it. As mentioned before, *most* of what we say day-to-day isn't going to make the cut for a piece of writing. "Ya gotta beat the best to be the best." That might make it. "Do you miss the fish?"

Now we're talking *tension*.

Façade

As you are well aware, people don't always say exactly what they mean. Much of the pleasure in reading dialogue is knowing more than a character or speaker knows about herself. Now that you have had practice layering dialogue and action to build tension, you want to *increase* the tension between what is said, thought, and done, between interior and exterior. There's a triangle here, an opportunity for opposition. In fact, in good creative writing, controlling tension in dialogue is not optional, it's required. And this technique, named by writer and teacher Jerome Stern, is called *façade*.

"Hey, how's it going," your friend says, but we can tell by her tone, how she is hanging her shoulders and dragging her toe around, making a bored circle, that she doesn't care how we are doing at all. She just wants us to ask her how *she's* doing.

That gap—the "false front" she is putting up—between what she presents to the outside and what is really going on inside her is a façade. We say "I hate you" when we mean "I love you."

PRACTICE

Read Peter Morris's short play, "Pancakes," on page 190. When do the characters say what they do not mean? How do you know this?

Dialogue in creative writing works best when it is used *not* to announce a character's thoughts or direct desires, *but to contradict them and create a gap, a false front.* Dialogue-action units let you juxtapose what's said with what's done; façade helps you broadcast the gap between what someone says and what they really think/feel/want.

In architecture, a façade is the front of a building. Think of a cheap building that has a fake brick front, but really is just a metal pole barn. There's a tension there. That building is pretending to be something it is not. Think of a house with an imposing façade—a grand entry, three stories of glass. But really, the house is just a three-bedroom tract house with a tiny kitchen, cheap carpet, and vinyl siding. A façade is a false front, and it's your most important dialogue tool. Without façade, most dialogue falls flat, and your readers will skip and skim.

When people talk to us in real life, they hint at things and focus on side issues, they beat around the bush. Usually, every conversation *that is interesting* has several levels. People have agendas.

Façade, layered on top of dialogue-action units, is the technique writers use to keep the tension levels in dialogue high.

> "I just can't do it," Valerie cried. "It's all those thirty-second notes. My fingers just won't let me do it!"
>
> "Yes they will. You just have to trust them," her instructor replied patiently.
>
> "But my concert is in five weeks! I'm never going to be ready by then!"
>
> "Well, with that attitude, you won't be. But I'll help you."
>
> "Okay," Valerie said.

What do you notice about this passage? There's an awful lot of time to get ready—five weeks. Not very tense. There's a helpful teacher who is kind and patient. Not a very good opponent! But also notice the dialogue, how it works against tension, not toward it. Valerie explains exactly what her problem is and tells us everything we need to know. Dialogue has to reveal new emotional nuances; it can't simply deliver information to the reader about character, situation, station in life.

She wants to play faster. Her talent isn't up to the demands of the piece at this moment. She lodges two complaints, *I can't*, and, *I won't be ready*, and then she says, "Okay!" This is the opposite of what you want to do.

It's much more interesting for your reader if the character is revealing more than she thinks she is. Gaps and misinterpretations give the reader a place to worm into your writing.

Some of your dialogue can use the dialogue-action technique to keep tension modulated. But not all your dialogue can be a direct statement. You need some false fronts in order for your piece to be complex and tense.

Examine this dialogue exchange from Marisa Silver's "What I Saw from Where I Stood."

> "We saw them," she said. "We know what they look like."
> "They weren't killers. They were thieves. There's a difference, I guess," I said.
> "No," she said, twisting her straight brown hair around her finger so tightly the tip turned white. "It doesn't make sense."
> Dulcie needs things to be exact.

In the passage above, Dulcie's dialogue lines are interesting, because we have to pay attention to understand what they are about. She hides as much as she reveals when she talks. The reader is *drawn in*. These are not talking heads, making a point to serve the writer's goal. These are stressed-out people, in pain, trying to communicate. They say the wrong thing, or try to impress the cops or come off as serious and devoted, when really they are terrified inside.

Dulcie is real to the reader. She is saying things do make sense and they don't make sense, at the same time. She is experiencing a great deal of tension inside herself. We feel for her.

Read the dialogue further on:

> "I should have noticed them tailing me," Dulcie said now. "How could I not notice a car that close?"
> "Don't do that," I told her. "Don't think about what could have happened."
> "I have to think about it," she said. "How can you not think about it? We were this close," she said, holding her fingers out like a gun and aiming at my chest.

What makes this dialogue passage tense? The use of façade. Dulcie has changed direction again: Earlier she said she noticed everything, now she is kicking herself for not noticing things right in front of her face. Usually, when people beat themselves up for something, there's something else in there bothering them too. What's on Dulcie's mind, besides the thieves? Then, her companion tells her not to worry about "what could have happened." But that isn't what she is worried about. When people are tense, they misunderstand. They hear what they need to hear. Their own motives and concerns come out in the dialogue. He's trying to help. But is he barking up the wrong tree? What's his agenda in that line?

To write façade, know what your character wants, and have him speak to it a little sideways. Have him talk about one thing *by way of* talking about what really bothers him, a whole other thing. Then, Dulcie yells at him. In the passage above, Silver heats up the exchanges beat by beat—each exchange a little more tense, a little edgier, than the one before. She saves her most dramatic part of the dialogue, which is Dulcie communicating with her fingers, for last. By "We were this close," do you think she means in more ways than one?

Usually, we reveal a lot more than we think we do when we talk to other people. When we are stressed and tense (those are the moments worthy of dramatizing through creative writing, remember!) our internal censors are less able to protect us. We say too much, or not enough. We don't mean to, but we reveal our deepest feelings and desires. That is probably the highest form of tension in literature.

This is a lot to practice.

What we are striving toward are dialogue-action units with internal tensions (what's said works against what the character is doing) working against the façade (what's said isn't what the character *really* means). That triangle is the essential heartbeat of tension.

In addition, the character's conversation and action lines work against the setting (you are close-up as you write all this), and her obstacles are *exactly* what she doesn't want. Set the thermostat, match your opponents, stay specific. Layer images, dialogue, and work toward false fronts—you'll be a tension-generating machine.

| PRACTICE |

Evaluate the changing levels of tension in Peter Morris's short play "Pancakes" (p. 191) by jotting a number in the margin to represent the tension level. When the level changes, write down a new number.

WRITING PROJECTS

1. Write a passage or poem utterly lacking in tension, interest, excitement: Be boring. Or, bring in the most boring piece of writing you can find. Read the boring passages aloud. Discuss: What are the most numbing, tension-killing things a writer can do? Long passages of description. Many difficult, look-it-up-in-a-dictionary word choices. What makes *boring* boring? Create a "what kills tension and reader interest" checklist. Avoid these pitfalls!

2. Write a narrative or poem detailing the actions and images that you experience on your route to work or school. Describe everything. Focus on what you do. Choose a day when things go fairly smoothly, fairly uneventfully. Set the tension in this short passage at a 1 or a 2, on a scale of 1 to 5. Then, draft a second short passage, same route, but this time let there be three subtle annoyances hindering your progress, and include another person, a passenger or another figure. Give one of the two of you some psychological quirk that makes your journey subtly more difficult. Try to make the tension somewhat higher than in your first passage; set the thermostat at 3 and try to take it to 5.

3. Write an argument between equals. Using only dialogue, and letting the conversation take up about two pages, write a dialogue in which two equally strong characters fight.

4. Write a poem or short-short in five lines or sentences. Use this recipe to adjust the tension of each line or sentence: 3, 2, 1, 4, 5. You may wish to write the parts in a different order, and then assemble them so that the tension meter reading fits the pattern. Title it using a word from the piece.

5. Write a piece of fiction or creative nonfiction that uses the tensions of a close game. The only subject you can't use is that of an actual sporting event. Write about a bad date, shopping with your father, babysitting the nightmare children; let the ups and downs—the tension—be inspired by the forward/backward rhythm of a fantastically close game, one that goes into triple overtime. It's that exciting. Use the chart on page 154 to guide your thermostat changes. Surprise your reader by letting the apparently weaker person win.

6. Layer your earlier work. Take a piece in progress from earlier this semester. With a writing partner, identify some of the images in the piece. Discuss oppositions you could make more out of, or add, in order to create at least three image layers. Rewrite the piece, working on layering images as a way of increasing the tension and power.

7. Write a story, poem, or creative nonfiction piece that uses four to six people. Present scenes or sections of three people, each of whom wants something different from the others. Cycle through at least three different combinations of your ensemble. Focus on images—don't explain what the people want. Simply show us.

8. Try layering dialogue and action. Using the following template, create a piece that alternates a line of speech and an action between two characters. Time yourself—keep your hand moving for 30 minutes. Briefly write a few sentences to set the scene, as in a play: Who is onstage, where are we, what's the weather/atmosphere/time of day/quality of the light? Then, divide your paper into two columns, as shown here.

Character 1	Character 2
Write a few sentences about Character #1: what he is wearing, how he is sitting, what he's fiddling with, his emotional state, desire.	Write a few sentences about Character 2, as you did for Character 1.
Write a line of dialogue for Character 1.	What is Character 2's response (first, in a line of dialogue)?
	What exact gesture or tiny action do you see Character 2 do? (Be sure you are *in* the image.)
What is Character 1's response to the comment/gesture by Character 2? Write the physical action, the tiny gesture you see. Your characters can get up, move around; the image is alive.	Character 2 responds, first with dialogue, then with a gesture. Repeat, following the pattern until the end of the time.
What does Character 1 say to Character 2? (Use your ears, don't make it up.)	

9. Try writing a short play using façade. Recall a conversation you had recently that was extremely personal and tense for you. You might begin with a quick list of ten tense conversations from the past month. Choose one and do a little sketch first, using your diagram to answer the questions above. Then, focus on the speech and tiny actions that make up the dialogue—however, the characters must be talking about something else (buying a house, picking out a puppy) besides the topic of the argument (one character wants to get married, the other doesn't, or one wants to have a baby, the other doesn't). Let the real fight come through in both dialogue and actions. But never mention the real fight directly!

10. Write a poem using only dialogue, using the principles of façade. Limit your poem to two speakers.

TENSION WORKSHOP

The prompts below will help you constructively discuss your classmates' work.

1. Write the tension formula—desire + danger = drama—for this piece. Describe the central *desire* in the main character/speaker. Is this danger presented clearly enough? How could the stakes or danger be increased? Could the desire part of the equation be intensified? How?

2. Create a tension map for the piece, assigning a number to represent the amount of tension in each paragraph (for prose) or line (for poetry). Are there places the piece "flatlines" (the same number repeats)? How could the numbers vary more? In which one place do you suggest the author work hardest to increase the tension?

3. Are there two or more characters to care about? Are they equally matched? How so?

4. What specific details and images function to *increase* the tension in this piece?

5. What's the central tension? Does the central tension have an internal as well as an external manifestation in this piece?

6. Identify one example of tension from the writer's use of closeups. Highlight or underline the passage where the writer employs this technique. Next, find a passage where the tension would increase if more closeups were used.

7. Identify three places in the piece where there could be more tension, and write in the margin one suggestion for a technique the writer could try from the following: triangles, layers, opposition. Try to suggest each technique if appropriate.

8. List at least two uses of triangles or potential triangles that could be developed. Are these passages also the places where the tension numbers are highest (from your mapping of the thermostat changes, above)?

9. Read just the dialogue aloud. Does it sound natural? Are there layers in what is said, and what is really meant? Are there oppositions? Is the dialogue tension-filled, or predictable? Note the best use of dialogue and say why. Note the weakest passage of dialogue and say why.

10. Is the writer using the façade technique? Where might the writer try to use façade more fully or boldly?

Marisa Silver
What I Saw from Where I Stood

Dulcie is afraid of freeways. She doesn't like not being able to get off whenever she wants, and sometimes I catch her holding her breath between exits, as if she's driving past a graveyard. So, even though the party we went to last week was miles from our apartment in Silver Lake, we drove home on the surface streets.

I was drunk, and Dulcie was driving my car. She'd taken one look at me as we left the party, then dug her fingers into my pants pocket and pulled out my keys. I liked the feel of her hand rubbing against me through my jeans; she hadn't been touching me much lately.

I cranked open the window to clear my head as we drove through Santa Monica. Nice houses. Pretty flowers. Volvos. Dulcie and I always say we'd never want to live out here in suburbia, but the truth is, we can't afford to, not on our salaries. Dulcie's a second-grade teacher in Glendale, and I'm a repairman for the telephone company.

When we reached Hollywood, things got livelier. There were skinny guitar punks patrolling the clubs on the strip with their pudgy girlfriends in midriff tops and thigh-high black skirts. A lot of big hair, big breasts, boredom. Farther east, there were boys strutting the boulevard, waiting to slip into someone's silver Mercedes and make a buck. One leaned against a fire hydrant and picked at his sallow face, looking cold in a muscle T-shirt.

We hit a red light at Vermont, right next to the hospital where Dulcie lost the baby, a year ago. She'd started cramping badly one night. She was only six months pregnant. I called the emergency room, and the attendant said to come right over. By the time we got there, the doctors couldn't pick up a heartbeat. They gave Dulcie drugs to induce labor and the baby was born. He was blue. He was no bigger than a football.

Dulcie looked up at the hospital and then back at the road. She's a small girl and she sank behind the wheel, getting even smaller. I didn't say anything. The light turned green. She drove across Vermont and I nodded off.

I woke up when a car plowed into us from behind. My body flew towards the windshield, then ricocheted back against my seat. Dulcie gripped the wheel, staring straight ahead out the windshield.

"Something happened," she said.

"Yeah," I heard myself answer, although my voice sounded hollow. "We had an accident."

We got out to check the damage and met at the back of the car. "It's nothing," Dulcie said, as we studied the medium-sized dent on the fender. It was nothing to us, anyway; the car was too old and beat-up for us to feel protective of it.

Behind me, I heard the door of a van slide open. I hadn't thought about the people who'd hit us, hadn't even noticed if they bothered to stop. I started to wave them off. They didn't need to get out, apologize, dig around for the insurance information they probably didn't have. But when I turned around, there were four or five men in front of me. They were standing very close. They were young. I was beginning to think that Dulcie and I should just get back into our car and drive away, when the van's engine cut out and a tall guy wearing a hooded sweatshirt called back towards it. "Yo, Darren! Turn it on, you motherfucker!"

His cursing seemed to make his friends nervous. Two of them looked at their feet. One hopped up and down like a fighter getting ready for a bout. Someone was saying "Shit, shit, shit" over and over again. Then I heard "Do it, do it!" and a short, wide kid with a shaved head and glow-in-the-dark stripes on his sneakers pulled out a gun and pointed it at my face. It didn't look like the guns in movies. Dulcie screamed.

"Don't shoot. Please don't shoot us!" Her voice was so high it sounded painful, as if it were scraping her throat.

"Your keys!" the tall one shouted. "Give us your motherfucking keys!"

Dulcie threw the keys on the ground at their feet. "Please! I don't have any money!"

"I'll get it," I heard myself say, as if I were picking up the tab at a bar. I was calm. I felt like I was underwater. Everything seemed slow and all I could hear was my own breathing. I reached into my back pocket and pulled out my wallet. I took out the bills and handed them over. The tall guy grabbed the money and ran back to the van, which made me feel better until I noticed that the kid with the shaved head was still pointing the gun at me.

That's when I got scared. As though someone had thrown a switch, all the sound returned, loud and close. I heard the cars roaring past on Sunset. I heard Dulcie screaming "No! No! No!" I heard an argument erupt between two of the guys. "Get in their car! Get in their fucking car or I'll do you too!" I grabbed Dulcie's hand, and I pulled her around the front of our car, crouching low. I could feel the heat of the engine under the hood. The van revved up. I stood, bringing Dulcie up with me, and there, on the driver's side, no more than three feet away, was the kid with the shaved head. He had the gun in one hand and Dulcie's keys in the other. I could see sweat glistening over the pimples on his face.

"Hey!" he said, looking confused. "What the fuck?"

Then it was as if I skipped a few minutes of my life, because the next thing I knew, Dulcie and I were racing down a side street toward the porch lights of some bungalows. We didn't look back to see if we were being followed. Sometimes Dulcie held my hand, sometimes we were separated by the row of parked cars. We had no idea where we were going.

After the police and their questions, and their heartfelt assurance that there was nothing at all they could do for us, we took a cab back to our apartment in Silver Lake. Dulcie was worried because the crack heads—that's what the police called them—had our keys, and our address was on the car registration. But the police had told us that the carjackers wouldn't come after us—that kind of thing almost never happened.

Still, Dulcie couldn't sleep, so we sat up all night while she went over what had happened. She'd seen the van on the street earlier, but hadn't it been in front of us, not behind? Why had they chosen our car, our sorry, broken-down mutt of a car? How close had we come to being shot?

"We saw them," she said. "We know what they look like."

"They weren't killers. They were thieves. There's a difference, I guess," I said.

"No," she said, twisting her straight brown hair around her finger so tightly the tip turned white. "It doesn't make sense."

Dulcie needs things to be exact. You have to explain yourself clearly when you're around her, so she's probably a good teacher. For a minute I wondered whether she wished we had been shot, just for the sake of logic.

She'd done this after losing the baby, too, going over and over what she might have done to kill it. Had she exercised too much? Not enough? Had she eaten something bad? She wanted an answer, and she needed to blame someone; if that person turned out to be her, that would still be better than having no one to blame at all. A few days after the delivery, a hospital social worker called to check on her. She reassured Dulcie that what had happened hadn't been her fault. It was a fluke thing, the woman said. She used the word *flukish*.

"I should have noticed them tailing me," Dulcie said now. "How could I not notice a car that close?"

"Don't do that," I told her. "Don't think about what could have happened."

"I have to think about it," she said. "How can you not think about it? We were this close," she said, holding her fingers out like a gun and aiming at my chest.

I drove Dulcie's car to work the next day. When I got home that night, Dulcie had moved our mattress from our bed into the living room, where it lay in the middle of the floor, the sheets spilling over onto the carpet. She'd taken a personal day to recover from the holdup. Her eyes were red, and she looked as though she'd been crying all afternoon.

"It's the rat," she said. "He's back."

A month earlier, a rat had burrowed and nested in the wall behind our bed. Every night, it scratched a weird, personal jazz into our ears. We told the landlord and he said he would get on it right away, which meant: You'll be living with that rat forever, and if you don't like it there're ten other people in line for your apartment. I checked around the house to make sure the rat couldn't find a way inside. I patched up a hole underneath the sink with plywood and barricaded the space between the dishwasher and the wall with old towels. After Dulcie was sure that there would be no midnight visitor eating our bananas, she was okay with the rat. We even named him—Mingus.

She wasn't okay with it anymore.

"He's getting louder. Closer. Like he's going to get in this time," she said.

"He can't get in. There's no way."

"Well, I can't sleep in that room."

"It's a small apartment, Dulcie." The living room was smaller than the bedroom, and the mattress nearly filled it.

"I can't do it, Charles. I can't."

"All right. We can sleep anywhere you want," I said.

"I want to sleep in the living room. And I want you to change the message on the answering machine," she said. "It has my voice on it. It should have a man's voice."

"You're worried about the rat hearing your voice on the machine?"

"Don't make fun of me, okay? Those guys know where we live."

Later that night, I discovered that she wanted to sleep with all the lights on.

"I want people to know we're home," she said. "People don't break in if they think you're there."

We were lying on the floor on our mattress. She felt tiny, so delicate that I would crush her if I squeezed too hard or rolled the wrong way.

"You don't mind, do you?" she said. "About the light. Is it too bright?"

She'd let me throw one of my shirts, an orange one, over the fixture hanging from the ceiling. It gave the room a muffled, glowy feel.

"No," I said. I kissed her forehead. She didn't turn to me. Since the baby, we've had a hard time getting together.

Dulcie sat up again. "Maybe it's a bad idea," she said. "Maybe a thief will see the light on at four A.M. and think that we're actually out of town. I mean, who leaves their light on all night when they're home?"

"No one."

"You know," she said, "I saw in a catalogue once that you could buy an inflatable man to put in a chair by your window. Or in your car. You could put him in the passenger seat if you were driving alone."

She looked at me, but I didn't know what to say. To me, driving with a plastic blow-up doll in the seat next to you seemed very peculiar.

"Lie down," I said, stroking her back beneath her T-shirt. Her skin was smooth and warm.

She lay down next to me. I turned over on my stomach and laid my hand across her chest. I liked the feel of the small rises of her breasts, the give of them.

Dulcie's milk had come in two days after the delivery. The doctor had warned her that this would happen and had prescribed Valium in advance. I came home from work and found Dulcie, stoned, staring at her engorged breasts in the bathroom mirror. I'd never seen anything like it. Her breasts were like boulders, and her veins spread out across them like waterways on a map. Dulcie squeezed one nipple, and a little pearl of yellowish milk appeared. She tasted it.

"It's sweet," she said. "What a waste."

For the next two days, she lay on the couch holding packs of frozen vegetables against each breast. Sometimes we laughed about it, and she posed for a few sexpot pictures, with the packs of peas pressed against her chest like pasties. Other times, she just stared at the living room wall, adjusting a pack when it slipped. I asked her if her breasts hurt, and she said yes, but not in the way you'd think.

I slid my hand off Dulcie's chest, turned back over, and stared at the T-shirt on the light fixture.

"Did you know," she said, "that when you're at a red light the person next to you probably has a gun in his glove compartment?"

"Defensive driving," I said, trying for a joke.

"Statistically speaking, it's true. Until yesterday, I never thought about how many people have guns," Dulcie said. "Guns in their cars, guns in their pocketbooks when they're going to the market, guns . . ."

A fly was caught between the light and my T-shirt. I could see its shadow darting frantically back and forth until, suddenly, it was gone.

The next evening as I was driving home from work, someone threw an egg at my car. I thought it was another holdup. I sucked in so much air that I started to choke and almost lost control. Two kids then ran by my window. One was wearing a Dracula mask and a cape. The other one had on a rubber monster head and green tights. I'd forgotten it was Halloween.

Dulcie takes holidays pretty seriously, and when I got home I expected to see a cardboard skeleton on the door, and maybe a carved pumpkin or two. Usually she greets the trick-or-treaters wearing a tall black witch hat that she keeps stashed in a closet the rest of the year. When she opens the door, she makes this funny cackling laugh, which is kind of embarrassing but also sweet. She's so waifish, there's not much about her that could scare anybody. But when I got home and climbed the outside stairs to our second-floor apartment, there was nothing on our door and the apartment was dark.

"What are you doing with all the lights off?" I asked when I got inside. She was sitting at the kitchen table, her hands folded in front of her as if she were praying.

"Shut the door," she said. "A whole pack of them just came. They must have rung the bell five times."

"They want their candy."

"We don't have any."

"Really? You didn't buy any?"

"Charles, we don't know who any of these people are," she said slowly, as if I were six years old. "I'm not going to open my door to perfect strangers."

"They're kids."

"What about the ones who come really late?" she asked. "All those teenagers. They're looking for trouble."

I sat down and reached across the table for her hands. "It's Halloween, Dulcie. It's just kids having fun."

"Plenty of people aren't home on Halloween. This is just going to be one of those places where nobody's home."

The doorbell rang.

"Dulcie—"

"Sh-h-h!" She hissed at me like a cat.

"This is ridiculous." I got up.

"Please, Charles!"

The bell rang again. I grabbed a box of cookies from the shelf and went to the door. A little kid was walking away, but he turned back when he heard the door open. He was six, eight years old. An old man I recognized from the neighborhood, maybe his grandfather, stood a few steps behind him.

The boy wore a cowboy outfit—a fringed orange vest over a T-shirt with a picture of Darth Vader on it, jeans mashed down into plastic cowboy boots, and a holster sliding down over his narrow hips. He took a gun out of the holster and waved it around in the air.

"Bang," he said, without enthusiasm.

"You got me," I answered, putting my hands to my chest and pretending to die.

"It's a fake gun," the boy said. "No real bullets."

"You mean I'm not dead?" I tried to sound amazed, and I got a smile out of the kid.

The grandfather said something impatiently in another language, Russian or maybe Armenian.

"Trick or treat," the boy said quietly. He held out a plastic grocery sack with his free hand.

I looked into the bag. There were only a few pieces of candy inside. Suddenly the whole thing made me sad. I offered my box of mint cookies.

The boy looked back at his grandfather, who shook his head. "I'm only allowed to have it if it's wrapped," the boy said to me.

I felt like a criminal. "We didn't have a chance to get to the store," I said, as the boy holstered his gun and moved off with his grandfather.

When I went back inside, Dulcie was standing in the middle of the dark living room, staring at me. Three months after the baby died, I came home from work and found her standing in that same place. Her belly underneath her T-shirt was huge, much bigger than when she'd actually been pregnant. For one crazy second, I thought that the whole thing had been a mistake, and that she was still pregnant. I felt a kind of relief I had never felt before. Then she lifted her shirt and took out a watermelon from underneath it.

A group of kids yelled "Trick or treat!" below us. They giggled. Someone said "Boo!" then there was a chorus of dutiful thank-you's. I heard small feet pound up the rickety wooden stairway to the second-floor apartments. I walked over to Dulcie and put my arms around her.

"We can't live like this," I said.

"I can," she said.

Dulcie went back to work three days after the carjacking. I dropped her off at school in my car, and she arranged for one of her teacher friends to give her a lift home. I took it as a good sign, her returning to work. She complains about the public school system, all the idiotic bureaucracy she has to deal with, but she loves the kids. She's always coming home with stories about cute things they did, or about how quickly they picked up something she didn't think they'd understand the first time. She was named Teacher of the Year last spring, and a couple of parents got together and gave her this little gold necklace. Her school's in a rough part of Glendale. The necklace was a big deal.

She was home when I got off work, sitting on the couch. She waved a piece of pink paper in the air.

"What's that?" I said.

"We're not allowed to touch the children anymore," she said.

"What are you talking about?"

She told me that a parent had accused a teacher of touching his daughter in the wrong way. Social Services came in, the works. When they finally got around to questioning the girl, she told them the teacher had just patted her on the back because she answered a question right.

"Now the district's in a panic—they don't want a lawsuit every time some kid exaggerates. So, no touching the students."

"That's nuts," I said. "Those kids need to be hugged every once in a while. They probably don't get enough affection at home."

"That's a racist generalization, Charles," she said. "Most of the parents try hard. They love their kids just as much as you and I would."

Neither of us said anything. Dulcie hadn't brought up the idea of our having kids since we'd lost the baby. She had just stepped on a grenade, and I was waiting through those awful seconds before it explodes.

"This is a fucked-up town," she said finally.

I wasn't sure what had made her say this. The school thing? The carjacking?

"Maybe if we turn on the TV we'll catch a freeway chase," I said.

"Or a riot."

"Or a celebrity bio."

She started laughing. "That's the real tragedy," she said. "The celebrity bio."

We laughed some more. When we stopped, neither of us knew what to say.

"I'm not racist," I said at last.

"I know. I didn't mean that."

"I may be prejudiced against celebrities, though."

She squeezed out a smile. It was worth the stupid joke.

The next Saturday, Dulcie called an exterminator. She'd decided that we should pay for one out of our own pocket, because she'd read that some rats carry airborne viruses.

"People died in New Mexico," she said. "Children too."

It turns out that the exterminator you call to get rid of bugs is not the kind you call to get rid of a rat. There's a subspecialty—Rodent Removal. Our rodent remover was named Rod. Rod the Rodent Remover. I was scared of him already.

When he came to the door, he was wearing a clean, pressed uniform with his name on it. "Rod," I said, "thanks for coming."

"It's really Ricardo, but I get more jobs as Rod. Ricardo is too hard for most people to remember. You have a problem with rats?" he said helpfully.

"Yeah. In here." I opened the door wider and led him into the apartment. "It's not really *in* the apartment, but we hear it from in here."

If Ricardo thought it was strange that the mattress was on the living room floor, he didn't say anything. Dulcie was waiting for us in the bedroom.

"It's there," Dulcie said, pointing to a gray smudge where the head of our bed frame met the wall. "He's in there."

Ricardo went over and tapped the wall with his knuckle. Dulcie held her breath. There was no sound from the rat.

"They usually leave the house during the day," Ricardo said.

"How does he get in?" Dulcie said.

Ricardo raised his finger toward the ceiling. "Spanish tile roof. Very pretty, but bad for the rat problem," he said. "They come in through the holes between the tiles."

"So there's nothing we can do?" Dulcie asked, alarmed.

"We can set a trap in the wall through the heating vent there," Ricardo said, pointing to the one vent in our entire apartment, which was, unhelpfully, in the hallway outside our bedroom.

"Then he'll die in the wall?"

"It's a bad smell for a few days, but then it goes away," Ricardo said.

I could see that none of this was making Dulcie feel any better.

"Or I can put a trap on the roof," Ricardo said.

"Do that," Dulcie said quickly.

"Okay," he said. "Now we have a plan."

He reached into his pockets and took out two yellow surgical gloves. Dulcie was horrified, the gloves confirming her suspicions about disease. But Ricardo smiled pleasantly. This was a guy who dealt with rats every day of his life, and it didn't seem to faze him.

"Why do they come inside?" Dulcie said, as we followed Ricardo towards the door. "The rats. Why do they live in the walls? There's no food there."

"To keep warm," Ricardo said. "Sometimes to have their babies."

He smiled and gave us a courtly nod as I let him out. When I turned back, Dulcie was still staring at the closed door, her hand over her mouth.

"It's just a rat," I said. I touched her shoulder. She was shaking.

A month after the baby died, the mailman delivered a package that I had to sign for. We don't get a lot of packages, so it was an event. The box was from a company called La Tierra. The name sounded familiar, but I couldn't place it; I was about to call back into the apartment for Dulcie when I remembered. La Tierra was the name of the company that cremated the baby.

"What is it?" Dulcie said from behind me. "Who was at the door?"

I turned around. This will kill her, I thought.

"What is it?" she said again, holding out her hand.

I had no choice but to hand it to her. She looked at it. Her face crumpled. "It's so light," she said finally.

I went to put my arms around her, but she stepped back. Then she started laughing. Her laughter became the kind of giggling you can't turn off. She bit her lips and clenched her teeth, but the giggles kept coming, as if they were tickling her insides in order to get out.

"You probably thought it was something from your mom," she said through her laughter. "Or some freebie from a computer company. Oh, my God," she said. "Can you believe this is our life?" I smiled, but it was that weird, embarrassed smile you offer when you feel left out of a joke.

We decided to take the ashes to the beach and scatter them on the water. We drove out to the Ventura County line, to a beach called El Pescador. You have to climb down a steep hillside to get to it, and there's usually no one there, especially in the off season. We parked and scrambled unsteadily down the trail. We were so busy concentrating on not falling that we didn't see the ocean until we were at its level. We both got quiet for a moment. The water was slate gray, pocked by the few white gulls that every so often swooped down to the surface and then rose up again. There were no boats in the ocean, only a couple of prehistoric oil derricks in the distance. "I think we should do it now," Dulcie said.

We opened the box. Inside was some Styrofoam with a hole gouged out. Nestled inside that hole, like a tiny bird, was a plastic bag filled with brown dust. There could not have been more than a tablespoonful. I took the bag and handed the box to Dulcie. Then I kicked off my shoes, rolled up my jeans, and walked out into the water. When I was calf deep, I opened up the bag. I waited for something to happen, for some gust of wind to kick up and take the ashes out to sea. But the day was calm, so I finally dumped the ashes into the water at my feet. A tiny wave moved them towards the shore. I worried that the ashes would end up in the sand, where somebody could step all over them, but then I felt the undertow dragging the water back towards the sea.

"I think that's the bravest thing I've ever seen a person do," Dulcie said as I came out of the water.

As we headed back to the trail, she picked up a smooth stone and slipped it into her pocket. Halfway up the path, she took the stone out and let it drop to the ground.

A week after the holdup, the police called. They had found our stolen car. Once the kids run out of gas, the officer explained, they usually abandon the car rather than pay for more. He gave us the address of the car lot, somewhere in South Central.

"Go early in the morning," the officer warned. "Before they get up."

" 'They'?" I asked.

"You a white guy?" the policeman asked.

"Yeah."

"You want to be down there before wake-up time. Trust me."

Dulcie said it was a self-fulfilling prophecy. Everybody expected things to be bad, so people made them bad. She saw it at her school. The kids who were expected to fail, well, they blew it every time out, even if they knew the work cold.

Still, we took the officer's advice and went down to the lot at seven in the morning. I admit I was nervous, driving through those streets. You like to think you're more open-minded than that, but I guess I'm not. I kept thinking about drive-by shootings and gangs and riots and all the things you read about, thinking, Those things don't happen near where I live, so I'm okay.

We found our car. It was a mess. It had been stripped; even the steering wheel was gone. There was every kind of fast-food wrapper scattered on the back seat, and French fries and old hamburger buns on the floor. You get hungry when you're high. It wasn't worth the price of towing, so we signed it over to the pound and left it there.

As I drove Dulcie to work, I told her the police had asked us to come identify the suspects in a lineup.

"But they'll know it was us who identified them," she said. "They know where we live."

"They were busy getting high. I don't think they were memorizing our address."

"I don't even remember what they looked like. It was dark."

"Once you see some faces, it might come back."

"Charles, don't make me do this. Don't make me!" she cried.

"I'm not going to make you do anything. Jesus. What do you think I am?"

She didn't answer me. I dropped her off at the school. She got out and walked towards the front door, then turned to wave at me, as if it were any regular day, as if we weren't living like some rat trapped in our own wall.

I took the day off. I'd already used up my sick days, and I knew we couldn't throw away the money, but I thought I'd go crazy if I had to be nice to a customer or listen to some technician talk about his bodacious girlfriend or his kid's troubles in school.

I didn't have a plan. I picked up a paper and got breakfast at a hipster coffee shop on Silver Lake Boulevard. There were a lot of tattooed and pierced people eating eggs and bacon; they looked as though they were ending a night, not beginning a day. I tried to concentrate on my paper, but nothing sank in. Then I got back into my car. I ended up driving along Vermont into Griffith Park, past the roads where guys stop to cruise, all the way up to the Observatory. I parked in the empty lot and got out.

The Observatory was closed; it was still early. I was trying to think of something to do with myself when I saw a trail heading up into the hills. The path was well worn; on the weekends, it was usually packed with tourists and families making a cheap day of it. But that morning I had it to myself. I wanted to walk. I walked for hours. I felt the sun rise up, and I saw the darkness that covered the canyons lift, as if someone were sliding a blanket off the ground.

By the time I stopped, others were on the trail — runners, or people walking their dogs, some kids who were probably playing hooky. I looked out over the canyon and thought about how I could go either way: I could stay with Dulcie and be as far away from life as a person could be, or I could leave.

I had been looking forward to the baby. I didn't mind talking to Dulcie about whether or not the kid should sleep in bed with us, or use a pacifier, or how long she would nurse him, or any of the things she could think about happily for days. I got excited about it, too. But I had no idea what it meant. What was real to me was watching Dulcie's body grow bigger and bigger, watching that stripe appear on her belly, watching as her breasts got fuller and that part around her nipples got as wide and dark as pancakes. When the doctors took the baby out of her, they handed him to me without bothering to clean him up; I guess there was no point to it. Every inch of him was perfectly formed. For a second, I thought he would open his eyes and be a baby. It didn't look like anything was wrong with him, like there was any reason for him not to be breathing and crying and getting on with the business of being in the world. I kept saying to myself, This is my baby, this is my baby. But I had no idea what I was saying. The only thing I truly felt was that I would die if something happened to Dulcie.

A runner came towards me on the trail. His face was red, and sweat had made his T-shirt transparent. He gave me a pained smile as he ran past. He kicked a small rock with his shoe, and it flew over the side of the canyon. For some reason, I looked over the edge for the rock. What I saw from where I stood was amazing to me. I saw all kinds of strange cactus plants—tall ones like base-ball bats, others like spiky fans. There were dry green eucalyptus trees and a hun-dred different kinds of bushes I couldn't name. I heard the rustle of animals, skunks or coyotes, maybe even deer. There was garbage on the ground and in the bushes—soda cans, fast-food drink cups, napkins with restaurant logos on them. I saw a condom hanging off a branch, like a burst balloon. For some rea-son, the garbage didn't bother me. For all I knew, this was one of those moun-tains that was made of trash, and it was nature that didn't belong. Maybe the trash, the dirt, the plants, bugs, condoms—maybe they were all just fighting for a little space.

I got home before Dulcie. I dragged the mattress back into the bedroom. I took my shirt off the light fixture in the living room and put it in the dresser. When Dulcie came back, she saw what I had done, but she didn't say anything. We ate dinner early. I watched a soccer game while she corrected papers. Then I turned off the lights in the living room, and we went into the bedroom. She knew my mind was made up, and she climbed into bed like a soldier following orders. When I snapped off the bedside lamp, she gave a little gasp.

We lay quietly for a while, getting used to the dark. We listened for the rat, but he wasn't there.

"You think the traps worked?" she said.

"Maybe."

I reached for her. At first it was awkward, as though we were two people who had never had sex with each other. Truthfully, I was half ready for her to push me away. But she didn't, and, after a while, things became familiar again. When I rolled on top of her, though, I felt her tense up underneath me. She started to speak. "I should go and get—"

I put my fingers on her mouth to stop her. "It's okay," I said.

She looked up at me with her big watery eyes. She was terrified. She started again to say something about her diaphragm. I stopped her once more.

"It's okay," I repeated.

I could feel her heart beating on my skin. I could feel my own heart beating even harder. We were scared, but we kept going.

Thomas Lux

The Man into Whose Yard
You Should Not Hit Your Ball

each day mowed
and mowed his lawn, his dry quarter acre,
the machine slicing a wisp
from each blade's tip. Dust storms rose
around the roar: 6:00 P.M., every day,
spring, summer, fall. If he could mow
the snow he would.
On one side, his neighbors the cows
turned their backs to him
and did what they do to the grass.
Where he worked, I don't know
but it sets his jaw too tight.
His wife a cipher, shoebox tissue,
a shattered apron. As if
into her head he drove a wedge of shale.
Years later his daughter goes to jail.

Mow, mow, mow his lawn
gently down a decade's summers.
On his other side lived mine and me,
across a narrow pasture, often fallow;
a field of fly balls, the best part of childhood
and baseball, but one could not cross his line
and if it did,
as one did in 1956
and another in 1958
it came back coleslaw—his lawn mower
ate it up, happy
to cut something, no matter
what the manual said
about foreign objects,
stones, or sticks.

Jessica Shattuck
Bodies

In the fluorescent light of the refrigerator, the halved parsnips look naked — pale and fleshy as limbs. Annie pauses before pulling them out. A refrigerator is like a hospital, a bright place that is not cheerful. A protective but uncertain place to wait.

"What are you doing?" Anthony says. He's standing in the doorway.

"Starting dinner," Annie says, flicking on the lights. They both blink in the sudden brilliance.

Anthony climbs up onto one of the tall stools on the other side of the kitchen island. He is five years old, blond, and freckled, with close-set blue eyes. Something about his mouth and his stubby but prominent little nose hints already at the old man he will be — stubborn, soft-spoken, a little unforgiving.

The music of *The Lion King* drifts toward them from the playroom.

"Not in the mood for the movie?" Annie asks.

Anthony shrugs and lays his head down on his outstretched arm.

Annie dabs small pieces of butter on the parsnips, draining water from the dish. Outside the window, twenty stories below, there is a bright stream of traffic on Fifth Avenue. Beyond that, Central Park is black — lit paths twist through it like constellations. She rinses beans, wraps bread in aluminum foil, rubs garlic and pepper on steaks, washes the pretty purple-and-white salad leaves whose name she can never remember. She and Anthony are comfortable with silence. When she first moved in with his family, he made her nervous. He is an intense child, with a sharp, scrutinizing gaze, and his frankness can be almost cruel. Annie tried to protect herself with chatter, elaborately inventive games, even bribes. But they are friends now. She feels more at home around Anthony than around anyone else she knows.

"Will you read to me?" Anthony asks after the steaks are in the broiler and the beans are steaming on the stove.

Annie looks at the clock. "For five minutes," she says.

"Yes, yes, yes," he chants, sitting up straight now.

Annie is in what her doctor refers to as the "hunker down and wait" period of treatment for Stage III Hodgkin's lymphoma. For the most part, she has been lucky. She has gone through ten remarkably smooth cycles of chemotherapy; the success has yet to be determined, but the side effects have been mild. Her straight, pale-brown hair is thinner, but she still has it. Though she needs at least twelve hours of sleep a day, she is not constantly exhausted. She takes her pills every morning — vitamins, herbs a Chinese doctor prescribed, green algae. She eats kale and radishes and drinks a full gallon and a half of water a day. She lives like someone who has built a home on the San Andreas Fault: she takes what small, possibly ridiculous precautions she can, and then chooses not to think about it.

Until November, Annie worked as a secretary for Anthony's mother, Cleo. Cleo is the creative director of a large international advertising agency — the first woman in the company's history to have this role. She is tall and levelheaded and big-boned, but glamorous. She works fifteen hours a day, and most weekends as well. She is an adept psychoanalyst of the public mind. "That'll make people think of getting old. People don't want to think of getting old," she'll say about a mockup of an ad for a real-estate Web site. Suddenly everyone will realize that the little boy bouncing his ball down the walk into his grandmother's garden reminds them of their lost childhoods — of time passing, of old dreams, and of dying. Cleo will substitute a girl for the boy, an older brother for the grandmother, and it will become an entirely different story. Annie would like to crawl into Cleo's confidence and curl up in her powerful vision of the world as an infinitely malleable, manageable place.

Annie's own days at the agency have been put on indefinite hold, and she misses them — the feeling of purpose and efficiency. Now she lives with Cleo and her family in their penthouse on Fifth Avenue, which has lots of extra room. It is a perfect arrangement, really; Annie did not have many people she could move in with when she got sick. There was her high-school sweetheart, who is now her ex-husband, in San Diego, and her brother, Todd, in Long Beach. But the last time she saw Todd he locked her in the closet and broke a bottle against the door. And her ex-husband has found God.

Besides, Cleo and her husband, Jay, need someone in addition to their babysitter to look after their two children. Mrs. Tibbs, they worry, will teach the children bad grammar and imperfect diction. Now Annie reads them stories and plays interesting, educational games, and is careful to choose her words exactly, hold on to silent "g"'s, never say "gonna" or use "real" as an adjective. She is used to this from the office — the only difference is that it is no longer a work-related necessity but something she has to do at home, because that is what Cleo and Jay's apartment has become.

Annie has made it to page 5 of *Goodnight Moon*, Anthony's favorite book, when the doorbell rings. "No," Anthony says, putting his hand on her hip as she starts to get up. "No." He is clingy and uncertain in the evenings.

"I have to get the door," Annie says gently. "It might be important."

But it is Cleo's niece Michele, who lives with her mother, Cleo's sister, two buildings down.

"Hi," Michele says with a bright, insincere smile. "Is Cleo home yet?" She peers over Annie's shoulder into the apartment as if Annie might not be trusted to tell the truth. Michele's mother drifts in and out of rehab programs, and Cleo worries about her niece. She is a beautiful girl: blond, long-legged, with perfectly straight, well-proportioned features. Tonight she is wearing a short, hot-pink skirt and impossibly high platform heels. Around Michele, Annie feels dumpy, prudish, and overwhelmingly average—average height (five feet five), average prettiness (small nose, brown eyes, and pale skin), average age (thirty-two), and average-sized breasts (34B). She remembers that she has not showered in two days, that her sweater is pilly, that her jeans are baggy at the knees.

"Not yet," she says. "Would you like to come in and wait for her?"

"Story!" Anthony demands from the couch.

Annie hopes Michele will say no.

"I can't," Michele says. "I'm on my way downtown, but I wanted to give her this." She holds out a thick silver-paper envelope with writing in metallic gold. "My sweet-sixteen party. At Au Bar," she adds, unable to restrain herself.

"Ooh," Annie says, "that'll be nice," hoping this is an appropriate response. But it sounds fraudulent, schoolteacherish. "I'll give it to her."

"Thanks," Michele breathes, and flashes another studied smile. "Say hi to Jay."

Annie closes the door behind her and walks back over to Anthony.

"O.K.," she says, settling onto the sofa. "Where were we?"

"Here," Anthony says, squirming closer, collapsing against her as soon as she leans back. She is thankful for his helplessness.

Since it is Thursday night, they are all eating together. This is Cleo's rule. Sundays and Thursdays, they dine at seven so that Anthony and his baby sister, Eden, can join them and afterward Cleo can put them to bed. On other nights, Cleo and Jay eat late, or have dinner engagements, or, often, Cleo is out of town. Tonight, Cleo has brought pink and orange dahlias home from the florist on Madison, which Annie has arranged in the center of the table. In the candlelight, they project pointed orange shadows onto the walls.

"What did you do, invite Alain Ducasse over to cook?" Jay says, surveying the food. "This looks fantastic." Jay is tall and in his early forties. He is technically good-looking, but there is something about him that seems still unformed, as if he had never, for even a moment, experienced pain.

"Abble, abble, abble, abble," Eden chants from her high chair. Saliva runs down her lower lip.

"Did you work out with Mel today?" Cleo asks Jay, wiping Eden's chin with her napkin. Mel is Jay's trainer. "I thought that was Monday, Wednesday, Friday."

"Bumped it up—Thursdays, too," Jay says, helping himself to a steak. Jay sold his Internet company for "a bundle," as he likes to say, before the market went bust, and since then he has devoted himself to "independent projects," which originally consisted of learning to play the guitar, writing a how-to (in his case, how to sell your startup company for millions) book, and getting in shape. Now his projects consist entirely of getting in shape—kick-boxing class, weight lifting, training for the New York marathon. In the four months since Annie moved in with them, he has gone way past "in shape." His muscles, which are by nature invisible, have become hard and round and move like an animal's beneath his skin. He can bench-press two hundred and thirty pounds and run to the tip of Manhattan and back in an hour and twenty minutes.

"Four times a week?" Cleo asks, her eyebrows raised.

"What's that supposed to mean?" Jay demands.

"Nothing," Cleo says. "Did you have a chance to call the Hornbys?"

Cleo is so smooth. Jay will have to run after this question now. He is volatile, but easily distracted. Annie has seen him agitated, cranky, even nasty a few times, but she has never seen Cleo so much as ruffled.

"They're coming on Saturday." Jay turns to Anthony and tousles his hair. "With Davey-boy, so you'll have a friend, too."

"I don't like him," Anthony says, slumping back in his chair.

"But he's your buddy," Jay says with a mixture of surprise and disappointment. "He's a good guy."

"Why not?" Cleo asks at the same time.

Anthony grunts and kicks the table leg. Annie has begun to notice that he is different with Cleo. Less communicative. More petulant. Gently, Annie stills his leg under the table.

"Na, na, na, na," Eden begins chanting. She has been released from her high chair and is crawling around under the table. Then she sits down and begins sucking on the remote control of Jay's new stereo.

"She loves to put things in her mouth," Annie says, removing the remote control gently from Eden's grasp.

"Well!" Jay says, standing up. "Just like your mother, aren't you?" He laughs and wiggles one of Eden's fat toes.

"Could you get the salt while you're up?" Cleo asks, with no hint that she has heard.

Annie suspects that Cleo and Jay have a wild and theatrical sex life. There is all of Jay's working out. There are his crass jokes. There is the way he smells when he comes into the kitchen for breakfast before showering. But these are merely complements of something Annie sees in Cleo. She is too confident, too invulnerable to be seductive. But when she is relaxed, when she and Jay come in from an evening out at a benefit, or a day of sailing on the Sound, there is something raw about her—a loose, substantial physicality that reminds Annie of a high-school athlete. It is slightly masculine. Unabashedly sexual.

The first time Annie thought about this, an image of Cleo, bent over, her brown hair trailing on the floor, popped into her mind. She was being fucked from behind. She was wearing a bustier and garters, and her wide pale feet with their unpainted toenails looked inanimate. The image was so vivid that Annie almost can't remember whether she has actually seen it. She imagines that Cleo likes frilly nighties in little-girl colors. That Jay, with his newly built body, comes out of the bathroom shirtless, in black briefs. That Cleo is coy, that Jay will do anything to get a blow job—David Hasselhoff impersonations, handsprings, a wrestling move in which he pins Cleo roughly against the headboard. It is both comical and dangerous. And Annie is shocked at how readily it springs into her imagination.

"Stop doing dishes," Cleo says, coming into the kitchen from the children's room. "Mrs. Tibbs will do those in the morning. You have better things to do."

"I like doing dishes," Annie says.

"Anthony would like you to go in and give him a kiss goodnight."

Annie tries to interpret Cleo's voice. Lately, when Cleo wants to read Anthony a story, he says no, he'd rather have Annie. Cleo turns it into a joke—you're a more fun mommy than I am, she says. But here, alone in the kitchen, Annie feels tension spring up between them like a wire. It makes Annie nervous; beneath Cleo's unflappable exterior, Annie has noticed lately, she has a capacity for cruelty.

"O.K." Annie wipes her hand on the dish towel and adds, "I feel a little woozy," which she does not, as if somehow this could make things equal.

Anthony's bedroom is at the far end of the apartment, across the darkened living room with its glass doors that lead out to a roof garden and the hollow rush of the city. Anthony is lying on his back, staring at the glow-in-the-dark stars Jay arranged on the ceiling in the shape of a baseball. "I knew you'd come," he says, turning onto his side as soon as she opens the door.

"Well, you asked for me, right?" Annie says gently. She sits down on the edge of his bed and can feel his legs, warm under the covers, pushing against her back.

"It's too dark," he says. "I want to sleep with the light on."

"Why?" Annie says. "Darkness is good. It's nothing to be afraid of."

"I'm not afraid," he says rolling onto his back. His voice has an anxious hitch to it, though.

"That's good."

"What is 'afraid'?" Anthony asks.

All around her the room is full of indistinguishable objects and flickering shadows from the roof garden—living things blowing, husk-like, in the March wind. A siren howls from below, muffled by the distance it has to travel.

"Annie?" Anthony is looking at her, his eyes demanding.

"It's a feeling," she says. "It's a way you feel." The words come out sounding thick and automatic. She concentrates on the pressure of his knee, bony and hard against the small of her back. "I think you know," she adds softly, when her voice seems more like her own again.

When she leans over to kiss him, he clasps her cheeks in his small damp hands. "Sleep tight," she whispers. Anthony doesn't let go. "Sleep tight," she repeats, gently peeling off his fingers.

In the front hall, Cleo has on the long tailored coat, gray slacks, and platform sneakers she refers to as her plane PJs. "Asleep?" she asks cheerfully. She already has more important things to think about.

"Almost," Annie says.

"I'm catching the red-eye. Be back Saturday at noon." She puts on a gray felt hat.

"You leaving, babe?" Jay comes in from the living room holding the *Wall Street Journal* in one hand.

"Mm-hmm," Cleo smiles, adjusting the hat just in time for Jay to knock it askew by enveloping her in his arms for a newspaper-crumpling bear hug and a kiss.

Cleo laughs and kisses him back. A firm but restrictive press of the lips.

"Call when you get there?" Jay says over his shoulder, already walking away across the hall.

"I will." Cleo makes a what-can-you-do face at Annie as she tucks her hair behind her ears and pulls the hat back into place. "Oh, will you make sure Mrs. Tibbs gets the envelope I put on the counter?"

Annie nods.

"You O.K.?" Cleo fixes Annie with her gaze, but there is something prohibitive about it, just as there was in her kiss.

"Yes," Annie says. "Have a safe trip."

"Be strong, kiddo." Cleo gives Annie a cool, dry kiss on the cheek.

Annie forces a smile and then closes the door after her.

In the kitchen she has the desire—the first in a long time—for a drink. She has not touched alcohol since she was diagnosed. In high school, there were two or three times she got really drunk—an exhilarating, freeing drunk where she became loud, sexy, and silly, the kind of girl who took drama instead of typing. This was a long time ago, when she was a Californian. When she was still living in Long Beach, answering phones at the tattoo parlor her brother worked at, and imagining she would go to design school, marry someone famous, live in a mansion. It was before junior college, before Todd really lost it, certainly before New York.

Annie opens Cleo and Jay's liquor cabinet, pulls out the Johnnie Walker, pours herself a glass. It tastes sharp and pure as medicine. Then she turns on the tap to finish the dishes. With her hands immersed in the warm water, the whiskey hot inside her, she tries to listen to her body—tries to feel the movement of her blood, the labored breathing of her cells. But she feels nothing— not even the beating of her heart.

"Hey, why don't you turn a light on?" Jay is standing in the doorway, where Anthony stood before.

"Oh," Annie says. "I forgot." But this isn't true. She has chosen the darkness. Seeing clearly seems like a distraction; she is surrounded by other people's clutter.

Jay flips the switch from the doorway but he hesitates before entering. Annie has the feeling he is afraid she is crying.

"Vitamins," he says. "Forgot my vitamins."

Annie wipes her face with her sleeve. She takes another sip of whiskey.

"Should you be drinking that—with—you know, your treatment and all?" Jays says the word "treatment" as if it were a euphemism for something sordid. He pours four pills as fat as roaches into his palm. In the refrigerator, bottles of zinc, vitamins C, A, and B, iron, protein powder, and Strong Body Multitabs occupy an entire shelf of the door.

She and Jay have never addressed her illness, a reticence that is not exactly strange but tiring. Cleo, with her strong sense of calm, her reliance on order and the ability to manipulate, has always been the arbiter of conversations about Annie's health. Jay usually pretends not to be listening, as if it were some other intimate, distinctly feminine problem they were discussing. "He doesn't get it," Cleo told Annie once. The comment was slightly unnerving—what was it, exactly, according to Cleo, that Jay didn't get?

Now, instead of looking at her, he occupies himself with a carton of skim milk.

"Here," Annie says, handing him a glass. When he pours the milk, the muscles under his taut, sallow skin rise and subside. Annie feels a corresponding rise of something unidentifiable in her gut.

"Your heart rate must be low," she says unsteadily.

"Forty-nine at rest." Jay brightens. "Last year it was seventy-two. Count it," he says, extending his arm.

Annie wraps her fingers around his warm wrist. His pulse crawls as sluggishly as ink through water. Annie counts forty-nine but doesn't let go. "Fifty, fifty-one, fifty-two, fifty-three," she recites out loud and tightens her grip. She concentrates on the flawless rhythm of his blood working its way through his body, nourishing his bones and muscles—she would like to absorb it, gobble it up, make it her own. Jay looks at her quizzically but doesn't pull away. She raises his wrist to his chest, bending his arm at the elbow, and watches his biceps swell. Suddenly, she can imagine it, pressed against her collarbone—his arm wrapped heavily around her neck and her teeth grazing the pale, damp, almost womanly skin at the crook of his elbow. Her own low breathing, she realizes when the hum of the refrigerator switches off, is the loudest sound in the room.

"Annie," Jay says, peeling her fingers from his wrist. "I think you need to get some sleep."

Annie removes her hand. "Maybe." She is surprisingly unembarrassed, even when she sways slightly against the door frame. She can feel Jay's eyes following her across the floor.

In the morning, Annie fixes herself breakfast. Early buds have appeared overnight on the trees in the Park, and the ground looks black and wet with spring. Friday mornings are when she usually goes in to see Dr. Tatel, but this week she is going in on Monday because Dr. Tatel is going out of town. This small irregularity feels exciting—evidence that she is well enough to be rescheduled.

In the last few months, she has learned how to turn her body over to medical science as if it were a sick pet. She can be poked and prodded now without feeling judged by the hands examining for error, can watch her blood coil up out of her arm without getting nauseated, can take the cold metallic sting of the stethoscope without feeling light-headed at the idea of her own beating heart. She has had practice, after all. She went to the emergency room at least four times with her brother before he took off. "Annie," he would joke afterward, "you watch those doctors like you're in training."

From the kitchen, Annie can hear Jay grunting on his chin-up bar. In about an hour, he will come out of the study and walk around the apartment, stretching his elbows behind his head, picking up newspapers and magazines, tossing them back down. At about eleven, he will try to sit at the computer and "organize his notes" before he goes to the gym at two o'clock, but will end up online playing a pro-sports betting game based on the stock market instead.

Annie puts on her sneakers and jacket to go for a walk. She has not left the apartment for four days. On Fifth Avenue, she is quickly swept up in the rush of taxis, buses, tourists, shoppers, and can collectors rattling their metal carts over the uneven sidewalk. At the corner of Park and Sixty-fifth Street, there is a Japanese man with thick glasses trying to feed a chocolate popsicle to a pigeon with a stump instead of a foot. Almost half the pigeons collecting tentatively around him have mutant feet—grotesque, fleshy bulbs or string-tangled toes. Annie can barely look at them, but at the same time cannot look away. She watches them hop around the cracked concrete eating invisible morsels, pecking at each other, and clumsily, violently, trying to mate. Why have they chosen this meagre, earthbound existence when they could be airborne, soaring up above the garbage and pollution—beyond the need to fight over an old man's crumbs?

It is almost noon by the time Annie realizes she is too cold to stay out any longer. The sun is flat and white and the budding trees cast a blurry shade on the path. Annie heads uptown, suddenly worried that she has exhausted herself, although she feels quite all right. Nannies and baby carriages and strollers have taken over the sidewalk. Nursery schools and half-day programs are getting out—it is the hour of the under-five-year-old. In the apartment, Jay will be fixing lunch—a protein shake, a bowl of cottage cheese, a chicken breast, and iceberg lettuce. The image of his biceps gathering into a round knot and then releasing under her hand appears in her mind. The thick skin, the light hairs, the full, invincible blue-green veins. Mrs. Tibbs will not bring Anthony home for another half hour.

Annie greets Philipe, the doorman. She suspects he sees her as some sort of charity case of Jay and Cleo's, or, worse yet, as a freeloader. But today her self-consciousness has vanished. Crossing the black and white marble tiles she feels transparent, like one of those tiny clear fish whose slippery bodies filter and refract light, break it into dancing pieces. A clammy layer of perspiration has built up on her lower lip and under her shirt, where the raggedy, nylon-covered underwire of her bra sits against her rib cage. Anticipation—Annie recognizes the same fluttering feeling that rose in her last night.

The elevator opens directly into the apartment, which takes up half the building's twentieth floor. It is bright inside, full of sunlight, dust particles hovering, visible in the air. She has started to shrug her coat off before she realizes there is a hysterical voice coming from the living room. Annie freezes with the coat around her elbows.

"Michele, you can't—" Jay's voice interrupts the higher sound of the girl's voice.

"I can't? Oh, really, I can't? You don't know anything about what I can do, Jay. You don't know shit about me." There is the sucking sound of the sliding door to the roof deck being opened.

The hazy bubble of expectation that has carried Annie upstairs bursts in an instant. Of course Jay has been sleeping with Michele. Hasn't she known this all along? It is her first thought, followed immediately by the urge to back up and away—to get into the elevator, go down to the lobby, out onto the cold street.

"Jesus Christ," Jay says. "What are you? Don't—"

But Annie is no longer listening to the words, just to the tense, terrified sound of his voice, which propels her forward, silently, across the sun-bright floorboards. When she gets to the entrance of the living room, she can see Jay standing in the open expanse of the sliding door and beyond him Michele, looking as though she's about to climb up onto the chest-high brick wall that marks the edge of the terrace. Her hair is pulled back in a severe ponytail that the wind is blowing up in all directions. She looks frightened, a little haggard. And she is high. Annie recognizes the signs from when she lived with Todd.

Both Jay and Michele turn at the same time to look at Annie, although she is not aware of having said anything. "Annie—" Jay says. It is possible that he is crying; his face has an ashen, uncomposed look to it. Annie averts her eyes. He is cowering in the doorway of his own living room, sucked dry by his own fear. The wall Michele is standing at is not even at the edge of the roof—beyond it there are several yards of tar and loose gravel.

Michele says nothing to Annie, but turns to Jay, wide-eyed with a new burst of rage. "You're probably sleeping with her, too. Aren't you? You're probably fucking her right under Cleo's nose. That's convenient. You don't even have to worry about the future, you sick asshole."

"No, no, no," Jay protests, and Annie stands absolutely still, bracing herself against the blow implicit in Michele's words. But they seem to float above her.

The girl looks almost shocked herself, still breathing too fast, but quiet now.

"I'm not dying," Annie says calmly. "I'm waiting."

She is aware of a new edge in her voice. A light, powerful feeling begins to course through her. She can feel her own blood finally—she is aware of its quick rhythm in the channels of her veins. She is aware of its feeding her bones and tissues, rushing from one region of her body to another, fuelled by something bright and strong and weightless, impervious to treatment or disease. It is as if some door had opened inside her and she could hear everything—not just her own heartbeat but the hollow, coddled ticking of Jay's body, the more chaotic, unformed racing of Michele's, and the troubled cacophony all three of them are making. The sound is real and essential and utterly irrelevant. It makes her think of the time her brother gave her a tattoo—a spindly leaf and its shadow curving along the jutting bone of her ankle. It had hurt like nothing she'd known before, and she'd squirmed and bit her lip until it was bloody, feeling nothing but the prick of the needle against delicate nerve endings, the burn of the ink under her skin. That's not you, Todd had said, pointing at her ankle. That's your body— leave it for a minute and come back.

"In fifteen minutes, Anthony will be coming home," Annie says to Michele. "And then Eden. You'd better go home before that."

From his place at the glass door, Jay is watching her.

"What makes you such an expert at what I should do?" Michele says. "You just live here. This isn't even really your home." But her voice is losing its conviction.

"No, it's not," Annie replies. "But I know you should leave now. You should go home and get some rest."

Michele heaves a deep sigh and runs her hand over her hair in a habitual gesture. "If I leave, it's for her sake, not yours, Jay," she says, in a voice that trembles, straining to be haughty. "And for poor Anthony. I'm sorry he has a twisted fuck of a father like you." Then she takes a few steps across the terrace and past Jay into the living room—stiff, careful steps shaped by some combination of pride and restraint. She plucks her leather jacket up off the sofa and walks across the beige-and-white Chinese carpet, leaving faint gray footprints on the plush surface which Carolita, the cleaning lady, will have to spend hours on her hands and knees scrubbing to remove. The thought flits through Annie's mind involuntarily.

When Michele gets to Annie, she pauses, close enough for Annie to smell the acrid, strung-out scent of her sweat. "Don't let him touch you," she says fiercely. There are little bubbles of saliva in the corners of her mouth. In a moment, she is gone, and the heavy oak door to the elevator vestibule clicks shut.

When Annie turns back toward Jay, he has sunk down onto the sofa with his knees wedged in against the coffee table and his head in his hands. He looks too big and ungainly for the spot he has climbed into. The curve of his back has the slump of defeat. What could she ever have thought his body had to offer?

"It's not what you think," Jay begins. "Michele is on something. She's upset—" He breaks off under Annie's gaze.

"It's not my business," she says. "It isn't my home."

"Of course it is. You live here. You take care of Anthony."

Jay shifts his gaze out toward the terrace in a self-conscious, nearsighted way. Looking at him, Annie is filled with the knowledge of things outside this room, of hospital waiting rooms and of the bowels of complicated machines that can see through flesh to what lies beneath it, of wet sidewalks and empty hallways, of the smell of new leaves and spring earth and grease coming out of coffee-shop air vents, of babies in the Park and the serious yellow of taxis and how simple it all looks from above. She is filled with the knowledge of loneliness and suspense and courage. Unlike this man protected by the mantle of good health and good fortune, she knows what is required not to be afraid.

Jay ventures a nervous glance up at her. His face is still pale and covered with a thin sheen of sweat. "I'm sorry—" he begins. "I'm sorry about what Michele—"

"It's all right," Annie interrupts. "It doesn't matter." And she means it.

From the hall, there is the whir of the elevator door opening and the sound of Anthony's high, excited voice, then Mrs. Tibbs's lower, wearier murmur of response. In a moment, Anthony is rushing toward Annie, flushed with fresh air and emotion. He is waving a sheet of paint-stiffened paper so that colored chips fall from it to the floor. "For you—" He is panting. "I made this. I didn't know if you'd be here."

Peter Morris

Pancakes

CHARACTERS

SAM, a businessman, late 20s–early 30s.
BUDDY, an unemployed man, late 20s–early 30s.

SETTING

An apartment.

TIME

The present.

Lights up on the table and two chairs. On the table are a butter dish, a knife and fork, a bottle of syrup, a glass of milk and a plate with an enormous stack of pancakes— four dozen at least. Sam sits at the table eating. He wears a blue business suit with a white shirt and red tie. Buddy enters, running in and sliding to a stop. He wears boxer shorts and a tee shirt and has a severe case of "bed head." He takes a deep breath, inhaling the pancake aroma, then crosses to the table and sits. He stares at Sam. There are several moments of silence with nothing being heard but the sound of Sam eating.

BUDDY: Good?
SAM: Uh huh.
BUDDY: They look good.
SAM: *(His mouth full.)* They are good.

   (Silence.)

BUDDY: Make 'em from scratch?
SAM: *(Mouth still full.)* Bisquick.
BUDDY: Bisquick is good.
SAM: I like Bisquick.
BUDDY: Makes a lotta pancakes.
SAM: I guess.
BUDDY: That's a lotta pancakes.
SAM: I like pancakes.

   (Silence. Buddy watches Sam pour more syrup on his pancakes. Buddy stands and exits. Sam continues to eat.)

BUDDY: *(Offstage.)* There's no more Bisquick.

(No response. Sam just smiles.)

BUDDY: I said, there's no more Bisquick.

SAM: *(His mouth full.)* So?

(Buddy re-enters with empty Bisquick box.)

BUDDY: You used it all up.

SAM: I know.

BUDDY: You could've left me some.

SAM: Well, I didn't.

BUDDY: That sucks. I live here too, you know.

SAM: Just barely.

BUDDY: You gonna bring that up again?

SAM: Just reminding you.

BUDDY: I don't need to be reminded. *(Silence. Buddy sits at the table opposite Sam.)*

BUDDY: Why won't you give me some of those pancakes?

SAM: Because they're mine.

BUDDY: You can't possibly eat them all.

SAM: Just watch me. *(He shoves an entire pancake in his mouth.)*

BUDDY: It's not fair.

SAM: Says you.

BUDDY: You have to give me some.

SAM: I do not. Who said I do? It's not a law. It's not in the Declaration of Independence or the Constitution. Nowhere do they say I have to give you some of my pancakes. What they *do* say is that everyone—*everyone*—is entitled to his own pancakes. This is a land of opportunity. Anyone is free to go out and get all the pancakes he can get his hands on.

BUDDY: What about the Bible?

SAM: What about it?

BUDDY: "Love thy neighbor"?

SAM: That only means you have to love him, not feed him.

BUDDY: You're taking it too literal. You're missing the spirit of the thing.

SAM: Spirit, schmirit, it doesn't say a fucking thing about pancakes.

BUDDY: I can't believe you're not going to give me any.

SAM: Make your own.

BUDDY: There's no more Bisquick.

SAM: Then eat something else.

BUDDY: There *is* nothing. Nothing but some pickle relish and a box of baking soda. I can't make anything out of that.

SAM: Not my problem.

BUDDY: Is that your attitude? "Not my problem"? You're satisfied so to hell with everybody else?

SAM: Not everybody else—just you. *(He resumes eating.)*

BUDDY: Look at you, stuffing your face. You should be ashamed.

SAM: Leave me alone. I'm trying to eat.

BUDDY: So am I! Only I have no food!

SAM: *(Stands and confronts Buddy.)* Then do something about it. Don't stand around begging. That's all you ever do and I'm sick of it. You want some food? Go get it.

BUDDY: Fine! I will! *(Buddy storms out. Beat. Sam sits back down and resumes eating. Buddy storms back in.)* Do you have ten bucks?

SAM: What?

BUDDY: Can you loan me ten bucks?

SAM: On top of the back rent you already owe me?

BUDDY: I said I'd pay you.

SAM: How? You have no job.

BUDDY: I'm looking.

SAM: Look harder.

BUDDY: I just need a little loan.

SAM: What about the big one I've already given you? I've been carrying you for months now but I'm through with it. Do you hear me? I work hard for my money, Buddy.

BUDDY: I'd be happy to work for mine too if someone would just let me. But I can't find a job, OK? I've looked and I've looked and I can't find a job. There's just not a big market these days for philosophers.

SAM: Then do something else.

BUDDY: But I was a philosophy major in college.

SAM: People don't need philosophers.

BUDDY: Yes, they do. They just don't know it. But they will. One day they'll wake up with a spiritual malaise, then they'll need me.

SAM: What the hell is a spiritual mayonnaise?

BUDDY: Malaise! Not mayonnaise! Spiritual malaise! And people like you are gonna get it bad! Trust me! Then I'll be in big demand! You wait and see! *(Pause. Buddy, realizing he is becoming unhinged, pulls himself together. He sits on the floor and begins meditating in the lotus position. Sam just looks at him.)*

SAM: You don't wanna work, do you?

BUDDY: *(In the same rhythm as his chanting.)* Yes, I do.

SAM: You don't. If you did, you wouldn't be sitting around unwashed, unshaved and undressed on a weekday.

BUDDY: It's eight o'clock in the morning.

SAM: Early bird catches the worm.

BUDDY: I don't want worms. I want pancakes.

SAM: Then earn them.

BUDDY: How?

SAM: You can do a little job for me.

BUDDY: What kind of little job?

SAM: You can shine my shoes.

BUDDY: You want me to shine your shoes?

SAM: I'll give you a pancake for each shoe.

BUDDY: One pancake for each shoe.

SAM: That's the offer.

BUDDY: Is that what you want, to humiliate me? Demean me? Well, forget it! I won't do it! I won't! I want at least two pancakes per shoe!

SAM: Deal.

BUDDY: Deal.

(They shake hands.)

BUDDY: Take off your shoes.

SAM: No.

BUDDY: Then how am I supposed to shine them?

SAM: Get down on your knees.

BUDDY: What?

SAM: Get down on your knees and shine my shoes.

BUDDY: Are you serious?

SAM: You want some pancakes, don't you?

BUDDY: You know I do.

SAM: Then get down on your knees.

BUDDY: Sam, please.

SAM: Down!

(Silence. Buddy gets down on his knees.)

BUDDY: What do I use to shine them with?

SAM: *(Deliberately, biting each word.)* Your tongue.

BUDDY: No.

SAM: *(Dangling a pancake in Buddy's face.)* Mmmmm, these are so good.

BUDDY: I won't do it.

SAM: They're so light and fluffy, sweet and delicious. Mmmm-mmmm-mmmm.

BUDDY: You're a pig.

(Sam pushes Buddy over with his foot.)

SAM: *(Seething.)* Watch your mouth, Buddy. You're only here thanks to my good graces. I could've thrown you out months ago. I could throw you out right now. But I won't. Because I pity you. Do you hear me? You're pathetic. Look at you, about to kiss my feet for some lousy pancakes.

BUDDY: I'm hungry. All I've eaten in the last week were some stale Saltines.

SAM: Those were *my* stale Saltines. Bought and paid for with my money. And you didn't even say thank you, did you?

BUDDY: *(Weakly.)* Thank you.

SAM: What was that?

BUDDY: Thank you. I said thank you.

SAM: That's better. *(Sam sits. Buddy slowly gets up off the floor.)* What is it with guys like you? You've always got your hand out. Soft, fleshy hands that haven't seen a day of work.

BUDDY: I need help.

SAM: "The Lord helps those who help themselves." Now *there's* a Bible quote for you.

BUDDY: That's not from the Bible.

SAM: Well, it should be. Now stop bothering me.

BUDDY: How can you be so heartless when you have so much? Look at you, you have all the pancakes.

SAM: That's right. They're all mine. And what, I should just give them to you?

BUDDY: You could share them.

SAM: Why in hell would I want to do that?

BUDDY: It might make you feel good.

(Sam bursts out laughing. Buddy watches in silence.)

SAM: That's the stupidest thing I ever heard.

BUDDY: Some people find great solace in charity.

SAM: What they find, Buddy boy, is a tax deduction. No one does anything without getting something in return. Now, can all the philosophical mumbo jumbo. I have to finish eating. I have a morning conference. They're putting me in charge of the national ad campaign for Good Will. *(He resumes eating.)*

BUDDY: Good Will. They're putting you in charge of "good will." Well, that's just perfect. It's like putting a fox in charge of the hen house.

SAM: *(His mouth full.)* Very funny.

BUDDY: It is. It's hilarious. But I just can't bring myself to laugh. It's a very amusing paradox but I just can't laugh. I'm too weak. I'm hungry and lightheaded and I just don't have the strength to laugh. But it is funny. Not slap-your-thigh funny but wry and ironic. Only God could make a joke like that. The same God that gets a kick out of holocausts and plagues and famines. What a sense of humor that guy's got. He gave you all the pancakes and he gave me none.

SAM: That's life. Some of us have pancakes and some of us have not.

BUDDY: Yup, and you have them. You're the pancake king.

SAM: That's me.

BUDDY: Here, your majesty, why don't I give you some more syrup?

SAM: I don't want any more syrup.

BUDDY: Sure you do. Everybody wants more syrup. *(He picks up the bottle of syrup and begins pouring it on Sam's head.)*

SAM: What the fuck!

BUDDY: And butter? What about some more butter? *(Buddy picks up the butter knife and plunges it in Sam's gut—one, two, three times. Sam falls to the floor.)* You want pancakes? Here, eat some pancakes! *(Buddy begins shoving pancakes into Sam's mouth. He coughs and hacks and begins choking.)* Have another! And another! And another!

(Suddenly, Sam's body goes limp. Buddy sits in his chair and begins ravenously eating pancakes.)

BUDDY: Hungry. So hungry. *(After a moment he looks down at Sam's body.)* You were right, the Lord does help those who help themselves. *(He kicks the lifeless body then resumes eating the pancakes.)*

(Fade to black.)

Ethan Canin
Fly-Fishing for Doctors

This was the summer of 1986, a hot one in Boston, but I never knew that it was summer, exactly, because in the mornings I left before dawn. The walk to my car along the sleeping street was my only time out in the world—a few moments in the dark, when the warm sidewalks were still giving off the evidence of yesterday's heat and walking on them was like passing by the oven in a kitchen. I drove to work along the river, where, by daylight, I knew lovers would come to spread out blankets along the shore, to pilot the little rented sailboats that tacked back and forth beneath the shining bridges, to lie arm in arm under the spreading oaks as lovers do in summertime. My own girlfriend had recently moved into my small apartment, but she was still just two unpacked suitcases and a lump on the other side of the bed. By the time I made it home, every second night, I was too exhausted to talk.

I was a third-year medical student, and in the hospital we were cutting people open. This was my rotation in surgery, the first real rotation I had done, and I was terrified and enthralled. I remember leaning in close while the vilest thing I had ever seen—the cracking of a man's chest—was performed by two surgeons, on either side of the table. The sternum was first split with an electric saw; then a steel spreader was inserted and its gears cranked apart until the ribs opened like a bear trap and revealed the shining organs inside, pulsing to a steady beat. That beat was where we were going.

At the time, I thought I wanted to become a surgeon. I was drawn to operating the way I was drawn to the Boston-style boxing matches that occurred nearly every weekend in my neighborhood—big, tight-shirted brawls outside the pubs in Kenmore Square. Surgery seemed, in a way, like a sport: a simple physical pastime that shot me full of adrenaline. And, though it horrified me, I loved it.

But I was also beginning to suspect—correctly, it turned out—that I would not spend my life in a hospital. Every second morning as I drove by the river, I felt the exquisite urge to keep on going, along Route 2 and straight out of Boston, past the suburbs and onward to the sweet country ponds where I had recently been teaching myself to fly-fish. Even then I must have known that this longing would turn out to be stronger than my ambition. The hospital was death. Summer was life.

I was still learning what is called aseptic technique—the ritual cleanliness that surrounds the operating room. This involved washing one's hands and arms with scrub brushes, donning mask and gown and gloves without touching them anywhere on the outside, and then, while assisting in surgeries that could take half a day, never allowing one's hands to move below the waist or above the shoulders. This last part was the most difficult, for the untrained hand reaches every few moments to the face—to brush back hair, to cough—and against these transgressions the scrub nurse stood careful watch, like a guard at a prison. Whenever my hand strayed—as every beginner's did—she instantly raised her finger and barked, in a satisfied voice, "Contamination!" Embarrassed, I would retreat to the scrub room, to rewash, reglove, and regown.

It was hot in the hospital, but the operating rooms were cool, and the coolest of all were the ones where heart surgery took place. These patients had to be kept chilled. Their open chests were packed with ice, and their blood, which was pumped through a bypass machine, was refrigerated before being returned to the arteries. My job was to hold the suction wand that pulled the blood out of the operating field. I was standing there one day, dreaming of water, of standing waist-deep in a sun-drenched pond in the woods, of arcing a frog-green popper across the cloudless New England sky, when I looked up and saw an ant crawl out of the surgeon's mask.

Nature! Summer! I was the only one who had noticed it, because I was the only one whose gaze was not fixed on the open heart in front of us. But then, seconds later, the ant turned around and disappeared. I wasn't quite sure that it hadn't been a hallucination. I kept my eyes on the surgeon's face, but nothing reappeared. Why did I want it to? What instinct for disorder was this?

Oh, how I longed then to be outside—to be at Baddacook Pond while the grasshoppers and dragonflies and honeybees made their crazy thrumming on the shore. It was blasphemous, I thought, to spend an entire summer inside. By evening, all the world would be pouring out onto the banks of the river—the lightning bugs would be blinking, the girls would be walking bare-armed in their summer dresses—and I would be in an operating room, scrubbed and masked.

A moment later, from beneath the surgeon's mask, a set of black feelers appeared again; then, after a pause, the ant itself emerged, not an illusion after all. It stood perched on the narrow brim of the mask, like a goat on a cliff. It paused there, tested the descent with its forelegs, then changed its mind and headed north, out onto the bridge of the surgeon's nose. I watched his head jerk back; I saw his eyes dart away from the beating heart and then cross as they squinted downward. The scrub nurse snatched her hand to her mouth in surprise. (Contamination! Contamination!) In a flash, she reached up and squashed the thing. Seconds later, she had replaced the surgeon's mask, then her own gown and gloves, then his entire gown. A moment after that we were back at work again. Oh, ant! Oh, summer!

CHAPTER SIX

PATTERN

Pattern is artful, intentional repetition. Pattern is a system of road signs or signals for your reader, designed to move her through your piece smoothly while guiding her attention to the most important parts of the work.

Pattern is how writers *make* meaning. A minister or an essay or a traffic light may *tell* you the meaning. Creative writers must *create meaning*.

Pattern makes any piece of art—dance, painting, sculpture—more complex, layered, and interesting. Pattern is partly why art is different from real life. Real life rambles. Pattern contains a piece, helps it have a shape, a design.

> *Art is pattern informed by sensibility.*
> — SIR HERBERT READ

When you were in secondary school, it's likely you were taught to write in three stages: generate, write, rewrite. You were supposed to brainstorm ideas, then write them all out, and then revise. However, few creative writers work this way. Usually writers enhance the patterns already organically in their writing, focusing on one area at a time: the sounds, the images, and the rhythms, both in terms of what appeals to the ear and what appeals to the eye.

Working with pattern doesn't always come easily, especially at first. Many of us have been taught that, like imitation, repetition is a fault and a flaw. Writing on your own, you might stay locked into preconceptions about repetition. "It's a pattern of behavior." "You're stuck in a pattern." But pattern is repetition on purpose, with a purpose. When we accuse someone of repetition, we imply they are using a pattern without purpose, repeating design elements that are either not worthy of repetition (recall the ultimate pattern song, "100 Bottles of Beer on the Wall") or repeated mindlessly, without a larger goal.

> *Art is the imposing of a pattern on experience, and our aesthetic enjoyment is recognition of the pattern.*
> — ALFRED NORTH WHITEHEAD

Repeating yourself is brave. Repeating yourself calls attention to what you are saying. It takes some confidence to believe your sounds, images, gestures, objects, ideas are worth repeating, and underscoring. Pattern is how you make a great poem out of a good poem, it's how you make fiction out of a stack of anecdotes, how you shape a play from snatches of dialogue. When you make patterns, you make art.

PATTERN BY EAR

Rhyme and Echoes

Perhaps the first pattern we encounter as young readers is rhyme. As tiny children, we are drawn to pattern and we find things that repeat and rhyme especially pleasing: "red fish, blue fish, old fish, new fish" is more intriguing to the ear than "miscellaneous finned creature."

For adult readers, rhyming for the sake of rhyming can be annoying:

> You are the one I love.
> More than the stars above.

The verse seems clunky, forced, amateur, because the word *above* is being used only to rhyme with *love*. It sounds goofy to describe stars and love this way when there are so many more interesting ways to describe them. This writer is not concerned with the image, and nothing pops into the reader's head. You can't see *above* — the word is the opposite of a specific, forcing the reader to think instead of see. The ear may be satisfied, but that is never enough in creative writing. Eyes, ears, mind's eye, touch — the whole system has to be activated.

> *For constructing any work of art you need some principle of repetition or recurrence; that's what gives you rhythm in music and pattern in painting.*
> — NORTHROP FRYE

In contrast, consider the rhymes from the final six lines of the poem "Squirt Gun" by Robert Morgan, which appears on page 98:

> You sprinkle dust along a step
> and scare the cat again and hit
> a June bug like a Messerschmidt.
> And when the gun is almost dry
> you place the barrel between your lips
> and close your eyes and fire a sip.

Here each word that rhymes also fits the poem, contributes to the visual image the poet wants to create. The rhymes aren't random. They serve the image, and the words are interesting and specific.

Rhyme isn't just for poets. Attention to the pattern of language is one of the most important features that distinguish creative writing from writing that informs, instructs, records, or explains.

Consider this line of fiction from short-story writer Aimee Bender: "The walk home from school was a straight line and the boy was not the wandering kind." Notice the rhyme. Bender's rhyme makes the sentence showy, interesting, fresh, and intriguing—good for a first sentence.

PRACTICE

Read the first paragraph of "Cathedral," Raymond Carver's short story on page 297. Make a list of all the words that have sounds that appear in other words in the paragraph. Do you notice a pattern? Do you think this is intentional on Carver's part? Practice substituting other words for some of his choices, ones that do not echo existing words in the passage. What changes?

Once creative writers discover the intricate nuances of sound, they use sound repetition to underline or highlight or even evoke, literally, specific moods and feelings in their readers. One tool writers can use to do this is echoes: sounds that are repeated throughout a piece. Notice how much power writing can generate just through the use of sound echoes. Instead of directly rhyming, and getting trapped into using simplistic or nonmagistic word choices, choose to use echoes. For example, reread "Squirt Gun" on page 98. Trace out the pattern of *s* sounds—how many *s* sounds do you find in the poem? Why would the poet choose to focus on *s*—does that sound go with the subject or the theme of the poem? Yes. "Sss" sounds like squirting. As you go over the poem, trace out other sound patterns—notice the *p* sounds in line one. Pay attention to the sounds Morgan uses to end each line. Do you see or hear sound patterns?

PRACTICE

Reread the page from Art Spiegelman's "Maus" (p. 59). Write a brief description of the kinds of sounds the words make. What kinds of vowels does Spiegelman use more of, long or short? What is the difference in effect of choosing one over the other? What consonants get repeated? What feeling do these consonants tend to evoke? Reread Rita Dove's poem "Driving Through" on page 124. Answer the same series of questions. How are the sound patterns—the sounds that are repeated, or echoed—underscoring the feelings you get from reading each piece?

Consonants and Vowels

Instead of thinking about sound simply as rhyme, pay attention to the vowels and consonants in your sentences. For practice, track the sound patterns — the repeated consonants and vowels — in this paragraph from Nick Flynn's memoir, *Another Bullshit Night in Suck City*. What sounds are repeated, and what are the effects of these sounds?

> In Boston the bars close at one. The next wave of revelers, more gregarious than the earlier crowd, bleary and headed home, push their way inside. Sometimes they give you a hassle, sometimes they flip you a few bucks. A little lit, sometimes they try to start up a conversation, sit on the floor next to you, offer you a drink, want to know your name.

The emphatic *b*'s in the first sentence give way, just as the night does, to looser, more open sounds. Notice the "eh," "ay," "eh," "ay" pattern of vowel sounds in the second sentence. Flynn's writing sounds good. We often take sound for granted when we read; sound can be very subtle.

> *When I write poetry, what I really get first is one or two phrases with a very insistent rhythm. The phrases keep insisting and the poem builds up by a process of accretion.*
> — KENNETH REXROTH

You might be thinking to yourself, "Do I really have to look at every single vowel, every single letter?" Yes. You do. Sound is going to come out of your piece, whether you want it to or not. You have a chance to shape the way your reader feels. Few writers are willing to leave that to chance.

What if Flynn had written without attention to sound and instead started his paragraph:

> In my town, stuff closes early.

And then:

> More people come into the bar after the first set goes home.

See the difference? The first passage sounds better. Why? The sound patterns aren't screaming for attention; Flynn pays attention to how he can connect words and sentences by using similar sounds. When this attention to sound is absent, we might say the writing "doesn't flow."

Some writers feel tempted to go crazy with sounds:

> Hilary heaped hundreds of hippos on the hydrodam.

Uh-oh. Now we are back to nursery-speak, hitting one sound *too* hard, way too hard. Fun to write, this kind of sound is unlikely to capture the attention of a serious audience. It's really fun to speak this way, and you'll evoke laughter in your reader unless your sound pattern is blended in, serves the purpose of the passage, and, like all good patterns, supports the rest of the piece instead of taking center

> *Refrain is one of the most valuable of all form methods. Refrain is a return to the known before one flies again upwards. It is a consolation to the reader, a reassurance that the book has not left his understanding.*
> — JOHN STEINBECK

stage. When a pattern of similar sounds evolves, the piece of writing feels more unified. It flows. Often, the consonant vowel pattern is subtle. You would only notice it if it weren't there. Read the following poem by Ofelia Zepeda. Inventory the sounds. Where are the patterns? What are they made of?

Ofelia Zepeda
Her Hair Is Her Dress

She lived to be over one hundred years old.
She told her children, "When I die, make a pillow for me out of my hair."
She had saved her hair all those years.
She used to say, "I don't want to be scratching through the ashes looking for
    my hair."
In the end her head did rest on her pillow of hair.

She pulls and twists, braiding.
Talking, pulling words down the length of the hair.
Make the part straight, be sure she is in balance.
Follow the path to the rabbit's nest.
That place at the base of the skull.
That private place that is hers alone.
That other place where the heartbeat is visible through the skin.

> *Writing is the science of the various blisses of language.*
> — ROLAND BARTHES

A tender place. Vulnerable.
Hit her there, her knees buckle and she falls face down at your feet.
A place so tender only a baby rabbit might sleep.

PRACTICE

Track the vowel sounds in Peter Meinke's "Atomic Pantoum" on page 330. What's the effect of these vowels on your mood or attitudes? How does Meinke use vowel patterns to make the poem have layers? Do the vowel sounds create any other effects that you notice?

Word Order

Compare:

He came. He saw. He conquered.

To:

He woke up when his alarm clock went off. It looked to be a great day. He thought about what to wear. Maybe he would get up and brush his teeth and wash his face and then get into his clothes or something.

Syntax is the order of the parts of the sentence. In the first example, notice how the syntax echoes—makes a pattern. Each sentence is two words, the parts of speech echoing. The second example doesn't pay attention to syntax. The writer hasn't paid any attention to how he might make a pattern with the sentences themselves. He is missing an opportunity to make his writing reader-friendly, powerful, and effective.

Syntax matters to writers in the same way reading music matters to composers, and the way strategy matters to military generals. The word *syntax* comes from a Greek word, *tassein*, meaning "to arrange" (the word *tactics* is closely related). To write "with syntax" means to write "with tactics." The order of the words matters. Writers *choose* the order, instead of leaving it to chance.

Let's look at Aimee Bender's sentence again:

The walk home from school was a straight line and the boy was not the wandering kind.

Notice how she repeats the same verb, "was," and sets up the syntax of the sentence so that its two parts mirror each other. How differently we would feel about this sentence if she wrote, "The boy walked home. He really didn't get lost much."

Many new writers rely on one basic sentence structure, learned early on. Their basic dance step uses the S-V-O syntax (Subject, Verb, Object). Like this:

I am good.
She left the building.
He woke up.
It was about time.

There is nothing inherently wrong with this syntax pattern. But when a writer uses only that one pattern the writing falls flat.

Notice in the following example from Tobias Wolff's memoir, *This Boy's Life*, how the author uses the basic pattern, inserts a variation, and returns to the basic pattern:

So I passed the hours after school. Sometimes, not very often, I felt lonely. Then I would go home to Roy.

The speaker is struggling with an abusive stepfather. He tries to have regular hours after school, messing around outside, hanging out by himself, avoiding his own house. When he feels lonely (the variation, not normal, not desired, not expected), Wolff uses an atypical sentence pattern to emphasize the unusual, the not-okay-ness—"sometimes, not very often,"—the sentence begins with a stutter-step, pauses—we breathe differently when we read it. It's a little jolt, a little break. The return to S-V-O matches the sense of inevitability—there is nowhere else for Tobias to go. He has to go home. Messing around with the basic sentence pattern creates energy and power. Notice the difference between "Good is what I am" and "I am good." Reread each sentence aloud. Do they sound the same? Do they even mean the same thing? Are there implications in the first version that aren't in the second?

| PRACTICE |

Write a short analysis of the syntax, pattern, and repetition Kathleen Norris uses in her memoir "Rain" on page 53.

Poet E. E. Cummings inverts word order so frequently, it becomes his signature move. Here is a Cummings poem about a mouse, poisoned by someone who doesn't want mice in the house.

E. E. Cummings
(Me up at does)

Me up at does

out of the floor
quietly Stare

a poisoned mouse

still who alive

is asking What
have i done that

You wouldn't have

What's important to remember is that our point of view is inverted in this poem—we are the mouse, looking up at the human. The words are reversed and so is our usual perspective—we don't typically identify with rodents. The syntax is jerky, words seem to be missing; do you almost hold your breath—choke?—as you read the poem? (Another pattern to notice: Why are some words capitalized? Do the capitalized words make a pattern you can make sense of? That's a visual pattern; more on that below.)

Readers appreciate "figuring out" the puzzle that is pattern, but the harder the puzzle is, the more payoff there better be. The mouse poem above is, like the mouse's life, quite brief. (Would you be likely to read a novel written in this style?)

PRACTICE

Read the story "How to Become a Writer" by Lorrie Moore on page 222. Track sound and syntax patterns, noting each example. Are there ways in which the author is "rhyming" sentences, sections, or paragraphs? Her short story imitates a self-help manual, or book on etiquette. What of the syntax of that form has she imported into her pattern? Read the poem "The Boy" by Marie Howe on page 228. Locate as many patterns of rhyme, sound, and syntax as you can.

Rhythm

Notice the differences in rhythm in the following two samples, one from a textbook, the other from the novel *Risk Pool* by Richard Russo:

> The preceding section illustrates the relationships between numerous cohesive devices.

> My father, unlike so many of the men he served with, knew just what he wanted to do when the war was over. He wanted to drink and whore and play the horses.

The rhythm in these two sentences is *very* different. The first is very monochromatic in tone, in part because the rhythm is flat. The second sentence bounces, moves, pulses. It has an interesting beat to it.

A beginning writer may write: "My father was a party animal."

Russo, an experienced novelist, writes: "He was celebrating life. His."

In the second example, Russo uses the typical S-V-O construction, but he slams on the brakes; instead of writing two S-V-O sentences in a row, he slaps down a one-word sentence. Both sentences begin with the "ha" sound of the letter *h*, creating a sound pattern that is counterpointed by the rhythms in the opposing sentences. Four words juxtaposed with one word: *his*. Russo creates humor and energy with syntax.

> *Meter is like the abstract idea of a dance as a choreographer might plan it with no particular performers in mind; rhythm is like a dancer interpreting the dance in a personal way.*
> — JOHN FREDERICK NIMS

The creative writer uses rhythm to punctuate, highlight, emphasize content, and to keep the reader engaged in the piece. Rhythmless writing = boring writing.

Law briefs lack rhythm. Memos from your boss lack rhythm. Bureaucratic writing is trying to be neutral, and creative writing is trying to be interesting, lively, memorable, enjoyable to read. Rhythm is a pattern that lets you do that.

Meter

We call the pattern of rhythms in creative writing *meter*. Just like a speedometer, meter measures how fast you are going, and it gives you information on what syllables or beats are stressed (emphasized) and which ones aren't. That's good information to have. Many new writers resist learning meter—it is complex, and there are a lot of impressive words that do have to be memorized—*spondee* and *trochee* and *pentameter*. But, if your class decides to spend some time on meter, try to remember this: Meter isn't a strict set of rules. Poets and writers make up their rules, use exceptions, reinvent the rules. Meter is feedback. It's information you get about how your poem is going to play out for the reader. Meter is a tool, a fine one. It's not a prison. Your teacher (especially if she or he is a poet) may decide to pursue an in-depth unit on meter. For now, if you choose to learn just one thing about meter, focus on iambic pentameter. You already know a lot about it, and you probably write in it even though you may not be aware you do! Read on.

> *I would sooner write free verse as play tennis with the net down.*
> — ROBERT FROST

Iambic Pentameter. Most poems are written in iambic pentameter. The term sounds fancy, but it isn't highbrow or obscure. It's our daily rhythm. It's a very natural way for speakers of English to put words together. Like the two-step in dance, or 4/4 time in music, it's a pattern of beats, or emphases on syllables, that is quite simple and direct. Chaucer, Shakespeare, Milton, Frost, and Stephen Crane wrote in iambic pentameter.

An iamb is a *da-DUM* sound; two syllables together, with the stress (the stress is the weight or the emphasis) on the second one, as in the word *adore*. The names Heather and Karen are *not* iambs. "Heh-THER" sounds wrong. Ka-REN sounds funny.

Because in English we usually begin sentences with an article—*the, an, a*—so the natural rhythm follows: the house, an egg, a boy. *Da-DUM, da-DUM, da-DUM.*

Set next to each other in a row, in a sentence, iambs always make a pattern:

i-AM-bic ME-ter GOES like THIS.

Some people say it echoes the pattern of a heartbeart (*da-DUM da-DUM*) or footfalls when people walk. It's a powerful pattern.

Pentameter means five units, so iambic pentameter means five *da-DUM*s per line, which is ten syllables per line, as in:

My mistress' eyes are nothing like the sun;

Why five? Humans like fives, we count in fives for a good reason (check your hand). There might be another reason: Take a deep breath. A good, very deep breath. Now, do that again, take a deep breath and this time, count how many times your heart beats. The poet John Frederick Nims calls iambic pentameter "a breathful of heartbeats." Have you taken CPR? What is the ratio of breaths to chest compressions, the substitute heartbeats?

If one purpose of poetry is to resuscitate the human soul, to give us back ourselves, it's no surprise iambic pentameter has become our most common rhythm.

| PRACTICE |

Compose five lines of poetry in iambic pentameter. Then rewrite them, trying to pay no attention to the beat at all. Do you feel like you have a good internal sense of rhythm? When you read the two versions out loud, does one sound better than the other?

Look back at some of your poetry. Are you writing in iambic pentameter without even knowing it? There's a good chance that if you are writing in English, you are using this meter—at least some of the time—unconsciously. Studying creative writing is all about becoming more aware of what you do, and how to direct your attention and your power to greater effect. Readers like iambic pentameter. It's reassuring, predictable, steady, controlled, and clear.

Free Verse. You may not want to write in iambic pentameter all the time. After experimenting with that specific rhythm, you may reject it as a pattern for your work. That's fine. Free verse is just as popular as iambic pentameter. When you write poetry with no rules about syllables or stresses or line length, when you are not following a preexisting pattern, you are writing free verse. In this case, the reader instead of the writer supplies the verbal emphases, and controls the rate of speed, the cadences.

Look at the following example, which does not follow the most common meter, iambic pentameter. Instead, it starts with two stresses together:

One, two
Buckle my shoe
Three, four
Shut the door

The pattern created by the short lines above—it's brisk, curt, peppy, bossy, isn't it? Nursery rhymes are not written in long lines, and you probably don't write a poem about the death of someone very important in two-syllable lines; the pattern is too curt. Consider Walt Whitman's poetry and rap lyrics: Both use long lines to talk about the dead and dying. Long lines create soothing, reflective patterns, and are well-suited to political or philosophical musings.

Think about the difference between saying, "Please consider allowing others to speak," and, "Shut the hell up!" Emphasis matters. Line length matters. Rhythm matters.

Notice how you have been working this semester. Experiment. Don't be stuck in a rut, writing all medium-length lines, medium paragraphs, medium sentences. What happens when you lengthen the line, the sentence? Does the meaning start to shift, too? The tone? What happens when you shorten and tighten, make lines, sentences, stanzas, paragraphs staccato, short? Does the meaning shift? Do you see the piece perhaps going in a new direction entirely? This is how writers work. Pattern isn't decoration or afterthought. It's the engine that drives a piece, the heartbeat. It can be used as a tool for discovery, a way of giving new energy to an old piece.

PRACTICE

Memorize a short poem in iambic pentameter (you may use one from this book, or find one on your own). Does the meter help you internalize the word patterns? Recite your poem aloud. When you say it aloud, do you keep to the meter, or do you vary it to add your own emphases?

PRACTICE

Reread the short story "Bodies" by Jessica Shattuck on page 180. Read and look (and listen!) for sound patterns. First, locate two or three interesting syntax patterns and copy these over in your assignment. Then, find three dialogue passages, and copy these out. Lastly, find a passage where iambs are repeated in a sequence. Noticing where she breaks the pattern each time, what can you say about how Shattuck is using sound to amplify the meaning and richness in the story?

PATTERN BY EYE

Objects

Writers also create patterns out of objects or images in a piece of writing in order to make for more meaningful, cohesive reading. This is called a unified pattern of imagery.

Take an inventory of the specific details, the objects, the "stuff" in your piece. Do you need to have a garage sale? Or do you need a personal shopper, and more carefully chosen objects to layer meaning into your piece?

> *Usually I begin with an image or a phrase; if you follow trustfully, it's surprising how far an image can lead.*
> — JAMES MERRILL

Many beginning writers need *more* stuff in their stories, poems, and plays. They refer to general worlds, but they don't populate these worlds with the details of real life, thereby missing an opportunity not just to be energetic, but to create a complex, interesting, layered pattern of imagery. Don't just stick in random stuff, choose objects that go with or work against the "stuff" in your piece, making interesting visual patterns. Some paper, an idea, blank walls. Hmm. What's the pattern? Vague emptiness? A cigarette, a broken baby stroller with a baby in it, a half-empty warm beer can — that's interesting. Those things make a pattern that affects the reader. There's a pattern of danger, neglect. The images make a pattern all on their own, and that pattern starts to tell a story.

The easiest way to learn more about creating a pattern of objects or images is to read as a writer. You'll need a sheet of paper with two columns. Label one column "animate" and the other "inanimate." Review the story "Bodies" by Jessica Shattuck on page 180. Record each object, as you come to it, in the appropriate column. Listing all the objects in the story, fill up your columns like this:

Object Patterns in Jessica Shattuck's "Bodies"

Animate objects	Inanimate objects
Long-legged, blond, shiny Michele	Halved parsnips like limbs
Glamorous, big-boned, cool Cleo, creative director for giant ad agency	Refrigerator like a hospital
Intense, frank Anthony, the kid	Gallon-and-a-half of water a day

Drooling Eden, the baby	Pilly sweater, baggy jeans, pills, vitamins
Animal-like Jay	Black Central Park
Annie, her body like a sick pet, sneakers, jacket	Pink and orange dahlias projecting pointy orange shadows on the walls

The pattern of objects tells us a lot about the deeper layers of the story. The objects are signals, they create a kind of lighted pathway for the reader. The objects, when strung together, make meaning. That's the power of pattern.

Notice on your object patterns worksheet the pairs that emerge. Michele, looking at the vegetables and seeing limbs. Cleo, hospital. Anthony, too much water. The people in this story, animate objects who have health, sexuality, and beauty, are accompanied by objects that evoke artifice, insensitivity, greed. The weaker characters—young Anthony, sick Annie—are trying, but drowning, turning limp. We know this partly because they are associated with objects that are losing strength or suffocating.

The pattern makes meaning.

Look at just the inanimate objects. Do they create a visual pattern? Do you hear echoes? Yes.

When pulled out and strung together, these objects spell, among other things, decay, loss, and fear.

Shattuck creates, by naming creepy inanimate things at regular intervals throughout her story, a background soundtrack that is thrumming, unnerving, slightly menacing, unpleasant. The reader has an uneasy feeling. That feeling is underscored by the pattern, and the breaks in the pattern; Shattuck includes *Goodnight Moon* and the soundtrack to *The Lion King*: moving, heartfelt pieces. The wholesome sweetness of these objects breaks the image pattern, breaks the sirens and the low-level fighting, underscoring the betrayal, sadness, and decay. To use heavy, dark, sad music in this story could have tipped the whole thing into melodrama.

If Shattuck had chosen to call our attention to the nice, brilliant nephew, the cute white doves in Central Park, the cheerful children in strollers, the helpful doorman in his pressed red suit, the fresh bread from the bakery on 107th Street, the crisp white paper it comes in—and all those things exist in this world, too—the tone of the piece, our feelings when we read, would be *quite* different.

A meaningful pattern of objects is key to a successful piece of creative writing.

When writing a piece set in a house, you don't describe every single room, you don't list everything in the fridge. You choose the items that go with the other items, items that underline or highlight the feeling you want to evoke in the reader. You are a set designer. You can only bring in *a few specific objects*. What do you select to best amplify the drama, your themes? The objects are going to create a pattern—you want to control that pattern. When you bring in flowers, you bring in clashing colors, to echo Michele and Cleo. Instead of providing beauty, these flowers make scary Halloween shadows, like weapons, on the walls. Everything you bring onto your set, you use. The gift of the flowers contrasts with and bounces off Anthony's gift in the final sentence of the story, the painting, so thick with color pieces of it are falling off as he gives it to Annie. Notice the patterns—saliva on Eden's face at the beginning of the story pairs with Michele's "little bubbles of saliva in the corners of her mouth" at the end of the story; Michele is a baby, a dangerous baby. Anthony is curved in a sofa at the beginning of the story, Jay is "sunk down into the sofa with his knees wedged against the coffee table and his head in his hands." A pattern of imagery that sharply underlines the differences in our desire to be comforted and our ability to give and receive love.

So, you do what good set designers do. You have a storehouse of stuff, and you pull out different items until you find a pattern.

PRACTICE

Go through a recent story or creative nonfiction piece of your own and do the animate/inanimate inventory. Consider the implications of the pattern, name the unified images. Are these pointing the reader in the emotional direction you want? What adjustments would you make to create a darker, more intense piece? What different inventory would you collect in order to emphasize the more comic, lighthearted aspects of the piece? Can you add some contrasting items (*Lion King* soundtrack playing while a family falls apart) to enhance the patterns?

Gestures

One of the most intriguing patterns to work with is that of movement—human physical movement, or gestures—throughout your piece. Consider the story of Cinderella, as in Disney's movie version for children. The first gestures are Cinderella's, dancing around the house getting her chores done. Imagine the footwork of the tale—that's the pattern we are tracking now. Then, the next movement pattern: the festive dance of birds and the fairy godmother, getting her ready for the ball. Another dance, with a different shape or pattern to it. It relates to the grand ball, where Cinderella *dances* again, for real this time, with the Prince. The final dance: It's the community's turn, as everyone is thrown into a tizzy while the prince fits the slipper, whirling through the town with his entourage until he finds his match. Tracking and working to align and intensify the patterns of movement in your creative writing gives you a chance to connect the parts of your piece cleverly. Movement attracts the reader. Pattern reinforces theme and meaning.

When the pattern changes, we have the same reaction as when a poet using iambic pentameter substitutes "Hark! Hark!" We pay attention.

Consider the patterns of gestures in Rick Moody's story "Boys" on page 94. Through the whole story, the boys are running and swooping and diving and dashing, tossing and digging, scratching and hollering. So when they stop, stand still, and whisper, that break in the pattern is going to heighten tension, gather our attention, and the writer will be able to make a major point. Pattern is a powerful tool; gestures are the way the writer choreographs her piece.

Notice the opening pattern of gestures in "Bodies" (look back at the opening paragraph on page 180). Annie makes dinner, turns on lights, a child lays his head down on his arm. Annie moves quietly through the kitchen, promises him attention; boy sits up straight. Summary flashback: Annie moves carefully through her days at Cleo's, dancing with her illness. Notice the pattern: In the first section (before the space break) we see up close Annie's moves through her life—they are tender, evenly paced, smooth. In the second section, the pattern her feet make on the floor of her life are the same, they have been static for a long time—since she got sick—and we see the dance from above, from farther back. Pattern. Pattern. Then, in the third section, the pattern changes, yes? The doorbell rings. Anthony puts his hand on his hip—two staccato gestures, boom, boom. It's like a time change in music, a couple of quick leaps in dance. Enter Michele. She *peers, breathes, flashes* and Anthony is *demanding, shouting, squirming, collapsing*. This is a new sequence, a new pattern. Notice the contrast, and how energy is created by establishing a pattern firmly and then changing it dramatically.

PRACTICE

In the Rick Moody story "Boys" on page 94, the movements and gestures are easy to track. Make a list of the gestures you find in the story. These will be different from the verbs you collected earlier; *gestures* refers to actions made by human bodies. What patterns do the gestures create?

Pattern on the Page

Another important aspect of pattern is the way the elements of your writing play out on the page. What's the pattern created by your paragraphs, your stanzas? There are concrete poems—where the poem is a two-dimensional portrait of its subject, a fire hydrant poem in the shape of a fire hydrant, a forsythia poem in the shape of a shrub—and we look at that structure in the next chapter.

> *Form is like asbestos gloves that allow you to pick up material too hot to handle otherwise.*
> — ADRIENNE RICH

A more subtle but just as creative way to approach pattern is to consider the visual patterns your work creates: How does your piece look on the page to the reader's eye? How does your writing cover — literally — the white page? If your paragraphs are taking up whole pages, can you initiate a more pleasing pattern of white space, indents, and breaks? Do your stanzas create a pattern — the same number of lines, lines about the same length? Are you deliberately changing the pattern, or is your creative writing sprawling across the page? Are your lines ragged on purpose? Or just because you haven't attended to that pattern yet?

White space matters. White space acts as a rest does in music; the reader gets to pause, breathe. White space alternating with short blocks of text speeds the pace (a staccato effect). Repeating visual elements — big block of text (paragraph, stanza, speech) with white space — create a polished, professional look and invite the reader in. The piece feels crafted, not dashed off. Long sections of text with no white space breaks are more difficult, the reader may become lost. Most writers employ *other patterns* — sound, syntax, rhythm, etc. — to help the reader stay on track through a long section.

The visual outline, or pattern, involves blocks of text and blocks of white space. Because as writers we are so limited by these two tools, it's absolutely essential we attend to the nuances of shape — literally, the way the piece looks on the page.

PRACTICE

Look back once again at Jamaica Kincaid's "Girl" (p. 55). If it were presented in many tiny paragraphs, how would that visual pattern affect your reading of the piece? What if Rick Moody's "Boys" (p. 94) was presented in stanzas, or sometimes in long paragraphs, sometimes in short? How would those pattern changes affect the meaning of the piece?

Where a piece begins on the page, where the title is, where a piece ends on the page — all of these things affect the pattern, the way the words are presented. Experiment to find the best pattern for your piece. Question why you indent where you do, be flexible when testing options. Don't settle for your first instinct. Play a little. We have text, and we have white space. How much pattern can you eke out of those two options without distracting or alarming your reader? As always, pattern supports, complements, and underscores the theme and purpose of the piece; pattern shouldn't try to take over. Good patterns enhance and support the meaning of creative writing.

LAYERING PATTERNS

Musicians like Jack White can write a song that repeats simple, everyday words:

No one never
No one never
No one never
Going to let you down now

> *It started as a lark and then became something beautiful.*
> — JACK WHITE

However, he also employs drums, marimba, and live sounds to create other inter-secting and overlapping patterns. Super-simple lyrics repeat effectively in music, but less successfully as standalone poems on the page. Often, song lyrics have to be sharp, hard, clear, and simple and straightforward in order to show up against all the other patterns in music. On the page, on their own, the words lack energy. What makes a beautiful wild paisley in the ear is a thin grey line on the page.

Creative writers, not supported by a three-piece band, have to write the bass line, the percussion, the melody, *and* the lyrics. Paged words *need* a higher vol-ume—more intricacy, subtle sounds, rhythms, visuals, etc.—much more so than sung words. In order to give our work proper backup, writers layer patterns, using more than one at a time. Just like a musician does.

After you have recorded the vocals, you're back in the studio, mixing, laying down new tracks, focusing each time on certain elements—the bass line, the percussion—and that's very much like the work we will do with pattern. While playing with pattern, think of yourself as the "mix master" and look for echoes. If you have something you like in your piece, repeat it.

PRACTICE

Rick Moody, in "Boys" on page 94, and Jamaica Kincaid, in "Girl" on page 55, provide examples of prose writers using sound, rhythm, rhyme—patterns of language—in addi-tion to physical pattern. Make two lists, one for each piece, where you list every single ele-ment that is used as part of a pattern.

Notice how writers use the principles of tension to make their patterns work harder. In Rick Moody's "Boys," the author uses a list pattern, like a grocery list, to name the kind of grief—sibling loss—that can hardly be spoken of coher-ently, that kind of pain that is with you every day, never goes away, but is as un-like a typical list item as you can get. We were running along, through our lives, the story suggests, and then the world broke into two pieces and we were never the same again. Instead of using a matching pattern, Moody chooses a syntax pattern that works *against* the other patterns of the piece.

PRACTICE

Read Lorrie Moore's story "How to Become a Writer" on page 220. How does the pattern (syntax and otherwise) create tension by working against the theme/subject/meaning of the overall story? List at least three examples, quoting sentences or short sections to explain how the pattern "goes against the grain" of the story.

Using clashing patterns on purpose creates energy, intensity, and can even allow you to discover insight into your own work. In the excerpt from *The Pharmacist's Mate* on page 60, Amy Fusselman uses the journal entries of her dad to write the history of his life; when she puts snapshots of her own life next to his pieces, she doesn't get a history of his life, as we might expect, she gets glimpses into the future—hers. Lorrie Moore writes many stories like the one included in this textbook, where she takes the conventional patterns of syntax, rhythm, and visuals found in self-help books and etiquette how-to guides and inserts images, gestures, and sound patterns associated with girls behaving badly or suburban families flailing. The controlled patterns of the how-to books, when juxtaposed with the messy, uneven, difficult traumas she writes about, create tension, friction, and irony.

It's *how* you say what you say that marks you as a successful writer. In creative writing, originality lies not in subject matter—it's unlikely you will be able to come up with a new subject—but rather in your prowess with pattern.

WRITING PROJECTS

1. Reread Mary Paumier Jones's "The Opposite of Saffron" on page 219. Make a catalog—a list—of each object (bed, desk, statue, dictionary, etc.) in this creative nonfiction. What can you say about the world evoked by this pattern of "stuff"? Create a story, poem, memoir, or monologue.

2. Make a list of *kinds* of writing with which you are quite familiar. The strategy guide for Halo or Zelda. The Chilton's manual for your Subaru. Liner notes. Field guides. Chemistry textbook-ese. Recipe books, comic books, yoga books. Choose one, and write a piece *about something very different*, just as Lorrie Moore marries the self-help book with the making of a writer. After you get a first draft down, go back and see if you can change any words to emphasize sound, rhythm. Is your syntax like that of your model? Try to work against pattern to create tension; if the hymn is your model for syntax, you

might write about doubting God (Emily Dickinson does this). Your piece may be poetry, creative nonfiction, a play, or fiction.

3. Construct a story from gesture patterns. Write a story that uses the same gesture pattern (simplify as needed, so that the first two sections would be "slow," "slow," and then "fast" for the third, etc.) as in "Bodies" (or another story of your or your teacher's choosing).

4. Take any poem or prose piece you have been working on this semester, and tune the sounds. Work in some near rhymes, echo words and sounds, and line up vowels and consonants. Read the new version aloud. What do your listeners think are the best parts of the piece?

5. Reread "af•ter•glow" by A. Van Jordan on page 55. List all the patterns you can find in this piece. Then, try a prose poem of your own, using a dictionary definition format, employing as many patterns as Jordan does.

6. Write a short piece (poem, story, memoir, or prose poem) in which you use lots of inverted syntax. Make your piece about a situation that is upside down, or tell it from a perspective that is the opposite of what we expect.

PATTERN WORKSHOP

The prompts below will help you constructively discuss your classmates' work.

1. Read your peer's work and with a highlighter or by underlining, identify patterns of rhyme and echo in this piece.

2. Locate at least three repeated consonant patterns and three repeated vowel patterns that serve to unify the piece, or emphasize words in a special way.

3. Comment on the rhythm in the piece. If the piece is poetry, does the poet use iambic pentameter? If the poet does not, rewrite one of the poem's lines, transforming it into iambic pentameter, making any changes you must in order to make the rhythm follow the pattern.

4. Visually, when you look at the work on the page, do you notice any interesting patterns? Any awkward widows or orphans, lines left stranded at the bottom or top of a page, or space breaks? Are there places or ways the writer could rework the piece in order to make it visually more interesting?

5. List the objects referred to in the writing. Is there a way—by either substituting objects or naming more specific, more specialized versions of the objects

already named—to create a pattern? Do the same for the gestures (human movements). Is there a pattern? Is the work choreographed?

6. End by giving the writer whose work you are examining four concluding comments: Name two aspects of pattern in the piece that are well done, and name the two techniques from this chapter that could use the most attention in revision.

Mary Paumier Jones
The Opposite of Saffron

MINNEAPOLIS, MINNESOTA

I don't remember this. I was too young. But my mother and father told of my childhood habit time and again. From their point of view: their first child wakes in the middle of the night, wakes them up too, not with cries but with giggles. She laughs and recites all the words they have taught her, her litany. I picture Mom getting back in bed after the first time. "What's the matter?" "Nothing, she's laughing and reciting her words." "Now?" "Yes, now." Night after night I did the same.

One day Dad taught me to say Minneapolis, Minnesota, a triumph of such magnitude it became my permanent finale, new words inserted before its resonance. When they heard "Minneapolis, Minnesota," my parents knew they could go back to sleep.

DICTIONARIES

One grade school summer I set myself a daily regime. In the room I shared with my sister at a small desk, I—what should I call it, played school? studied? Nothing sounds exactly right. But I allotted time for this and that, and day after day found satisfaction there alone.

Praying was one thing I did, or my version of it, which had a lot in common with daydreaming, a blue and white statue of the Virgin Mary with the snake under her foot there to inspire me to fantasies of sainthood in which I was beloved and admired by millions.

And I read the dictionary—yes, read the dictionary. My goal was to get through it in the course of the summer—which I'm sure I didn't do, but no matter. The column of words were an endless feast.

Some forty years later I bought a used set of the tiny print edition of the Oxford English Dictionary. I had to find a stand magnifier for it because using the hand-held one that comes with it makes me nauseous. So now I can look up any English word and get its entire history complete with examples of use through the centuries, right in the comfort of my own home.

I lust after the large print edition—or the regular size print edition, I should say—the new updated twenty-four volume $2500.00 one. A set sits proudly on the ledge behind the cash registers in a bookstore I frequent. Whenever I buy anything—which is appallingly often—I look at it and fantasize saying, "Oh, and throw in the OED too."

SYZYGY

A word I looked up: syzygy. (File it away in case you ever have three y's in Scrabble—or can you have three y's in Scrabble?) The morning paper announced that the moon's perigee was falling on its syzygy. The paper called these words "cold and rational," an odd description because syzygy sounds to me as if it sizzles, which indeed it does, coming from the Greek for yoke, pair, conjunction, copulation. (Remember *copulative* verbs? What a shame they've been demoted to *linking*.)

A curious thing has happened to syzygy; time can do strange things to words as well as people. Originally referring to the conjunction of two heavenly bodies, since sometime in the 1700's syzygy has included both conjunction and opposition, so the word has become one of those few whose meaning has extended to include its opposite.

I knew there was a full moon coming. The full is the opposition, the syzygy when the sun and the moon are aligned on opposite sides of the earth. The moon's perigee is the point in its orbit where it is closest to earth. About once a year or so, the full moon occurs at the point when the moon is closest, the perigee and syzygy together. If the clouds clear off, we'll see a big moon tonight.

THE POSSIBLE SUNSHINE

All February the clouds refused to clear off. "Cold air moving over Lake Ontario formed the clouds that blocked the sun," the paper said. "The city got only twenty percent of the possible sunshine."

Then one morning it is over. Objects have volume in space, reflect light, take up room. We have been looking at the world with one eye closed, thinking it flat, circle outlined on a two-dimensional page instead of crosshatched sphere bulging forward, casting shadow.

Telephone wires scallop the road. Cars trail bulbous gray shapes. I'll need my sunglasses—where might they be? Porch railings stripe porch and wall. My old dog feels a rush of youth, pulls against the double leash. And I—even I—am here, my being unmistakable. I cast a shadow, therefore I am.

Odd, but we don't think about it, how the absence of sun is also the absence of shadow.

JUST THE OPPOSITE

In T'ai Chi class Dr. Young talked about yin and yang. In the beginning square form, each movement is followed by a pause: the movement is yin, the pause yang. To my Western ears this smacks of sexism; the masculine principle acting, the feminine doing nothing. But I eventually begin to learn the pause is not nothing. Given its proper weight, gravity, and time, the pause does its work, its stretch, its subtle modification of the quality of the move before and the one to come. Later in the round form, the movement is continuous. Yin and yang, though still opposite, are inscrutably simultaneous, engaged in an ancient abstract intercourse.

In Sunday's *New York Times* David Richards reviews a stage performance by George C. Scott. To encompass it he proposes what he calls a "theory of contradictory impulses." Scott excels in a mediocre role, Richards says, because before giving the audience one emotion, he gives a hint of its opposite: laughter before tears, hate before love. This works because it reflects how life is, each emotion closer to its opposite than to anything like itself.

As a child in Eastern Europe, fiber artist Neda Al-Hilali knit a lot of gray socks for the family, always gray. She lusted for color and when she once managed to get some bright yarn, she hid it as an American boy might his copy of *Playboy*, looking at it, touching, working in secret ecstasy under her bedcovers.

Now she is internationally known for her mastery of color. And personally known as a wonderful cook—her classes usually end with festive party meals. When asked how she gets her colors so vibrant, she replies that she always puts a dash of the opposite color dye in the pot. "You know," she says, as if everyone does, "just like you put in a bit of an opposite spice when you cook."

Carolyn Kizer
Parents' Pantoum
for Maxine Kumin

Where did these enormous children come from,
More ladylike than we have ever been?
Some of ours look older than we feel.
How did they appear in their long dresses

More ladylike than we have ever been?
But they moan about their aging more than we do,
In their fragile heels and long black dresses.
They say they admire our youthful spontaneity.

They moan about their aging more than we do,
A somber group—why don't they brighten up?
Though they say they admire our youthful spontaneity
They beg us to be dignified like them

As they ignore our pleas to brighten up.
Someday perhaps we'll capture their attention
Then we won't try to be dignified like them
Nor they to be so gently patronizing.

Someday perhaps we'll capture their attention.
Don't they know that we're supposed to be the stars?
Instead they are so gently patronizing.
It makes us feel like children — second-childish?

Perhaps we're too accustomed to be stars,
The famous flowers glowing in the garden,
So now we pout like children. Second-childish?
Quaint fragments of forgotten history?

Lorrie Moore
How to Become a Writer

First, try to be something, anything, else. A movie star/astronaut. A movie star/missionary. A movie star/kindergarten teacher. President of the World. Fail miserably. It is best if you fail at an early age — say, fourteen. Early, critical disillusionment is necessary so that at fifteen you can write long haiku sequences about thwarted desire. It is a pond, a cherry blossom, a wind brushing against sparrow wing leaving for mountain. Count the syllables. Show it to your mom. She is tough and practical. She has a son in Vietnam and a husband who may be having an affair. She believes in wearing brown because it hides spots. She'll look briefly at your writing, then back up at you with a face blank as a donut. She'll say: "How about emptying the dishwasher?" Look away. Shove the forks in the fork drawer. Accidentally break one of the freebie gas station glasses. This is the required pain and suffering. This is only for starters.

In your high school English class look at Mr. Killian's face. Decide faces are important. Write a villanelle about pores. Struggle. Write a sonnet. Count the syllables: nine, ten, eleven, thirteen. Decide to experiment with fiction. Here you don't have to count syllables. Write a short story about an elderly man and woman who accidentally shoot each other in the head, the result of an inexplicable malfunction of a shotgun which appears mysteriously in their living room one night. Give it to Mr. Killian as your final project. When you get it back, he has written on it: "Some of your images are quite nice, but you have no sense of plot." When you are home, in the privacy of your own room, faintly scrawl in pencil beneath his black-inked comments: "Plots are for dead people, pore-face."

Take all the babysitting jobs you can get. You are great with kids. They love you. You tell them stories about old people who die idiot deaths. You sing them songs like "Blue Bells of Scotland," which is their favorite. And when they are in their pajamas and have finally stopped pinching each other, when they are fast asleep, you read every sex manual in the house, and wonder how on earth anyone could ever do those things with someone they truly loved. Fall asleep in a chair reading Mr. McMurphy's *Playboy*. When the McMurphys come home, they will tap you on the shoulder, look at the magazine in your lap, and grin. You will want to die. They will ask you if Tracey took her medicine all right. Explain, yes, she did, that you promised her a story if she would take it like a big girl and that seemed to work out just fine. "Oh, marvelous," they will exclaim.

Try to smile proudly.

Apply to college as a child psychology major.

As a child psychology major, you have some electives. You've always liked birds. Sign up for something called "The Ornithological Field Trip." It meets Tuesdays and Thursdays at two. When you arrive at Room 134 on the first day of class, everyone is sitting around a seminar table talking about metaphors. You've heard of these. After a short, excruciating while, raise your hand and say diffidently, "Excuse me, isn't this Birdwatching One-oh-one?" The class stops and turns to look at you. They seem to all have one face—giant and blank as a vandalized clock. Someone with a beard booms out, "No, this is Creative Writing." Say: "Oh—right," as if perhaps you knew all along. Look down at your schedule. Wonder how the hell you ended up here. The computer, apparently, has made an error. You start to get up to leave and then don't. The lines at the registrar this week are huge. Perhaps you should stick with this mistake. Perhaps your creative writing isn't all that bad. Perhaps it is fate. Perhaps this is what your dad meant when he said, "It's the age of computers, Francie, it's the age of computers."

Decide that you like college life. In your dorm you meet many nice people. Some are smarter than you. And some, you notice, are dumber than you. You will continue, unfortunately, to view the world in exactly these terms for the rest of your life.

The assignment this week in creative writing is to narrate a violent happening. Turn in a story about driving with your Uncle Gordon and another one about two old people who are accidentally electrocuted when they go to turn on a badly wired desk lamp. The teacher will hand them back to you with comments:

"Much of your writing is smooth and energetic. You have, however, a ludicrous notion of plot." Write another story about a man and a woman who, in the very first paragraph, have their lower torsos accidentally blitzed away by dynamite. In the second paragraph, with the insurance money, they buy a frozen yogurt stand together. There are six more paragraphs. You read the whole thing out loud in class. No one likes it. They say your sense of plot is outrageous and incompetent. After class someone asks you if you are crazy.

Decide that perhaps you should stick to comedies. Start dating someone who is funny, someone who has what in high school you called a "really great sense of humor" and what now your creative writing class calls "self-contempt giving rise to comic form." Write down all of his jokes, but don't tell him you are doing this. Make up anagrams of his old girlfriend's name and name all of your socially handicapped characters with them. Tell him his old girlfriend is in all of your stories and then watch how funny he can be, see what a really great sense of humor he can have.

Your child psychology advisor tells you you are neglecting courses in your major. What you spend the most time on should be what you're majoring in. Say yes, you understand.

In creative writing seminars over the next two years, everyone continues to smoke cigarettes and ask the same things: "But does it work?" "Why should we care about this character?" "Have you earned this cliché?" These seem like important questions.

On days when it is your turn, you look at the class hopefully as they scour your mimeographs for a plot. They look back up at you, drag deeply, and then smile in a sweet sort of way.

You spend too much time slouched and demoralized. Your boyfriend suggests bicycling. Your roommate suggests a new boyfriend. You are said to be self-mutilating and losing weight, but you continue writing. The only happiness you have is writing something new, in the middle of the night, armpits damp, heart pounding, something no one has yet seen. You have only those brief, fragile, untested moments of exhilaration when you know: you are a genius. Understand what you must do. Switch majors. The kids in your nursery project will be disappointed, but you have a calling, an urge, a delusion, an unfortunate habit. You have, as your mother would say, fallen in with a bad crowd.

Why write? Where does writing come from? These are questions to ask yourself. They are like: Where does dust come from? Or: Why is there war? Or: If there's a God, then why is my brother now a cripple?

These are questions that you keep in your wallet, like calling cards. These are questions, your creative writing teacher says, that are good to address in your journals but rarely in your fiction.

The writing professor this fall is stressing the Power of the Imagination. Which means he doesn't want long descriptive stories about your camping trip last July. He wants you to start in a realistic context but then to alter it. Like recombinant DNA. He wants you to let your imagination sail, to let it grow big-bellied in the wind. This is a quote from Shakespeare.

Tell your roommate your great idea, your great exercise of imaginative power: a transformation of Melville to contemporary life. It will be about monomania and the fish-eat-fish world of life insurance in Rochester, New York. The first line will be "Call me Fishmeal," and it will feature a menopausal suburban husband named Richard, who because he is so depressed all the time is called "Mopey Dick" by his witty wife Elaine. Say to your roommate: "Mopey Dick, get it?" Your roommate looks at you, her face blank as a large Kleenex. She comes up to you, like a buddy, and puts an arm around your burdened shoulders. "Listen, Francie," she says, slow as speech therapy. "Let's go out and get a big beer."

The seminar doesn't like this one either. You suspect they are beginning to feel sorry for you. They say: "You have to think about what is happening. Where is the story here?"

The next semester the writing professor is obsessed with writing from personal experience. You must write from what you know, from what has happened to you. He wants deaths, he wants camping trips. Think about what has happened to you. In three years there have been three things: you lost your virginity; your parents got divorced; and your brother came home from a forest ten miles from the Cambodian border with only half a thigh, a permanent smirk nestled into one corner of his mouth.

About the first you write: "It created a new space, which hurt and cried in a voice that wasn't mine, 'I'm not the same anymore, but I'll be okay.' "

About the second you write an elaborate story of an old married couple who stumble upon an unknown land mine in their kitchen and accidentally blow themselves up. You call it: "For Better or for Liverwurst."

About the last you write nothing. There are no words for this. Your typewriter hums. You can find no words.

At undergraduate cocktail parties, people say, "Oh, you write? What do you write about?" Your roommate, who has consumed too much wine, too little cheese, and no crackers at all, blurts: "Oh, my god, she always writes about her dumb boyfriend."

Later on in life you will learn that writers are merely open, helpless texts with no real understanding of what they have written and therefore must half-believe anything and everything that is said of them. You, however, have not yet reached this stage of literary criticism. You stiffen and say, "I do not," the same way you said it when someone in the fourth grade accused you of really liking oboe lessons and your parents really weren't just making you take them.

Insist you are not very interested in any one subject at all, that you are interested in the music of language, that you are interested in—in—syllables, because they are the atoms of poetry, the cells of the mind, the breath of the soul. Begin to feel woozy. Stare into your plastic wine cup.

"Syllables?" you will hear someone ask, voice trailing off, as they glide slowly toward the reassuring white of the dip.

Begin to wonder what you do write about. Or if you have anything to say. Or if there even is such a thing as a thing to say. Limit these thoughts to no more than ten minutes a day; like sit-ups, they can make you thin.

You will read somewhere that all writing has to do with one's genitals. Don't dwell on this. It will make you nervous.

Your mother will come visit you. She will look at the circles under your eyes and hand you a brown book with a brown briefcase on the cover. It is entitled: *How to Become a Business Executive.* She has also brought the *Names for Baby* encyclopedia you asked for; one of your characters, the aging clown–school teacher, needs a new name. Your mother will shake her head and say: "Francie, Francie, remember when you were going to be a child psychology major?"

Say: "Mom, I like to write."

She'll say: "Sure you like to write. Of course. Sure you like to write."

Write a story about a confused music student and title it: "Schubert Was the One with the Glasses, Right?" It's not a big hit, although your roommate likes the part where the two violinists accidentally blow themselves up in a recital room. "I went out with a violinist once," she says, snapping her gum.

Thank god you are taking other courses. You can find sanctuary in nineteenth-century ontological snags and invertebrate courting rituals. Certain globular mollusks have what is called "Sex by the Arm." The male octopus, for instance, loses the end of one arm when placing it inside the female body during intercourse. Marine biologists call it "Seven Heaven." Be glad you know these things. Be glad you are not just a writer. Apply to law school.

From here on in, many things can happen. But the main one will be this: you decide not to go to law school after all, and, instead, you spend a good, big chunk of your adult life telling people how you decided not to go to law school after all. Somehow you end up writing again. Perhaps you go to graduate school. Perhaps you work odd jobs and take writing courses at night. Perhaps you are working on a novel and writing down all the clever remarks and intimate personal confessions you hear during the day. Perhaps you are losing your pals, your acquaintances, your balance.

You have broken up with your boyfriend. You now go out with men who, instead of whispering "I love you," shout: "Do it to me, baby." This is good for your writing.

Sooner or later you have a finished manuscript more or less. People look at it in a vaguely troubled sort of way and say, "I'll bet becoming a writer was always a fantasy of yours, wasn't it?" Your lips dry to salt. Say that of all the fantasies possible in the world, you can't imagine being a writer even making the top twenty. Tell them you were going to be a child psychology major. "I bet," they always sigh, "you'd be great with kids." Scowl fiercely. Tell them you're a walking blade.

Quit classes. Quit jobs. Cash in old savings bonds. Now you have time like warts on your hands. Slowly copy all of your friends' addresses into a new address book.

Vacuum. Chew cough drops. Keep a folder full of fragments.

An eyelid darkening sideways.
World as conspiracy.
Possible plot? A woman gets on a bus.
Suppose you threw a love affair and nobody came.

At home drink a lot of coffee. At Howard Johnson's order the cole slaw. Consider how it looks like the soggy confetti of a map: where you've been, where you're going—"You Are Here," says the red star on the back of the menu.

Occasionally a date with a face blank as a sheet of paper asks you whether writers often become discouraged. Say that sometimes they do and sometimes they do. Say it's a lot like having polio.

"Interesting," smiles your date, and then he looks down at his arm hairs and starts to smooth them, all, always, in the same direction.

Marie Howe

The Boy

My older brother is walking down the sidewalk into the suburban summer night:
white T-shirt, blue jeans—to the field at the end of the street.

Hangers Hideout the boys called it, an undeveloped plot, a pit overgrown
with weeds, some old furniture thrown down there,

and some metal hangers clinking in the trees like wind chimes.
He's running away from home because our father wants to cut his hair.

And in two more days our father will convince me to go to him—you know
where he is—and talk to him: No reprisals. He promised. A small parade of kids

in feet pajamas will accompany me, their voices like the first peepers in spring.
And my brother will walk ahead of us home, and my father

will shave his head bald, and my brother will not speak to anyone the next
month, not a word, not *pass the milk*, nothing.

What happened in our house taught my brothers how to leave, how to walk
down a sidewalk without looking back.

I was the girl. What happened taught me to follow him, whoever he was,
calling and calling his name.

CHAPTER SEVEN

INSIGHT

Before you edit your work and think about turning in a final draft or sending it off to a literary magazine or publisher, make sure your creative writing includes insights. *Insights* are your careful, specific observations about how and why people behave as they do. Insights add up to wisdom. In this chapter, we'll look at how to go about deepening and intensifying creative writing so that it is insightful and, sometimes, wise. Creative writing—literature—is devoted to exploring the complex aspects of human experience. We read to be entertained, yes, but also to learn and understand more about who we are, how we function, why we are here, and what our lives mean.

"Cathedral," the short story by Raymond Carver on page 297, contains numerous insights into how sighted people behave around the blind and how married people behave, resulting in wisdom about human growth, the potential for people to change their vision of the world. *The Pharmacist's Mate* (excerpted on p. 60), Amy Fusselman's memoir, contains wisdom about asking questions, changing your mind, and passing a habit of observation down through the generations. If you look closely at your subjects, you probably notice the interesting features of human nature—why we do the things we do, why we avoid certain situations, why we repeat behaviors that are clearly counterproductive.

In presenting her portrait of truants in "We Real Cool" (p. 292), poet Gwendolyn Brooks presents insight into the romanticized attitudes toward death held by members of a gang. In "How to Become a Writer" (p. 222), Lorrie Moore presents the wisdom a student writer struggles to apprehend and questions what we think we are learning when we attend college, how school affects our dreams. Having survived high school, you know a lot more about human nature than you might think. How to bring the insights—your inner wisdom—up from within your soul and out onto the page, reflected in the images you present your reader—is a core part of your lifelong work as a writer.

PRINCIPLES OF INSIGHT

"War is bad" isn't really an insight; it may be based on wisdom, but creative writing almost always finds its gold in the tiny crevices of human experience. Good writers don't sit down and plunk down brilliant insights, poking in bits of wisdom here and there throughout a piece like gelled fruit in a fruitcake. Good creative writers learn how to reenter the scenes and moments in their writing that might yield up an insight, and they let the speakers, and the characters in their work discover insights. Working with the strategy of insight is really just a matter of *practicing* noticing and recording in this new way: Creative writers are explorer-discoverers, finding insights as they work rather than working from conclusions, and then using the work to illustrate canned or packaged ideas. For example, if you take six photographs of your mother and study them closely, and work hard to write images that reveal specific aspects of her, you will likely discover more than one or two insights about your mother. Parts of her personality will come into focus. The reasons why she does things the way she does might become suddenly clear. This is much more interesting for your reader than you deciding, in advance, "I will write an essay about my mother the nut," and then proceeding to marshal evidence you have already decided will fit your thesis.

> *There is only one trait that marks the writer. He is always watching. It's a kind of trick of mind and he is born with it.*
> — MORLEY CALLAGHAN

Sometimes we come up with an insight separate from the writing process; but most often, we find our insights, the essential wisdom in our works, while we are writing, during the process of shaping energy, increasing tension, playing with pattern. Those very strategies are what lead us to wisdom. It's more fun to know what you are going to find out; it's scary to write in this open-ended discovery mode. But knowing ahead of time what you want to say too often leads to clichés, not wisdom. War is bad. (We already know.) Love is difficult. (We already know.) Road trips are fun. (Sometimes, sort of.) Good writers stay open-ended. They use the writing to search for *new ways of looking at a topic*. And good writers stay small. Instead of trying for the big statement, they focus on getting the exact nature of the truth of an afternoon. Wisdom is more reliably found in the very specific parts of your piece, not in the lofty ideas in your head.

You won't ever know exactly what it is you are going to produce. Most experienced writers say this uncertain, slightly daft feeling doesn't go away. Good writers — smart writers — trust the process. They trust, like a diver, that if they enter the depths the same way, each time, focusing on their technique, using visual cues, they will sometimes produce insights — true, organic, and whole. And those kinds of insights *are* wisdom.

"A writer is not so much someone who has something to say as he is someone who has found a process that will bring about new things he would not have thought of if he had not started to say them," William Stafford writes in *Writing the Australian Crawl*. "That is, he does not draw on a reservoir; instead he engages in an activity that brings to him a whole succession of unforeseen stories, poems, essays, plays." It's this activity—creative writing, our method for launching and staying hooked into an image—that is the process of wisdom-finding.

Wisdom is strongest when it emerges out of the work rather than when it's imposed on it. So, keep focused tightly to the images, work small, and trust your material to reveal insights rather than forcing them into your works. What follows are some specific techniques you can practice to increase the level of insight in your creative writing.

> *A writer's mind seems to be situated partly in the solar plexus and party in the head.*
>
> — ETHEL WILSON

PRACTICE

Reread one of your favorite published pieces. What is directly stated in the piece that could be considered an insight of some kind? Are there indirect statements that show the author's wise mind at work? Stepping back and taking a look at the overall wisdom of the piece, how does the writer contribute to our collective understanding of a particular aspect of human experience?

Accuracy

In order to be considered a wise, deep, true, and lasting writer, you must be dead-on accurate in your observations and details. Comedian Jerry Seinfeld's television show, *Seinfeld*, was popular partly because Seinfeld and his friends on the show spent an enormous amount of time simply naming, with great precision, everyday things we experience all the time but never notice: the low talker, the close talker. That's in large part what "smart" is: accurate. Noticing tiny true things everyone else glides by. Seeing closely. You don't have to be "deep." You just have to get it *exactly* right.

How? By paying close attention to your subject.

Strive in your writing for scientific accuracy (describing things exactly as they are) and psychological accuracy (presenting human behavior exactly as you see it, not slanting actions one way or the other to make a particular point). Always, what you discover *by writing* is going to be more revealing, more likely to produce insight than what you *think of ahead of time*.

You want to look more closely at two specific areas as you work over a piece of writing, moving in closer with accuracy, carefully observing people and their reactions.

People. When you write about people, write from close up and focus tightly on their gestures—how they move their bodies and what those gestures imply about what they want and how they are feeling. You want to focus on action— it's behavior that reveals our character. What kind of things, large and small, do the people you are writing about do? How do they do it, exactly, and what tiny distinctions do you notice between one person's little actions and another's way of doing the exact same thing? Coach football, take drugs, throw parties, vacation in Las Vegas, walk too fast?

In addition to the insights that come from watching human behavior as closely and carefully as a scientist, you also find insight by listening to exactly how people really talk. There's a kind of shorthand, faked dialogue that marks amateur creative writing: Avoid writing down what you *think* people sound like, and be like a reporter and get the exact things people say. Instead of giving your characters lines, let them surprise you. Interview them. Your characters may or may not speak wisdom (notice who does, and when, in the dialogue in Raymond Carver's story). But your reader will find your insights into human behavior compelling if you record the ways in which people say and misstate what they mean, often hiding what they really think.

Actions/Reactions. Every action inspires a reaction, and reactions are at least as revealing of human nature as action itself. How do others cause the flawed, struggling humans in your creative writing to behave *differently*, to alter their actions, to speak differently, to move differently? Track reactions, and you will discover insights into human psychology that will add layers and depth to your writing.

How do your characters/speakers visibly respond, what actions do you see when you watch them from close up *after* they are antagonized or delighted? All dialogue is a pattern of action/reaction—that is what a conversation *is*. There's not only drama in action/reaction, there's insight to be found by looking closely at patterns of response and trying to understand how and why.

Practice simply looking more closely at action and reaction, gesture and response; soon, your writing will be more accurate and hence more insightful. When you write *accurately* about your mother, your breakfast, your best friend, war, or a cocktail party, it's going to contain wisdom, as long as you get the people, their movements, and the tiny chain reactions that underlie all human interaction exactly right. That is the life's work of a writer.

When you analyze the Michael Cunningham short story "White Angel" in terms of accuracy, a pattern of insights emerges. The 1960s and 1970s were a time of great American freedom and pursuit of individual happiness. Concern moved away from protecting borders and maintaining defenses, both nationally and personally. This vulnerability allowed for great pleasure (sex, drugs, rock and roll), but also a greater potential for invasion, injury, accident, loss. In the story, notice how the actions (lighting up, throwing a party, dancing) and the reactions (younger brother to older brother, older brother to culture, adults to teenagers, adults to culture, etc.) move us toward this wisdom.

In creative writing, wisdom is a passage in the work where the reader says, "That is exactly right. That's *exactly* how it is."

PRACTICE

Read the story "White Angel" by Michael Cunningham on page 243. To analyze the insights in the piece, you will probably want to read it twice. Make a two-columned table. Label the columns "People" and "Actions/Reactions." Then, list in each category three places where Cunningham's details are so well-crafted, so perfectly revealing of time, place, personality, psychology, that they could count as *insights*.

Generosity

Perhaps you used to write for yourself, and maybe you still do. But now you are doing something different: You now write for readers. Good writers are generous to their readers. They create experiences for them to have (not just hear about). They set up a series of images, and little by little, a more significant truth emerges. Readers feel smart when they feel like they are making sense out of real life. The writer creates a pattern of insights, the reader solves for x. Writers don't spell it out, pandering to their readers and dumbing it all down. Writers are generous, not only in working hard to make sure the reader has a rewarding, interesting reading experience, but also by making sure there is some insight in the piece. Writers portray how we live, why we do the things we do; creative writing can be defined as a collection of small, precise observations pointing toward insights the casual observer would probably not notice. Creative writers are generous with their vision.

In addition to being generous with our observations on human behavior, creative writers also try to be generous in how they present humans. We are all flawed. If, as a writer, you write from "on high," hypercritical of everyone and everything you write about, showing humans only at their most petty, most violent, most unaware, you will not be writing lasting, insightful work. You won't have wisdom. Recall the story by Raymond Carver, "Cathedral," on page 297. Carver is generous in his insights. He shows Robert's annoying qualities as well as his good ones. He does the same for the wife, and, most importantly, for the narrator. The narrator has a lot of limitations. But he has some good points, too. Carver explores all these angles. He's a master of tension, and he uses these tensions to draw conclusions—insights—about how human psychology works.

We don't always act in ways that get us what we want. Sometimes, we can't see what's right in front of us. We put on acts, try to impress others, when really we are insecure, afraid. Carver, like any highly evolved human, is generous to the narrator. He sees the man's limitations, and the context for those limitations. He shows the reader what the narrator is trying to do. When the narrator fails, Carver shows us his pain. He shows his humanity.

> *A writer is someone who can make a riddle out of an answer.*
> — KARL KRAUS

Smart writers seek to understand human flaws, see weakness and strength, and balance their description by looking at a moment from many sides. Even artists famous for a dark or despairing view of the world, such as Franz Kafka or Quentin Tarantino or Art Spiegelman (*Maus*, excerpted on p. 59), thread humor or compassion or earnest attempts at human connection into their work. They are generous. "If it could happen to you, it could happen to me." That's the basic premise of *generosity* in art, and that's why art connects us.

Questioning

Children and artists, it's often said, are more alike than different. One crucial way they are connected is in their sense of curiosity, of wonder. Art, like children, asks questions. Questions usually lead us closer to the truth, toward deeper insights, and into the realm of wisdom. Asking the right question—specific, targeted, precise—*is* wisdom. When writing pretends to have all the answers, readers often keep the work at arm's length. "Hmm," they say. "How do you know for sure?" Certainty can close things down, end things too quickly, cut off the very curiosity that keeps us learning, moving us toward insight.

Getting in the habit of questioning gives you a direct line to your innate wisdom. Practice letting your work pose small, pointed questions, so the reader remains engaged, active, and alive right along with you.

PRACTICE

Read the poem "Bad Cello" by Marianne Boruch on page 256 and make a list of the questions the poems leads us to ask about human experience. Come up with ten tiny different questions. Next, come up with a list of fifteen questions Michael Cunningham may have been thinking about when he wrote "White Angel" (p. 243). What insights do you come to when you discuss some of these questions? Are these insights in the story? Provoked by the story?

Instead of recording your feelings in your journal, get in the habit of keeping a writer's notebook in which you ask questions. Tiny questions. What is it like when you realize you have been operating under limiting stereotypes? What is the nature of your father's essential personality, and what of that — good and bad — have you inherited? Why do we drive too fast, drink too much, act irresponsibly: What motivates us? Why do we keep dating *the same wrong person*? Why is doing the wrong thing sometimes *pleasurable*?

Instead of having ideas for writing projects, get in the habit of asking questions — little questions are often more productive for creative writers than big questions. Questions about human behavior and motivation. Questions about what you resist. Gentle, nonjudgmental questions. "Why is my roommate such a jerk?" is probably not going to produce great art. "What does a room look like when two people aren't in agreement?" might be more provocative, more interesting. We've all noticed how a room changes in appearance — our experience of the objects in the room changes — depending on what kind of conversation is happening there.

Asking good questions requires you to develop a habit of paying very close attention to exactly what you were wondering at an exact moment. This takes time and practice, but you can do it just as well as anyone else — just ignore the uncomfortable feelings that will come when you first give it a try.

| PRACTICE |

Read the poem "Carpe Diem" by Lynne McMahon on page 257. Discuss the kinds of questions she asks. How do the questions create energy? Tension? Are the questions supposed to be answered?

Good questions are usually not the first ones you think of. Use listing as your technique — before, during, and after writing — in order to generate insight-bearing questions. Wise questions often come in clusters — not freewriting, not thinking out loud, but a calculated, forceful deepening of the narrator's hopes and considerations.

The selection by Adam Gopnik, an essay about kids and football (p. 258), poses this initial question: How would he teach these eight-year-olds to play football? This is followed by a tight cluster of three follow-up questions: "Orate at them? Motivate them? Dazzle them with plays and schemes?" The questions reveal Gopnik's capacity for wonder. They also direct the reader to consider things he or she maybe hasn't ever before — the various styles of coaching, for instance, as well as the worried-parent nature of Gopnik.

Sure, writers answer questions.

But really good writers keep asking new ones.

Yes, literature contains Big Questions. Why does a good man die young? What's the point of trying when you know you'll lose? How do we keep hope alive in the face of tragedy?

But creative writers achieve wisdom by asking little questions, wondering about the things everyone else glides right past. We are the ones who say, "Wait. Stop. Did you notice that? Do you wonder why?"

WAYS TO BE WISE: CREATING INSIGHT

Creative writing is all about providing readers with a sensory experience. Creative writing works on your body as it enters your mind. It comes in through your ears, your pores, your eyes. We can wave at the author on shore, as Billy Collins suggests in "Introduction to Poetry" (p. 277), acknowledge someone created this thing, but ultimately, our interactions with the poem, the text, are more like our experience of a ballet, a concert, or a movie—we enter into the thing with our senses, attending to our emotional responses. We don't really (though we have often been taught to) beat "a meaning" out of creative writing. Instead, we enjoy the sensations a piece creates in us. We can talk about our reading experiences. In creative writing wisdom is lodged inside images, layered between experiences; it's seen and felt and touched. *In art, wisdom is always anchored in the sensory world.*

> *A writer is not someone who expresses his thoughts, his passion, or his imagination in sentences, but someone who thinks sentences.*
> *A Sentence-Thinker.*
> — ROLAND BARTHES

The most powerful way to cue the sensory world in your reader's mind is to provide "moving pictures" that will play out in the reader's mind. In order to write wisdom, you must show other people engaged in meaningful action. Along with action comes dialogue—which, as you have studied, is a kind of action. Creative nonfiction provides a terrific opportunity to study wisdom in action and dialogue. "Last of the Metrozoids," Adam Gopnik's story on page 258, is a wise piece about a wise teacher. It's an analysis of a friendship, a prayer, perhaps, and an investigation into death and dying, kid's football, and the Meaning of Life. Gopnik demonstrates the various ways a writer uses the scenic, sensory, physical world to generate insight and wisdom. The brilliance of his essay comes from within the deeper actions and movements and the accurate dialogue of the piece. The wisdom is in Gopnik's ability to be generous: He's on the side of the underdog, always, and willing to expose his own flaws and shortcomings. The insights aren't laid down on top, like icing. Gopnik embeds wisdom in actions and speech and questions.

| PRACTICE |

Read the essay by Adam Gopnik, "Last of the Metrozoids," on page 258. Make a list of ten dialogue examples and ten action-images (a person doing something) that may reveal the deeper wisdom embedded in this piece. Look for dead-on accurate places where the dialogue and the action seem particularly revealing, perhaps alluding to more than just what's on the surface.

Insight in Action

Look at the second paragraph of "Last of the Metrozoids": "Football had replaced Yu-Gi-Oh cards and the sinister water yo-yo (poisonous) as a preoccupation and a craze." That's an insight. Not earth-shattering, but an insight nonetheless. A perception, based in human action, that explains a tiny piece of the human world to us.

> *The role of the writer is not to say what we can all say, but what we are unable to say.*
>
> — ANAÏS NIN

Notice that in the first paragraph, the author's friend is sick, preoccupied with *his* new "craze": all the varieties of chemotherapy, a crazy-making endeavor, "none of which did much good, at least not for very long." The first paragraph focuses on the sequences of adult life, work as hobby—curating and lecturing as one focus, replaced by another, illness. In the second paragraph, on the micro-level, the boys move from the "work" of cards and "sinister water yo-yo (poisonous)," like chemotherapy, obviously, to football, the Super Bowl, their next obsession. By presenting their actions side by side, Gopnik connects Kirk Varnedoe and Gopnik's eight-year-old son Luke. Insight! In their own very different ways, these two people are taking similar journeys, moving from something less profound to something weighty and large and life-changing.

People's movements, habits, and actions give us clues to who they are. Juxtaposing the actions of two different characters allows the reader to see more deeply into both characters, and their larger situations.

Gopnik links *actions*—the game of naming with a football play—and subtly implies that the *making* of a team is half the fun, and where a lot of the energy and interest is. That's a wise observation; it's really true, isn't it?

They aren't even on the field; heck, they don't even have anyone to *play* yet, but already the game is well underway for the boys—their spirit, their love for life, and the tension in the ranks (cool "Freakazoid" kids versus the traditional "Giants"). Gopnik's insights—his writer's wisdom—is lodged *inside* the piece.

> *Art-speech is the only truth. An artist is usually a damned liar, but his art, if it be art, will tell you the truth of his day.*
>
> — D. H. LAWRENCE

Notice how Gopnik doesn't state, "Preparing to play is as much fun as the game itself." We *see* the truth of this because he shows us how people act. In creative writing, wisdom is buried in human actions.

PRACTICE

Work through the Gopnik essay on your own, listing other actions that reveal aspects of human nature. Then, reread the short essay on page 137 by Aleida Rodríguez and make a list of the significant actions, the ones that let you see the psychology and the meanings of the people and events in the piece.

Insight in Speech

Whether it's a poem, play, prose narrative, or love letter, successful pieces of writing often include wisdom in the form of dialogue, often from a minor character or speaker. Again, it's *sensory* wisdom that will stick with your reader. When people speak, usually we have an image of them talking. That's what we always want—that movie playing in the reader's head.

"If you're going to spend your life coaching football," Varnedoe says, in the Gopnik essay on page 259, "you have to be smart enough to do it well and dumb enough to think it matters."

You could put a witticism like that on a bumper sticker. It's an insight, offered by a man who thinks, who notices, who cares, who is committed to a life of the mind as well as a life of the body. Making a career choice, he has *thought*, this Varnedoe, about his own strengths, weaknesses, and the various characters of men of letters, men of sport.

> *Art must take reality by surprise.*
> — FRANÇOISE SAGAN

People who are unhappy often haven't made distinctions about what they are well-suited to, driven by, or drawn to. Character is complex. Varnedoe knows his, and he has clearly spent some time reading about and thinking over the character traits of successful football coaches.

Readers like to be around minds like this. Gopnik is a smart writer—he lets Varnedoe speak for himself, and we get a triple hit—a sound bite of wisdom, insight into Varnedoe, and a present moment—and this happens on the sensory level because it is in dialogue. Gopnik doesn't try to be smart himself in his writing. He uses the writing as a stage, onto which he brings smart people and lets them talk. Use this strategy in your own writing to add depth and wisdom to your work.

PRACTICE

Reread "Bodies" by Jessica Shattuck on page 180, or "Telling Tales" by Migdalia Cruz on page 272. Where do you find "wisdom lines" or insights in the words that are spoken aloud? Make a list of the lines that are most illuminating.

WAYS TO BE UNWISE: WHAT NOT TO DO

There are a few pitfalls to avoid when you are working with insight as a strategy for generating and working on your creative writing. Literature isn't a code, it isn't designed to hold hidden meanings that torture readers. Creative writing isn't about tricks. Billy Collins, a poet and a teacher, takes this as his subject in the poem "Introduction to Poetry." We could look at this poem as presenting four guidelines for what not to do when looking for ways to work in insight and layer in wisdom in creative writing:

PRACTICE

Read the poem "Introduction to Poetry" by Billy Collins on page 277. By asking students to skate across, nestle into, and practically get bitten or stung by poetry, what does Collins want them to understand about the nature of meaning and insight in creative writing?

---

1. Do Not Preach. If you focus your story, poem, or play around a single idea, from a single simple vantage point (abortion should be legal, homelessness is bad), you are likely writing a sermon or a position paper. Didactic writing—writing that exists in order to, in a narrow sense, instruct the reader—is not creative writing. It's the opposite. Creative writing teaches by showing people involved in actions, from very close up, so that the reader *sees* things about her or his own life simply by watching these moments and overhearing the dialogue. The less the writer states directly, the more powerful the creative writing.

> *It is the function of art to renew our perception. What we are familiar with we cease to see. The writer shakes up the familiar scene, and as if by magic, we see a new meaning in it.*
>
> — ANAÏS NIN

   Unwise: Your personal diatribe on the conflict in Iraq (when you've never been there).

   Wise: Poem from the point of view of a soldier-friend of yours, struggling back here at home with how to act, while you are shooting pool at the local pub.

2. Do Not Use Overly Poetic or Writerly Diction. If you are writing in order to sound smart or "be poetic," by using lots of words you don't normally use in conversation, trying to sound lofty, trying too hard to be difficult and complex, you will sound amateur, not

> *The most important thing in a work of art is that it should have a kind of focus, i.e., there should be some place where all the rays meet or from which they issue. And this focus must not be able to be completely explained by words.*
>
> — LEO TOLSTOY

wise. If you are writing in a flowery or fancy way, readers may conclude you are trying to be ironic or funny. If they read you at all. Pretentious is the opposite of wise.

Unwise: It was back when things were really crazy.
Wise: "We lived then in Cleveland, in the middle of everything. It was the sixties—our radios sang out love all day long." (Cunningham, "White Angel," p. 243)

3. Do Not Spell Everything Out. Treat your reader as a smart, informed, savvy person. Readers *want* to figure things out. They want to come up with multiple interpretations of events—just as we do in real life.

Unwise: A poem about the meaning in life written in vague abstract statements:
Life is a mystery
We do not know why
We struggle so much
And then we die.

Wise: Lynne McMahon's poem "Carpe Diem" on page 257, where each time you read it, you consider the questions a little more, a little differently; every reader has a unique reaction to the poem, different "answers." There's more than one meaning.

4. Do Not Fear You Have Nothing to Say. You have plenty of insights. It's all based on seeing, observing, noticing. You can stare, peer, and pry at least as well as anybody else on this planet. Looking and noticing are habits. You practice, and you get better. You can easily become a better observer and a more astute writer: Just use your eyes. Remember, you have been studying human nature your whole life. For years, you have been reading, seeing plays, watching television and movies. Whether you are young, old, book-smart, street-smart, or none of these, you know *a lot* about how art and literature operate, and you know a lot about people, situations, how they change, what's important. Don't *think* too much—you'll likely end up in a rut. Write, focusing on the action and the dialogue, what people do and what they say. Most writers claim their writing is smarter than they are. If you focus on images, you will find your wisdom.

> *A man will turn over half a library to make one book.*
> — SAMUEL JOHNSON

PRACTICE

Reread the poem by Billy Collins on page 277. Who is the "they" in Collins's poem? What kind of readers? Why do people often want "a meaning" out of a poem or story? Collins lists five ways of getting at the meaning of a poem—what kinds of meanings are going to reveal themselves given his approach? Can you use his directions for reading when you read *his* poem? Have you been in classes where the discussion was similar to this one?

WRITING PROJECTS

1. Write a scene from your life where you really made a mistake — small or large. Show no mercy. Show yourself completely wrecking things, behaving badly; it's all your fault. Present other people in the scene in their best light — show them as helpful, concerned versions of themselves, while sticking to the truth. Focus, highlight the bad in you and the good in those around you. (This might be really hard to do!) Next, do a completely opposite version. Write about the same screwup, which was in fact your fault, but present the details, setting, action, and dialogue (stick to the truth) that explains why you did this thing. Present you as a hero who made a small mistake in service of the greater good, or you as a hero who was tricked, or trapped, or victimized by circumstances, bad childhood — whatever the case may be. In this second version, present all the negative gestures, speech, action, stuff, and habits of the other people in this scene. Share both; which one is closer to the real truth? Which one is more popular with your reader/listeners? Is the truth somewhere in the middle?

2. Write a poem that is a list of questions. Make sure each of your questions is surprising, fresh, unexpected. Try to include images — specifics, concrete words — in as many of the questions as you can. If you use images, you will likely find your questions might be smarter than you are! Try to steer toward the questions that are in front of us every day, but that few slow down enough to really notice or articulate. If you like, and you know small kids, incorporate into your question-poem some of the questions you directly overhear them posing; listen closely and get the quotes exactly. Let your poem be at least twenty lines long.

3. Write a piece about a teacher whose lessons went well beyond his or her assigned subject matter. Use specific moments from three different settings (as Gopnik shows field, classroom, hospital room) and let the teacher speak for herself. Use images to find out new information about this person from your past. In showing the teacher in action, you will discover and collect insights into the person's character. Let the writing help you discover new insights; avoid relying on your preexisting assumptions.

4. Write a poem or an essay in which someone's question to you changes everything you think. One caveat: You can't tell us how your thinking changed, you can only show us your interaction with the person before, during, and after The Question. Leave it to the reader to figure out what changed.

5. Take two things you know quite a bit about that are very different from each other—such as football and art history, or Nintendo and Lutheranism—and write a piece of creative nonfiction that shows scenes of your actions and dialogue as you encounter these two worlds. Can you use action and gesture to show how the lessons of one world inform and apply to the other world's wisdom?

6. Using a piece you have worked on in this class, move in closer in six different places, using your image-creating skills to see more closely, to present more tiny details with greater accuracy. Continue rewriting the piece, making the following additional changes: Add two more reactions (carefully observed), two more revealing actions, and two questions (that you do not answer; your characters can ask them, or your narrator).

INSIGHT WORKSHOP

The prompts below will help you constructively discuss your classmates' work.

1. In the student piece you are reading, highlight two examples of accuracy, places where the writer names something small that we take for granted or just don't notice because we don't pay close enough attention.

2. Find two examples of generosity, where the writer shows both the good and the bad in a character, speaker, or situation.

3. Underline passages where the writer asks questions that are then left unanswered.

4. Identify three to five places in the student piece where an insight could be made more accurate, more generous, or a question inserted.

5. Identify any passages in the student's work that preach, overexplain, state the obvious, or sound grandiose or forced, like the writer is trying too hard to sound smart and not trusting his or her own voice and inner wisdom.

6. Identify your favorite piece of wisdom in this piece.

Michael Cunningham
White Angel

We lived then in Cleveland, in the middle of everything. It was the sixties—our radios sang out love all day long. This of course is history. It happened before the city of Cleveland went broke, before its river caught fire. We were four. My mother and father, Carlton, and me. Carlton turned sixteen the year I turned nine. Between us were several brothers and sisters, weak flames quenched in our mother's womb. We are not a fruitful or many-branched line. Our family name is Morrow.

Our father was a high school music teacher. Our mother taught children called "exceptional," which meant that some could name the day Christmas would fall in the year 2000 but couldn't remember to drop their pants when they peed. We lived in a tract called Woodlawn—neat one- and two-story houses painted optimistic colors. Our tract bordered a cemetery. Behind our back yard was a gully choked with brush, and beyond that, the field of smooth, polished stones. I grew up with the cemetery, and didn't mind it. It could be beautiful. A single stone angel, small-breasted and determined, rose amid the more conservative markers close to our house. Farther away, in a richer section, miniature mosques and Parthenons spoke silently to Cleveland of man's enduring accomplishments. Carlton and I played in the cemetery as children and, with a little more age, smoked joints and drank Southern Comfort there. I was, thanks to Carlton, the most criminally advanced nine-year-old in my fourth-grade class. I was going places. I made no move without his counsel.

Here is Carlton several months before his death, in an hour so alive with snow that earth and sky are identically white. He labors among the markers and I run after, stung by snow, following the light of his red knitted cap. Carlton's hair is pulled back into a ponytail, neat and economical, a perfect pinecone of hair. He is thrifty, in his way.

We have taken hits of acid with our breakfast juice. Or rather, Carlton has taken a hit and I, considering my youth, have been allowed half. This acid is called windowpane. It is for clarity of vision, as Vicks is for decongestion of the nose. Our parents are at work, earning the daily bread. We have come out into the cold so that the house, when we reenter it, will shock us with its warmth and righteousness. Carlton believes in shocks.

"I think I'm coming on to it," I call out. Carlton has on his buckskin jacket, which is worn down to the shine. On the back, across his shoulder blades, his girlfriend has stitched an electric-blue eye. As we walk I speak into the eye. "I think I feel something," I say.

"Too soon," Carlton calls back. "Stay loose, Frisco. You'll know when the time comes."

I am excited and terrified. We are into serious stuff. Carlton has done acid half a dozen times before, but I am new at it. We slipped the tabs into our mouths at breakfast, while our mother paused over the bacon. Carlton likes taking risks.

Snow collects in the engraved letters on the headstones. I lean into the wind, trying to decide whether everything around me seems strange because of the drug, or just because everything truly is strange. Three weeks earlier, a family across town had been sitting at home, watching television, when a single-engine plane fell on them. Snow swirls around us, seeming to fall up as well as down.

Carlton leads the way to our spot, the pillared entrance to a society tomb. This tomb is a palace. Stone cupids cluster on the peaked roof, with stunted, frozen wings and matrons' faces. Under the roof is a veranda, backed by cast-iron doors that lead to the house of the dead proper. In summer this veranda is cool. In winter it blocks the wind. We keep a bottle of Southern Comfort there.

Carlton finds the bottle, unscrews the cap, and takes a good, long draw. He is studded with snowflakes. He hands me the bottle and I take a more conservative drink. Even in winter, the tomb smells mossy as a well. Dead leaves and a yellow M & M's wrapper, worried by the wind, scrape on the marble floor.

"Are you scared?" Carlton asks me.

I nod. I never think of lying to him.

"Don't be, man," he says. "Fear will screw you right up. Drugs can't hurt you if you feel no fear."

I nod. We stand sheltered, passing the bottle. I lean into Carlton's certainty as if it gave off heat.

"We can do acid all the time at Woodstock," I say.

"Right on. Woodstock Nation. Yow."

"Do people really *live* there?" I ask.

"Man, you've got to stop asking that. The concert's over, but people are still there. It's the new nation. Have faith."

I nod again, satisfied. There is a different country for us to live in. I am already a new person, renamed Frisco. My old name was Robert.

"We'll do acid all the time," I say.

"You better believe we will." Carlton's face, surrounded by snow and marble, is lit. His eyes are bright as neon. Something in them tells me he can see the future, a ghost that hovers over everybody's head. In Carlton's future we all get released from our jobs and schooling. Awaiting us all, and soon, is a bright, perfect simplicity. A life among the trees by the river.

"How are you feeling, man?" he asks me.

"Great," I tell him, and it is purely the truth. Doves clatter up out of a bare tree and turn at the same instant, transforming themselves from steel to silver in the snow-blown light. I know at that moment that the drug is working. Everything before me has become suddenly, radiantly itself. How could Carlton have known this was about to happen? "Oh," I whisper. His hand settles on my shoulder.

"Stay loose, Frisco," he says. "There's not a thing in this pretty world to be afraid of. I'm here."

I am not afraid. I am astonished. I had not realized until this moment how real everything is. A twig lies on the marble at my feet, bearing a cluster of hard brown berries. The broken-off end is raw, white, fleshly. Trees are alive.

"I'm here," Carlton says again, and he is.

Hours later, we are sprawled on the sofa in front of the television, ordinary as Wally and the Beav. Our mother makes dinner in the kitchen. A pot lid clangs. We are undercover agents. I am trying to conceal my amazement.

Our father is building a grandfather clock from a kit. He wants to have something to leave us, something for us to pass along. We can hear him in the basement, sawing and pounding. I know what is laid out on his sawhorses—a long raw wooden box, onto which he glues fancy moldings. A single pearl of sweat meanders down his forehead as he works. Tonight I have discovered my ability to see every room of the house at once, to know every single thing that goes on. A mouse nibbles inside the wall. Electrical wires curl behind the plaster, hidden and patient as snakes.

"Shhh," I say to Carlton, who has not said anything. He is watching television through his splayed fingers. Gunshots ping. Bullets raise chalk dust on a concrete wall. I have no idea what we are watching.

"Boys?" our mother calls from the kitchen. I can, with my new ears, hear her slap hamburger into patties. "Set the table like good citizens," she calls.

"Okay, Ma," Carlton replies, in a gorgeous imitation of normality. Our father hammers in the basement. I can feel Carlton's heart ticking. He pats my hand, to assure me that everything's perfect.

We set the table, spoon fork knife, paper napkins triangled to one side. We know the moves cold. After we are done I pause to notice the dining-room wallpaper: a golden farm, backed by mountains. Cows graze, autumn trees cast golden shade. This scene repeats itself three times, on three walls.

"Zap," Carlton whispers. "Zzzzzoom."

"Did we do it right?" I ask him.

"We did everything perfect, little son. How are you doing in there, anyway?" He raps lightly on my head.

"Perfect, I guess." I am staring at the wallpaper as if I were thinking of stepping into it.

"You guess. You guess? You and I are going to other planets, man. Come over here."

"Where?"

"Here. Come here." He leads me to the window. Outside the snow skitters, nervous and silver, under streetlamps. Ranch-style houses hoard their warmth, bleed light into the gathering snow. It is a street in Cleveland. It is our street.

"You and I are going to fly, man," Carlton whispers, close to my ear. He opens the window. Snow blows in, sparking on the carpet. "Fly," he says, and we do. For a moment we strain up and out, the black night wind blowing in our faces—we raise ourselves up off the cocoa-colored deep-pile wool-and-polyester carpet by a sliver of an inch. Sweet glory. The secret of flight is this—you have to do it immediately, before your body realizes it is defying the laws. I swear it to this day.

We both know we have taken momentary leave of the earth. It does not strike either of us as remarkable, any more than does the fact that airplanes sometimes fall from the sky, or that we have always lived in these rooms and will soon leave them. We settle back down. Carlton touches my shoulder.

"You wait, Frisco," he says. "Miracles are happening. Fucking miracles."

I nod. He pulls down the window, which reseals itself with a sucking sound. Our own faces look back at us from the cold, dark glass. Behind us, our mother drops the hamburgers sizzling into the skillet. Our father bends to his work under a hooded lightbulb, preparing the long box into which he will lay clockworks, pendulum, a face. A plane drones by overhead, invisible in the clouds. I glance nervously at Carlton. He smiles his assurance and squeezes the back of my neck.

March. After the thaw. I am walking through the cemetery, thinking about my endless life. One of the beauties of living in Cleveland is that any direction feels like progress. I've memorized the map. We are by my calculations three hundred and fifty miles shy of Woodstock, New York. On this raw new day I am walking east, to the place where Carlton and I keep our bottle. I am going to have an early nip, to celebrate my bright future.

When I get to our spot I hear low moans coming from behind the tomb. I freeze, considering my choices. The sound is a long-drawn-out agony with a whip at the end, a final high C, something like "ooooooOw." A wolf's cry run backward. What decides me on investigation rather than flight is the need to make a story. In the stories my brother likes best, people always do the foolish, risky thing. I find I can reach decisions this way, by thinking of myself as a character in a story told by Carlton.

I creep around the side of the monument, cautious as a badger, pressed up close to the marble. I peer over a cherub's girlish shoulder. What I find is Carlton on the ground with his girlfriend, in an uncertain jumble of clothes and bare flesh. Carlton's jacket, the one with the embroidered eye, is draped over the stone, keeping watch.

I hunch behind the statue. I can see the girl's naked arms, and the familiar bones of Carlton's spine. The two of them moan together in the dry winter grass. Though I can't make out the girl's expression, Carlton's face is twisted and grimacing, the cords of his neck pulled tight. I had never thought the experience might be painful. I watch, trying to learn. I hold on to the cherub's cold wings.

It isn't long before Carlton catches sight of me. His eyes rove briefly, ecstatically skyward, and what do they light on but his brother's small head, sticking up next to a cherub's. We lock eyes and spend a moment in mutual decision. The girl keeps on clutching at Carlton's skinny back. He decides to smile at me. He decides to wink.

I am out of there so fast I tear up divots. I dodge among the stones, jump the gully, clear the fence into the swing-set-and-picnic-table sanctity of the back yard. Something about that wink. My heart beats fast as a sparrow's.

I go into the kitchen and find our mother washing fruit. She asks what's going on. I tell her nothing is. Nothing at all.

She sighs over an apple's imperfection. The curtains sport blue teapots. Our mother works the apple with a scrub brush. She believes they come coated with poison.

"Where's Carlton?" she asks.

"Don't know," I tell her.

"Bobby?"

"Huh?"

"What exactly is going on?"

"Nothing," I say. My heart works itself up to a hummingbird's rate, more buzz than beat.

"I think something is. Will you answer a question?"

"Okay."

"Is your brother taking drugs?"

I relax a bit. It is only drugs. I know why she's asking. Lately police cars have been browsing our house like sharks. They pause, take note, glide on. Some neighborhood crackdown. Carlton is famous in these parts.

"No," I tell her.

She faces me with the brush in one hand, an apple in the other. "You wouldn't lie to me, would you?" She knows something is up. Her nerves run through this house. She can feel dust settling on the tabletops, milk starting to turn in the refrigerator.

"No," I say.

"Something's going on," she sighs. She is a small, efficient woman who looks at things as if they give off a painful light. She grew up on a farm in Wisconsin and spent her girlhood tying up bean rows, worrying over the sun and rain. She is still trying to overcome her habit of modest expectations.

I leave the kitchen, pretending sudden interest in the cat. Our mother follows, holding her brush. She means to scrub the truth out of me. I follow the cat, his erect black tail and pink anus.

"Don't walk away when I'm talking to you," our mother says.

I keep walking, to see how far I'll get, calling, "Kittykittykitty." In the front hall, our father's homemade clock chimes the half hour. I make for the clock. I get as far as the rubber plant before she collars me.

"I told you not to walk away," she says, and cuffs me a good one with the brush. She catches me on the ear and sets it ringing. The cat is out of there quick as a quarter note.

I stand for a minute, to let her know I've received the message. Then I resume walking. She hits me again, this time on the back of the head, hard enough to make me see colors. "Will you *stop*?" she screams. Still, I keep walking. Our house runs west to east. With every step I get closer to Yasgur's farm.

Carlton comes home whistling. Our mother treats him like a guest who's overstayed. He doesn't care. He is lost in optimism. He pats her cheek and calls her "Professor." He treats her as if she were harmless, and so she is.

She never hits Carlton. She suffers him the way farm girls suffer a thieving crow, with a grudge so old and endless it borders on reverence. She gives him a scrubbed apple, and tells him what she'll do if he tracks mud on the carpet.

I am waiting in our room. He brings the smell of the cemetery with him, its old snow and wet pine needles. He rolls his eyes at me, takes a crunch of his apple. "What's happening, Frisco?" he says.

I have arranged myself loosely on my bed, trying to pull a Dylan riff out of my harmonica. I have always figured I can bluff my way into wisdom. I offer Carlton a dignified nod.

He drops onto his own bed. I can see a crushed crocus, the first of the year, stuck to the black rubber sole of his boot.

"Well, Frisco," he says. "Today you are a man."

I nod again. Is that all there is to it?

"*Yow,*" Carlton says. He laughs, pleased with himself and the world. "That was so perfect."

I pick out what I can of "Blowin' in the Wind."

Carlton says, "Man, when I saw you out there spying on us I thought to myself, *yes.* Now *I'm* really here. You know what I'm saying?" He waves his apple core.

"Uh-huh," I say.

"Frisco, that was the first time her and I ever did it. I mean, we'd talked. But when we finally got down to it, there you were. My brother. Like you *knew.*"

I nod, and this time for real. What happened was an adventure we had together. All right. The story is beginning to make sense.

"Aw, Frisco," Carlton says. "I'm gonna find you a girl, too. You're nine. You been a virgin too long."

"Really?" I say.

"*Man*. We'll find you a woman from the sixth grade, somebody with a little experience. We'll get stoned and all make out under the trees in the boneyard. I want to be present at your deflowering, man. You're gonna need a brother there."

I am about to ask, as casually as I can manage, about the relationship between love and bodily pain, when our mother's voice cuts into the room. "You did it," she screams. "You tracked mud all over the rug."

A family entanglement follows. Our mother brings our father, who comes and stands in the doorway with her, taking in evidence. He is a formerly handsome man. His face has been worn down by too much patience. He has lately taken up some sporty touches—a goatee, a pair of calfskin boots.

Our mother points out the trail of muddy half-moons that lead from the door to Carlton's bed. Dangling over the foot of the bed are the culprits themselves, voluptuously muddy, with Carlton's criminal feet still in them.

"You see?" she says. "You see what he thinks of me?"

Our father, a reasonable man, suggests that Carlton clean it up. Our mother finds that too small a gesture. She wants Carlton not to have done it in the first place. "I don't ask for much," she says. "I don't ask where he goes. I don't ask why the police are suddenly so interested in our house. I ask that he not track mud all over the floor. That's all." She squints in the glare of her own outrage.

"Better clean it right up," our father says to Carlton.

"And that's it?" our mother says. "He cleans up the mess, and all's forgiven?"

"Well, what do you want him to do? Lick it up?"

"I want some consideration," she says, turning helplessly to me. "That's what I want."

I shrug, at a loss. I sympathize with our mother, but am not on her team.

"All right," she says. "I just won't bother cleaning the house anymore. I'll let you men handle it. I'll sit and watch television and throw my candy wrappers on the floor."

She starts out, cutting the air like a blade. On her way she picks up a jar of pencils, looks at it and tosses the pencils on the floor. They fall like fortune-telling sticks, in pairs and crisscrosses.

Our father goes after her, calling her name. Her name is Isabel. We can hear them making their way across the house, our father calling, "Isabel, Isabel, Isabel," while our mother, pleased with the way the pencils had looked, dumps more things onto the floor.

"I hope she doesn't break the TV," I say.

"She'll do what she needs to do," Carlton tells me.

"I hate her," I say. I am not certain about that. I want to test the sound of it, to see if it's true.

"She's got more balls than any of us, Frisco," he says. "Better watch what you say about her."

I keep quiet. Soon I get up and start gathering pencils, because I prefer that to lying around trying to follow the shifting lines of allegiance. Carlton goes for a sponge and starts in on the mud.

"You get shit on the carpet, you clean it up," he says. "Simple."

The time for all my questions about love has passed, and I am not so unhip as to force a subject. I know it will come up again. I make a neat bouquet of pencils. Our mother rages through the house.

Later, after she has thrown enough and we three have picked it all up, I lie on my bed thinking things over. Carlton is on the phone to his girlfriend, talking low. Our mother, becalmed but still dangerous, cooks dinner. She sings as she cooks, some slow forties number that must have been all over the jukes when her first husband's plane went down in the Pacific. Our father plays his clarinet in the basement. That is where he goes to practice, down among his woodworking tools, the neatly hung hammers and awls that throw oversized shadows in the light of the single bulb. If I put my ear to the floor I can hear him, pulling a long low tomcat moan out of that horn. There is some strange comfort in pressing my ear to the carpet and hearing our father's music leaking up through the floorboards. Lying down, with my ear to the floor, I join in on my harmonica.

That spring our parents have a party to celebrate the sun's return. It has been a long, bitter winter and now the first wild daisies are poking up on the lawns and among the graves.

Our parents' parties are mannerly affairs. Their friends, schoolteachers all, bring wine jugs and guitars. They are Ohio hip. Though they hold jobs and meet mortgages, they think of themselves as independent spirits on a spying mission. They have agreed to impersonate teachers until they write their novels, finish their dissertations, or just save up enough money to set themselves free.

Carlton and I are the lackeys. We take coats, fetch drinks. We have done this at every party since we were small, trading on our precocity, doing a brother act. We know the moves. A big, lipsticked woman who has devoted her maidenhood to ninth-grade math calls me Mr. Right. An assistant vice principal in a Russian fur hat asks us both whether we expect to vote Democratic or Socialist. By sneaking sips I manage to get myself semi-crocked.

The reliability of the evening is derailed halfway through, however, by a half dozen of Carlton's friends. They rap on the door and I go for it, anxious as a carnival sharp to see who will step up next and swallow the illusion that I'm a kindly, sober nine-year-old child. I'm expecting callow adults and who do I find but a pack of young outlaws, big-booted and wild-haired. Carlton's girlfriend stands in front, in an outfit made up almost entirely of fringe.

"Hi, Bobby," she says confidently. She comes from New York, and is more than just locally smart.

"Hi," I say. I let them all in despite a retrograde urge to lock the door and phone the police. Three are girls, four boys. They pass me in a cloud of dope smoke and sly-eyed greeting.

What they do is invade the party. Carlton is standing on the far side of the rumpus room, picking the next album, and his girl cuts straight through the crowd to his side. She has the bones and the loose, liquid moves some people consider beautiful. She walks through that room as if she'd been sent to teach the whole party a lesson.

Carlton's face tips me off that this was planned. Our mother demands to know what's going on here. She is wearing a long dark-red dress that doesn't interfere with her shoulders. When she dresses up you can see what it is about her, or what it was. She is responsible for Carlton's beauty. I have our father's face.

Carlton does some quick talking. Though it's against our mother's better judgment, the invaders are suffered to stay. One of them, an Eddie Haskell for all his leather and hair, tells her she is looking good. She is willing to hear it.

So the outlaws, house-sanctioned, start to mingle. I work my way over to Carlton's side, the side unoccupied by his girlfriend. I would like to say something ironic and wised-up, something that will band Carlton and me against every other person in the room. I can feel the shape of the comment I have in mind but, being a tipsy nine-year-old, can't get my mouth around it. What I say is, "Shit, man."

Carlton's girl laughs at me. She considers it amusing that a little boy says "shit." I would like to tell her what I have figured out about her, but I am nine, and three-quarters gone on Tom Collinses. Even sober, I can only imagine a sharp-tongued wit.

"Hang on, Frisco," Carlton tells me. "This could turn into a real party."

I can see by the light in his eyes what is going down. He has arranged a blind date between our parents' friends and his own. It's a Woodstock move—he is plotting a future in which young and old have business together. I agree to hang on, and go to the kitchen, hoping to sneak a few knocks of gin.

There I find our father leaning up against the refrigerator. A line of butterfly-shaped magnets hovers around his head. "Are you enjoying this party?" he asks, touching his goatee. He is still getting used to being a man with a beard.

"Uh-huh."

"I am, too," he says sadly. He never meant to be a high school music teacher. The money question caught up with him.

"What do you think of this music" he asks. Carlton has put the Stones on the turntable. Mick Jagger sings "19th Nervous Breakdown." Our father gestures in an openhanded way that takes in the room, the party, the whole house—everything the music touches.

"I like it," I say.

"So do I." He stirs his drink with his finger, and sucks on the finger.

"I *love* it," I say, too loud. Something about our father leads me to raise my voice. I want to grab handfuls of music out of the air and stuff them into my mouth.

"I'm not sure I could say I love it," he says. "I'm not sure if I could say that, no. I would say I'm friendly to its intentions. I would say that if this is the direction music is going in, I won't stand in its way."

"Uh-huh," I say. I am already anxious to get back to the party, but don't want to hurt his feelings. If he senses he's being avoided he can fall into fits of apology more terrifying than our mother's rages.

"I think I may have been too rigid with my students," our father says. "Maybe over the summer you boys could teach me a few things about the music people are listening to these days."

"Sure," I say, loudly. We spend a minute waiting for the next thing to say.

"You boys are happy, aren't you?" he asks. "Are you enjoying this party?"

"We're having a great time," I say.

"I thought you were. I am, too."

I have by this time gotten myself to within jumping distance of the door. I call out, "Well, goodbye," and dive back into the party.

Something has happened in my small absence. The party has started to roll. Call it an accident of history and the weather. Carlton's friends are on decent behavior, and our parents' friends have decided to give up some of their wine-and-folk-song propriety to see what they can learn. Carlton is dancing with a vice principal's wife. Carlton's friend Frank, with his ancient-child face and IQ in the low sixties, dances with our mother. I see that our father has followed me out of the kitchen. He positions himself at the party's edge; I jump into its center. I invite the fuchsia-lipped math teacher to dance. She is only too happy. She is big and graceful as a parade float, and I steer her effortlessly out into the middle of everything. My mother, who is known around school for Sicilian discipline, dances freely, which is news to everybody. There is no getting around her beauty.

The night rises higher and higher. A wildness sets in. Carlton throws new music on the turntable—Janis Joplin, the Doors, the Dead. The future shines for everyone, rich with the possibility of more nights exactly like this. Even our father is pressed into dancing, which he does like a flightless bird, all flapping arms and potbelly. Still, he dances. Our mother has a kiss for him.

Finally I nod out on the sofa, blissful under the drinks. I am dreaming of flight when our mother comes and touches my shoulder. I smile up into her flushed, smiling face.

"It's hours past your bedtime," she says, all velvet motherliness. I nod. I can't dispute the fact.

She keeps on nudging my shoulder. I am a moment or two apprehending the fact that she actually wants me to leave the party and go to bed. "No," I tell her.

"Yes," she smiles.

"No," I say cordially, experimentally. This new mother can dance, and flirt. Who knows what else she might allow?

"Yes." The velvet motherliness leaves her voice. She means business, business of the usual kind. I get myself out of there and no excuses this time. I am exactly nine and running from my bedtime as I'd run from death.

I run to Carlton for protection. He is laughing with his girl, a sweaty question mark of hair plastered to his forehead. I plow into him so hard he nearly goes over.

"Whoa, Frisco," he says. He takes me up under the arms and swings me a half-turn. Our mother plucks me out of his hands and sets me down, with a good farm-style hold on the back of my neck.

"Say good night, Bobby," she says. She adds, for the benefit of Carlton's girl, "He should have been in bed before this party started."

"*No,*" I holler. I try to twist loose, but our mother has a grip that could crack walnuts.

Carlton's girl tosses her hair and says, "Good night, baby." She smiles a victor's smile. She smooths the stray hair off Carlton's forehead.

"*No,*" I scream again. Something about the way she touches his hair. Our mother calls our father, who comes and scoops me up and starts out of the room with me, holding me like the live bomb I am. Before I go I lock eyes with Carlton. He shrugs and says, "Night, man." Our father hustles me out. I do not take it bravely. I leave flailing, too furious to cry, dribbling a slimy thread of horrible-child's spittle.

Later I lie alone on my narrow bed, feeling the music hum in the coiled springs. Life is cracking open right there in our house. People are changing. By tomorrow, no one will be quite the same. How can they let me miss it? I dream up revenge against our parents, and worse for Carlton. He is the one who could have saved me. He could have banded with me against them. What I can't forgive is his shrug, his mild-eyed "Night, man." He has joined the adults. He has made himself bigger, and taken size from me. As the Doors thump "Strange Days," I hope something awful happens to him. I say so to myself.

Around midnight, dim-witted Frank announces he has seen a flying saucer hovering over the back yard. I can hear his deep, excited voice all the way in my room. He says it's like a blinking, luminous cloud. I hear half the party struggling out through the sliding glass door in a disorganized, whooping knot. By that time everyone is so delirious a flying saucer would be just what was expected. That much celebration would logically attract an answering happiness from across the stars.

I get out of bed and sneak down the hall. I will not miss alien visitors for anyone, not even at the cost of our mother's wrath or our father's disappointment. I stop at the end of the hallway, though, embarrassed to be in pajamas. If there really are aliens, they will think I'm the lowest member of the house. While I hesitate over whether to go back to my room to change, people start coming back inside, talking about a trick of the mist and an airplane. People resume their dancing.

Carlton must have jumped the back fence. He must have wanted to be there alone, singular, in case they decided to take somebody with them. A few nights later I will go out and stand where he would have been standing. On the far side of the gully, now a river swollen with melted snow, the cemetery will gleam like a lost city. The moon will be full. I will hang around just as Carlton must have, hypnotized by the silver light on the stones, the white angel raising her arms up across the river.

According to our parents the mystery is why he ran back to the house full tilt. Something in the graveyard may have scared him, he may have needed to break its spell, but I think it's more likely that when he came back to himself he just couldn't wait to get back to the music and the people, the noisy disorder of continuing life.

Somebody has shut the sliding glass door. Carlton's girlfriend looks lazily out, touching base with her own reflection. I look, too. Carlton is running toward the house. I hesitate. Then I figure he can bump his nose. It will be a good joke on him. I let him keep coming. His girlfriend sees him through her own reflection, starts to scream a warning just as Carlton hits the glass.

It is an explosion. Triangles of glass fly brightly through the room. I think for him it must be more surprising than painful, like hitting water from a great height. He stands blinking for a moment. The whole party stops, stares, getting its bearings. Bob Dylan sings "Just Like a Woman." Carlton reaches up curiously to take out the shard of glass that is stuck in his neck, and that is when the blood starts. It shoots out of him. Our mother screams. Carlton steps forward into his girlfriend's arms and the two of them fall together. Our mother throws herself down on top of him and the girl. People shout their accident wisdom. Don't lift him. Call an ambulance. I watch from the hallway. Carlton's blood spurts, soaking into the carpet, spattering people's clothes. Our mother and father both try to plug the wound with their hands, but the blood just shoots between their fingers. Carlton looks more puzzled than anything, as if he can't quite follow this turn of events. "It's all right," our father tells him, trying to stop the blood. "It's all right, just don't move, it's all right." Carlton nods, and holds our father's hand. His eyes take on an astonished light. Our mother screams, "Is anybody *doing* anything?" What comes out of Carlton grows darker, almost black. I watch. Our father tries to get a hold on Carlton's neck while Carlton keeps trying to take his hand. Our mother's hair is matted with blood. It runs down her face. Carlton's girl holds him to her breasts, touches his hair, whispers in his ear.

He is gone by the time the ambulance gets there. You can see the life drain out of him. When his face goes slack our mother wails. A part of her flies wailing through the house, where it will wail and rage forever. I feel our mother pass through me on her way out. She covers Carlton's body with her own.

He is buried in the cemetery out back. Years have passed—we are living in the future, and it's turned out differently from what we'd planned. Our mother has established her life of separateness behind the guest-room door. Our father mutters his greetings to the door as he passes.

One April night, almost a year to the day after Carlton's accident, I hear cautious footsteps shuffling across the living-room floor after midnight. I run out eagerly, thinking of ghosts, but find only our father in moth-colored pajamas. He looks unsteadily at the dark air in front of him.

"Hi, Dad," I say from the doorway.

He looks in my direction. "Yes?"

"It's me. Bobby."

"Oh, Bobby," he says. "What are you doing up, young man?"

"Nothing," I tell him. "Dad?"

"Yes, son."

"Maybe you better come back to bed. Okay?"

"Maybe I had," he says. "I just came out here for a drink of water, but I seem to have gotten turned around in the darkness. Yes, maybe I better had."

I take his hand and lead him down the hall to his room. The grandfather clock chimes the quarter hour.

"Sorry," our father says.

I get him into bed. "There," I say. "Okay?"

"Perfect. Could not be better."

"Okay. Good night."

"Good night. Bobby?"

"Uh-huh?"

"Why don't you stay a minute?" he says. "We could have ourselves a talk, you and me. How would that be?"

"Okay," I say. I sit on the edge of his mattress. His bedside clock ticks off the minutes.

I can hear the low rasp of his breathing. Around our house, the Ohio night chirps and buzzes. The small gray finger of Carlton's stone pokes up among the others, within sight of the angel's blank white eyes. Above us, airplanes and satellites sparkle. People are flying even now toward New York or California, to take up lives of risk and invention.

I stay until our father has worked his way into a muttering sleep.

Carlton's girlfriend moved to Denver with her family a month before. I never learned what it was she'd whispered to him. Though she'd kept her head admirably during the accident, she lost her head afterward. She cried so hard at the funeral that she had to be taken away by her mother—an older, redder-haired version of her. She started seeing a psychiatrist three times a week. Everyone, including my parents, talked about how hard it was for her, to have held a dying boy in her arms at that age. I'm grateful to her for holding my brother while he died, but I never once heard her mention the fact that though she had been through something terrible, at least she was still alive and going places. At least she had protected herself by trying to warn him. I can appreciate the intricacies of her pain. But as long as she was in Cleveland, I could never look her straight in the face. I couldn't talk about the wounds she suffered. I can't even write her name.

Marianne Boruch
Bad Cello

My bad cello! I love it
too much, my note to almost note,
my almost Bach, my almost Haydn, two who
heard things falling off a shelf—
they never thought that
was music. Try wind at night. Try that
against your good night's
sleep. Still, something's passing, same
as grief—there's no
word for it. Same as joy
but only in the flourish of up and down, the way
a note is held—or held off—
too long.
　　　　　　Certain afternoons are
private, forsythia against the window,
its hundreds of branches I should have

cut in summer, their
scratch-scratch-scratchity. So I practice
to them, so I practice
with them.
               I keep thinking
how Brahms slept right through
my childhood, that print in a frame
above my grandmother's threadbare couch, and how
I loved his face completely. His eyes
were closed. He leaned against the piano.
And above him all those
other faces—Beethoven and Bach and Mozart—
misty currents they floated in said *dream*, said
go away, Brahms is having a vision right now,
said *Brahms needs his nap.*
                       It's just that—bad cello!—
the rondo? I like it, like to play it twice because
no words! Because *I do it*
so badly! Delicious part
going minor, right
down the hole, neither what-I-thought nor
what-I-dreamt. Dark in there. Strange.

Lynne McMahon
Carpe Diem

Is it memory that makes us whole?
The question was posed by the ten o'clock news
investigating Alzheimer's and stroke,
the key network of synaptic fuses
blinking out, the brain's small cities polled,
found empty across the vacant mews.
Where are the poplar trees, where's the bench
you made, the wallpaper irises you glued
in strips? Home vanishes inch by inch.
Is love, too, cobbled out of past?
What will become of us, landmarks gone?
Dante's worst pang, the knowledge of happiness
lost, would be mine, but wrong

to think you'd feel it less—
you might sense an absence dawning,
it dawns on me, in another's face,
a bewildered sorrow you'd try to calm,
too instinctive in you to be erased.
But I'm willfully naive, I'm told.
Instinct, too, can be extinguished,
the present tense grotesquely folding
in and over on itself, contextless
and dangerous in an endless scroll
of carpe diem. Where's the face I know,
the hands I've memorized and kept?
Is it memory that makes us whole?
Is love over when memory is spent?

Adam Gopnik
Last of the Metrozoids

In the spring of 2003, the American art historian Kirk Varnedoe accepted the title of head coach of a football team called the Giant Metrozoids, which practiced then every week in Central Park. It was a busy time for him. He had just become a member of the Institute for Advanced Study, in Princeton, after thirteen years as the chief curator of painting and sculpture at the Museum of Modern Art in New York, and he was preparing the Mellon lectures for the National Gallery of Art in Washington—a series of six lectures on abstract art that he was supposed to deliver that spring. He was also dying, with a metastasis in his lung of a colon cancer that had been discovered in 1996, and, at Memorial Sloan-Kettering Cancer Center, in New York, he was running through all the possible varieties of chemotherapy, none of which did much good, at least not for very long.

The Giant Metrozoids were not, on the face of it, much of a challenge for him. They began with a group of eight-year-olds in my son Luke's second-grade class. Football had replaced Yu-Gi-Oh cards and the sinister water yo-yo (poisonous) as a preoccupation and a craze. The boys had become wrapped up in the Tampa Bay Buccaneers' march to victory in the Super Bowl that winter, and they had made up their minds to be football players. They wanted a team—"a real team that practices and has T-shirts and knows plays and everything"—that could play flag football, against an as yet unknown opponent, and I set about trying to organize it. (The name was a compromise: some of the boys had wanted to be called the Giants, while cool opinion had landed on the Freakazoids; Metrozoids was arrived at by some diplomatic back formation with *Metropolitan*.)

Once I had the T-shirts, white and blue, we needed a coach, and Kirk, Luke's godfather, was the only choice; during one of his chemotherapy sessions, I suggested, a little tentatively, that he might try it. He had been a defensive-backfield coach at Williams College for a year after graduation, before he went to Stanford to do art history, and I knew that he had thought of taking up coaching as a full-time profession, only to decide, as he said once, "If you're going to spend your life coaching football, you have to be smart enough to do it well and dumb enough to think it matters." But he said yes, eagerly. He gave me instructions on what he would need, and made a date with the boys.

On the first Friday afternoon, I took the red cones he had asked for and arranged them carefully on our chosen field, at the corner of Fifth Avenue and Seventy-ninth Street. I looked over my shoulder at the pseudo-Renaissance mansion that houses N.Y.U.'s Institute of Fine Arts, right across the street. We had met there, twenty-three years earlier, his first year at the Institute of Fine Arts, and mine, too. He had arrived from Stanford and Paris and Columbia, a young scholar, just thirty-four, who had made his reputation by cleaning up one of the messier stalls in the art-historical stable, the question of the authentic Rodin drawings. Then he had helped revive some unfairly forgotten reputations, particularly that of the misunderstood "academic" Impressionist Gustave Caillebotte.

But, as with Lawrence Taylor's first season with the Giants, though we knew he was supposed to be good, nobody was this good. He would come into the lecture room, in turtleneck and sports jacket, professor-wear, and, staring at his shoes, and without any preliminaries, wait for the lights to dim, demand, "First slide, please," and, pacing back and forth, look up at the image, no text in his hand but a list of slides. "Last time, we left off looking at Cezanne in the eighties, when the conversation between his code, registered in the deliberately crippled, dot-dot-dash, telegraphic repetition of brushstrokes, and his construction, built up in the blocky, stage-set recessional spaces, set out like flats on a theater," he would begin, improvising, spitballing, seeing meaning in everything. A Judd box was as alive for him as a Rodin bronze, and his natural mode was to talk in terms of tension rather than harmony. What was weird about the pictures was exactly what there was to prize about them, and, his style implied, all the nettled and querulous critics who tried to homogenize the pictures into a single story undervalued them, because, in a sense, they undervalued life, which was never going to be harmonized, either.

It was football that made us friends. In that first fall, he had me typed as a clever guy, and his attitude was that in the professions of the mind clever guys finish nowhere at all. Then, that spring, we organized a touch-football game at the institute, and although I am the most flat-footed, least gifted touch-football player in the whole history of the world, I somehow managed to play in it. A bunch of us persuaded our young professor to come out and join in one Sunday. The game was meant to be a gentle, co-ed touch game. But Kirk altered it by his presence. He was slamming so many bodies and dominating so much that a wary, alarmed circle of caution formed around him.

Finally, I insisted to John Wilson, the Texan Renaissance scholar in the huddle, that if he faked a short pass, and everybody made a lot of noise—"I got it!" "There it is!," and so on—Kirk would react instantly and run toward the sound, and I could sneak behind him for the touchdown.

Well, the play worked, and, perhaps recognizing that it was an entirely verbal construction, he spotted its author and came right over, narrow-eyed and almost angry. "Smart play," he said shortly, with the unspoken words "Smart-ass play" resonating in the leaves above our heads. But then he shook his fist happily, a sign meaning O.K., nice one. He turned away. He sees right through me, I thought; he knows exactly what I'm up to. I began working harder, and we became friends.

A quarter-century later, he was coming to the same field from the hospital. He was a handsome man, in a big-screen way, with the deep-set eyes and boyish smile and even the lumpy, interesting complexion of a Harrison Ford or a Robert Redford. The bull-like constitution that had kept him alive for seven years, as the doctors poured drugs into him like Drano into a clogged sink, might have explained why the chemo, which thinned and balded almost everyone else, had somehow made him gain weight and grow hair, so, though he was a little stocky now, and a little gray, his step was solid and his eyes were rimmed with oddly long Egyptian lashes.

The boys came running from school, excited to have been wearing their Metrozoid T-shirts all day, waiting for practice: Eric and Derek and Ken, good athletes, determined and knowing and nodding brief, been-there-before nods as they chucked the ball around; Jacob and Charlie and Garrett talking a little too quickly and uncertainly about how many downs you had and how many yards you had to go; Will and Luke and Matthew very verbal, evangelizing for a game, please, can't we, like, have a game with another team, right away, we're ready; and Gabriel just eager for a chance to get the ball and roll joyfully in the mud. I was curious to see what Kirk would do with them. He was, first and foremost, a teacher, and his lectures still resonated in the halls of the institute. But how would he teach these eight-year-olds to play football? Orate at them? Motivate them? Dazzle them with plays and schemes?

"O.K.," he said, very gently, as the boys gathered around him in an attentive, slightly wary circle. "Let's break it down. First thing is how you stand. Everybody get down in a three-point stance."

The boys dropped to their haunches confidently.

Kirk frowned. He walked up and down the line, shoving each one lightly on a shoulder or a knee, and showing how a three-point stance could be a weak or strong tripod, a launching pad or a stopping place, one that let you push off strongly or one that held you back. At last, he got everybody's stance correct. "O.K., let's run," he said. "Just run the length of the field, from these cones to those cones, and then turn back. Last guy does fifteen pushups." Luke stumbled and was the last guy, and Kirk had him do fifteen pushups. The point was made: No favorites.

Right around then, a young park worker came up in one of those officious little green carts the park people ride around in. "I'm sorry," he said, "you can't play here. It's ruled off for games."

I was ready to get mad—I mean, hey, who was making these rules? We had been playing touch football here for years—when Kirk stepped in.

"We-ell," Kirk said, and the Southern accent he brought with him from his youth in Savannah was suddenly more intense, an airplane captain's accent. "Well, uh, we got ten young men here eager to play football. Where can we take them to play?"

To my surprise, the park worker was there for the enlisting. "Let me see— I'll come back," he said. We went on with the drills, and ten minutes later the guy scooted up again in his cart.

"I think I've found just the place," he said. "If you go off there, right over the road, and take the left fork, you'll find this field that's hidden there behind the parking lot." He added, almost confidentially, "It's just opposite the toilets near the Ramble, but it's flat and large, and I think it's perfect."

"Much obliged," Kirk said, and he gestured to the boys, a big arm-sweeping gesture, and led them off in search of the promised field. They followed him like Israelites. We walked across the road, took the left, and went down a hill, and there it was—a little glade that I had never seen before, flat and fringed by tall trees, offering shade to the waiting moms and dads. It had a slightly derelict look—I could imagine that in a livelier era this field might have been a Francis Bacon mural, men struggling in the grass—but today it was perfect.

"Gentlemen," Kirk said clearly to the boys as they straggled on, looking around a little dubiously at the tufts of grass and the facing bathrooms. "Welcome to Metrozoid Field. This is the place we have been looking for." He set out the red cones again around the fringes.

"O.K., let's scrimmage," he ordered. He divided the guys in half with a firm, cutting gesture, and they began an intense, slightly nervous touch-football game. Kirk watched them, smiling and silent.

"Shouldn't we teach them a play?" I suggested.

"No," he said. "They're off to a good start. Running and standing is a good start."

The scrimmage ended, and the winning team began to hurrah and high-five.

"Hey," he said, stepping forward, and for the first time I heard his classroom voice, his full-out voice, a combination of Southern drawl and acquired New England sharpness.

"No celebrations," he said, arriving at the middle of the field. "This is a scrimmage. It's just the first step. We're all one team. We are the Giant Metrozoids." He said the ridiculous name as though it were Fighting Irish, or Rambling Wrecks, an old and hallowed name in the American pigskin tradition. The kids stopped, subdued and puzzled. "Hands together," he said, and stretched his out, and solemnly the boys laid their hands on his, one after another. "One, two, three, together!" and all the hands sprang up. He had replaced a ritual of celebration with one of solidarity—and the boys sensed that solidarity was somehow at once more solemn and more fun than any passing victory could be.

He had, I realized on the way home, accomplished a lot of things. He had taught them how to stand and how to kneel—not just how to do these things but that there was a right way to do these things. He had taught them that playing was a form of learning—that a scrimmage was a step somewhere on the way toward a goal. And he had taught them that they were the Giant Metrozoids. It was actually a lot for one hour.

When I say that I began working harder, I can barely begin to explain what his idea of working hard meant: it was Bear Bryant's idea of hard work circa 1955, it was General Patton's idea of being driven, only more military. It was coupled with a complete openness and equality, a vulnerability to his students' criticisms so great that it was almost alarming. He was working that hard, and was as eager to have you spot his weights as he was to spot yours. In what now seems like the halcyon days of 1984, a Saturday morning in winter would begin with a phone call and a voice booming, breaking right through the diaphanous protection of the answering machine, "Hey, folks, it's Kirk. I got up early to walk the pooch and I think I got some progress made on this here problem. What say we meet at eleven and trade papers?" I would curse, get out of bed, get to work, and be ready three hours later, with a new draft of whatever the hell I was supposed to be working on. We would meet at the little island that separates SoHo, where we lived, and Tribeca, where he and his wife, the artist Elyn Zimmerman, had their loft, and, standing there, he would turn the pages, and I would turn the pages, and he would show me all the ways in which I had missed the boat. Above all, he would insist, break it down: Who were the artists? What were the pictures? Give me the dates. Compile lists, make them inclusive, walk through it. You break it down in order to build it back up. What does it mean, why does it matter, for this artist, for art history, for the development of human consciousness? I would go back to work and the phone would ring again at three. "Hey, folks, it's Kirk. What do you say we meet and go over this new draft I've done and then maybe get some dinner?" And we would meet, and all four — or six or eight or ten — people would come together around him, and have dinner, and drink a good bottle of white wine and a good bottle of red wine and finally, exhausted, I would get to bed.

And then the phone would ring again. "Hey, folks, it's Kirk. I got to walk the pooch one last time, and I was just thinking that I may finally have sorted out the locomotive from the caboose in this thing. What do you say . . ." And I would put a coat on over my pajamas and go out one last time, in the whipping cold of midnight, and he would open the envelope right there and start reading, signalling to me to do the same, while his black Chow raced around, and we would try one more time to clarify exactly why Picasso looked at African art or why Gauguin went to Tahiti, while a generation walked by us in Astor Place haircuts and long vintage coats on their way to the Odeon.

I had always loved football, too, and we watched it together on Saturday afternoons and Monday nights for years. We saw a lot of good games, but we missed the big one. In 1984, we went up to New England to celebrate Thanksgiving, and we were supposed to watch what promised to be the greatest college football game of all time, Boston College–Miami, Doug Flutie versus Bernie Kosar. But our wives wanted to do something else — go look at things at a Shaker fair, I think — and we came home to find that we'd skipped the greatest college football game of all time, which Flutie had won by a Hail Mary, a long, desperation heave, on the last play of the game. We stared at each other in disbelief — we missed that? — and for the next twenty years "Boston College–Miami" was code between us for something you really, really wanted to do but couldn't, because your wife wanted to do something else. "You want to try and grab a burger at six?" "Uh — Boston College–Miami." It was code between us also for the ironies of life, our great, overlooked game, the one that got away.

"I think I'm going to make the motivational speech," I said to Luke as we walked over to Metrozoid Field the next Friday. I had been working on the motivational speech for several days. I didn't see a role for myself on the Metrozoids as a leader, and I thought I might make a contribution as the Tommy Lasorda type, raising everyone's spirits and bleeding Metrozoid blue.

"O.K.," he said, relenting for the moment. "Tell it to me again."

"We're here to separate the men from the boys," I said, stopping at the Miner's Gate entrance to the Park, at Seventy-ninth Street, and trying to growl like Gary Busey as the Bear, "and then we're going to separate the warriors from the men." I paused to let this sink in. "And then we're going to separate the heroes from the warriors — and then we're going to separate the legends from the heroes. And then, at last, we're going to separate the gods from the legends. So, if you're not ready to be a football god, you don't want to be a Metrozoid." Long pause. "Now, won't that make the guys motivated?"

He reflected. "I don't know if they'll be motivated. They'll certainly be nauseated. Nobody wants to be motivated to play football, Dad. They want to play football."

Kirk ran another minimalist practice on this second week, and he missed the next because he was too sick from the chemo. I ran the session, and I thought, ambitiously, that it would be good to try a play at last, so I set about teaching them a simple stop-and-go. I got them to line up and run short, stop, and then go long. They ran it one by one, but none of them could get the timing quite right, and the boy who was supposed to be quarterbacking the thing couldn't get the right zip on the ball. Everyone was more annoyed than motivated, so I stopped after ten minutes, and sent them back to scrimmaging. They were restless for their coach.

It wasn't any surprise that he missed a practice; the surprise was that he made as many as he did. The chemo he was getting was so caustic that it had to be infused gradually, over sessions lasting three or four hours. Years of chemotherapy had left the veins in his arms so collapsed that sometimes it took half an hour for a nurse just to find an entry. He would grimace while being poked at with the needle, and then go on talking. He had the chemotherapy at one of the midtown extensions of the hospital, where the walls were earnestly decorated with Impressionist posters, Manet and Monet and Renoir—the art that he had taught a generation to relish for its spring-coiled internal contradictions and tensions there as something soothing for dying patients to look at.

He would talk, for hours. Sometimes he talked about the Metrozoids, and sometimes about Dylan or Elvis, but mostly he tried to talk through the Mellon lectures he was to give in Washington. He was, he said, going to speak without a text, just with a slide list. This was partly a bravura performer's desire to do one last bravura performance. It was also because he had come to believe that in art history description was all the theory you needed; if you could describe what was there, and what it meant (to the painter, to his time, to you), you didn't need a deeper supporting theory. Art wasn't meaningful because, after you looked at it, someone explained it; art explained itself by being there to look at.

He thought that modern art was a part of modern life: not a reaction against it, or a subversion of it, but set within its values and contradictions, as surely as Renaissance art was set in its time. His book on the origins of modernism, *A Fine Disregard,* used an analogy from the history of rugby to illuminate the moment of artistic innovation: during a soccer game at the Rugby School, in England, an unknown young man named William Webb Ellis picked up the ball and ran with it, and a new game came into being. A lot of people thought that Kirk was celebrating a Romantic view of invention. But his was a liberal, not a Romantic, view of art. It began with an individual and extended to a community. What fascinated him was the circumstances that let someone act creatively and other people applaud instead of blowing the whistle.

That was what he loved to talk about when he talked about Elvis. He revered the moment when, in 1954, Elvis walked into a studio and played with Scotty and Bill and Sam, and everything suddenly came together. Had any of the elements been absent, as they easily might have been, as they usually are—had the guitarist Scotty Moore been less adaptable, the producer Sam Phillips less patient—then Elvis would have crooned his songs, no one would have cared, and nothing would have happened. The readiness was all. These moments were his faith, his stations: Picasso and Braque in their studios cutting the headlines right out of the newspapers and pasting them on the pictures to make collage, Richard Serra (first among Kirk's contemporary heroes) throwing hot lead in a studio corner and finding art in its rococo patterns.

Toward the end of one chemotherapy session, as he worried his way through his themes, a young man wearing the usual wool cap on his head came around the usually inviolable barrier of drapery that separated one "suite" from the next.

"You are professor?" he asked shyly, with a Russian accent, and Kirk shook his head.

"No, you are professor. I know. We have treatment at same time, every week. Same three hours," and he gestured toward his cap, with a short, we're-in-this-together smile. "I used to bring book, but now I just listen to you."

That Sunday of the first Mellon lecture, Kirk walked to the lectern after an introduction. The room was sold out, and the overflow had been sent to another lecture room. "Can I have the lights down, please," he said, and I saw that he had kept his word: he had no text, no notes, just a list of slides. He began to show and describe objects from sixties American minimalism—plywood boxes and laid-out bricks and striped paintings. He didn't offer a "theory," or a historical point. He tried, instead, to explain that a landscape that looked simple—there had been Abstract Expressionist splashes, and then there were all these boxes—was actually extraordinarily complex: there was a big difference between the boxes of Donald Judd, elegizing New York Canal Street culture, and the gleaming, body-shop boxes of the West Coast minimalists, glorifying California car culture.

"The less there is to look at," he said, pacing, as he always did, "the more important it is that we look at it closely and carefully. Small differences make all the difference. So, for example, the next time somebody tries to sell you on the mechanical exactitude of Frank Stella's stripes, think again about the beautiful, delicate breathing space in these stripes, the incredible feathered edge of the touch of the picture, which has everything to do with its kind of espresso-grounds, Beat Generation blackness that gives the picture its particular relationship to its epoch and time."

So he walked people through it. There were the bright, Matissean stripes of Ellsworth Kelly, made from the traced shapes of Parisian shadows, and those dark, espresso-bar simplicities of Stella. There was the tradition of the Bauhaus diaspora, all those German refugee artists who had been forced to go to South America, and who had proselytized for a kind of utopian, geometric abstraction—which had then appeared in New York just as New York artists were using geometric forms to indicate a cool-guy stoical distaste for utopian aspirations, creating a comedy of misunderstanding and crossbreeding. An art that had seemed like a group of quadratic equations set by a joyless teacher had been revealed as a sequence of inventions thought up by people. Where there seemed to be things, there were stories. The audience, at the end of the hour, was riveted. Someone was breaking it down, and then was going to build it back up. You didn't want to miss it.

"O.K., we're going to learn a play," he said, the next Friday at Metrozoid practice.

The boys were standing on Metrozoid Field in their Metrozoid shirts in a semicircle around him. He showed them the play he had in mind, tracing it in the dirt with a stick: the quarterback takes the ball from the center and laterals to the halfback, who looks for one of three downfield receivers, who go in overlapping paths down the right sideline—one long, one medium, one short. The boys clapped hands and ran to the center of the field, terrier-quick and terrier-eager.

"No, no. Don't run. Just walk through it the first few times."

The boys then ostentatiously walked through the play, clowning around a bit, as though in slow motion. He laughed at that. But he had them do it anyway, five or six times, at a walk.

"Now let's just amble through it, same thing." The play took on a courtly quality, like a seventeenth-century dance. The boys did it at that pace, again and again: hike and pitch and look and throw.

"Now let's just run easy." The boys trotted through their pattern, and Garrett, the chosen quarterback, kept overthrowing the ball. Gently but firmly, Kirk changed the running back with the quarterback, Ken for Garrett, so that Garrett had the honor of being official quarterback but wouldn't have to throw, and then had them trot through it again. Ken threw hard, and the ball was caught.

After twenty minutes, Kirk clapped his hands. "Full speed. Everybody run." The boys got in their stances, and took off—really zoomed. The ball came nervously back, the quarterback tossed it to the halfback, he turned and threw it to the short receiver.

"Great!" At top eight-year-old speed, the ball had been thrown for a completion. The Metrozoids had mastered a play.

"Now let's do it again," Kirk said. I heard him whisper to Matthew, the short receiver, as he lined up, "Fall down!" They started the play, Garrett to Ken. Matthew fell down. Ken's eyes showed a moment of panic, but then he looked up, and saw the next boy, the middle receiver, Luke, waiting right in line, and he threw there. Complete.

"Nice read," Kirk said, clapping his hands. "Nice read, nice throw, nice catch. Well-executed play."

The boys beamed at each other.

"You break it down, and then you build it back up," Kirk said as they met at the center of the field to do the pile of hands. "The hardest play you learn is just steps put together."

By the fourth and fifth weeks of the Mellons, the scene at the National Gallery was almost absurd. People were lining up at nine in the morning for the two-o'clock lecture; I met a woman who had driven down from Maine to be there. The overflow room had to be supplied with its own overflow room, and the museum finally printed a slightly short-tempered handout. ("But what if I need to use the restroom while standing in line?" "If you need to use the restroom while in line, ask your neighbor to save your place.")

The fifth lecture would, he thought, be the toughest to put over. He found it easy to make an audience feel the variety, the humanity, of abstract art, even an art as refined and obstinate as the art of Judd or the young Frank Stella. But it was harder to make people accept, and relish, that art's perversity, and harder still to make them see that its perversity was exactly the humanism it offered. In the lecture hall, he explained that, as E. H. Gombrich had shown half a century ago in his Mellon lectures, representational artists were always making forms and then matching them—taking inherited stereotypes and "correcting" them in the light of new things seen. Leonardo, for instance, had inherited the heraldic image of a horse, and he had bent it and reshaped it until it looked like an actual animal. Abstract artists were always making forms and then trying to unmatch them, to make sure that their art didn't look like things in the world. Sooner or later, though, they always did, and this meant that, alongside abstraction, there was a kind of sardonic running commentary, which jumped on it anytime that it did look like some banal familiar thing.

Pop art was the most obvious source and form of this mockery: Roy Lichtenstein made fun of the abstract Op artist Victor Vasarely for making pictures that looked like the bottom of a sneaker, and Andy Warhol thumbed his nose at Barnett Newman for making pictures that looked like matchbook covers, and so on. But this counter-tradition wasn't mere jeering. It was generative, too: it forced and inspired new art. It kept abstraction from wallowing complacently in a vague mystical humanism. In the parody and satire of abstraction, its apparent negation, lay its renewal.

This process, Kirk explained, easily visible in the dialogue of minimalism and Pop, was just as vital, if less obvious, in the relationship between Jackson Pollock and Cy Twombly, two of his heroes. Twombly's squiggles and scribbles were not dutifully inspired by but actually parodied Pollock's method: "Everything that Twombly achieves he achieves by the ironic distancing of himself from Pollock. Everything that is liquid is turned dry. Everything that is light is turned dark. Everything that is simple and spontaneous and athletic is turned obsessive, repetitive, self-conscious in Twombly. By this kind of negation, he re-realizes, on a completely different scale and completely different terms, the exact immediacy of energy conveyed to canvas that Pollock has." Negation and parody were forms of influence as powerful as any solemn "transmission" of received icons. Doubt led to argument; argument made art.

That Friday, out on Metrozoid Field, Kirk divided the boys into two teams. "A team runs the play and B team defends," he said.

"But they'll know what we're gonna do," someone on the A team complained.

"That's O.K. Most of the time, the other team knows what you're gonna do. That's called your tendency. The key is to do it anyway."

"But if they know—"

"Just run the play. Most of the time, the other team knows. The hard part is doing it right even when you know exactly what's coming."

The offense boys ran their one play, the flea-flicker, and the defense boys ran around trying to stop it. Standing on the sidelines, I was amazed to see how hard it was to stop the play even if you did know it was coming. The boys on defense ran around, nettled, converging on the wrong receiver and waving their hands blindly at the ball. The boys on offense looked a little smug.

He called them together. "You know what they're going to do. Why can't you stop it?"

The boys on the B team, slightly out of breath, shrugged.

"You can't stop it because they know what they're going to do but you don't know what you're going to do against it. One team has a plan and the other team doesn't. One team knows what it's doing, and the other team knows what they're doing but it doesn't know what it's doing. Now let's figure out what you're going to do."

He went to work. Who's the fastest kid they have? O.K., let's put the fastest kid we have on him. Or, better, what if each guy takes a part of the field and just stays there and knocks the ball down if it comes near him? Don't move now; just stay there and knock it down. They tried both ways—man-to-man and zone—and found that both ways worked. The play lost its lustre. The boys on the B team now seemed smug, and the boys on the A team lost.

"Maybe you need another wrinkle," he said to the A team. "Let's work on it."

Watching him on Metrozoid Field, you could see what made him a great teacher on bigger questions for bigger kids. Football was a set of steps, art a set of actions. The mysterious, baffling things—modern art, the zone defense—weren't so mysterious or baffling if you broke them down. By the end of the spring practice, the eight-year-olds were instinctively rotating out of man-to-man into a zone and the offense audibling out of a spread formation into a half-back option, just as the grownups in Washington were suddenly seeing the differences and similarities between Pollock's drips and Twombly's scrawls.

One particularly bright kid, Jacob, was scared of the ball, the onrushing object and the thousand intricate adjustments you had to make to catch it. He would throw his arms out and look away, instead of bringing his hands together. Kirk worked with him. He stood nearby and threw him the ball, underhanded, and then got him to do one thing right. When he caught it, Kirk wasn't too encouraging; when he dropped one he wasn't too hard. He did not make him think it was easy. He did not make him think that he had done it when he hadn't. He made him think that he could do it if he chose.

It is said sometimes that the great teachers and mentors, the rabbis and gurus, achieve their ends by inducting the disciple into a kind of secret circle of knowledge and belief, make of their charisma a kind of gift. The more I think about it, though, the more I suspect that the best teachers—and, for that matter, the truly long-term winning coaches, the Walshes and Woodens and Weavers— do something else. They don't mystify the work and offer themselves as a model of rabbinical authority, a practice that nearly always lapses into a history of acolytes and excommunications. The real teachers and coaches may offer a charismatic model—they probably have to—but then they insist that all the magic they have to offer is a commitment to repetition and perseverance. The great oracles may enthrall, but the really great teachers demystify. They make particle physics into a series of diagrams that anyone can follow, football into a series of steps that anyone can master, and art into a series of slides that anyone can see. A guru gives us himself and then his system; a teacher gives us his subject, and then ourselves.

If this story was the made-for-television movie that every story about early death threatens to become, we would have arranged one fiery game between the Giant Metrozoids and another team, a bigger, faster, slightly evil team, and the Metrozoids would win it for their coach. It didn't happen like that. Not that the Metrozoids didn't want a game. As their self-confidence increased, they kept urging us to find some other team of eight-year-olds that they could test themselves against. I was all for it, but Kirk, I sensed, was not. Whenever the boys raised the possibility, he would say, diffidently, "Let's wait till the fall," knowing, of course, that the fall, his fall, would never come.

I understood the hold he had on the Metrozoids. But when I thought about his hesitation I started to understand the hold that the Metrozoids had on him. I had once said something fatuous to him about enjoying tonight's sunset, whatever tomorrow would bring, and he had replied that when you know you are dying you cannot simply "live in the moment." You loved a fine sunset because it slipped so easily into a history, yours and the world's; part of the pleasure lay in knowing that it was one in a stream of sunsets you had loved, each good, some better, one or two perfect, moving forward in an open series. Once you knew that this one could be the last, it filled you with a sense of dread; what was the point of collecting paintings in a museum you knew was doomed to burn down?

But there were pleasures in life that were meaningful in themselves, that did not depend on their place in an ongoing story, now interrupted. These pleasures were not "aesthetic" thrills—not the hang gliding you had never done or the trip to Maui you had never taken—but things that existed outside the passage of time, things that were beyond comparison, or, rather, beside comparison, off to one side of it. He loved the Metrozoid practices, I came to see, because for him they weren't really practicing. The game would never come, and the game didn't matter. What mattered was doing it.

At the last practice of the school year, the boys ran their plays and scrimmaged, and the familiar forms of football, of protection and pass routes and coverages, were all there, almost magically emerging from the chaos of eight-year-olds in motion. At the end, the boys came running up to him, and he stood in place, and low-fived each one of them. "See you in September," the kids cried, and Kirk let the small hands slap his broad one, and smiled. "We'll work again in the fall," he said, and I knew he meant that someone would.

That Sunday, he did something that surprised me. It was the last lecture of the Mellons, and he talked about death. Until then, I had never heard him mention it in public. He had dealt with it by refusing to describe it—from Kirk the ultimate insult. Now, in this last lecture, he turned on the audience and quoted a line from a favorite movie, *Blade Runner*, in which the android leader says, "Time to die," and at the very end he showed them one of his favorite works, a Richard Serra *Torqued Ellipse*, and he showed them how the work itself, in the physical experiences it offered—inside and outside, safe and precarious, cold and warm—made all the case that needed to be made for the complexity, the emotional urgency, of abstract art. Then he began to talk about his faith. "But what kind of faith?" he asked. "Not a faith in absolutes. Not a religious kind of faith. A faith only in possibility, a faith not that we will know something, finally, but a faith in not knowing, a faith in our ignorance, a faith in our being confounded and dumbfounded, as something fertile with possible meaning and growth. . . . Because it can be done, it will be done. And now I am done." The applause, when it came, was stadium applause, and it went on a long time.

By July, the doctors had passed him right out of even the compassionate trials, and were into the world of guesses and radiation. "It's a Hail Mary," he said of a new radiation therapy that they were proposing. "But, who knows, maybe I'll get the Doug Flutie of radiologists." Then a slight ache in his back which he thought was a disk he'd hurt water-skiing turned out to be a large tumor in his spine, and the end came quickly.

His wife, Elyn, had to be out of the city, and I spent the last Saturday afternoon of his life with him. In the old way, I went into his office to work on something I was writing. Kirk went to see what was on television. He had, I noticed, a team photograph of the Metrozoids at their last practice propped up on the coffee table. By then, he could hardly walk, and his breath came hard.

But he called out, "Yo. You got to come here."

"What?"

"You won't believe this. Boston College–Miami."

Damned if it wasn't. ESPN Classics had a "Hail Mary" Saturday, all the great games decided on the last play, and now, twenty years late, they were showing the game from beginning to end: the whole game, with the old graphics and the announcer's promos, exactly as it had first been shown.

So we finally got to watch the game. And it was 1984 again, and the game was still thrilling, even though you knew what the outcome would be, and how it would happen. Kirk's brother, Sam, came around, and he watched, too, the three of us just enjoying a good game, until at last here we were, at that famous, miraculous, final Hail Mary, Doug Flutie dropping back and rolling out, to heave the ball desperately downfield.

"Look at that!" Kirk cried, and the ball was still in midair out of view, up above the television screen.

"What?" I asked, as the ball made its arc and fell into the hands of Gerard Phelan and the announcers went wild.

"That's no Hail Mary. Watch it again and you'll see. That's a coverage breakdown." The old defensive-backfield coach spoke evenly, as, twenty years before, the crowd jumped and screamed. "Safety steps up too soon because he doesn't think Flutie can make that throw on the run. What he doesn't see is that Flutie has time to square around and get his feet set on the rollout, which adds fifteen yards to his range. Safety steps up too soon, Phelan runs a standard post route, and that's it. That safety sees Flutie get his feet set, makes the right read, and there's no completion." Turning to us, he said, "That is no Hail Mary, friends. That's no miracle. That is just the play you make. That is one gentleman making the right read and running the right pattern and the other gentleman making the wrong read." And for one moment he looked as happy as I had ever known him: one more piece of the world's mysteries demystified without being debunked, a thing legendary and hallowed broken down into the real pattern of human initiative and human weakness and human action that had made it happen. We had been waiting twenty years to see a miracle, and what we saw—what he saw, once again, and showed us—was one more work of art, a pattern made by people out of the possibilities the moment offered to a ready mind. It was no Hail Mary, friends; it was a play you made.

He turned to me and Sam, and, still elated by the revelation of what had really happened all those years ago, we began to talk about Ralph Emerson and Richard Serra. And then Kirk said, heavily, "There is nothing in the world I would rather be doing than taking part in this conversation. But I have to lie down." He died four days afterward, late at night, having spent the day talking about Hitchcock films and eighteenth-century hospital architecture.

Luke and Elyn and I went up to the football field at Williams last fall and, with some other friends, spread his ashes in the end zone, under the goalposts. At his memorial, at the Metropolitan Museum of Art, Renee Fleming sang and the violinist Arnold Steinhardt played and the art world of New York turned out and listened and recalled him. I think a lot of them must have been puzzled, in the slide show that Elyn had prepared to begin the evening, and which recapitulated his career, from Savannah to Princeton, to see toward the end a separate section gravely entitled "The Giant Metrozoids," with the big figure surrounded by small boys. But I'm sure he would have been glad to see them there. The Metrozoids are getting back in business again, with an inadequate coach. I've thought about finally making the motivational speech, but I don't think I need to. The Metrozoids don't need to learn how to separate the men from the heroes. They know.

Migdalia Cruz
From Telling Tales

This play is dedicated to Gloria, Pedro, Nancy and Virginia Cruz.

SAND

She wasn't supposed to go on the roof. I tole her not to. But she wouldn't listen to me. She never listens to me. She's always the brave one.

I cried for a long time after that. I cried for her and I cried for me, because I din't go with her. I din't know what was gonna happen. And now I'll always wonder what woulda happened if I'da gone.

I was on the fire escape when they caught him. A whole army of men from the neighborhood were carrying him up above their heads. And he squirmed like a rat, like a fucking rat in a corner surrounded by hungry cats.

They took him into the playground and threw him down into the sandbox. Everybody stood around him and screamed at him. You couldn't even understand what they were saying.

I closed my eyes for a minute and when I opened them again, he was buried in the sand. Two men held him down while everybody else threw sand in his face. His eyes were filled with it and he was screaming. Then they filled up his mouth and the screaming stopped. He threw up and choked and he kept choking on his own blood and spit and sand.

And I smiled. . . .

That's when I thought there must be a God, because there was justice.

They picked him up and my daddy tied his legs to the back of his '58 Plymouth Valiant. He got that car the day I was born — two months before Anita was born. That car was us. It was as old as us. Eight years old. So wise for eight. So strong. Stronger than we could ever be. Stronger than my father. They dragged him through the streets he knew so well. The streets we played in. Where he watched us and made his plan. I hoped that car would climb to the roof and jump over — like Anita. Rip him up, like he ripped Anita. Take his hands and make him pull his own guts out. And then the balls. Slash. Cut. Tear.

He tore her clothes off with his teeth. He ripped her open with his teeth. His teeth were yellow and sharp — like gold. Golden teeth. Now he had vomit and blood caked onto his teeth. They weren't so pretty like they used to be. They looked good now. Like they were supposed to look.

We keep away from the sandbox now. It's strange when people from an island are scared of sand.

JESUS

I don't understand anything. I just keep seeing a pincushion shaped like a heart. It's pink with yellow fringe and where the pins are stuck, there's blood dripping. I remember where that comes from. . . .

When I was very little, about one, my sister Tati, who was two, got very sick. I didn't see my parents much for the next five years because they were always at the hospital. Turns out she had lead poisoning. My mom gave me a picture of Jesus when I was two and told me to pray to it — that Tati would get better if only I did this.

Jesus had light brown hair and blue eyes and his heart showed and it was bluish red with swords going through it and blood dripping from the wounds. But he was smiling.

For Mother's Day, when I was in first grade, we had to sew pincushions for our moms. I made mine heart-shaped. The teacher liked it very much. So did my mother. Everytime she stuck a pin in it, I snuck a look. Would it bleed? I wondered.

Tati was pale when she came back. I missed her. We played rocking horse together. That's where you cradle each other and rock back and forth in the middle of the sofa where the springs are loosest. After awhile only I could do the cradling. That was okay. But nobody ever explained it to me.

YELLOW EYES

I'm sitting in front of my great-grandfather. He is telling me a story about how he fell in love with my great-grandmother, but I can't hear him. He has beautiful yellow eyes and I'm hypnotized by them. I just sit staring at him. I can see every line of his skull. Every vein. His skin is like coffee with milk, like my father's coffee with milk. He doesn't get out of bed anymore. He sits up though and we dress him. He's wearing a brownish-green sweater, a cardigan. His dirty undershirt shows beneath it. It is stained with cherry chewing tobacco. His words smell like mucus and tobacco. People think mucus doesn't smell. But I think it smells. It smells yellow. His pants are brown; they are too short and cuffed. One cuff is torn and hanging off his thin, long legs. He has the longest legs I've ever seen. He's the tallest man I've ever known. He has scars on his arms and his legs from chains. He is strong.

He used to hold me over his head with his feet. Like a circus act. Like a balancing act. We could be famous I always thought. He's so strong and I'm so graceful.

He has on the socks I bought him for Christmas. My ma said to buy him socks because old people's feet get very cold.

He was one hundred six when he died and she was ninety-nine. She was also nuts. She'd wake up a different person every day. We always had to guess three or four times before we hit on the right name to call her. She thought she lived in a great manor in the country and my great-grandfather was her valet instead of her husband. My mother was the poor woman who came in once a week to do laundry. She pitied all of us and gave us chocolates because "Poor people like chocolates. It takes their minds off their little problems. . . ." They weren't really chocolates though—she used to cut out cubes from bars of soap and pretend they were chocolates. She'd watch you too. She'd watch you put 'em in your mouth and wait till your mouth foamed up before she'd turn away. "Good chocolates, huh? You people always enjoy my chocolates. You're like dogs for them. Hungry for them. I never liked sweets myself. They weaken your heart. People fall in love when they eat too much candy. Always with the wrong person. That's why so many children have children. They don't know. Their minds are in the sweets, covered with sugar. No sense."

PAPO CHIBIRICO

Papo Chibirico was fifteen when I was seven. He was my first love. He bought me coloring books and candy and took me to the zoo. Anthony Vargas tried to give me coloring books too, but I punched him in the nose and made him bleed. Papo thought it was a good idea. "Don't let the boys bully you," he always said.

Every summer we formed softball teams. Once we were playing and I walked backwards to make a catch. I didn't know I was on a hill and fell off into a pile of beer bottles. Papo carried me the fifteen blocks home with one hand holding my left knee together. He pulled the glass out of the wound and went with my Mom and me to the hospital. He was mature for a kid. That's what I thought.

When I turned eleven, I went to P.R. for the summer. I returned a foot and a half taller and five shades darker. Papo was six inches shorter than me then. How could he be six inches shorter, if he was eight years older? Papo changed that summer too, he got more muscles and was training to become a wrestler. My dad and I watched his first televised fight on Channel Forty-seven. That's when I found out he was a midget—because he was a midget wrestler.

Papo fought the Jamaican Kid. The strength was in their arms really. Their little legs just kicked the air. With their arms they pinned each other to the floor. My Dad laughed and I wondered what was so funny. He explained to me that it was supposed to be funny—that's why you watch midget wrestling, to laugh. The Jamaican Kid won.

The next day I saw Papo. He was still friendly to me even though he was a TV star. All the kids on the block wanted to talk to him. But he talked just to me. The big kids were always challenging him to a fight. He would say "No," but they would push him and hit him until there was nothing left to say. Sometimes three or four would gang up on him and hold him up in the air. His useless legs would swing wildly at his attackers always missing their mark. "Some tough guy!" Then they'd throw him into a dumpster. I used to watch and cry because I didn't know what else to do. All I could do was wait for them to leave and help Papo out of the garbage. He always got mad at me then. "Don't you know you could get hurt?! Stay away from me, will you! I don't need your help!" But he always needed my help.

He got to be a really good wrestler. The kind the crowd stands up for. He got tougher too. Carried a knife and stabbed somebody, so I couldn't see him anymore. He'd look at me from across the street when I was sitting on the fire escape doing my homework. He waved and I waved back, but he always turned away before he saw me wave. I guess he was afraid I wouldn't.

When he got a little money saved, he got a special bicycle on which he could reach the pedals. He spent hours on that bike, circling the neighborhood. I watched him go by and go by and go by again. He looked normal on that bike—happy. He walked with a limp now. The Jamaican Kid went crazy one night and bit a chunk out of his calf. He got an infection from it. The Jamaican Kid never even apologized. I know because I asked. That's the last thing we ever talked about.

It was one of those real hot August nights, when everybody's on the street because nobody can sleep. Some guys are playing the congas in the playground, small children are playing tag, mothers are gossiping and the men are playing dominoes. Papo comes by on his bike. It's a pretty one—black with a red seat and Papo's in red and black too. He looks sharp. His face is pretty. He's the only one on the block with green eyes. Everybody wanted those eyes. Everybody says hello. He starts showing off, making the bike jump and taking turns real fast and low. People applaud. He does this over and over, people finally stop watching but he keeps saying "Look at me, look at me!" Now people are embarrassed to look. Papo goes by one more time. . . .

I don't know where the car came from. It was a new car, I think. Shiny. Maybe just freshly waxed. People always wax their cars in the summer. He wouldn't have lived long anyway—that's what people said. "God bless him. Midgets don't live very long."

But he wasn't a midget, he was a dwarf.

PARCHEESI

The stage of a school auditorium. The walls are mint green. The stage is just a platform. No walls. The floor of the stage is brown. It's two thirty in the afternoon. Assembly time. All the children are saying the pledge of allegiance, except the Jehovah's Witnesses. The principal is seated in the front row. She's seven and a half feet tall with long, blonde hair and long, white teeth. Her bangs touch her eyebrows. Her ears touch her chin. Whenever there's an announcement made, she yells at the child to speak up. "How can you say something on a stage that no one can hear?!" I hated that stage.

I was My Fair Lady on that stage. Eliza Doolittle. I had a voice then. My friend Sharon Gray always forgot her lines and the principal would yell at her. "How can we enjoy the show if we can't hear you? Only stupid people forget their lines."

Sharon was very pretty . . . she's a cop now. I used to hate cops but I could never hate Sharon. She was my dumbest best friend. She didn't know how to read in the fifth grade and I taught her.

On my eleventh birthday, she came to my house with a Parcheesi game. I already had a Parcheesi game. I said "Oh, I have one just like that." I felt bad because as soon as I said it I knew she was embarrassed, so then I knew she had brought it for me. She was going to take it back, but I told her I lost all the pieces out of my other game and so it was a good thing she had bought this new set. It was prettier than the one I had. She bought it at John's Bargain Store. That was our favorite store because everything was either fifty-nine cents or eighty-eight cents. I couldn't believe she had bought me anything . . . it was a lot of money to spend on a friend.

We sat right in front of the television and watched Captain Jack's Popeye cartoons first—"Ahoy, ye maties!"—"Ahoy, Captain Jack." And then we played Parcheesi. She ate me first and went twenty spaces. I hate when someone eats me first because then I'm bound to lose. The first eater always wins in Parcheesi. She ate me second and third too. But then she stopped eating me even though she could. I guess because it was my birthday. I ended up winning.

Sharon had the blackest skin I've ever seen except in *National Geographic*. It was polished wood. My mother used to say she must use lemon Pledge on her face because it was so shiny. And she smelled like lemons too, because of our business. We sold coconut ices and lemonade. My dad showed us how to make the ices so we gave him part of our profits — that was Sharon's idea. Sharon made the lemonade because she was an expert. Her mother made lemonade for her to take to school on Pot Luck Lunch Day and all the kids loved it. It had rosehips in it. But we didn't know what they were then — we thought it was a drug because it tasted so good.

In sixth grade, we got separated by Mrs. Newman because she said Sharon wasn't smart enough to be in the same class with me. I was in six-one and they put her in six-twelve. That wasn't too bad though because we had up to six-twenty-six. The kids in six-twenty-six were called the F-Troop. They weren't bad but they were stupid. The kids in six-twelve weren't real stupid, they just smoked too much. The kids in six-fifteen were the school terrors. They started a war against all the other classes. Sharon got stabbed in the stomach after she stood up for me when some girls from six-fifteen tried to steal my bus pass. The next day they were waiting for her in the yard and worked her over. Sharon said if there'd only been three she could have handled it, but there were five.

I used to wonder what happened to Sharon until I met her on the bus. She saw me first and came over and hugged me. She remembered me. I was so glad to see her because I almost never stop thinking about her. She's always there in the back of my head — like a soft spot that babies have that if struck kills them instantly. Dogs have a spot like that too. It's on their sides.

Sharon had a dog. His name was Don. Junie, her little brother named him — he just couldn't say dog, it came out like don. It was a big poodle with all its hair — not a clipped, ugly, French one. We took Don everywhere with us. He would come into the bathroom and watched everything you did in there. He was curious and I don't blame him. I always liked watching dogs pee in the street. So shameless. I wanted a life like that. Sharon wanted order. She wanted money. She wanted to have a history and I wanted to have a past.

So now she can blow your head off with a three fifty-seven magnum and I can tell you about it.

Billy Collins
Introduction to Poetry

I ask them to take a poem
and hold it up to the light
like a color slide

or press an ear against its hive.

I say drop a mouse into a poem
and watch him probe his way out,

or walk inside the poem's room
and feel the walls for a light switch.

I want them to waterski
across the surface of a poem
waving at the author's name on the shore.

But all they want to do
is tie the poem to a chair with rope
and torture a confession out of it.

They begin beating it with a hose
to find out what it really means.

CHAPTER EIGHT

STRUCTURE: ELEMENTS

Structure is the conscious, purposeful arrangement of your material. Sometimes writers get lucky, and images seem to arrange themselves. Some pieces come out whole, in the right order. That "flow" happens automatically *some of the time.* But, because writers can't count on structure to "just happen" all the time, we must spend time learning the basic principles of ordering images.

What is true for the writing strategies—energy, tension, pattern—is true for structure: Creative writers attend to structure in different ways at different times in their writing process. Structure is a shaping strategy that helps you generate new work as well as deepen existing work.

In some cultures and time periods, writers have enjoyed working strictly within established structures. In other places and periods in our history, experimentation and originality—*unstructured writing*—have been valued most highly. Think about what you enjoy

> *Style and structure are the essence of a book; great ideas are hogwash.*
>
> — VLADIMIR NABOKOV

reading the most. Dense, formless rants? Short snappy plots? Novels with long introductions, long chapters? Graphic novels? Reading with attention to structure—paying attention to how a structure keeps your interest level high—helps you create inventive, workable structures for your own readers. Most readers want to be informed *and* entertained.

Structure isn't a straitjacket. It's a blueprint that you use, or design yourself, to organize your work. In fact, many times readers aren't even aware you are using a specific structure. Structure in creative writing, as in building, does its work behind the walls, in the ceiling, underneath the floors. It's the framework that holds the building together, and then when we enter the grand hall, our attention as readers is captured by the details, the feelings, the emotions of the experience. Structure doesn't constrain your writing, it lets you create a floor for the reader, so she can move around in your piece easily.

This chapter discusses the component parts of narrative. Narrative, as you may know, means telling a story, and creative writers use storytelling techniques in fiction, of course, but also in creative nonfiction essays and in narrative poetry. The next chapter offers a kind of recipe book of specific instructions for expanding your structure repertoire. Some story and poem forms—structures—have been so successful with readers over the centuries that creative writers continue to use, combine, and reinvent them. So, after learning the basic moves (elements) that make up structure, you'll practice some more complex dances (forms).

> *The higher your structure is to be, the deeper must be its foundation.*
> — SAINT AUGUSTINE

Keep an open mind—most students find that once they get a piece started, paying attention to structure makes creative writing vastly easier and more rewarding. Learning a new way to see the pieces of a text and learning some new recipes for writing will help you later as you come up with your own innovations.

IMAGES

Images transport readers. Structure *keeps* the reader transported, sustaining the sensory experience. At its most basic, structure is simply *a sequence of images*. All semester, you have been working to create pieces of alive, interesting, focused writing—images. When you string together a series of these images in meaningful sequences, you are making a structure. It's like preparing a fine dinner. Your meal is only as great as the ingredients. The key to success with structure is to use strong, vivid, transporting images.

Images are your building blocks. For the structure exercises you will practice in this chapter and the next, it's often easiest to start with an image from previous work, your journal, or work in progress. You can also start from the ground up, but it's usually easier to start with an image extracted from an existing piece. Just as woodworkers take scraps and create new pieces, writers gather up their fits and starts; it's always easier to start with something—an image—than the blank page. Many creative writers recycle their best image. Faulkner reuses many of the same images, as does Hemingway, Willa Cather, Victor Hugo, and the poets William Carlos Williams and Gwendolyn Brooks. These writers do not suffer from a dearth of material. When the same image is used in a *new and different structure*, new things happen for the reader. Feel free to "steal" from yourself, and recast your best images in new "shows."

In poetry, you have words, lines, stanzas, and sections to work with. In narratives—any time you are assembling *a story*, whether as short fiction, novel, creative nonfiction, play, screenplay, or one of the many hybrid forms, including the graphic novel—you play with bits, beats, scenes, sequences, or chapters. Note that though we call them by different labels, the elements of structure apply to both poetry and prose:

Elements of Structure

Prose	Poetry
Bits	Words/Phrases
Beats	Lines
Scenes	Stanzas

Structure is the art of combining these component parts—all of which are based on the image. Let's take a look at each one, starting with story structure—the component parts of essays, stories, novels, and plays.

PRACTICE

Read "Cathedral" by Raymond Carver on page 297. Write a paragraph about how the story is put together. What are the bits, the beats? What are the scenes? In what order has Carver placed the parts of the story?

PARTS OF NARRATIVE

Learning to more carefully identify the parts of prose lets you expand your options as an artist. Narratives are made up of four basic moves: bits, beats, scenes, and sequences. "Cathedral" is made up of small bits and emotional beats, forming scenes strung together to make the story.

The one overall structure in my plays is language.
— EDWARD BOND

Learning to use that intuitive, emotional thing is important. But to understand dramatic structure, to learn what literature really is; those things are valuable, too.
— JIMMY SMITS

Bits

Bits are the tiny pieces of your prose, sentences, half-sentences, lines, riffs—the tiny moments, always images, that show us who the people in your piece really are and what they are doing. Creative writers rely on bits; they're the lifeblood of narrative, the tiny pieces of mosaic that contribute to the whole. Bits can be used to fulfill four different story functions: to reveal something about a character (how she orders a drink, plays pinball); to establish relationships (a mother needles her daughter, a boy is kicked out of the playground by his buddies); to move the plot forward (your character loads boxes into her car, a teenager is arrested); and as backstory bits that give your story depth (one- or two-sentence flashes into past actions, images from the past). Bits are brief, active, and they make a single point. They are simple.

Examine some bits from Raymond Carver's story "Cathedral":

Character-revealing bit: "She was at the draining board doing scalloped potatoes. She put down the knife she was using and turned around."

Relationship-establishing bit: "I reached to draw her robe back over her, and it was then that I glanced at the blind man. What the hell! I flipped the robe open again."

Plot-advancing bit: " 'Get us a pen and some heavy paper. Go on, bub, get the stuff,' he said."

Backstory bit: "She'd seen something in the paper: HELP WANTED — *Reading to Blind Man,* and a telephone number. She phoned and went over, was hired on the spot."

PRACTICE

Find an example of each type of bit in Carver's story "Cathedral" on page 297. Find an example of each type of bit in Jessica Shattuck's "Bodies" on page 180.

In an amateur story, the writer may reveal character to the reader by telling: "They fought in the kitchen." That's not a bit. It's not an image: It's a summary. Get into the habit of writing prose in bits, and you keep your readers involved in the story.

Summary doesn't allow the writer to establish relationships quickly or efficiently, and its use often marks writing as amateur. What's so useful about thinking in terms of story bits is you capture those tiny actions that reveal many layers of motivation and behavior. Amateurs tend to write in broad strokes — "They hated each other," or, "It had been years since they got along well." Human behaviors are shaded, complex, nuanced. In "Cathedral," when "Bub" covers and then uncovers his wife, in that little bit of action he reveals a lot about himself, his views of his wife, and his feelings toward the blind in general and Robert in particular. A bit is a powerful thing. It's a micro-movie. The reader sees *everything*.

Backstory is when the writer pauses to fill in some background on the characters or the situation. Here, the temptation to stop using images and write summary is probably greater than anywhere else in narrative. But backstory is much more vivid and effective when it is studded with bits. In the example above we can *see* the newspaper, imagine in our mind's eye this woman, her life, the circumstances of her first meeting with Robert. In the character-revealing bit above, notice how Carver chooses to give us a sharp image, fully focused, of the wife — she's deliberate, focused, controlled. She puts down the knife and turns around. Drops her weapon, opens herself up to what's going on next.

Give them a bit, and readers see a world. Give them a bit, and readers see *into* your writing. Bits are tiny images, the cells of the body of your work.

PRACTICE

Locate a piece of summary from your own work, from earlier this semester. Translate the summary into a bit. Which one is more effective? Compare.

Beats

Beats are the essential "what happens" moments, the blow-by-blow of the emotional track of the story. You must have beats to have a story. Beats are bits with *plot implications*. In a bit, we see your characters. In a bit, we see why and what happens.

Imagine your four-year-old niece, telling you a story about her dream. The dragons were chasing her and she fed them. And then they were chasing her. And they turned purple. And then she was hungry and she was chasing them. And she turned green! And they went to the store and there were dragons there too. And she got . . . And so on.

What's *wrong* with this narrative? Nothing, if you adore this child.

What's *missing*? Implications.

A ton of stuff happens in her story, but nothing really *matters*. She's fine. The monsters are fine. The store is fine. There aren't *implications, stakes, results. Beats.*

> There's something about free play within an ordered and disciplined structure that resonates for readers. And there's something about complete caprice and flux that's deadening.
>
> — DAVID FOSTER WALLACE

Beats are cause-and-effect situations, rendered in image. In a beat, the *direction of the story changes*. There's a "so what."

Dragons are chasing you? If you get eaten, there's a story. (For someone to tell, perhaps the dragon.) You go to the store? If there's a robbery, and the dragons save the day because you fed them, and the robbers happened to be terrified of the color purple, you have the makings of a story. X causes Y causes Z, and the results are *big*! And they *matter*!

That's beats. Beats serve the story. They are its rhythm.

Learning to recognize a beat may take practice. To locate story beats, extrapolate the *emotional* turning points from the key actions. There have to be three beats in any story in order for it to be a story: beginning, middle, end.

To find the first story beat in "Cathedral," look for the opening emotional declaration. It occurs when the husband says, cruelly, that he could take the blind man bowling. The beat establishes the ordinary world of their relationship—about to be radically changed forever by Robert. The first beat tells readers: This man is not connected to his wife, or himself. He is pretending to be funny, and really, he is scared to death. Of alive things, of blindness, of closeness. But he doesn't know any of this. That's a powerful opening beat. A lot is at stake.

The next beat, the next intense emotional point to the story, is when the narrator watches his wife guide Robert into their house. We know this isn't a bit, because it takes several paragraphs and there's detailed description accompanying the arrival. What's the point? The wife is happier than the narrator imagined she would be. This is going to be much, much worse than he thought. We see he is jealous. As readers, maybe we feel something like pity or empathy for "Bub." Again, there are implications. There are things that could really go wrong here. Beats always move us closer to unstable moments, moments of conflict, pain, or intensity.

Beats are the emotional hits experienced by the readers, the ups and downs felt as they *see* the scenes of the story play out.

PRACTICE

List the beats in the short story "Cathedral" on page 297. Then, look back at one of your own narratives and create another "beat sheet"—a list of the points that are shown in images, the points of weighted emotional intensity. Compare the structures. Are there things you would do differently if you revised your piece?

One problem in many unsuccessful stories is that the beats don't matter. In the four-year-old's dream rendition, it doesn't matter if the dragons ate everyone, because in the next scene, the people are encountering different dragons. People come back to life easily, so it doesn't matter that they die. Beats are the opposite of blabbing. Beats are what matters.

> Any structure is mutable, but once you've chosen it, then you have to accept it—if you're ever going to get any depth.
> — PETER COYOTE

Practice noticing narrative beats. When your friends converse, notice which of them are natural storytellers, directing attention to the beats—the emotional hits—and which are less artful, telling a lot of extra information that doesn't really matter? When you watch television and movies, take a notebook and make a beat sheet—many new writers train in this fashion. After only a couple of intentional viewings like this, you will be stunned at how much tighter and crisper your prose can be. When you view DVDs, the "Scene Selection" screens are often (though not always) broken into the story beats, based on the writers' actual beat sheet. Watch the film on your own, make your beat sheet, and compare to the scenes as they are broken out in the Scene Selection portion of the DVD. Practice as much as you can. If this work is difficult for you, working in a group often makes it easier to see the beats more clearly and quickly.

PRACTICE

Watch a sitcom of your choice. With a sheet of paper divided lengthwise down the middle, track the bits versus the beats: the emotional moments of impact. (If you choose a program that is on DVD, you will be able to review the scenes, but you can do this either way.) Television writing is highly structured and perfectly disciplined. There's no excess. *Everything* is either a bit or a beat. You can learn a lot about narrative structure watching television with pen and paper in hand.

PRACTICE

Read "Proofs" by Richard Rodriguez, on page 308. For this piece of creative nonfiction, create a beat sheet, or emotional outline. (Remember: The beats are always tied to visuals.) Focus on *images where the emotional exchange is clear and dramatic.* How many beats are there in the piece?

Scenes

Beats combine to make up scenes. A scene is like a tennis match: The power in the scene moves back and forth from one person to the other. This movement — positive emotion, negative emotion, positive emotion, this essential action-reaction movement — is the heartbeat of writing narrative and creating drama.

We know a scene by its shape: It's a box containing drama, delimited by time. A scene starts at a certain point in time — 2 p.m. at Sally's Boutique — and it presents two or three or four emotional beats: Sally is ticked off because she dyed Bob's hair green, which is what he asked for, but he doesn't like it; Bob's wife is flirting with Sally's fifteen-year-old son; Sally refuses to refund Bob. The scene stops, at say, 2:20, when Bob and his adorable wife storm out of the salon yelling, "We will ruin your business!" When you change your location — the parking lot in front of Sally's — you change scenes. When you change *time* — picking up the story the next day, for example — you change scenes. Prose writers work *exactly as filmmakers and playwrights* do: envisioning their work as a series of scenes. Time change? New scene. Location change? New scene.

A scene, then, is a dramatic unit. If you choose not to write in scenes, you risk losing your reader. Scenes break your narrative into manageable chunks. Like periods in a basketball game, or innings in baseball, scenes give the piece structure, so your reader knows where he is, and where things stand. And, just as in a game, where many points or only a few are scored in a given period, a scene may contain one beat or a series of beats. You will want to practice writing simple one-beat scenes, as well as more complex multi-beat scenes.

So, the beats combine into sequences to make a scene, and scenes provide the large plot points for your story: the beginning, the middle, the end. A beat is a micro-scene. A scene is a string of beats arranged to build up to a moment of high intensity.

The Four Features of Scenes. To write a scene, be conscious of the four features of scenes: problem, polarity, time, and space. To improve an existing scene, increase the intensity of the problem and the polarity, and tighten the time and space.

Problem. Conflict drives scenes and gives them shape and dramatic interest. (The four-year-old's dream story lacks conflict—things happen freely, randomly, with no opposing force.) As you already know, weak characters without strong agendas (desires, needs) will not generate much conflict, or much reader interest. Your main character needs a clear problem. And he or she must be *opposed* by a worthy opponent. As in football, a blowout is not that fun for the audience; readers want a fair fight between equally matched characters.

Polarity. Polarity is the *direction* the fight goes, the impact of the solution to the problem, the energy of the scene. Every scene has to move from one point to another point (or else it is static, and not effective). To find out the polarity of a scene (think of a battery, with the + and the – on either end), ask yourself how it starts, up or down. And then where does it go? Do things get better, or worse? In the story "White Angel" by Michael Cunningham, on page 243, notice where the first scene starts—when the author writes "Here is Carlton," locating the characters in space, starting the movie—now we see the boys. In action. What's the polarity? The scene starts with "cold" and "shocks" and drugs and terror; it ends, right before the space break on page 245, with "how real everything is" and Carlton as a source of deep comfort and security. It goes from negative (death) to positive (life and heightened sensory experience).

Time Limitations. Scenes in which there is time pressure—the boss is coming, the rent is due, you're late to get home and the fairy godmother is going to freak out—are stronger than scenes where time is *not* a factor. Dark is falling, the clock is ticking, capture is imminent—consider ways to tighten the time around your scenes. Every scene starts at a certain precise time. As the writer, you need to be conscious of *real time*. Condense time to create structures that attract readers, and organize your images concisely.

Space Limitations. Scenes take place in specific, boundaried settings: a kitchen, a park, a car, a living room, a cliff. The writer must be able to see, in her or his mind's eye, every detail of the setting before she or he writes the scene. Good scenes take place in tight spaces. Your trip down Route A1A to Key West—that's not a scene, it's a saga. A scene takes place in a defined location, and the tighter the "walls" of the scene, the more interesting the scene is. The kitchen, the bathroom, the walk-in freezer. The hallway, the rooftop garden, the pumpkin patch—as you practice, you will develop an eye for what makes an exciting scene location. To tell the story of your Key West trip, what are the three most interesting scenes you could use? Make a list of potentials, and choose the most vibrant three—you are looking for space limitations, and also keeping in mind *conflict*—at what point are the problems between people most interesting? That's how you find the scenes you need to write. The rest? You don't need it.

How do you locate the scenes in a narrative? You make a kind of blueprint of the story, looking at the location and time changes. For example, in "Cathedral," does the story open with a scene? No. The narrator is reporting, using bits from the past, laying out the emotional and historical setting and landscape. After the series of bits that comprise the first six paragraphs of the story, we are anchored in time and space. The first scene opens with the cooking bit at the top of page 299. The curtain rises. What has come before is like a voice-over, the narrative bits spoken to us, the

> *Structure is more important than content in the transmission of information.*
>
> — ABBIE HOFFMAN

reader. And then we see a woman cooking, and we hear an argument between this woman and her husband. We see the potato roll under the stove. Real time. A real space. We're in a scene. "Pieces of the story began to fall into place," the narrator says, to show us, the reader, that his wife talks and he half-listens.

PRACTICE

Take any scene from the Akhil Sharma short story on page 125 and locate the four essential scene components. Do the same for any scene in the story "White Angel" by Michael Cunningham on page 243.

Reading Scenes in Raymond Carver's "Cathedral." Break down the first scene in "Cathedral": Scene 1 is kitchen scene, blind man history, argument.

Beat one: Wife to husband: "The man's lost his wife!" Text: Stop being a jerk. Subtext: Do you not value wife/loss/love?

Beat two: (We expect the husband to back down and stop being a jerk.) He says something very offensive and also just plain stupid on purpose: "Was his wife a Negro?" Text: Adding fuel to the fire; I will not cooperate. Subtext: I don't want this man in my house, or you to like him. Your past connection threatens me.

Beat three: "Pathetic." After the long backstory bits, the narrator's reaction provides the emotional hit that ends the scene. It's a "game over" kind of one-word sentence, harsh, short, final. Subtext: I will not invest emotionally in these people, I will not care.

The polarity is positive, because the narrator believes he is winning. He believes he is handling this well. He has listened while his wife talked. By enduring the evening, he pretends to himself he is a good husband. By rejecting the poignancy in the blind man's story, he feels on top, in control.

Where does scene 2 start and stop? Look for time and location changes. Scene 2 begins with the phrase "So when the time rolled around." First, there's a bit—having a drink, getting up from the sofa, looking out the window. Then, the scene begins with what the narrator sees through that window. If you can film it, it's a scene. This one plays out as Robert enters the house, the husband makes drinks, and Robert does that weird thing with his beard.

> I think that as a director you have to at the very least shape the script; structure it. Otherwise you're not really doing your job.
> — JOHN BOORMAN

Three bits then move the plot forward: drinks, talking, more drinks. Quick, quick, quick, we cover time, the plot moves, we understand the relationships between the three people. The next scene opens at dinner with the sentence, "When we sat down at the table" (location change, time change) and slides—imagine the camera not stopping, just one long fluid shot—"We didn't look back"—it's all one big gesture, the big feast, the move to the sofa to recover. The scene climaxes with the television beat ("This is a color TV") where the blind man is scoring point after point on the narrator, refusing to be flustered by the narrator's discomfort, rudeness, or fear.

When the wife departs the scene, that scene is over. A new scene, the pot-smoking scene, begins when Robert and the husband listen to the weather and sports. The wife is gone a long time. She enters the scene midway through. This scene climaxes when she touches Robert—no matter what the narrator does to try to numb all feeling, those two remain connected, kind, and focused on each other.

As you read for structure, and begin to intentionally and artfully construct scenes to contain your prose, you may feel you are practically a film or stage director. Plays, of course, are entirely composed of scenes, and fiction and creative nonfiction writers often practice seeing their narratives in terms of dramatic structure. Imagine, always, your characters are actual actors, just as the screenwriter or playwright does. And, when you change their location, or move back or forward in time, you start a new scene. If a character leaves the scene and the dynamic changes, and/or there's a leap forward in time, a new scene begins. Labelling these scene changes as you are first learning structure helps you keep your transitions crisp, your scenes necessary, and your action humming along.

| PRACTICE |

Read through "Cathedral" again. List the scenes to break the story down into an outline of its scenes. Label the time, the locale, and the polarity of each scene.

PARTS OF POEMS

Poems, like stories, essays, and plays, are made up of pieces—images. They are broken into sections (stanzas) and they can employ many kinds of formal structures. The sonnet and the haiku are examples of formal structures you may already be familiar with. We will look at those kinds of "recipes" for structures in the next chapter; here, we take a close look at the building blocks poets use to make a well-crafted poem. Many poems use narrative structure and tell a story. As you practice writing different kinds of poetry, the rhythms and movements of narrative structure that you practiced above will strengthen the power of your poems. Structuring a poem, though, involves special attention to every word, line, stanza, and section.

Words

In a poem, every single word matters. Because there are usually fewer words in poetry than in prose (stories, essays, memoir), each word has more attention on it, and carries more weight. The sound of the word, its history, the feel of the word in the reader's mouth, the resonances of the word, the connotations, the associations, and how a word interacts with the other words in the poem, especially in terms of echoes—all these create an effect on the reader—and the effect can be powerful. Words matter. Words start battles and stop them. (Try being silent for an entire day.)

> *Training is fabulous because it gives you a basis, a strong structure, so that when you're unbelievably nervous and you think that you can't get a word out, you will get the word out.*
> — CHARLOTTE RAMPLING

We live *in words*, and without them, our lives are profoundly different. Place a single word on a sheet of paper. It draws a lot more attention than the page you are reading right now, covered with words. Poetry is the one place in the world where we return our focus to *words*. Tiny, simple, dangerous, mighty words.

In a poem, words provide the foundation for your piece. Each word has to be selected individually. Like a bricklayer laying a path, individual bricks are chosen or rejected based on how well they will fit the overall pattern, and how sturdy and perfectly formed they are.

Beginning writers must work to avoid word packages—words that come in groups mostly through habit. "Tears rolling down her cheeks," "beautiful blue sky," "pleasantly surprised"—words that frequently travel in little packs together usually need to be broken up and reconsidered when structuring a poem. They're prefabricated, these packages, and poems require each word to be carefully and individually selected. Poets are the most economical of writers, and any word you want that is anticipated by the reader *is already in the reader's head.* So it need not be written, and in fact, must not be.

PRACTICE

If you can predict the next word in a poem, chances are you may be experiencing a word package. Try this: Fill in the blanks for the following prompts. If what you fill in is what most other people would fill in, that's a word package, and you should avoid placing those words together in your poetry.

Shining _____.

Eyes like _____.

_____ _____ hair.

_____ mist.

A _____ moon.

Joy and _____.

Nice and _____.

Contrast the beginning first draft of a poem with a professional, published poem. What do you notice about the word choices?

1

I have taught her all she needs
And now it's up to her
I want to be there with her and for her
But she won't let me in.

2

across the Passaic's asphalt drawbridge into the heart of Kearny—
my cheeks flushed with wine—you the muse I didn't choose
dragging danger down in chains across the hangdog face of me

See the difference? In the second example, an excerpt from the poem "In Hot Pursuit" on p. 313, the author Timothy Liu chooses words that have spark and flash, each one earns its place, works hard in the poem. In the first sample, the words are bland by comparison. They're everyday, any-old-word words.

PRACTICE

Read the entire poem by Timothy Liu on page 313. Underline the words that function as beats—words specific and powerful enough to create an image unit. How many words—what percentage—in the poem carry beat weight? How does this compare to early work by yourself?

Choosing good, crisp words is just as important in narrative as it is in poetry, but in poetry the words show up as though each one is boldface. In narrative, a good bit—a bit of action—can provide the flourish and activity, the vibrance and electricity you need to keep the reader's attention glued to your pages. Words in poetry are absolutely as important as bits in prose. Each must sing. Each word must stand on its own. Each word in a poem must *earn* its keep. Many poets keep in their notebook a special section where they collect favorite words for use in future poems.

> *I always felt if we were going in to do an album, there should already be a lot of structure already made up so we could get on with that and see what else happened.*
>
> — JIMMY PAGE

Lines

Lines in poetry, like the beats in a story, make up the structure of the piece. Words are the cells, lines are the bones. Think of the line the same way you were taught to think of paragraphs in essay writing in composition class. What's the thesis of the line? How does it develop your overall argument or story? The line has to accomplish a lot—as much as a whole paragraph. The line needs to have a polarity, too, just like a beat. It has to *move*. Avoid lines that simply recast or repeat what came before or what comes after. Each line in a poem is a micro-moment. Unlike sentences in a paragraph, which can link and build and clarify and explain, a poem's lines must move from point A to point B, every time. Poetry is condensed. If a story is like a house, a poem is like a tree fort or a house-boat. Every board matters. Every nail is serving at least one purpose. Poetry isn't prose with shorter margins. Many early poem drafts are baggy, sloppy, because of a lack of attention to the line: Each line has to work hard to earn its right to stay in the poem. (You may wish to review the discussion of the line in Chapter 5, on tension.)

| PRACTICE |

Choose any poem in this book with long lines. Now, find another poem in this book that has very short lines. Using a plus sign (+) or a minus sign (–), mark the polarity of each line in both poems. Look at the emotional hit. Is what *happens* in the line going in a positive direction? Or is it a negative, a loss, a slipping back? Think about what you know about tension as you look at the pattern of plusses and minuses that make up the beats of each poem. What do you notice about beats and structure? Does your long-line poem example have more than one beat, ever, in a line? Is each line a single beat in the short-line poem?

> *I will take form and say what*
> *I want to say; the form will*
> *not deform me.*
> — SONIA SANCHEZ

A line in a poem can be as short as one word ("O" and "I" being the shortest words we have available to us) or take up more than one line on the page.

Read the following poems by Gwendolyn Brooks and Beth Bachmann. As you examine the line lengths, pay special attention to the emotional beat—what *happens*—in the line. Also, notice that when a line indents, it signals that the line doesn't really break—the limits of the page's dimensions force an indent—but we read the line as if it is a continuation of the one before.

Gwendolyn Brooks
We Real Cool

The Pool Players.
Seven at the Golden Shovel.

We real cool. We
Left school. We

Lurk late. We
Strike straight. We

Sing sin. We
Thin gin. We

Jazz June. We
Die soon.

Now read this poem by Beth Bachmann, "Colorization." Consider the same issues you did for the Brooks poem above.

Beth Bachmann
Colorization

Black and white distances the viewer.

Take, for instance, a split crow dropped from the jaw of some animal into
the snow.
If we were to encounter it, with our heads tucked to our chests to block the
blizzard,
we might think of it as shadow, but, in truth, the body is red.

There are two ways to name this: restoration and desecration.
It comes down to a question of actuality and intent.

When you enter my room, it is dark. What you can see
are broad shapes, the lines the blinds throw onto the bed.

If this were in color, would you know whether or not to be afraid?

The longer the line, the more attentive the poet must be to the principles of
structure discussed above; the longer the line, the more narrative structure tools
are necessary in order to keep the reader's attention engaged with the poem. If
your poem is one long line, you may well be writing a prose poem, a time-
honored structure that appeals to many poets and prose writers.

PRACTICE

Does more happen in the Bachmann lines than in the Brooks lines? What's different at
the end of each line, above, than at the opening of the line—what's the polarity of the
individual lines? Retype the Brooks lines into long, long lines and read the new version
aloud. What's different? Retype Bachmann's long lines into short bits. What changes
when you read the new version aloud?

Stanzas

In poetry, stanzas are groups of lines, separated by white space. Some poems are not
broken into individual stanzas, but many are. The stanza operates like a paragraph
in an essay, a scene in a story, or a chapter in a novel. Each stanza contributes a
micro-story that stops at a high point of interest, so readers will *not* put the writing down, but read on because they must know: Where will the poet go next?

Often, stanzas in narrative poems are arranged in a structure that parallels
classic story structure. The stanzas build an idea by 1, introducing the central

conflict or tension; 2, deepening and intensifying, complicating that central idea; and 3, building toward the climax, the highest, most intense moment in the story.

In lyric poetry, stanzas may be crafted to reveal different approaches to the feeling, mood, or emotion being portrayed. Wallace Stevens's lyric poem "Thirteen Ways of Looking at a Blackbird" doesn't tell a story, it presents a variety of ways of considering nature, and life. A narrative poem moves through a sequence of events, while a lyric poem circles, hovers, dwells, intensifies, presenting a variety of angles, or points of view.

We will look more at stanzas in the next chapter, where forms — recipes for poems — give you very specific directions on what to do in, and with, a stanza. At first, stanza forms can feel restricting, but once student writers get over their initial resistance, most love the freedom that having a map or structural blueprint allows them. Instead of wandering all over the place, worrying about when to break a line, start a new stanza, or just hitting the "enter" key randomly, forms give you a structure, so you are free to be wildly creative in your poetry's content.

WRITING PROJECTS

1. Craft a scene with a positive-negative-positive beat structure. Your main character is winning, then losing, then winning. For example, he asks a girl out, and she says she has seen him around a lot. She smiles. This is a "positive" charge for the bit. Write a negatively charged bit to follow (using this example to start, or your own) and end on a positively charged exchange, creating a scene with movement.

2. Write a story that takes exactly the same amount of time to read as is played out on the page.

3. Take an older story of your own. How much time do you cover? Restructure the story so that it takes place in three hours or less. What scenes will you need to tell the story in this new form? Write the story, and compare the two pieces. Which one is more successful? What do you gain? What is lost in the new, more tightly timed version?

4. Write a story structured in three scenes. Use three different locales. Use a short amount of time, and keep the time of each scene brief. Each scene should have three to six beats. Write the scenes with a positive-negative-positive polarity pattern.

5. Invent a polarity pattern for a story and write the scenes to fit your pattern.

6. As a class, create a list of as many clichés and word packages as you can. "Put the pedal to the medal," "work like beavers," and "hit this one out of the park." Then, craft a poem, using the cliché form as your structure, but mixing and matching to create the most surprising word unpackages you can. Title your poem and share it with the class.

7. Write a poem of exactly 100 words (delicious words) and keep it to one stanza.

8. Write a poem using only one-word lines. Make your poem at least thirty lines or longer, but not longer than one page. Choose a subject that fits this staccato structure. Choose words that stand out; avoid mundane, predictable, flat words. As always, create images even with just these deft, short strokes; avoid abstract words like "love," "freedom," "pain," "insinuating." "Black" and "cat" give us images; "yearning" does not. Then, write a poem using five lines, but make sure each line is at least thirty-five words long! Read these aloud to the class, and vote on which you prefer. Next, take your short-line poem and rewrite it, using long lines for your structure. What happens to the polarities when you work against structure in this way? Is there more tension, or is the poem ruined? Do the same thing with your long-line poem — condense it into thirty single-word lines. Do you accomplish less? More? Is much of your original meaning lost?

9. Take one of your stories from this semester and translate it into a narrative poem, substituting words as needed to emphasize sound, meaning, and clarity and interest. Does each scene in your story need to be its own stanza, or do you prefer to structure the stanzas differently? Be ready to discuss your choices.

STRUCTURE WORKSHOP

The prompts below will help you constructively discuss your classmates' work.

1. *Prose.* Label one effective (image-based) example of each of the elements of structure — bit, beat, scene, or line and stanza — in the student piece you are reading.

2. *Prose.* Identify a place in the student piece where the writing could be made more vivid by *condensing* the section into a bit (prose) or a single word (if you are reading a peer poem) — by doing more with less.

3. *Prose.* Label the parts of the strongest scene or stanza in the piece. Bracket the section off, and tell the writer what you like best about it.

4. *Prose.* Create a beat sheet or a line map for this piece, making a list of what happens at each pulse point (beat) in the piece. What are the three strongest, most vivid, transporting beats or lines? Which three are the weakest? Say why you believe those three points to be weak. Is it because they are not in image? Repetitive? Not presenting a new emotional hit?

5. *Poetry.* Circle all the words that you consider packaged—words with which you would be able to fill in the blank, given the preceding word or words. Underline the vivid, sparkly, fresh, interesting words and phrases.

6. *Poetry.* Does each line have a polarity—a movement from positive to negative, or vice versa? Label each line that does with a + or a – and use a ? to indicate you aren't sure or the line does not have enough energy to move the reader from a negative emotion or feeling to a positive (or the reverse).

7. *Poetry.* Write a brief note to the author, telling her or him why you think she or he chose the stanza structure she or he did for this poem. Do you see reasons to vary the stanza structure?

Raymond Carver
Cathedral

This blind man, an old friend of my wife's, he was on his way to spend the night. His wife had died. So he was visiting the dead wife's relatives in Connecticut. He called my wife from his in-laws'. Arrangements were made. He would come by train, a five-hour trip, and my wife would meet him at the station. She hadn't seen him since she worked for him one summer in Seattle ten years ago. But she and the blind man had kept in touch. They made tapes and mailed them back and forth. I wasn't enthusiastic about his visit. He was no one I knew. And his being blind bothered me. My idea of blindness came from the movies. In the movies, the blind moved slowly and never laughed. Sometimes they were led by seeing-eye dogs. A blind man in my house was not something I looked forward to.

That summer in Seattle she had needed a job. She didn't have any money. The man she was going to marry at the end of the summer was in officers' training school. He didn't have any money, either. But she was in love with the guy, and he was in love with her, etc. She'd seen something in the paper: HELP WANTED—*Reading to Blind Man*, and a telephone number. She phoned and went over, was hired on the spot. She'd worked with this blind man all summer. She read stuff to him, case studies, reports, that sort of thing. She helped him organize his little office in the county social-service department. They'd become good friends, my wife and the blind man. How do I know these things? She told me. And she told me something else. On her last day in the office, the blind man asked if he could touch her face. She agreed to this. She told me he touched his fingers to every part of her face, her nose—even her neck! She never forgot it. She even tried to write a poem about it. She was always trying to write a poem. She wrote a poem or two every year, usually after something really important had happened to her.

When we first started going out together, she showed me the poem. In the poem, she recalled his fingers and the way they had moved around over her face. In the poem, she talked about what she had felt at the time, about what went through her mind when the blind man touched her nose and lips. I can remember I didn't think much of the poem. Of course, I didn't tell her that. Maybe I just don't understand poetry. I admit it's not the first thing I reach for when I pick up something to read.

Anyway, this man who'd first enjoyed her favors, the officer-to-be, he'd been her childhood sweetheart. So okay. I'm saying that at the end of the summer she let the blind man run his hands over her face, said goodbye to him, married her childhood etc., who was now a commissioned officer, and she moved away from Seattle. But they'd kept in touch, she and the blind man. She made the first contact after a year or so. She called him up one night from an Air Force base in Alabama. She wanted to talk. They talked. He asked her to send him a tape and tell him about her life. She did this. She sent the tape. On the tape, she told the blind man about her husband and about their life together in the military. She told the blind man she loved her husband but she didn't like it where they lived and she didn't like it that he was a part of the military-industrial thing. She told the blind man she'd written a poem and he was in it. She told him that she was writing a poem about what it was like to be an Air Force officer's wife. The poem wasn't finished yet. She was still writing it. The blind man made a tape. He sent her the tape. She made a tape. This went on for years. My wife's officer was posted to one base and then another. She sent tapes from Moody AFB, McGuire, McConnell, and finally Travis, near Sacramento, where one night she got to feeling lonely and cut off from people she kept losing in that moving-around life. She got to feeling she couldn't go it another step. She went in and swallowed all the pills and capsules in the medicine chest and washed them down with a bottle of gin. Then she got into a hot bath and passed out.

But instead of dying, she got sick. She threw up. Her officer—why should he have a name? he was the childhood sweetheart, and what more does he want?—came home from somewhere, found her, and called the ambulance. In time, she put it all on a tape and sent the tape to the blind man. Over the years, she put all kinds of stuff on tapes and sent the tapes off lickety-split. Next to writing a poem every year, I think it was her chief means of recreation. On one tape, she told the blind man she'd decided to live away from her officer for a time. On another tape, she told him about her divorce. She and I began going out, and of course she told her blind man about it. She told him everything, or so it seemed to me. Once she asked me if I'd like to hear the latest tape from the blind man. This was a year ago. I was on the tape, she said. So I said okay, I'd listen to it. I got us drinks and we settled down in the living room. We made ready to listen. First she inserted the tape into the player and adjusted a couple of dials. Then she pushed a lever. The tape squeaked and someone began to talk in this loud voice. She lowered the volume. After a few minutes of harmless chitchat, I heard my own name in the mouth of this stranger, this blind man I didn't even know! And then this: "From all you've said about him, I can only conclude—" But we were interrupted, a knock at the door, something, and we didn't ever get back to the tape. Maybe it was just as well. I'd heard all I wanted to.

Now this same blind man was coming to sleep in my house.

"Maybe I could take him bowling," I said to my wife. She was at the draining board doing scalloped potatoes. She put down the knife she was using and turned around.

"If you love me," she said, "you can do this for me. If you don't love me, okay. But if you had a friend, any friend, and the friend came to visit, I'd make him feel comfortable." She wiped her hands with the dish towel.

"I don't have any blind friends," I said.

"You don't have *any* friends," she said. "Period. Besides," she said, "goddamn it, his wife's just died! Don't you understand that? The man's lost his wife!"

I didn't answer. She'd told me a little about the blind man's wife. Her name was Beulah. Beulah! That's a name for a colored woman.

"Was his wife a Negro?" I asked.

"Are you crazy?" my wife said. "Have you just flipped or something?" She picked up a potato. I saw it hit the floor, then roll under the stove. "What's wrong with you?" she said. "Are you drunk?"

"I'm just asking," I said.

Right then my wife filled me in with more detail than I cared to know. I made a drink and sat at the kitchen table to listen. Pieces of the story began to fall into place.

Beulah had gone to work for the blind man the summer after my wife had stopped working for him. Pretty soon Beulah and the blind man had themselves a church wedding. It was a little wedding—who'd want to go to such a wedding in the first place?—just the two of them, plus the minister and the minister's wife. But it was a church wedding just the same. It was what Beulah had wanted, he'd said. But even then Beulah must have been carrying the cancer in her glands. After they had been inseparable for eight years—my wife's word, *inseparable*—Beulah's health went into a rapid decline. She died in a Seattle hospital room, the blind man sitting beside the bed and holding on to her hand. They'd married, lived and worked together, slept together—had sex, sure—and then the blind man had to bury her. All this without his having ever seen what the goddamned woman looked like. It was beyond my understanding. Hearing this, I felt sorry for the blind man for a little bit. And then I found myself thinking what a pitiful life this woman must have led. Imagine a woman who could never see herself as she was seen in the eyes of her loved one. A woman who could go on day after day and never receive the smallest compliment from her beloved. A woman whose husband could never read the expression on her face, be it misery or something better. Someone who could wear makeup or not—what difference to him? She could, if she wanted, wear green eye-shadow around one eye, a straight pin in her nostril, yellow slacks and purple shoes, no matter. And then to slip off into death, the blind man's hand on her hand, his blind eyes streaming tears—I'm imagining now—her last thought maybe this: that he never even knew what she looked like, and she on an express to the grave. Robert was left with a small insurance policy and half of a twenty-peso Mexican coin. The other half of the coin went into the box with her. Pathetic.

So when the time rolled around, my wife went to the depot to pick him up. With nothing to do but wait—sure, I blamed him for that—I was having a drink and watching the TV when I heard the car pull into the drive. I got up from the sofa with my drink and went to the window to have a look.

I saw my wife laughing as she parked the car. I saw her get out of the car and shut the door. She was still wearing a smile. Just amazing. She went around to the other side of the car to where the blind man was already starting to get out. This blind man, feature this, he was wearing a full beard! A beard on a blind man! Too much, I say. The blind man reached into the back seat and dragged out a suitcase. My wife took his arm, shut the car door, and, talking all the way, moved him down the drive and then up the steps to the front porch. I turned off the TV. I finished my drink, rinsed the glass, dried my hands. Then I went to the door.

My wife said, "I want you to meet Robert. Robert, this is my husband. I've told you all about him." She was beaming. She had this blind man by his coat sleeve.

The blind man let go of his suitcase and up came his hand.

I took it. He squeezed hard, held my hand, and then he let it go.

"I feel like we've already met," he boomed.

"Likewise," I said. I didn't know what else to say. Then I said, "Welcome. I've heard a lot about you." We began to move then, a little group, from the porch into the living room, my wife guiding him by the arm. The blind man was carrying his suitcase in his other hand. My wife said things like, "To your left here, Robert. That's right. Now watch it, there's a chair. That's it. Sit down right here. This is the sofa. We just bought this sofa two weeks ago."

I started to say something about the old sofa. I'd liked that old sofa. But I didn't say anything. Then I wanted to say something else, small-talk, about the scenic ride along the Hudson. How going *to* New York, you should sit on the right-hand side of the train, and coming *from* New York, the left-hand side.

"Did you have a good train ride?" I said. "Which side of the train did you sit on, by the way?"

"What a question, which side!" my wife said. "What's it matter which side?" she said.

"I just asked," I said.

"Right side," the blind man said. "I hadn't been on a train in nearly forty years. Not since I was a kid. With my folks. That's been a long time. I'd nearly forgotten the sensation. I have winter in my beard now," he said. "So I've been told, anyway. Do I look distinguished, my dear?" the blind man said to my wife.

"You look distinguished, Robert," she said. "Robert," she said. "Robert, it's just so good to see you."

My wife finally took her eyes off the blind man and looked at me. I had the feeling she didn't like what she saw. I shrugged.

I've never met, or personally known, anyone who was blind. This blind man was late forties, a heavy-set, balding man with stooped shoulders, as if he carried a great weight there. He wore brown slacks, brown shoes, a light-brown shirt, a tie, a sports coat. Spiffy. He also had this full beard. But he didn't use a cane and he didn't wear dark glasses. I'd always thought dark glasses were a must for the blind. Fact was, I wished he had a pair. At first glance, his eyes looked like anyone else's eyes. But if you looked close, there was something different about them. Too much white in the iris, for one thing, and the pupils seemed to move around in the sockets without his knowing it or being able to stop it. Creepy. As I stared at his face, I saw the left pupil turn in toward his nose while the other made an effort to keep in one place. But it was only an effort, for that eye was on the roam without his knowing it or wanting it to be.

I said, "Let me get you a drink. What's your pleasure? We have a little of everything. It's one of our pastimes."

"Bub, I'm a Scotch man myself," he said fast enough in this big voice.

"Right," I said. Bub! "Sure you are. I knew it."

He let his fingers touch his suitcase, which was sitting alongside the sofa. He was taking his bearings. I didn't blame him for that.

"I'll move that up to your room," my wife said.

"No, that's fine," the blind man said loudly. "It can go up when I go up."

"A little water with the Scotch?" I said.

"Very little," he said.

"I knew it," I said.

He said, "Just a tad. The Irish actor, Barry Fitzgerald? I'm like that fellow. When I drink water, Fitzgerald said, I drink water. When I drink whiskey, I drink whiskey." My wife laughed. The blind man brought his hand up under his beard. He lifted his beard slowly and let it drop.

I did the drinks, three big glasses of Scotch with a splash of water in each. Then we made ourselves comfortable and talked about Robert's travels. First the long flight from the West Coast to Connecticut, we covered that. Then from Connecticut up here by train. We had another drink concerning that leg of the trip.

I remembered having read somewhere that the blind didn't smoke because, as speculation had it, they couldn't see the smoke they exhaled. I thought I knew that much and that much only about blind people. But this blind man smoked his cigarette down to the nubbin and then lit another one. This blind man filled his ashtray and my wife emptied it.

When we sat down at the table for dinner, we had another drink. My wife heaped Robert's plate with cube steak, scalloped potatoes, green beans. I buttered him up two slices of bread. I said, "Here's bread and butter for you." I swallowed some of my drink. "Now let us pray," I said, and the blind man lowered his head. My wife looked at me, her mouth agape. "Pray the phone won't ring and the food doesn't get cold," I said.

We dug in. We ate everything there was to eat on the table. We ate like there was no tomorrow. We didn't talk. We ate. We scarfed. We grazed that table. We were into serious eating. The blind man had right away located his foods, he knew just where everything was on his plate. I watched with admiration as he used his knife and fork on the meat. He'd cut two pieces of meat, fork the meat into his mouth, and then go all out for the scalloped potatoes, the beans next, and then he'd tear off a hunk of buttered bread and eat that. He'd follow this up with a big drink of milk. It didn't seem to bother him to use his fingers once in a while, either.

We finished everything, including half a strawberry pie. For a few moments, we sat as if stunned. Sweat beaded on our faces. Finally, we got up from the table and left the dirty plates. We didn't look back. We took ourselves into the living room and sank into our places again. Robert and my wife sat on the sofa. I took the big chair. We had us two or three more drinks while they talked about the major things that had come to pass for them in the past ten years. For the most part, I just listened. Now and then I joined in. I didn't want him to think I'd left the room, and I didn't want her to think I was feeling left out. They talked of things that had happened to them—to them!—these past ten years. I waited in vain to hear my name on my wife's sweet lips: "And then my dear husband came into my life"—something like that. But I heard nothing of the sort. More talk of Robert. Robert had done a little of everything, it seemed, a regular blind jack-of-all-trades. But most recently he and his wife had had an Amway distributorship, from which, I gathered, they'd earned their living, such as it was. The blind man was also a ham radio operator. He talked in his loud voice about conversations he'd had with fellow operators in Guam, in the Philippines, in Alaska, and even in Tahiti. He said he'd have a lot of friends there if he ever wanted to go visit those places. From time to time, he'd turn his blind face toward me, put his hand under his beard, ask me something. How long had I been in my present position? (Three years.) Did I like my work? (I didn't.) Was I going to stay with it? (What were the options?) Finally, when I thought he was beginning to run down, I got up and turned on the TV.

My wife looked at me with irritation. She was heading toward a boil. Then she looked at the blind man and said, "Robert, do you have a TV?"

The blind man said, "My dear, I have two TVs. I have a color set and a black-and-white thing, an old relic. It's funny, but if I turn the TV on, and I'm always turning it on, I turn on the color set. It's funny, don't you think?"

I didn't know what to say to that. I had absolutely nothing to say to that. No opinion. So I watched the news program and tried to listen to what the announcer was saying.

"This is a color TV," the blind man said. "Don't ask me how, but I can tell."

"We traded up a while ago," I said.

The blind man had another taste of his drink. He lifted his beard, sniffed it, and let it fall. He leaned forward on the sofa. He positioned his ashtray on the coffee table, then put the lighter to his cigarette. He leaned back on the sofa and crossed his legs at the ankles.

My wife covered her mouth, and then she yawned. She stretched. She said, "I think I'll go upstairs and put on my robe. I think I'll change into something else. Robert, you make yourself comfortable," she said.

"I'm comfortable," the blind man said.

"I want you to feel comfortable in this house," she said.

"I am comfortable," the blind man said.

After she'd left the room, he and I listened to the weather report and then to the sports roundup. By that time, she'd been gone so long I didn't know if she was going to come back. I thought she might have gone to bed. I wished she'd come back downstairs. I didn't want to be left alone with a blind man. I asked him if he wanted another drink, and he said sure. Then I asked if he wanted to smoke some dope with me. I said I'd just rolled a number. I hadn't, but I planned to do so in about two shakes.

"I'll try some with you," he said.

"Damn right," I said. "That's the stuff."

I got our drinks and sat down on the sofa with him. Then I rolled us two fat numbers. I lit one and passed it. I brought it to his fingers. He took it and inhaled.

"Hold it as long as you can," I said. I could tell he didn't know the first thing.

My wife came back downstairs wearing her pink robe and her pink slippers.

"What do I smell?" she said.

"We thought we'd have us some cannabis," I said.

My wife gave me a savage look. Then she looked at the blind man and said, "Robert, I didn't know you smoked."

He said, "I do now, my dear. There's a first time for everything. But I don't feel anything yet."

"This stuff is pretty mellow," I said. "This stuff is mild. It's dope you can reason with," I said. "It doesn't mess you up."

"Not much it doesn't, bub," he said, and laughed.

My wife sat on the sofa between the blind man and me. I passed her the number. She took it and toked and then passed it back to me. "Which way is this going?" she said. Then she said, "I shouldn't be smoking this. I can hardly keep my eyes open as it is. That dinner did me in. I shouldn't have eaten so much."

"It was the strawberry pie," the blind man said. "That's what did it," he said, and he laughed his big laugh. Then he shook his head.

"There's more strawberry pie," I said.

"Do you want some more, Robert?" my wife said.

"Maybe in a little while," he said.

We gave our attention to the TV. My wife yawned again. She said, "Your bed is made up when you feel like going to bed, Robert. I know you must have had a long day. When you're ready to go to bed, say so." She pulled his arm. "Robert?"

He came to and said, "I've had a real nice time. This beats tapes, doesn't it?"

I said, "Coming at you," and I put the number between his fingers. He inhaled, held the smoke, and then let it go. It was like he'd been doing it since he was nine years old.

"Thanks, bub," he said. "But I think this is all for me. I think I'm beginning to feel it," he said. He held the burning roach out for my wife.

"Same here," she said. "Ditto. Me, too." She took the roach and passed it to me. "I may just sit here for a while between you two guys with my eyes closed. But don't let me bother you, okay? Either one of you. If it bothers you, say so. Otherwise, I may just sit here with my eyes closed until you're ready to go to bed," she said. "Your bed's made up, Robert, when you're ready. It's right next to our room at the top of the stairs. We'll show you up when you're ready. You wake me up now, you guys, if I fall asleep." She said that and then she closed her eyes and went to sleep.

The news program ended. I got up and changed the channel. I sat back down on the sofa. I wished my wife hadn't pooped out. Her head lay across the back of the sofa, her mouth open. She'd turned so that her robe had slipped away from her legs, exposing a juicy thigh. I reached to draw her robe back over her, and it was then that I glanced at the blind man. What the hell! I flipped the robe open again.

"You say when you want some strawberry pie," I said.

"I will," he said.

I said, "Are you tired? Do you want me to take you up to your bed? Are you ready to hit the hay?"

"Not yet," he said. "No, I'll stay up with you, bub. If that's all right. I'll stay up until you're ready to turn in. We haven't had a chance to talk. Know what I mean? I feel like me and her monopolized the evening." He lifted his beard and he let it fall. He picked up his cigarettes and his lighter.

"That's all right," I said. Then I said, "I'm glad for the company."

And I guess I was. Every night I smoked dope and stayed up as long as I could before I fell asleep. My wife and I hardly ever went to bed at the same time. When I did go to sleep, I had these dreams. Sometimes I'd wake up from one of them, my heart going crazy.

Something about the church and the Middle Ages was on the TV. Not your run-of-the-mill TV fare. I wanted to watch something else. I turned to the other channels. But there was nothing on them, either. So I turned back to the first channel and apologized.

"Bub, it's all right," the blind man said. "It's fine with me. Whatever you want to watch is okay. I'm always learning something. Learning never ends. It won't hurt me to learn something tonight. I got ears," he said.

We didn't say anything for a time. He was leaning forward with his head turned at me, his right ear aimed in the direction of the set. Very disconcerting. Now and then his eyelids drooped and then they snapped open again. Now and then he put his fingers into his beard and tugged, like he was thinking about something he was hearing on the television.

On the screen, a group of men wearing cowls was being set upon and tormented by men dressed in skeleton costumes and men dressed as devils. The men dressed as devils wore devil masks, horns, and long tails. This pageant was part of a procession. The Englishman who was narrating the thing said it took place in Spain once a year. I tried to explain to the blind man what was happening.

"Skeletons," he said. "I know about skeletons," he said, and he nodded.

The TV showed this one cathedral. Then there was a long, slow look at another one. Finally, the picture switched to the famous one in Paris, with its flying buttresses and its spires reaching up to the clouds. The camera pulled away to show the whole of the cathedral rising above the skyline.

There were times when the Englishman who was telling the thing would shut up, would simply let the camera move around over the cathedrals. Or else the camera would tour the countryside, men in fields walking behind oxen. I waited as long as I could. Then I felt I had to say something. I said, "They're showing the outside of this cathedral now. Gargoyles. Little statues carved to look like monsters. Now I guess they're in Italy. Yeah, they're in Italy. There's paintings on the walls of this one church."

"Are those fresco paintings, bub?" he asked, and he sipped from his drink.

I reached for my glass. But it was empty. I tried to remember what I could remember. "You're asking me are those frescoes?" I said. "That's a good question. I don't know."

The camera moved to a cathedral outside Lisbon. The differences in the Portuguese cathedral compared with the French and Italian were not that great. But they were there. Mostly the interior stuff. Then something occurred to me, and I said, "Something has occurred to me. Do you have any idea what a cathedral is? What they look like, that is? Do you follow me? If somebody says cathedral to you, do you have any notion what they're talking about? Do you know the difference between that and a Baptist church, say?"

He let the smoke dribble from his mouth. "I know they took hundreds of workers fifty or a hundred years to build," he said. "I just heard the man say that, of course. I know generations of the same families worked on a cathedral. I heard him say that, too. The men who began their life's work on them, they never lived to see the completion of their work. In that wise, bub, they're no different from the rest of us, right?" He laughed. Then his eyelids drooped again. His head nodded. He seemed to be snoozing. Maybe he was imagining himself in Portugal. The TV was showing another cathedral now. This one was in Germany. The Englishman's voice droned on. "Cathedrals," the blind man said. He sat up and rolled his head back and forth. "If you want the truth, bub, that's about all I know. What I just said. What I heard him say. But maybe you could describe one to me? I wish you'd do it. I'd like that. If you want to know, I really don't have a good idea."

I stared hard at the shot of the cathedral on the TV. How could I even begin to describe it? But say my life depended on it. Say my life was being threatened by an insane guy who said I had to do it or else.

I stared some more at the cathedral before the picture flipped off into the countryside. There was no use. I turned to the blind man and said, "To begin with, they're very tall." I was looking around the room for clues. "They reach way up. Up and up. Toward the sky. They're so big, some of them, they have to have these supports. To help hold them up, so to speak. These supports are called buttresses. They remind me of viaducts, for some reason. But maybe you don't know viaducts, either? Sometimes the cathedrals have devils and such carved into the front. Sometimes lords and ladies. Don't ask me why this is," I said.

He was nodding. The whole upper part of his body seemed to be moving back and forth.

"I'm not doing so good, am I?" I said.

He stopped nodding and leaned forward on the edge of the sofa. As he listened to me, he was running his fingers through his beard. I wasn't getting through to him, I could see that. But he waited for me to go on just the same. He nodded, like he was trying to encourage me. I tried to think what else to say. "They're really big," I said. "They're massive. They're built of stone. Marble, too, sometimes. In those olden days, when they built cathedrals, men wanted to be close to God. In those olden days, God was an important part of everyone's life. You could tell this from their cathedral-building. I'm sorry," I said, "but it looks like that's the best I can do for you. I'm just no good at it."

"That's all right, bub," the blind man said. "Hey, listen. I hope you don't mind my asking you. Can I ask you something? Let me ask you a simple question, yes or no. I'm just curious and there's no offense. You're my host. But let me ask if you are in any way religious? You don't mind my asking?"

I shook my head. He couldn't see that, though. A wink is the same as a nod to a blind man. "I guess I don't believe in it. In anything. Sometimes it's hard. You know what I'm saying?"

"Sure, I do," he said.

"Right," I said.

The Englishman was still holding forth. My wife sighed in her sleep. She drew a long breath and went on with her sleeping.

"You'll have to forgive me," I said. "But I can't tell you what a cathedral looks like. It just isn't in me to do it. I can't do any more than I've done."

The blind man sat very still, his head down, as he listened to me.

I said, "The truth is, cathedrals don't mean anything special to me. Nothing. Cathedrals. They're something to look at on late-night TV. That's all they are."

It was then that the blind man cleared his throat. He brought something up. He took a handkerchief from his back pocket. Then he said, "I get it, bub. It's okay. It happens. Don't worry about it," he said. "Hey, listen to me. Will you do me a favor? I got an idea. Why don't you find us some heavy paper? And a pen. We'll do something. We'll draw one together. Get us a pen and some heavy paper. Go on, bub, get the stuff," he said.

So I went upstairs. My legs felt like they didn't have any strength in them. They felt like they did after I'd done some running. In my wife's room, I looked around. I found some ballpoints in a little basket on her table. And then I tried to think where to look for the kind of paper he was talking about.

Downstairs, in the kitchen, I found a shopping bag with onion skins in the bottom of the bag. I emptied the bag and shook it. I brought it into the living room and sat down with it near his legs. I moved some things, smoothed the wrinkles from the bag, spread it out on the coffee table.

The blind man got down from the sofa and sat next to me on the carpet.

He ran his fingers over the paper. He went up and down the sides of the paper. The edges, even the edges. He fingered the corners.

"All right," he said. "All right, let's do her."

He found my hand, the hand with the pen. He closed his hand over my hand. "Go ahead, bub, draw," he said. "Draw. You'll see. I'll follow along with you. It'll be okay. Just begin now like I'm telling you. You'll see. Draw," the blind man said.

So I began. First I drew a box that looked like a house. It could have been the house I lived in. Then I put a roof on it. At either end of the roof, I drew spires. Crazy.

"Swell," he said. "Terrific. You're doing fine," he said. "Never thought anything like this could happen in your lifetime, did you, bub? Well, it's a strange life, we all know that. Go on now. Keep it up."

I put in windows with arches. I drew flying buttresses. I hung great doors. I couldn't stop. The TV station went off the air. I put down the pen and closed and opened my fingers. The blind man felt around over the paper. He moved the tips of his fingers over the paper, all over what I had drawn, and he nodded.

"Doing fine," the blind man said.

I took up the pen again, and he found my hand. I kept at it. I'm no artist. But I kept drawing just the same.

My wife opened up her eyes and gazed at us. She sat up on the sofa, her robe hanging open. She said, "What are you doing? Tell me, I want to know."

I didn't answer her.

The blind man said, "We're drawing a cathedral. Me and him are working on it. Press hard," he said to me. "That's right. That's good," he said. "Sure. You got it, bub. I can tell. You didn't think you could. But you can, can't you? You're cooking with gas now. You know what I'm saying? We're going to really have us something here in a minute. How's the old arm?" he said. "Put some people in there now. What's a cathedral without people?"

My wife said, "What's going on? Robert, what are you doing? What's going on?"

"It's all right," he said to her. "Close your eyes now," the blind man said to me.

I did it. I closed them just like he said.

"Are they closed?" he said. "Don't fudge."

"They're closed," I said.

"Keep them that way," he said. He said, "Don't stop now. Draw."

So we kept on with it. His fingers rode my fingers as my hand went over the paper. It was like nothing else in my life up to now.

Then he said, "I think that's it. I think you got it," he said. "Take a look. What do you think?"

But I had my eyes closed. I thought I'd keep them that way for a little longer. I thought it was something I ought to do.

"Well?" he said. "Are you looking?"

My eyes were still closed. I was in my house. I knew that. But I didn't feel like I was inside anything.

"It's really something," I said.

Richard Rodriguez
Proofs

You stand around. You smoke. You spit. You are wearing your two shirts, two pants, two underpants. Jesús says, if they chase you throw that bag down. Your plastic bag is your mama, all you have left; the yellow cheese she wrapped has formed a translucent rind; the laminated scapular of the Sacred Heart nestles flame in its cleft. Put it in your pocket. The last hour of Mexico is twilight, the shuffling of feet. A fog is beginning to cover the ground. Jesús says they are able to see in the dark. They have X-rays and helicopters and searchlights. Jesús says wait, just wait, till he says. You can feel the hand of Jesús clamp your shoulder, fingers cold as ice. *Venga, corre.* You run. All the rest happens without words. Your feet are tearing dry grass, your heart is lashed like a mare. You trip, you fall. You are now in the United States of America. You are a boy from a Mexican village. You have come into the country on your knees with your head down. You are a man.

Papa, what was it like?

I am his second son, his favorite child, his confidant. After we have polished the DeSoto, we sit in the car and talk. I am sixteen years old. I fiddle with the knobs of the radio. He is fifty.

He will never say. He was an orphan there. He had no mother, he remembered none. He lived in a village by the ocean. He wanted books and he had none.

You are lucky, boy.

In the nineteenth century, American contractors reached down into Mexico for cheap labor. Men were needed to build America: to lay track, to mine, to dredge, to harvest. It was a man's journey. And, as a year's contract was extended, as economic dependence was established, sons followed their fathers north. When American jobs turned scarce—during the Depression, as today—Mexicans were rounded up and thrown back over the border. But for generations it has been the rite of passage for the poor Mexican male.

I will send for you or I will come home rich.

In the fifties, Mexican men were contracted to work in America as *braceros*, farm workers. I saw them downtown in Sacramento. I saw men my age drunk in Plaza Park on Sundays, on their backs on the grass. I was a boy at sixteen, but I was an American. At sixteen, I wrote a gossip column, "The Watchful Eye," for my school paper.

Or they would come into town on Monday nights for the wrestling matches or on Tuesdays for boxing. They worked over in Yolo county. They were men without women. They were Mexicans without Mexico.

On Saturdays, they came into town to the Western Union office where they sent money—money turned into humming wire and then turned back into money—all the way down into Mexico. They were husbands, fathers, sons. They kept themselves poor for Mexico.

Much that I would come to think, the best I would think about male Mexico, came as much from those chaste, lonely men as from my own father who made false teeth and who—after thirty years in America—owned a yellow stucco house on the east side of town.

The male is responsible. The male is serious. A man remembers.

The migration of Mexico is not only international, South to North. The epic migration of Mexico and throughout Latin America, is from the village to the city. And throughout Latin America, the city has ripened, swollen with the century. Lima. Caracas. Mexico City. So the journey to Los Angeles is much more than a journey from Spanish to English. It is the journey from *tu*—the familiar, the erotic, the intimate pronoun—to the repellent *usted* of strangers' eyes.

Most immigrants to America came from villages. The America that Mexicans find today, at the decline of the century, is a closed-circuit city of ramps and dark towers, a city without God.

The city is evil. Turn. Turn.

Mexico is poor. But my mama says there are no love songs like the love songs of Mexico. She hums a song she can't remember. The ice cream there is creamier than here. Someday we will see. The people are kinder—poor, but kinder to each other.

Men sing in Mexico. Men are strong and silent. But in song the Mexican male is granted license he is otherwise denied. The male can admit longing, pain, desire.

HAIII—EEEE—a cry like a comet rises over the song. A cry like mock-weeping tickles the refrain of Mexican love songs. The cry is meant to encourage the balladeer—it is the raw edge of his sentiment. HAIII—EEEE. It is the man's sound. A ticklish arching of semen, a node wrung up a guitar string, until it bursts in a descending cascade of mockery. HAI. HAI. HAI. The cry of a jackal under the moon, the whistle of the phallus, the maniacal song of the skull.

Tell me, Papa.

What?

About Mexico.

I lived with the family of my uncle. I was the orphan in the village. I used to ring the church bells in the morning, many steps up in the dark. When I'd get up to the tower I could see the ocean.

The village, Papa, the houses too . . .

The ocean. He studies the polished hood of our beautiful blue DeSoto.

Mexico was not the past. People went back and forth. People came up for work. People went back home, to mama or wife or village. The poor had mobility. Men who were too poor to take a bus walked from Sonora to Sacramento.

Relatives invited relatives. Entire Mexican villages got recreated in three stories of a single house. In the fall, after the harvest in the Valley, families of Mexican adults and their American children would load up their cars and head back to Mexico in caravans, for weeks, for months. The school teacher said to my mother what a shame it was the Mexicans did that—took their children out of school.

Like wandering Jews. They carried their home with them, back and forth: they had no true home but the tabernacle of memory.

Each year the American kitchen takes on a new appliance. The children are fed and grow tall. They go off to school with children from Vietnam, from Korea, from Hong Kong. They get into fights. They come home and they say dirty words.

The city will win. The city will give the children all the village could not— VCRs, hairstyles, drum beat. The city sings mean songs, dirty songs. But the city will sing the children a great Protestant hymn.

You can be anything you want to be.

We are parked. The patrolman turns off the lights of the truck—"back in a minute"—a branch scrapes the door as he rolls out of the van to take a piss. The brush crackles beneath his receding steps. It is dark. Who? Who is out there? The faces I have seen in San Diego—dishwashers, janitors, gardeners. They come all the time, no big deal. There are other Mexicans who tell me the crossing is dangerous.

The patrolman returns. We drive again. I am thinking of epic migrations in history books—pan shots of orderly columns of paleolithic peoples, determined as ants, heeding some trumpet of history, traversing miles and miles . . . of paragraph.

The patrolman has turned off the headlights. He can't have to piss again? Suddenly the truck accelerates, pitches off the rutted road, banging, slamming a rock, faster, ignition is off, the truck is soft-pedalled to a stop in the dust; the patrolman is out like a shot. The cab light is on. I sit exposed for a minute. I can't hear anything. Cautiously, I decide to follow—I leave my door open as the patrolman has done. There is a boulder in the field. Is that it? The patrolman is barking in Spanish. His flashlight is trained on the boulder like a laser, he weaves it along the grain as though he is untying a knot. He is: Three men and a woman stand up. The men are young—sixteen, seventeen. The youngest is shivering. He makes a fist. He looks down. The woman is young too. Or she could be the mother? Her legs are very thin. She wears a man's digital wristwatch. They come from somewhere. And somewhere—San Diego, Sacramento—somebody is waiting for them.

The patrolman tells them to take off their coats and their shoes, throw them in a pile. Another truck rolls up.

As a journalist, I am allowed to come close. I can even ask questions.

There are no questions.

You can take pictures, the patrolman tells me.

I stare at the faces. They stare at me. To them I am not bearing witness; I am part of the process of being arrested. I hold up my camera. Their eyes swallow the flash, a long tunnel, leading back.

Your coming of age. It is early. From your bed you watch your Mama moving back and forth under the light. The bells of the church ring in the dark. Mama crosses herself. From your bed you watch her back as she wraps the things you will take.

You are sixteen. Your father has sent for you. That's what it means: He has sent an address in Nevada. He is there with your uncle. You remember your uncle remembering snow with his beer.

You dress in the shadows. Then you move toward the table, the circle of light. You sit down. You force yourself to eat. Mama stands over you to make the sign of the cross on your forehead with her thumb. You are a man. You smile. She puts a bag of food in your hands. She says she has told *La Virgin*.

Then you are gone. It is gray. You hear a little breeze. It is the rustle of your old black *Dueña*, the dog, taking her shortcuts through the weeds, crazy *Dueña*, her pads on the dust. She is following you.

You pass the houses of the village; each window is a proper name. You pass the store. The bar. The lighted window of the clinic where the pale medical student from Monterrey lives alone and reads his book full of sores late into the night.

You want to be a man. You have the directions in your pocket: an address in Tijuana, and a map with a yellow line that leads from the highway to an "X" on a street in Reno. You are afraid, but you have never seen snow.

You are just beyond the cemetery. The breeze has died. You turn and throw a rock back at *La Dueña*, where you know she is—where you will always know where she is. She will not go past the cemetery, not even for him. She will turn in circles like a *loca* and bite herself.

The dust takes on gravel, the path becomes a rutted road which leads to the highway. You walk north. The sky has turned white overhead. Insects click in the fields. In time, there will be a bus.

I will send for you or I will come home rich.

Timothy Liu
In Hot Pursuit

across the Passaic's asphalt drawbridge into the heart of Kearny—
my cheeks flushed with wine—you the muse I did not choose
dragging danger down in chains across the hangdog face of me

as I followed you upriver, wanting you to cleanse me like a sari
pulled through a virgin's wedding band—why else would I cruise
across the Passaic's asphalt drawbridge into the heart of Kearny

still hot on your brand-new tail?—yes, you—my spanking Jersey
princess with a papa's pocketbook good for nothing but booze
and chains of smoke you'll drag across the hangdog face of me

until I cry myself to sleep in the priest's confessional, unworthy
of your whorish looks and your windows down blasting blues
across the Passaic's asphalt drawbridge into the heart of Kearny

with a fifth of Maker's Mark sloshing in your lap more empty
than the gas was ever gonna get when I got through—win or lose—
love but a daisy chain dragged across the hangdog face of me

until crush felt more like crash upside another tab of Ecstasy
hurled overboard with seat belts coming loose and pairs of shoes
spilled across Passaic asphalt straight into the heart of Kearny
where danger dragged its tread across the hangdog face of me.

CHAPTER NINE

STRUCTURE: FORMS

FORMS FOR ANY GENRE

In your composition class, you may have learned to write a comparison/contrast essay, or other papers with a set form or structure: the process essay (the "how to"), the definition essay, the profile of a person or a place. In a ready-made structure, or *form*, you follow a recipe and put the parts of writing together in the designated order.

> *When forced to work within a strict framework the imagination is taxed to its utmost—and will produce its richest ideas. Given total freedom the work is likely to sprawl.*
>
> — T. S. ELIOT

Creative writers, like cooks and composers, work with a number of these basic structures—forms—that allow us to shape our writing into reader-friendly formats. Specific forms can be used to generate new work, as in "write a sonnet" or "draft a three-act play by Friday." Structure can also be applied to your existing pieces of writing, helping you see new and different possibilities in your work.

Linear Structure

Some structure "recipes" are so basic to good writing, they can apply to poems, plays, stories, novels—any genre. These structures have been around for hundreds or even thousands of years, and are basically instruction manuals for writers. Sometimes, writers *want* to reinvent the wheel. But often, using an existing structure as a template forces you to go deeper into what you can say, surprising not just the reader, but also yourself in the process. Think about it: Dancers, athletes, musicians, architects, and cooks, just like creative writers, use basic sequences or blueprints—rumba, baseball, ballad, three-bedroom ranch, appetizer–main course–dessert—because they *work*.

Some very basic structural forms work equally well for poets *and* prose writers, for playwrights and experimentalists. All of these structures may be used to generate work, or deepen work you may have already begun. For example, if a story isn't working, try it as a journey poem. If you are blocked, try writing an alphabet essay, just as a warm-up. If a poem is stalled, what if you turn it into a visitation? Like all the tools for writers in this book, structure works at the beginning, middle, and end of the creative writer's process. "Cathedral," in Chapter 8, can be seen as a journey—the narrator's voyage from blindness to seeing. Meeting a blind man on the road to enlightenment is an aspect of the journey story that has been used in many cultures, for thousands of years! When you take apart a text, from Homer to Homer Simpson, you will often see that essential journey structure, the move from ignorance to knowledge, from home to world, from innocence to experience.

> I learned that you should feel when writing, not like Lord Byron on the mountain top, but like a child stringing beads in kindergarten: happy, absorbed, and quietly putting one bead after another.
>
> — BRENDA UELAND

The Song of Solomon, from the Bible, is a list, as are many love poems, where the poet simply mentions everything she or he considers particularly wonderful about the beloved. The alphabet, hours in the day, numbers, or any system of your own devising can determine the order of the list items. There are also specific structures that apply to certain genres, especially for poetry. In the second part of the chapter, you can experiment with pantoums, ghazals, sestinas, and villanelles. Like sudoku or crossword puzzles, poem forms can be maddening, frustrating, elegant, and fun—usually all at once.

Try to think of forms as road maps; form is a strategy that actually takes some of the work of writing out of your hands, freeing you to be more wild and creative.

Classical Dramatic Structure. Classic dramatic structure dates back to Aristotle, who first described it. It's the foundation of creative writing in Western civilization. If a story *is* a story, it probably has three parts to it, parts that even a small child can identify: beginning, middle, end. In high school you may have learned this pattern as: conflict, crisis, resolution.

Classic dramatic structure is a way of presenting your chunks of narrative in order to give the reader/viewer a dramatic story experience, focused on forward motion. By analyzing beginning-middle-end in terms of how they relate to each other, you use the tool of classic dramatic structure to strengthen your poems, fiction, creative nonfiction, and plays, as well as the stories you tell as part of the conversations you have on a daily basis with friends and family.

Conflict. Classic dramatic structure has three parts. The first part is *conflict*. Instead of warming up, instead of wandering around, always start with a battle: one character's strong unmet desire set against, and directly opposing, another equally viable character's strong unmet desire (as you learned in the previous chapter, this is the heart of writing good scenes). Remember, a battle takes place when two characters (or, in a poem, two speakers, entities, or desires) have conflicting agendas. The characters must each want something, and the wants must conflict, which means something in *one person's action* blocks the desire of the other. For example: Joe takes Olivia to a fancy restaurant to break up with her; just before he drops the bomb over crème caramel, she presents a man's engagement ring to him and proposes. The climax comes from what happens *next*.

Readers aren't interested in the build-up—how Olivia got ready for the date, the cab ride to the restaurant, Joe's protracted ordering process. Readers are interested in how the conflict plays out, and *beginnings always contain the first stage of the high-stakes conflict.*

In a short poem, the opening conflict could be one line; in a short story or piece of creative nonfiction, the opening might be one scene or three, that establish and develop the opening battle. In a novel, the conflict that opens the book can be developed, intensified step by step, and expanded to many chapters. The classic story form is flexible enough to meet the needs of your topic and the dimensions inherent in your conflict.

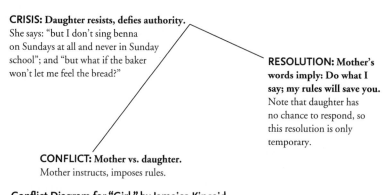

CRISIS: Daughter resists, defies authority.
She says: "but I don't sing benna on Sundays at all and never in Sunday school"; and "but what if the baker won't let me feel the bread?"

RESOLUTION: Mother's words imply: Do what I say; my rules will save you. Note that daughter has no chance to respond, so this resolution is only temporary.

CONFLICT: Mother vs. daughter. Mother instructs, imposes rules.

Conflict Diagram for "Girl," by Jamaica Kincaid

Crisis. Section two in this structure, the middle, is called the *crisis*. If you are using multiple scenes, place the crisis moment at the end of the sequence, at the end of this second phase in the action. A crisis is when the battle is at its very, very worst. When the loser loses, things can't get any worse in the narrative. In some large, significant, or subtle and moving way, the world as these characters know it seems to have come to an end.

Regardless of the genre in which you are working, crisis requires tension. To create an effective crisis, remember these principles for creating and sustaining tension:

1. Make sure the two opposing forces are equally strong.
2. Make the reader wonder how the battle will come out.
3. Make sure the crisis comes out of the opening conflict.
4. Reverse the direction of the battle.

| PRACTICE |

Reread "Girl" by Jamaica Kincaid on page 55. Write a brief paragraph that argues for or against "Girl" as an example of classic dramatic structure. Now, make the opposite argument. Which is more convincing?

When you reread "Girl," what do you notice in terms of story structure? Does Kincaid utilize the classic structure in "Girl"? Where is the conflict, what's the crisis, which sentence or sentences contain the resolution? Identify what you *think* they each might be.

The conflict is clearly between a mother and a daughter. The mother is the speaker in the piece, and the daughter is hearing this onslaught of directives, which plays in her head like a tape she can't shut off. The conflict is mother versus daughter, rules versus freedom. The crisis occurs three lines from the end of this short-short story, in italics, when the daughter asks her mother a question, daring to interrupt the monologue of commands: *"but what if the baker won't let me feel the bread?"* By breaking the sequence, disrupting the flow, Kincaid has cleverly brought her piece to a climax—we know this mother is incredibly strong, controlling, bossy, militant, protective, even harsh. How will she respond to being questioned? That's the moment of high tension, that's the crisis point. Can you ask this kind of mother a question? What happens if you do? The daughter is prepared for this battle—how much trouble can you get in for asking a simple question? Well, a lot. As we all know. You open yourself up to humiliation. So, as readers, we hold our breath for a quick second, and speed on to read the answer—the mother trumps us. She has an answer for everything. She uses the daughter's question to shame her into mature adulthood, just as she always does. Game over.

Resolution. Do you have to have a resolution? Art is not life. Art demands you deliver significance to the reader. In her classic textbook *Writing Fiction*, Janet Burroway suggests thinking about resolution in this way. She lays out six choices for writers looking for ways to resolve the crises in their works:

1. The two fighting forces call a truce.
2. The two fighters call a truce, and agree to fight again later.
3. Declaring victory, the hero lives happily ever after, the loser suffers.
4. Losing, the main character offers insight into life with loss.
5. The two fighters both realize no one will ever win.
6. Each side thinks it has won.

Essential with any of these six choices for resolution is your ability to show *the newly changed life* of your main character (or in a poem, speaker). Usually, in contemporary creative writing, the change is small, interior, subtle, psychological, well-observed. Also remember that you don't have to resolve the conflict itself (stating a clear winner and loser—usually that isn't how life works). You just have to resolve the *story line*.

With these concepts in mind, how do you see Kincaid's ending? Is there a resolution to the conflict? How does the *story* resolve? Some readers see the daughter as defeated. The mother will always win; that's the archetypal conflict resolution for mother-daughter stories. Other readers see the daughter as winning: She has a strong brilliant mother who always has an answer for everything; this girl will make it through the hard parts of life. The resolution isn't overtly presented in a scene or an image, but implied. We imagine a plucky, savvy daughter, growing up to be strong like her mother. And other readers see the mother as the loser: If she keeps acting like this, she will lose her daughter; she is pushing her away. Your feelings about the resolution may change as you read and reread.

> *Architecture starts when you carefully put two bricks together. There it begins.*
> — LUDWIG MIES VAN DER ROHE

Good artists make their resolutions complex, but not murky. It's good for your ending to provoke discussion, which is different from confusion. When in doubt, look back to your opening, be sure it links clearly and logically to your crisis, and let your resolution reverse something already established in the piece. Focus on the *point of the change*. Focus on the psychology of your characters, watching the impact of the battle, the conflict, in their lives. That's the key to writing resolution.

Mystery, yes. Confusion, no.

PRACTICE

Reread the short-short story by Lorraine López on page 52 and "White Angel" by Michael Cunningham on page 243. Locate the conflict, crisis, and resolution. Now, do the same for a narrative poem of your choosing, such as "Buying Wine" by Sebastian Matthews on page 53 or "Driving Through" by Rita Dove on page 124. Outline the three pieces by simply listing the author, title, and conflict, crisis, and resolution for each.

Journey.   The journey structure is simple, straightforward, and powerful. Most myths and fairy tales use it. A journey is a literal trip your main character takes, and along the way he is tested, ultimately returning home with new knowledge. *Peter Pan* is a journey. The King Arthur legend is a journey. The Narnia books by C. S. Lewis use the journey structure. *Star Wars, Thelma and Louise, On the Road* by Jack Kerouac, and *The Sisterhood of the Traveling Pants* by Ann Brashares are all journeys.

Cinderella is on a journey: She works and toils, the invitation to the ball provides her errand/quest, and the fairy godmother assists, providing the time element that will keep tension high on the trip. Cinderella returns after the ball to the ordinary world with the knowledge that she is not a greedy, self-serving person, this is not her real family, and her prince is out there. The road back is a tough one. Cinderella toils, while her grotesque stepsisters try to wedge their hideous feet into the slipper. But Cinderella's foot fits — her reward is the prince, and the kingdom. The world is a better place with Cinderella on a throne. The whole community benefits. (And, notice, she's off again! On the Journey of Royal Marriage/Life in a Castle.)

Rick Moody uses the journey structure in "Boys" on page 94: coming of age, which is the journey from childhood to adulthood, provides the structure for his narrative. Thinking of the beats in your story as pieces of a journey, and organizing them that way, helps you structure your poem, play, essay, or story so that the reader can follow along happily.

We don't learn much sitting on the couch, and readers don't care to watch passive humans musing, eating potato chips, staring off into space. Action and enlightenment happen when we leave home, comfort, security, and routine.

> *Structure is one of the things that I always hope will reveal itself to me.*
> — RICHARD RUSSO

That's the premise of the journey structure. If the travelers don't go through tests along the way, they don't change or transform — the energy fades quickly. The reader will say, "Are we there yet?"

Journey structure is natural and simple to organize. Give your characters a destination, and make it difficult for them to get there. The stops along the way are where you insert your obstacles and insights. It is essential when writing a journey that you not report on the trip (our natural tendency), but that you render the key points of the journey *in images*. That is, we have to be there. We have to experience what your characters experience, as they do it. You as writer know the ultimate outcome. But you have to write as though you don't.

Journeys are most interesting when there are at least two people involved — the other person serves as a foil, so we can measure and address the main character's change and growth. If your character journeys alone, she is alone with her thoughts. In a shorter narrative poem, the reader will tag along, but for longer narratives, readers need to have another person along so we can see/feel/sense our main character on stage, and not be trapped in her head, with her thoughts.

The Six Components of the Journey. The journey uses story beats to present the six key emotional or action points listed below.

1. Ordinary World.   The ordinary world is either the opening location or implied. The main character has an errand or a quest, a problem to be solved — the call to adventure. The image or images the author uses to present the ordinary world show the mix of feelings in the main character — he wants to obey his parents, but he also wants to marry his love.

2. Call to Adventure.   The conflict here is between the main speaker or central character and the ordinary world, but also between this figure and the unknown world he will be entering; additionally, a lone traveler is bound to have boring sections of journeying, as anyone who has driven cross-country, or just upstate, knows. Add a companion, and let the call to adventure spark tension between the two sojourners.

3. Mentor.   A mentor provides encouragement, wisdom, or magical gifts to push the main character onward. The trip itself is a special world, with different rules and tests from the traveler's home world. There is usually a time element (remember: tension!), and a crisis where the hero's central strengths are tested. Her fidelity, ethics, sense of right and wrong, something grand and huge (Westerns, video games) or something subtle and fine (literary fiction, poems) may provide the tension in the image or images that make up the crisis.

4. Tests and Ordeals.   Here is the accordion part of the journey structure. A Norse saga has thousands of tests and ordeals; the first three components can be handled in a single sentence, opening the saga. A narrative poem might have one test or ordeal. The main character solves problems, creates problems, is overwhelmed by problems, and his or her problems generate new problems. Apply what you know about bits and beats to keep these scenes crisp and interesting.

5. Reward.   After the final test/ordeal (the crisis), we move into Act Three, the beginning of the resolution. What has the journey taught the main character? How is this person different now? What does he return to the ordinary world *with*? A chalice, super powers, a spouse, a baby, the anti-virus, wisdom, experience?

6. Return.   Finally the main character returns (or return is implied). The hero has new information, wisdom, or insight, and often the suggestion is that this new self will benefit the ordinary world. This is the resolution, the ending. In many short pieces, the return is implied, or the reader is left to conjecture. In other pieces, a full scene or scenes will be devoted to the return.

In every journey, there is a nested classic dramatic structure. Notice how the Call to Adventure is equivalent to "conflict." The final Test and Ordeal will contain the "crisis" from classic structure. And the "resolution" is going to be in numbers 5 and 6—where we see the change in the character, as she deals with the outcome of the big crisis battle.

PRACTICE

Find the Six Components of the Journey in works from each genre: fiction, nonfiction, and poetry. Try using Marisa Silver's "What I Saw from Where I Stood," page 167, or Michael Cunningham's "White Angel," page 243. The essay by Naomi Shihab Nye, "How to Get There" on page 346 has a classic journey structure, as does the poem by Dana Levin, "Techno," on page 347. Can you find the basic journey structure? List each stage, and provide a few quotes from the piece you are examining to designate that stage of the journey. Do this for each of the three pieces.

Interior/Exterior Aspects of the Journey.   The inward journey is just as important as the outward journey; write in images, and those inner layers will come through. Amy Fusselman's memoir excerpt (p. 60) is a journey—a woman's journey through the loss of her father, and the medical establishment's fertility protocols. Michael Chabon's short story "Along the Frontage Road" (p. 348) is a journey that starts at the destination—the pumpkin patch. The characters journey through a microcosm of today's society, dealing with race, loss, grief, and parenting along the way.

In order to go deeper with your practice of this form—in poetry, nonfiction, and/or fiction—study the two levels: psychological and physical.

After you have gotten clear on the basic steps that make up the exterior journey, then ask yourself: What is the interior journey?

In Sebastian Matthews's poem "Buying Wine" (p. 53), the ordinary world is presented in the first line: "Stay in the car." The car is where kids wait. The call to adventure, the choice: car or Wine Mart. Car = safe and known. Wine Mart = adult world, danger and drama.

The mentor is the father ("circus master"), and this same figure also provides the tests and ordeals

> *Dreaming is a form of planning.*
> — GLORIA STEINEM

for the young boy speaker in the poem. The mentor-father knows everything about wine. As he shops, it's like he's gathering "fruit," collecting something nourishing and good and innocent. But often, the speaker doesn't meet the call to adventure with action. He stays in the car, where he is safe. He grows impatient—the Wine Mart is an ordeal; the promise the father makes that he will return quickly is often broken. The father fills a cart with wine bottles. This is too much wine, isn't it? The father seems to be consumed by planning sumptuous meals, matching wines and foods, and oblivious to his children. That's an ordeal for a child.

What is the reward? When we read the poem again, we see in stanzas 2, 3, 6, and 7 that the author/speaker of the poem knows *an awful lot about wine*. So, education, epicurean knowledge of food and drink, sophistication—that's a reward, possibly. "The dream party" is his quest, this boy's, and we have a strong sense this speaker could cook a fabulous meal, throw a fine party.

But, what's the elixir? What does he return to the ordinary world with? Well, it sounds like by waiting in the car, calling his father out, passing his tests by peering in, listening to the jukebox, and running around in the parking lot, not going into the store much—"once I slipped back into the store . . . master of my own cart"—the speaker has a kind of sense, groundedness, frugality perhaps, or "good values." When he is back in his own life, in adulthood, the poem shows us how he is fully capable of walking down wine aisles and remembering his father, being just as stimulated and delighted by sensory passions, perhaps, as his father, but *he is not his father*. The interior journey reflects and echoes the exterior one. They do not walk down the wine aisles together. They are different men.

> *Many poets argue that traditional forms give us something to work against, a kind of resistance training. That is how we build muscles, that is how we build power.*
> — JIM FERRIS

As an adult, the speaker shops very differently. He realizes wine was more important than children to his father. Our speaker is torn—maybe he spends a little too much time on an "Umbrian red," but he knows his limits. Twelve dollars. He might be "drifting," but he doesn't go off course, as his father did.

Consider how the journey helps you add depth and meaning and shape to your story (in whatever genre). If you want to tell us about your father's drinking habits, and compare and contrast them with your own, making some observations about maturity and parenting and pleasure, you have many forms to choose from. Matthews probably noticed the parallels between walking up and down aisles and following (or not) in your father's footsteps. The physical journey mirrors the interior one.

The process of discovering those twin journeys is something writers work at, trying different topics, shapes, and angles of approach. When you *force* an exterior and interior journey—a walk down the beach parallels your spiritual development, for example—your writing may or may not cooperate. The only way to know is to try it and see.

Visitation. The journey inverted is called a visitation. A visitation is a story that takes place in the character's ordinary world. Instead of leaving the ordinary world to have tests, adventures, growth, etc., someone (or something) comes to the ordinary world, and this visitor creates problems, a series of ordeals and tests, and that's what creates the plot. *E. T.* is a visitation; the little alien transforms the ordinary world of a boy, and creates all of the key journey features. "The Three Little Pigs" is a visitation (that uninvited carnivore creating all the plot points). In this book, Jessica Shattuck's "Bodies" (p. 180) and Raymond Carver's "Cathedral" (p. 297) provide excellent examples of the visitation structure.

Visitation structures begin with a knock on the door, a car in the driveway, someone entering your room. In visitation, you are attacked on your home turf. The visitor disrupts ordinary life, and this disruption can be comic (*Home Alone*), terrifying (*Alien*), pleasant (*Splash*), annoying (*What About Bob?*), or useful (*Mary Poppins*). The battle is that of the main character as he conquers or is conquered by this visitor. And in the process, he transforms or becomes transformed—as in the classic structure, the journey, change is at the heart of this form. The story starts with the arrival and ends with the departure of the visitor; any preface or follow-up will probably fall flat.

PRACTICE

Discuss "Surrounded by Sleep" (p. 125) as a visitation. Now, argue that it is a journey. Which lens is most helpful to you in understanding the structure of the story?

As with the journey, skillful writers work hard to have the inner experiences of the character move the reader. In a blockbuster movie, the visitation can rely on special effects and action, sex, and violence. On the page, the reader is expecting a writer to show off her insights, psychological observations, wisdom, and accurate understanding of how people do what they do, and why.

Jessica Shattuck layers visitations into her story "Bodies." Illness visits the main character, wreaking havoc on her body and her spirit. Sexy, vampy Michele visits the home, and takes its married patriarch as her lover. The main character herself is a visitor in this drama, and as a visitor, her place in the family is inherently unstable.

PRACTICE

Read the Sharon Olds poem "Visiting My Mother's College" on page 354. What kind of journey gives the structure to this poem? Can you find all the journey elements in the poem? Is it a visitation structure, as the title strongly suggests?

Note: If you are trying to figure out if you want to use the journey lens or the visitation lens to analyze the structure of a piece, focus on who in the story undergoes the most difficulty. To whom does the story "happen"? Who is changed most in the story? To whom do the events *mean or matter* the most? If, in Chabon's story, we had access to the pumpkin seller, the story would be a visitation.

But because Nicky and his dad are on an errand, the story is best viewed through the lens of journey. When you are the visitor, you're on a trip. When you are the center of the story, you must undergo a change. Carver's blind man is a catalyst—he initiates change in others. He is the same wise, funky, cool guy at the ending as he was at the beginning of "Cathedral." Focus on who changes, and make sure that's your point-of-view character as you try on different structures for different stories.

Nonlinear Structure

The three previous structures—classical drama, journey, and visitation—are closely related. They are all lenses for looking at conflict, and tools for shaping the transformation of your main characters. Classical drama and journey are very much alike; visitation is the inverse of journey.

However, there is an alternate way of constructing creative writing, one which doesn't use conflict and resolution to drive the engine of the story. This alternate way is called modular, mosaic, or nonlinear structure, which can be used for any genre. Use it at the beginning, to create a piece from scratch, or later, to revise a piece that is bogged down in the middle, or flat, or confusing or boring.

Some writers just do not want to focus on conflict, battles, tension, and transformation, and some life experiences do not fit that way of measuring and framing human experience. Rarely do our days move along, increasing in tension, climaxing just after dinner, and resolving before bedtime. Creative writers need options. Three options that many students enjoying experimenting with include: list, alphabet, and braid.

Good thinking—like life—doesn't always follow a straight line. Hardly ever do our own conflicts follow classic story structure. Sometimes, a relationship may reach a climactic moment, and segue logically to resolution, but usually life is messier, with grey areas, gaps in understanding, and overlaps. Good narrative structures, like good lives, don't always have to follow the classic-drama, or Aristotelian, model of dramatic form. Art can be like life. Also, it can be very rewarding for a reader to have to find the connections between the images himself.

List. Lists allow you to organize the elements of a piece of creative writing easily and quickly. Anyone can make a list; you probably have made one already this week, at least in your head. The list structure is a wonderfully easy method used not only to structure existing drafts of pieces, but to generate new material. Humans are natural-born list makers. Think of your birthday list, your grocery list, your goals list, your list of titles, your list of places where you want to submit job applications, the to-do list in your notebook, the real to-do list in your head. We basically move through our day, every day, making lists.

The tension in a list structure comes from juxtaposition, and the energy comes from brevity, image, and leaping. The dramatic power of list pieces comes not from a big blow-out fight or a journey, but rather from the gaps between the sections and the intensity of the images, as the reader supplies the narrative threads.

The recipes that help us craft sophisticated dramatic narratives, above, are very clear and orderly. Working with modular forms is more like cooking *without* a recipe, an inherited form. You lay out the ingredients you want to consume, and put them together however you please, thinking on the fly, working from intuition. Like the three structures above, lists, alphabets, and braids work well for all genres of writing.

The lists you generated in the first unit of the semester, when you focused on the images of your life story—the things on your bedroom walls, the cars of your life, blue things from your life, shoes, boys, hotels, lies—these can turn into wonderful poems and list stories. These lists are called catalogs, and they can provide specificity and energy for all genres of creative writing; when they alone form the basis of the piece, you have a list structure.

An alternative to the list of "stuff" is a list of images. And image lists aren't just structures for poets; Jamaica Kincaid's piece, which we analyzed for classic structure elements above, is a list of things heard by the speaker.

Other types of lists to explore include the List of Instructions (a recipe poem or story), the List of Questions or Commands (most commonly seen in poems, but possible for adventurous prose writers), and the List of What I Did or Noticed Today. In his poem "Introduction to Poetry" on page 277, Billy Collins lists ways he wishes readers would approach reading poetry, along with some things he wishes they would not do. The list strategy keeps his poem focused, and helps the reader pay attention to his main points. Similarly, Lynne McMahon, author of "Carpe Diem" on page 257, uses a simple list of questions to examine some very complicated aspects of memory, forgetting, and consciousness itself. Jamaica Kincaid's "Girl" (p. 55) and Rick Moody's "Boys" (p. 94) are two short stories which use the list structure as their organizing principle, presenting a list of parental rules and a list of boys' actions respectively. Notice how the repetition in a list always creates energy. Notice how in these two poems and two stories, as in most creative writing list pieces, the list is always a list of *images*.

Another way of using lists to structure a piece of creative writing is to use the same repeated word ("red," or someone's name) in every line in the poem or sentence in the prose piece. Other list forms use the same opening words for each line or paragraph; every line starts with "I remember," or, "I can't tell you," or, "In America."

PRACTICE

Read the short story by Lorrie Moore on page 222. In what ways does the author use lists to organize and structure the material in her story?

Lorrie Moore uses the format of the self-help book to structure her list story, "How to Become a Writer." Self-help books list steps one can take to improve one's love life or get more organized, or lose weight, or be more or less sensitive, with a sequence of rules, what to do, what not to do—a handy checklist for simple problem-solving. In real life our attempts to figure out who we are, work on our personal weaknesses, declare a major, or fall in love rarely fit into checklist form. Usually, our own lives are much messier.

Often our own personal story unfolds without a clear conflict, a climax, and a neat resolution. So Lorrie Moore rejects traditional construction methods. She doesn't try to tell her story in terms of conflict/crisis/resolution. She takes a well-known structure—the self-help book, which always uses listing as part of its structure—and she tells the story of a girl trying to figure out her family, her life, and her major using that form. Lorrie Moore is suggesting life is more like a list, a sequence of events that may or may not lead to climactic insights. Maybe, the story suggests, real life *is* the self-help book.

"How to Become a Writer" is built by stringing together twenty-two modules, organized into a list, that answer the question posed by the title. Each section lists another step in the quest to become a writer. Each module has a conflict of its own—each module is a miniature story.

Unless your sections are superbly short, like Dinty W. Moore's and Rick Moody's, you have to use what you know about conflict and story structure to construct the modules. If you don't, you risk losing your reader: Without conflict, without being equipped to wonder what will happen, who will win, how the story will end, the reader may easily put down all your beautiful modules.

PRACTICE

Make a list of things you could list in a story, essay, or poem. It's absolutely fine—encouraged—for you to "steal" from your work in progress. Here are some examples: a list of single words, a list of swears, a list of people you've loved, a list of actions, a list of kinds of one thing (blue, darkness, sons, anger), a list of what you hate, a list of What Doug Doesn't Do, a list of postcards received, a list of weather you have known well, a list of people who irritate you, a list of things you have not said.

Alphabet. When creative writers use the alphabet to provide the structure for a piece of writing, it's called an *abecedarius.*

To experiment in this form, start every line of poetry or prose—this will be a twenty-six-line poem or twenty-six-paragraph prose piece—with a different letter of the alphabet. *A* or a word that begins with *A* starts you off. Your second line in this piece begins with a word that starts with *B*. And so on, down to *Z*. The limits, or rules, are what make the poem interesting. How can you work out some surprises, some inventive ways around the restrictions of *X* and *Q*? How can you make the poem flow *in spite of the restrictions*? The puzzle makes your mind leap, and that is just what you want. You may have already worked with the related form, acrostics, in school—perhaps spelling out the letters of your name, or your boyfriend's or your father's, to make a poem which you then gave as a present.

Forcing yourself into a box like this does interesting things to your creativity. You end up surprising yourself. Oftentimes, the letters for which you "can't think of anything" provide the most fresh, original sections. The renowned poet Ezra Pound wrote an entire book, *The ABC of Reading*, using this form. Other well-known examples include Czeslow Milosz's *Milosz's ABC's*, a book of brief prose essays. A. J. Jacobs's *The Know-It-All* is a memoir of reading the *Encyclopedia Britannica* in alphabetical order.

Instead of writing a "whole," you craft twenty-six tiny parts, and string them together, like beads on a strand, like knots on a rope. Don't feel you have to work in order, straight through from A to Z. If you love this kind of intellectual wordplay and these kinds of structures, there are a number of brain-busting structural variations on the alphabet form at the end of this chapter. In the appendix, you will find a list of books that present the recipes for even more complex list-based, word-based structure puzzles.

PRACTICE

Read the alphabet pieces by Dinty W. Moore, "Son of Mr. Green Jeans: An Essay on Fatherhood, Alphabetically Arranged," page 355 and David Lehman, "Abecedarius," page 360.

When reading these two abecedarius prose pieces, notice the specificity, the strong verbs, the tension, and the energy. Each piece, each "letter," on its own is interesting and alive. Because there is no classic structure—conflict, crisis, resolution—each little bit or beat in the piece has to have enough energy and tension to sustain reader interest.

PRACTICE

Reread David Lehman's poem (p. 360) and Dinty W. Moore's essay (p. 355); both use the alphabet, but very differently. Do you see other structural principles at work besides the alphabet? Are there elements of classic dramatic structure, for example? Are there any components of the journey structure? Visitation?

Braid. With braid structures—in poems, essays, and short stories or novels—
you as writer have to keep three balls in the air at once. It's a good structure to
practice after you have done some work with classic structure and listing. It combines the best elements of both: classical story structure (you are telling three stories simultaneously) and listing (setting unlike things next to each other).

To braid a text, you usually have three pieces that you layer into one piece,
one after the other. The three pieces are *story strands.* If you have ever braided
someone's hair, or your own, you know two pieces just don't have enough traction to get a good braid going and four, five, or six different strands can be fun or
unwieldy, depending on hair texture.

Sometimes a writer will take two of the strands and tell them, in interlocking
fashion, using journey or classic structure, and then a third strand will provide a
counterpoint. For example, you tell the story of your mother and her mother,
during the Runaway Fiancé Crisis of 1942, breaking the story into tense, brief
scenes. Between each of that story's steps, you play out piece by piece the story of
you and your roommate dating the same guy. Interspersed between those two interlocking narratives, you include diary entries from your mother's college diary.
Two traditional stories, and one alternative modular strand. That story might
look something like this if you graphed it:

X = mother story
O = you/roommate story
! = diary entry excerpts

X O ! X O ! X O ! X O ! X O ! X O ! X

Amy Fusselman's piece (p. 60) provides a terrific example of the braid form.
The story of her attempts to get pregnant is counterpointed with her family
story. In between these two narratives, she braids in examples from her father's
diaries. The diaries inform the other two stories.

There are three keys to successful braiding:

1. Pick topics that don't have immediate obvious connections. Three stories
   about three friends all having a fairly similar experience isn't a braid, it's blah.
   The energy in braiding comes from *unlike things next to each other.*
2. Allow the juxtapositions to surprise you; don't impose order on the pieces.
3. Write in short sections. Readers need to be able to keep all three stories in
   their heads—use one- or two-paragraph sections.

Short sections with strong images, solid, clear action lines, and complete
emotional micro-moments compose the braid. The energy comes from the leaps,

gaps, and juxtapositions. The reader figures out connections; the writer doesn't explain. The braid sections can be like snapshots or postcards. Because the narrative line is suppressed, braided pieces are usually shorter rather than longer. The longer your sections, the more you must pay attention to conflict and crisis action.

Notice braided art forms around you. Many television shows braid two or three different story lines into each episode. When you look back over the works in this textbook, do you find braided pieces? Braiding is instantly interesting to readers; they have to pay closer attention to what you have to say. Connections evolve. Simple becomes complex.

FORMS FOR POEMS

Recipes for form poems always look much more intimidating than they really are. Once you start actually *doing* the poem, the poem will write itself, and the rules will serve as a guide to keep you on track, sort of like guardrails on curvy highways. You needn't memorize these forms—poets consult the sample poems and the recipe as they work, and you should too. You will have on your desk your own poem, the recipe, and a few samples of the form. You'll constantly go back and forth.

> *"Formal": a ball gown and tuxedo come to mind, attire uncomfortable and constricting, designed to impress. Classy, right? But no: the word "formal" drives from a proletarian source, for in Latin it described the molds used by potters.*
> — PATRICIA MONAGHAN

Writing form poems is a lot like reading music. Once you know the code, you can read any recipe for a form poem—a pattern to go— and you are on your way. There are hundreds of forms, and much pleasure to be had in practicing new forms and discovering old traditions. It's like the workouts you get from your coach or out of magazines. Do twenty reps of this, circle back, ten of these, then rest. You don't think about what you have to *do* next, and so you can concentrate on the quality of the repetitions themselves.

Above all, be patient with yourself. When you are trying something new, it's normal to feel frustrated. Keep your sense of humor: The mistakes, missteps, and parts of your poem that don't "fit" the structural demands are part of the fun of creating within forms. Your best approach: Read a few examples of the form. Review the recipe. Take an existing image, some nugget of something from existing work, and then let the form take you for a ride.

So, read the poems, skim over the instructions, and learn the patterns by writing the poems. You'll know you've written a good form poem when your audience doesn't even notice the rules.

In order to avoid natural frustration at the outset, many students work closely with the recipe as they create their first pantoum, ghazal, sestina, or villanelle. It is heartily recommended you try each one *twice*; the first time to learn the moves, and the second so you can begin to have fun with the form.

Pantoum

The *pantoum* has been around for over 500 years. It's a Malayan form of poetry with Persian and Chinese influences, composed of four-line stanzas (quatrains). The pantoum is very nonlinear, forcing the reader to circle back, circle back, revisit. It's the opposite of classic dramatic structure, as pantoums move in spirals. A pantoum is made up of a sequence of *refrains*—or lines that are repeated. In pantoum, the journey *is* the destination. That's a very different approach than classic structure, what you may be used to reading. A pantoum is the opposite, actually, of conflict-crisis-resolution. A pantoum is devoted to zigzagging, circling, interlocking, unfolding. It's a perfect form for those experiences in your life you wish to write about that just don't fit into classic dramatic structure.

The pantoum is much more interesting and clear when it is read aloud.

Reading Pantoums. Read the pantoum below out loud. Then, have someone read it to you. How much of the form do you notice when you listen? As with all structures, if the structure is truly effective, it's not the most prominent feature of the piece. The tension, the energy, the images—that's what you pay attention to. The structure is the *infrastructure*, a hidden thing inside the piece. So don't worry if you don't notice the structure right away. That's a sign the poet has been successful. In the pattern below, each repeated letter of the alphabet shows you where lines repeat.

Peter Meinke
Atomic Pantoum

In a chain reaction
the neutrons released
split other nuclei
which release more neutrons

The neutrons released
blow open some others
which release more neutrons
and start this all over

Blow open some others
and choirs will crumble
and start this all over
with eyes burned to ashes

And choirs will crumble
the fish catch on fire
with eyes burned to ashes
in a chain reaction

The fish catch on fire
because the sun's force
in a chain reaction
has blazed in our minds

Because the sun's force
with plutonium trigger
has blazed in our minds
we are dying to use it

With plutonium trigger
curled and tightened
we are dying to use it
torching our enemies

Curled and tightened
blind to the end
torching our enemies
we sing to Jesus

Blind to the end
split up like nuclei
we sing to Jesus
in a chain reaction

What feeling do you get as you read and then listen to this poem? You are probably aware of the repetitions, the urgency, and the circling. Words and lines are repeated. This is a poem about obsession. It keeps going over and over certain images. That's the province of the pantoum, which is suited to its structure.

The pantoum repeats whole lines rather than words. The lines can be of any length. The second and fourth lines of the first stanza are used again, and repeated exactly to become the first and third lines of the second stanza. This same pattern is used to complete the entire poem. You can end whenever you like—there are pantoums that are *pages* long. However, a four-stanza pantoum is common, and in the final stanza, you could simply repeat lines one and three from the first stanza, or write new lines. You have options.

Here's the pantoum recipe:

STANZA 1	STANZA 2	STANZA 3	STANZA 4
A	B	E	G
B	E	G	I (or A or C)
C	D	F	H
D	F	H	J (or A or C)

Notice the elegant simplicity of this form: The second and fourth lines of each stanza become the first and third lines of the following stanza.

PRACTICE

Read the pantoum by Carolyn Kizer on page 221. Have the poem read out loud to you, as well. It's important to always both see and hear a pantoum, to see the structure and hear its effect. Now examine the lines and place the corresponding letters by them, so that you see the pattern very clearly. How does Kizer's use of the form compare to Meinke's? Which do you like better?

Writing Pantoums. When you write a pantoum, you only need two lines you like. Many poets find "cast away" lines from other poems, so as to not start with a blank page. It's okay to get a little frustrated when you first start writing your pantoum. Learning a new dance step or a new guitar lick is hard at first, and then you have a feeling of "breaking the code." Know that once you get your two basic lines, the pantoum *will* bow to you.

Do not expect this to become clear or easy until you're in the midst of experimenting with it. Most students do not feel at this point that this makes perfect sense. Confusion, frustration, and uncertainty are good signs—this means that you are on the right track. It's going to click after you write your first pantoum.

As you compose these first two lines, which will give birth to all the other lines in the pantoum, consider what the pantoum *does* to the reader: It makes the reader feel edgy, nervous, a bit boxed in.

Good topics for pantoums include those things in your life that cause you to obsess, to go back and forth, to repeat yourself. Bad break-ups, where you go back, back, back, over all the same old fights. Addictions—to food, people, drugs, ideas. Bad television, endless reruns, shopping malls, and strip malls where everything and everyone looks just the same.

A pantoum can make something that bores you out of your mind—a bad lecture, a tedious summer painting houses, your constantly breaking-down car—into something humorous, weirdly fascinating, or beautiful. Swimming laps. Teaching kids to make the letter *A*. Where in your life are you locked into repetition? The pantoum gives you a lens for looking at repetition; you might be surprised at what you discover about the same-old, same-old.

> *I like using forms like pantoums because I feel a set form, far from being restrictive, is very liberating and forces your imagination to explore possibilities it might not otherwise consider.*
>
> — SOPHIE HANNAH

PRACTICE

Before sitting down to write your first pantoum, focus on good topics for this back-and-forth form. Make a list of twenty-five things that cause your mind or body to go over and over the same ground, again and again. Work quickly—limit your allotted time to work on this list to ten minutes. If, with three minutes left, you don't have twenty-five—press yourself to come up with *anything*. If your last items don't "fit," just write them down anyway.

Once you have tried the traditionally structured pantoum, use the basic recipe to make your own kind of pantoum. Break the rules, invent your own structure to support what it is you want to say. Use the pantoum's interesting back-and-forth structure to inspire you in a new creative direction. Sometimes when you break the rules, that breach becomes the most interesting part of the pattern. Musicians do this frequently. Consider a live performance, where a singer will substitute another word, maybe a rhyme, or maybe something else altogether, into a part of the song everyone knows by heart. This is part of the fun—the surprise, the play. And it calls the reader's attention to something important. As with Lorrie Moore's story ("How to Become a Writer," p. 222), real life doesn't follow the rules.

PRACTICE

Alternative pantoums are those inspired by the pantoum form, but deviating in interesting ways. Try a pantoum that loosely follows the recipe, breaking out of the form at necessary points.

Ghazal

The *ghazal* is a poetic form that comes out of Persian poetry; it appears in Arabic, Urdu, and Turkish traditions. This poetic form, at least 1,300 years old, probably older, was mostly used to write about religion and love, specifically the mystical aspects of devotion and the pain and longing that comes from lost love. For a ghazal, the writer composes five to twelve two-line stanzas.

Reading Ghazals. The ghazal is associative (like a list). Instead of the poet taking one idea and developing it, as in a sonnet, the poet takes disparate images, and lays them next to each other, as you might on your coffee table—your personal arrangement of beautiful or intriguing things. The two-line stanzas (couplets) sit in the reader's mind side by side, not in order to develop a linear argument.

Here's a ghazal by Ellen Doré Watson. What do you notice about the structure?

Ellen Doré Watson
Ghazal

Newly happy in my body, blind to the lie at the core,
I toy with forbidden self, tantalized to the core.

She leaves behind black tights & "creative movement"
for pink and a bun: how will she find her "I" in the corps?

Kelly blades growing from cinders: some call dubious
proof there's new life in what dies at the core.

Are waves deaf? asks Michaux. Sometimes it's
other's music we covet—to get a rise at the core.

Teen-angry, innocent of what "it" was, I yelled Eat it raw!
Among the underpants they found a good-sized apple core.

For days she's acted years older; when she starts sobbing
I'm lost to my effort not to capsize at the core.

Songs we mumble, melodies we hum, dreams burrowing
upwards—hints for who listens: noise from the core.

I bloom to the click & thrill of a stranger, then flood
with blueish relief: he's not my size at the core.

Gutter is a word hurled: who lives there is tattered.
But aren't we owners uncivilized at the core?

Fire doesn't know how to be small for five minutes. No
apology blooms from his mouth, I ignite at the core.

In search of seals, beach glass, shooting stars, we go
from zoom-mode to wide-angle: we have eyes at the core.

In the wake of your leaving, no sleep—but at dawn
I find I still smell of last night at the core.

Dream: I eat the shelled egg a white hen offers held
in her claw-foot. We are all disguised to the core.

Notice how each couplet's second line repeats the same word. That's the hallmark of the ghazal. What holds the ghazal together? A formal unity based on pattern: rhyme and repetition. So, like the modular narrative forms, the pieces have their own integrity. The most important aspect of the ghazal is that the couplets are completely separate miniature poems. In the example above, all the couplets relate closely, but they do not have to.

Writing Ghazals. If you hate writing five-paragraph essays on a specific theme, you will probably love ghazal writing. The ghazal leaps from image to image, avoiding predictability.

Here's your recipe for writing a ghazal. Each letter here stands for the last word in the line. So, *a* in lines 1 and 2 means you are repeating the word at the end of each of those lines. In line 3, you end your line with a new word, which should not rhyme with your *a* word. Notice that line 4 ends with the same word that ended lines 1 and 2. In Watson's ghazal, she uses the word *core* and also *corps*, which is an interesting and creative way of "breaking the rules." Feel free to do the same, choosing words like *son* and *sun* or *be* and *bee*, words that sound alike but have different meanings.

As always with form poems, you read the recipe, study a few examples, and feel daunted. It's in writing the poem that it all comes together, so be patient. Give yourself time to work through the instructions. The pattern is shown below; each new letter of the alphabet shows you where your line ends with a new word:

STANZA 1	STANZA 2	STANZA 3	STANZA 4	STANZA 5
a	b	c	d	e
a	a	a	a	a

This recipe shows how to construct the first five couplets—a ghazal must have five couplets but you can continue on up to twelve couplets. There is no need to link the couplets together. Each couplet is a separate poem. Each couplet line in the poem is the same length.

Historically, the last couplet is supposed to be the "signature" couplet, where the poet includes his or her own name. Feel free to include this aspect of the ghazal in your drafts, but you can ignore this rule; both ghazals in this chapter do.

| PRACTICE |

Continue to label the lines of the Ellen Doré Watson ghazal, above, using the recipe as your guide. Discuss what you notice about the structure of the poem.

| PRACTICE |

Write a five-to-twelve stanza ghazal about love or obsession. Include your first name in the final line if you like. Use the recipe, and make your lines roughly the same length.

Sestina

With a sestina, you have six stanzas, each with six lines, plus a little ending stanza of one to three lines, like a P.S. on a letter.

Invented in France in probably the twelfth century, the sestina repeats lines instead of repeating words. The Italian poets Petrarch and Dante made the form famous (and Dante gave it its name). As with the pantoum, poets often write sestinas when they want to tackle topics involving obsession. When you land on the right topic, you render a haunting experience, the kind of feeling and worry that's very hard to talk about in regular conversation.

The sestina adds a slightly more intricate pattern of words to the brooding, worrying, obsessive feeling that you get from a pantoum and a ghazal. The sestina, as you may have already guessed from the name, is made up of a pattern based on the number six. Safe to say, if you like sudoku, you are going to love the sestina! In order to create a sestina, choose six words for your end words. You write six stanzas, recycling these words that end your lines in a different order each time. On page 341, Wesli Court uses the words *last, again, father, dreamed, died,* and *night.* All the lines in the poem end with one of those words. The order is dictated by the recipe on page 338. A final stanza uses all six words in a much smaller amount of space. You will be surprised at the things you are able to say; limiting your word choices really increases your creativity.

You will probably want to choose your end words first, to build a frame you then fill in. It can be maddening, but also fun. John Ashbery, the famous poet, once said that writing a sestina is like riding downhill on a bicycle and having the pedals push your feet. Keep your sense of play and your sense of humor as you explore this form.

Reading Sestinas. As with all poems, you must read a sestina more than one time, and you must hear it aloud as well as read it aloud. The first time you read this poem, just listen to it as you would any other poem. Then go back and notice the way the words are repeated, the pattern.

Wesli Court
The Obsession

Last night I dreamed my father died again,
a decade and a year after he dreamed
of death himself, pitched forward into night.
His world of waking flickered out and died —
an image on a screen. He is the father
now of fitful dreams that last and last.

I dreamed again my father died at last.
He stood before me in his flesh again.
I greeted him. I said, "How are you, father?"
But he looked frailer than last time I'd dreamed
we were together, older than when he'd died —
I saw upon his face the look of night.

I dreamed my father died again last night.
He stood before a mirror. He looked his last
into the glass and kissed it. He saw he'd died.
I put my arms about him once again
to help support him as he fell. I dreamed
I held the final heartburst of my father.

I died again last night: I dreamed my father
kissed himself in glass, kissed me goodnight
in doing so. But what was it I dreamed
in fact? An injury that seems to last
without abatement, opening again
and yet again in dream? Who was it died

again last night? I dreamed my father died,
but it was not he — it was not my father,

only an image flickering again
upon the screen of dream out of the night.
How long can this cold image of him last?
Whose is it, his or mine? Who dreams he dreamed?

My father died. Again last night I dreamed
I felt his struggling heart still as he died
beneath my failing hands. And when at last
he weighed me down, then I laid down my father,
covered him with silence and with night.
I could not bear it should he come again —

I died again last night, my father dreamed.

When you read the sestina by Court, what do you notice about the pattern? Can you figure it out just by listening? By looking? In a good sestina, the pattern isn't completely obvious; it's supposed to be subtle, a little hidden. If the poet is doing his or her job, you notice the images, and the feelings the poem creates in you.

Writing Sestinas. The recipe for a sestina follows. Here, the capital letters stand for the word at the end of each line. Can you see the logic in the pattern? Here's a hint for unlocking the logic of the pattern: Stanza 2 takes the ABC and inter-splices DEF, backwards. If all this patterning gives you a headache, don't worry about it. Just follow the guide.

STANZA 1	STANZA 2	STANZA 3	STANZA 4
A	F	C	E
B	A	F	C
C	E	D	B
D	B	A	F
E	D	B	A
F	C	E	D

STANZA 5	STANZA 6	FINAL STANZA
D	B	AB
E	D	CD
A	F	EF
C	E	
F	C	
B	A	

For the final stanza, you can follow the recipe above and write three lines. When there are two letters shown in a poem recipe, as above, it means that you put the A word (the word that ended your first line in stanza 1, your second line in stanza 2, etc.) in the middle of the line, and your B word (same word you used in B, above) at the end of line 1 of this final stanza. Line 2 of the final stanza, CD, puts the C word in the middle of the line, and the D word at the end; line 3, the last line of the whole poem, places the E word in the middle of the line, and your poem ends with whatever word you have been using in the F slot.

Or, you can make your final stanza just one line long, as Wesli Court does in "The Obsession." Notice how all six words are packed into that last, final sentence.

The challenge of the sestina is to draw attention *away from* (not toward) the end words (the repeating words). So, poets often break their lines so that the phrases with the repeating word flow down into the next line. Also part of the fun of a sestina is finding phrases like *blowing wind* and *wind the clock* in order to achieve visual, but not aural, repetition.

PRACTICE

Label the lines in Wesli Court's sestina with the corresponding letters from the recipe, page 337, and discuss what you notice about the pattern.

PRACTICE

Read the sestina by Diane Wakoski on page 361 and label the lines with the corresponding letters from the recipe above. Do you notice any variations? Do they add anything to the meaning of the poem?

Poems such as Wakoski's "Sestina to the Common Glass of Beer: I Do Not Drink Beer" and Wesli Court's "The Obsession" give voice to the creepier, more puzzling aspects of life: What it is to go over and over something painful and terrible. Poets hope that by writing these darker, more difficult poems, they'll help readers feel less alone in their own obsessions. The sestina can function as a song does. Singing someone else's lyrics can soothe, heal, uplift. Reading someone else's sestina can get us unstuck, and resolve, perhaps, a piece of one of our personal obsessions.

The author of "The Obsession" uses the words from the repetition for his final stanza, the short one, and that might be a good way to start your own sestina—write a sentence, let it be compressed, mysterious, surprising, or unusual, and draw your sestina's key words from that sentence. See if the triggering sentence can serve as the inspiration for your final stanza, the three compressed lines that end the poem.

Another way to begin the sestina is to come up with a "grab bag" of good, usable, end words that can work in many different situations. Here's a list to choose from, or to prompt you to find words from your own poem drafts that might be worthy of using again:

red	house	child
book	love	Spanish
six	black	letters
wind	clock	purple
green	love	uncle
kitchen	dog	mystery
cheeks	car	paper

Plain words are easier to work with as you knit your stanzas together. The sestina project is more like sewing, more like carpentry, as you shuffle your choices, your words, and your lines.

Experiment with a few sestinas before you decide you loathe the form. After trying a classic, strict sestina, play a little and fudge the rules. Sometimes, for example, poets drop the final stanza (the three-line one) completely. That is perfectly legal. Other poets use closely related words to make patterns—*light, night, enlightened.* Or, *sun, son, sunned.* Breaking the rules for pattern, you create a new pattern. Adjusting the rules for a form, you invent new ones.

PRACTICE

Make a list of six solid end words, words that leave you some flexibility, that aren't too specific, like *hasenpfeffer*. Words you won't mind hearing over and over. Choose for your topic something that weighs on your mind, something that you go over and over: failed love, running track, worry about the future. Try a sestina.

Villanelle

Developed in Italy, where it was the basic pattern for folksongs, the villanelle became very popular in France in the seventeenth century; today, however, it's seen as a kind of poet's Mount Everest: You attempt it because it's there.

Reading Villanelles. The villanelle is a nineteen-line poem of five tercets (three-line stanzas) completed by a quatrain (a four-line stanza). Two lines in the poem repeat throughout the entire poem, in a specific order (just like in the sestina). Here, a capital letter means the whole line is repeated, and a lowercase letter means a word is rhymed or repeated. In the villanelle recipe you will see the symbols A¹ and A². The first A is the first line of your poem, and each time it's repeated, you use the exact same line again—the poem truly writes itself. When you see A² in the recipe, you are writing a new line, but the end word *rhymes* with A¹.

There's also a rhyme scheme sandwiched in between those repeating lines. It goes *aba* for the tercets, and ends *abaa* for the quatrain. Again, as you read, you probably don't overtly notice the structure, if the villanelle is doing its job. As always, it's easiest to begin a form poem by reading an example, and then labeling the lines so you can see the form. The notation is confusing and frustrating until you practice writing a few. Be patient.

A very famous poem, one you may have read or heard before, is actually a villanelle. Watch for the repeated lines, and the rhyme scheme, as you read and listen.

Dylan Thomas
Do Not Go Gentle into That Good Night

Do not go gentle into that good night,
Old age should burn and rave at close of day;
Rage, rage against the dying of the light.

Though wise men at their end know dark is right,
Because their words had forked no lightning they
Do not go gentle into that good night.

Good men, the last wave by, crying how bright
Their frail deeds might have danced in a green bay,
Rage, rage against the dying of the light.

Wild men who caught and sang the sun in flight,
And learn, too late, they grieved it on its way,
Do not go gentle into that good night.

Grave men, near death, who see with blinding sight
Blind eyes could blaze like meteors and be gay,
Rage, rage against the dying of the light.

And you, my father, there on the sad height,
Curse, bless me now with your fierce tears, I pray.
Do not go gentle into that good night.
Rage, rage against the dying of the light.

What do you hear, when you read the poem aloud? Have someone read it aloud to you, or read aloud it as a group. There is much power in the repetitions. The cycle of refrains underscores much of the meaning in the poem — can you comment on that meaning? What does the reader come away with after reading this poem? If it wasn't written in the form of a villanelle, what important parts or emphases might be lost?

Here is the recipe for the villanelle. The nineteen lines can be of any length. There have to be five tercets, one quatrain, and two rhymes, plus two refrains.

STANZA 1	STANZA 2	STANZA 3
A^1 — refrain	a	a
b	b	b
A^2 — refrain	A^1 — refrain	A^2 — refrain

STANZA 4	STANZA 5	STANZA 6
a	a	a
b	b	b
A^1 — refrain	A^2 — refrain	A^1
		A^2

PRACTICE

Read the villanelle by John Yau on page 362: "Chinese Villanelle." Read it aloud, and to yourself, looking closely for patterns you notice with your ear, and then again with your eyes. Which villanelle do you prefer, Yau's or Thomas's? Go ahead and use the recipe to label the lines of Yau's villanelle, to help you get used to the structure.

Writing Villanelles. The successful villanelle has refrain (repeated) lines that blend and flow into the poem. You want the lines to change meaning in their varied contexts. By paying attention to the pattern you create both with rhyme and with repetition, you return to your writing, whether prose, free verse, or some combination, with a better ear for the way repetition can underline, emphasize, and shift meaning. The villanelle is one of those poems that will, like a pantoum, almost write itself, once you have settled on two lines that you think are interesting enough to repeat (that also rhyme). Be patient with yourself as you write your villanelle — you are building new writing muscles as you work in this form, and you will surely feel some resistance, annoyance, frustration. Let that be part of your writing and learning process. Most students find that in each case — pantoum, ghazal, sestina, villanelle — learning *about* the poem is difficult, much more difficult than

> *Pay attention only to the form; emotion will come spontaneously to inhabit it. A perfect dwelling always finds an inhabitant.*
> — ANDRÉ GIDE

actually doing it. Try taking older, failed poems and reworking them into one or more of these forms. And, again, allow yourself to break the rules and reinvent the forms — to claim these techniques for yourself.

| PRACTICE |

Write two villanelles about love, death, or family. For your first attempt, stick absolutely to the pattern. In your second attempt, bend the rules to suit yourself and your poem.

WRITING PROJECTS

1. Write a piece that carefully follows the principles of classic narrative structure. Keep the piece — whatever genre — to one page. Can your audience find the conflict, the crisis, and the resolution?

2. Draw a six-panel comic (this is not art class, so feel free to use rudimentary stick figures; you are practicing the journey elements here, not your drawing skill). Outline the basic moves of a journey story. Write the story (a poem, an essay, a memoir, a short story, or a novel chapter). Let the cartooning process help you save time by focusing your attention on the *key scenes you need to tell the story.*

3. Write a journey poem in six lines. Make sure one line (a beat) encompasses each of the six stages of the journey.

4. Construct a journey story — as a poem, story, or memoir. Begin by writing images that connect to the six steps. Don't feel you have to compose your images in order, and draw from material you have already written, if you like.

5. Write a visitation. Make sure to include an external and internal story line.

6. Write a list poem, using six to ten images of a place you know well, viewed at various times of the day or year. Come at the place from different angles, moods, points of view. Make each image transporting.

7. Try a story, poem, or creative nonfiction essay, like Dinty W. Moore's on page 355, using the alphabet as your structural map. Don't feel you have to start with *A* as you begin composing — you can put the sections of lines in alphabetical order later. Let your sections be brief, specific, and stand-alone. It may be easiest to start with a topic (fighting with my mother, dog-love) or to go back through your work from the class, and find a few images you'd like to plug in, and then go from there.

8. Write a braided poem, story, play, or essay. Select three story lines that don't go together; one can be "found": diaries, blogs, letters, etc. Consider using, for one of your strands, a visual story, photographs, or cartooning, either your own or from another source.

9. Write a new pantoum. Choose a subject that has an inherent back-and-forth energy. Don't try to get anywhere.

10. Write a purposely Not-Perfect Pantoum. Borrow two lines from any piece—prose or poetry—in this textbook, or as directed by your teacher. Use those lines to launch your pantoum, laying them out as your A line and B line. Complete your pantoum, cheating wherever you need to in order to keep the images, the energy, and the tension alive.

11. Write two ghazals. Do one "loose" ghazal, following most, but not all of the rules. In your second attempt, follow the rules exactly. Choose two very different topics, befitting the "looseness" and "structure" of your assignment.

12. Create two different sestinas on two different topics. Let your first deviate from the rules. Let your second attempt follow the recipe (which is on page 338) very carefully. When you read them to your audience, let them choose the one they like the best.

13. Write a villanelle on the topic of your choice. Consider using Yau's example on page 362 for inspiration when choosing your topic.

14. Invent a new form for poetry: Write out the rules, write a sample poem that fits the form, and name it. You may even wish to compose a bogus history, or loftily explain the way the form came about. Ask the class or your writing group to write in the new form. Does your new form lend itself to a particular *type* of topic, as the pantoum lends itself to obsession?

15. Use what you know about form to revise a weak piece of your own writing from earlier in this course. Redo your work (it might change a lot or a little) using any one of the forms in this chapter. The piece you choose to rework in a form could be a poem, but also consider your prose pieces, too.

FORMS WORKSHOP

When addressing a piece written in a form, first consider how the piece follows the conventions, or rules, of the form. Second, see where the piece deviates. Then examine how the deviations add to or detract from the reading experience. Finally, give the writer feedback on her or his use of the tools writers use—images, tension, structure, pattern, insight. The prompts below will help you constructively discuss your classmates' work.

1. What structural devices is the writer using? Briefly describe all the elements of structure you find. Is the piece a specific form with rules, or based on a form with rules? Does it have a crisis and resolution? Is it braided in construction? Is there a journey or a visitation in this piece? Describe how the parts are arranged.

2. Are there places where the structure is weak? Soft or vague spots? Places you as reader are expecting something to happen, and then it doesn't? Are there extra parts, more than necessary?

3. Revisit the instruction in this chapter that seems to most accurately apply to this piece. What can the writer do a better job of?

4. Are there other structures this material might be well suited for?

5. Is the beginning of the piece interesting, fresh, and arresting? Or does it feel like a preface, a warm-up? Is there a better place to begin? Often the first few lines or paragraphs can be cut. Do you see a natural opening line buried in the beginning section of this piece?

6. Do the same as in question 5 for the ending: Does the piece end at the right point? Is there a cool-down, a summing up, too much explanation?

7. What is the point of greatest tension in this piece? Does it come at the best possible time? Usually, the climax is "the beginning of the end."

8. List six places in this piece that contain a lot of energy. List three spots that lack energy.

9. Make a list of the most memorable visual images in this piece.

10. Name two insights that this piece offers, either directly or indirectly.

Naomi Shihab Nye
How to Get There

At 7 a.m. a driver from a car service comes to collect me on the drizzly upper east side of Manhattan, where I'm a houseguest. I need to go to Paterson, New Jersey, to stomp around with junior high school students for the day. *Paterson, New Jersey, please*, I say. And the driver with his beautiful accent says, *Tell me, how do you get to New Jersey?* Is he kidding? I live in Texas. I know how to get from San Antonio to San Angelo. Obviously we must cross a bridge or traverse a tunnel to go from Manhattan to Jersey, but which one? Beats me. *Call your office*, I say. He doesn't have a phone in the vehicle.

So I urge him, *Pull over* and find myself trumpeting out the window, *How do we get to New Jersey?* at every third corner. No one looks surprised. Lean Latino men step closer to help us. Sleepy grandmas point damp newspapers. And they know. They all know something. If we don't speak to strangers—what will we do in a moment like this? I translate everybody's fast English into slower English for my driver. He is careful with his pedals. He bobs his head in that graceful subcontinental way. As soon as we're safely tucked onto the George Washington Bridge, I ask where he's from. *Bangladesh*. I've been there. *Twice*, I tell him. He turns his whole head around to look at me. Smiles. Every driver I've had in this city is from Pakistan, Palestine, Trinidad. It's a federation of bravery—the city's wheels steered by the wide world. *You saw my country?* he says brightly. *I saw it. I didn't drive there though. I didn't either*, he says. *I just got my first driver's license. Three months ago when I arrived here.*

We miss an exit. Actually, we miss a whole level of road. He says cheerfully, *Oh my goodness! We wanted to be up, but we are down.* Then he says, *The first time I was driving, someone wants to go to Newark Airport. I don't know it. I say where is it and they get very angry. They are shouting, Drive! Drive! They are telling me where to go. Actually that is what my company says—you only learn by going. When I leave them, I try to come back to New York City, but two hours later it is dark and a policeman by the side of road tells me I am going to Florida. Florida! Did you ever go to Florida? Pull over*, I say.

We roar into a gas station where I ask a lavishly tattooed man about Paterson and he tells me. Luckily there is not much traffic in our direction this morning. We are able to ease in and out of the flow. Now I am growing worried about my driver getting back into Manhattan with the horrendous traffic moving the other way. We pass houses with their eyes still shut, worlds we know not of and worlds we know too well. Kids with book bags. A thousand little turn-offs. Graffiti and pink trees. *Is it nice in Texas?* he asks me. *Very nice,* I say. *You could drive there. A lot.* Finally we pull up in front of a brick building in Paterson where I think I am supposed to be. Fifteen minutes early. *We made it!* He turns around to shake my hand a long time. *My friend!* he says, *We made it, yes we did! And I don't even know how to ride a bicycle!*

Dana Levin
Techno

I was tracking the stars through the open truck window,
    my friend speeding the roads through the black country —
and I was thinking how the songs coming from the radio
    were like the speech of a single human American psyche —
the one voice of the one collective dream, industrial, amphetamine,
    and the stars unmoving —
the countryside black and silent, through which a song pumped serious killer
    over and over —
and I could feel the nation shaping, it was something about the collective dream
    of the rich land and the violent wanting —
the amphetamine drive and the cows sleeping, all along the sides
    of the dark road —
never slowing enough to see what we might have seen if the moon rose up
    its pharmaceutical light —
aspirin-blue over the pine-black hills what was rising up —
mullein or something else in the ditches their flameless tapers —
world without fire the song heralded a crystal methedrine light —
while the sky brought its black bone down around the hood of the truck
    the electronic migration —
    we were losing our bodies —
    digitized salt of bytes and speed we were becoming a powder —

light—
bicarbonate—
what we might have seen, if we had looked—

Michael Chabon
Along the Frontage Road

I don't remember where we used to go to get our pumpkins when I was a kid. I grew up in a Maryland suburb that, in those days, had just begun to lay siege to the surrounding Piedmont farmland, and I suppose we must have driven out to somebody's orchard or farm—one of the places we went to in the summer for corn and strawberries, and in the fall for apples and cider. I do remember the way that my father would go after our pumpkins, once we got them home, with the biggest knife from the kitchen drawer. He was a fastidious man who hated to dirty his hands, in particular with food, but he was also a doctor, and there was something grimly expert about the way he scalped the orange crania, excised the stringy pulp, and scraped clean the pale interior flesh with the edge of a big metal spoon. I remember his compressed lips, the distasteful huffing of his breath through his nostrils as he worked.

Last month I took my own son down to a vacant lot between the interstate and the Berkeley mudflats. Ordinarily no one would ever go to such a place. There is nothing but gravel, weeds, and the kind of small, insidious garbage that presents a choking hazard to waterfowl. It is a piece of land so devoid of life and interest that from January to October, I'm certain, no one sees it at all; it ceases to exist. Toward the end of the year, however, with a regularity that approximates, in its way, the eternal rolling wheel of the seasons, men appear with trailers, straw bales, fence wire, and a desultory assortment of orange-and-black or red-and-green bunting. First they put up polystyrene human skeletons and battery-operated witches, and then, a few weeks later, string colored lights and evergreen swags. Or so I assume. I have no idea, actually, how this kind of business operates. There may be a crew of Halloween men, who specialize in pumpkins, and then one of Christmas men, who bring in the truckloads of spruce and fir. The Halloween men may be largely Iranian and the Christmas men Taiwanese. And I don't know if someone actually owns this stretch of frontage, or if it lies, despised and all but invisible, open to all comers, a freehold for the predations of enterprising men. But I don't want to talk about the contrast between the idyllic golden falls of my Maryland youth and the freeway hum, plastic skeletons, and Persian music that spell autumn in the disjointed urban almanac of my four-year-old son. I don't want to talk about pumpkins at all, really, or about Halloween, or, God knows, about the ache that I get every time I imagine my little son wandering in my stead through the deepening shadows of a genuine pumpkin patch, in a corduroy coat, on a chilly October afternoon back in, say, 1973. I don't mean to imply that we have somehow rendered the world unworthy of our children's trust and attention. I don't believe that, though sometimes I do feel that very implication lodged like a chip of black ice in my heart.

Anyway, Nicky loves the place. Maybe there is something magical to him in the sight of the windswept gray waste transfigured by an anomalous outburst of orange. In past years, the rubber witch hands and grinning skulls had intimidated him, but not enough to prevent him from trying to prolong our visits past the limits of my patience and of my tolerance for the aforementioned ache in my chest. This year, however, was different, in a number of ways. This year he took the spooky decorations in stride, for one thing.

"Dad. Look. Look, Dad. There's a snake in that skull's eyehole," he said.

We were just getting out of the car. The gravel parking strip was nearly empty; it was four o'clock on a Monday afternoon, with three weeks still to go until Halloween. So I guess we were a little early. But we had both wanted to get out of the house, where ordinary sounds—a fork against a plate, the creak of a stair tread—felt like portents, and you could not escape the smell of the flowers, heaped everywhere, as if some venerable mobster had died. In fact the deceased was a girl of seventeen weeks, a theoretical daughter startled in the darkness and warmth of her mother's body, or so I imagine it, by a jet of cool air and a fatal glint of light. It was my wife who had suggested that Nicky and I might as well go and pick out the pumpkin for that year.

There was only one other car in the lot, a late-model Firebird, beer-cooler red. Its driver's-side door stood open. In the front passenger seat I saw a little boy, black, not much older than my Nicky. The Firebird's radio was on, and the keys were in the ignition: a sampled Clyde Stubblefield beat vied with the insistent pinging of the alarm that warned of the open car door. The little boy was looking out, toward a small brown structure beyond the wire fence that in my three years of visiting this forlorn place had escaped my attention completely. It was hardly bigger than a drive-in photomat. On its sign there was a picture of a fish struggling with a bobber and a hook and the single word *Bait*. From the muscle car, the bait shop, and a deadened air of resentment exuded by the kicking, kicking foot of the little boy left alone, I inferred that he was waiting for his father.

"What if that snake was for real?" Nicky said, pointing to the skull that sat atop a bale of straw. It was hollow, like the genuine article, and some clever person had arranged a rubber snake so that it coiled in and out of the eye sockets and jaws. Nicky approached it now, boldly, one hand plunged into the rear of his polar-fleece trousers to scratch at his behind.

"That would be very cool," I said.

"But it's only rubber."

"Thank goodness."

"Can we get a skull, too, and put a snake inside it?"

"We only do pumpkins in our family."

"Is that because we're Jewish?"

"Why, yes, it is," I said. "Come on, Nick." I tugged his hand out of his pants and gave him a helpful nudge in the direction of the pumpkins. "Start shopping."

The pumpkins lay spilled like marbles in scattered bunches around the cashier's stand, which was tiny, a rudimentary wooden booth painted red and white to remind somebody—myself alone, perhaps—of a barn. Straw bales stood posed awkwardly here and there, exuding a smell of cut grass, which only intensified my sense of having borne my son into a base and diminished world. There was also straw strewn on the ground, I suppose to provide a rural veneer for the demolition-rubble paving material of the vacant lot. And there was a scarecrow, a flannel shirt and blue jeans hastily stuffed with crumpled newspaper, and token shocks of straw protruding from the cuffs and throat of the shirt. The legs of the blue jeans hung empty from the knee, like the trousers of a double amputee. The head was a pumpkin fitted out with a *Friday the 13th*–style goalie's mask. I forbid myself, absolutely, to consider the proposition that in the orchards of my youth it would never have occurred to anyone to employ a serial-killer motif as a means of selling Halloween pumpkins to children.

Nicky walked slowly among the pumpkins, pondering them with the toe of his sneaker. If the past two years were any guide, he was not necessarily looking for the largest, the roundest, or the most orange. The previous lucky victims had both been rather oblong and irregular, dented and warty specimens that betrayed their kinship to gourds, and scarred with that gritty cement that sometimes streaks the skin of pumpkins. Last year's had not even been orange at all but the ivory that lately seemed, at least in our recherché corner of California, to have become popular. I had no idea what Nicky's criteria for selecting a pumpkin might be. But I had remarked certain affinities between my son and the character of Linus in *Peanuts*, and liked to imagine that he might be looking for the most sincere.

"Cute," said the man in the cashier's stand. He was of indeterminate ethnicity—Arab, Mexican, Israeli, Armenian, Uzbek—middle-aged, with a grizzled mustache and thick aviator-style glasses. He sat behind a table laid out with a steel cash box, a credit-card press, a cellular telephone, and five demonstration models, XS, S, M, L, and XL, priced according to size from ten to twenty-two dollars. "How old is he?"

"Four," I said.

"Cute," the pumpkin man said again. I agreed with him, of course, but the adjective was offered without much enthusiasm, and after that we let the subject drop. A door banged, and I looked across the lot. A man was walking from the bait shack out to the frontage road. He was tall and light-skinned, with a kettle-drum chest and the kind of fat stomach that somehow manages to look hard: the body of a tight end. He wore white high-tops, big as buckets, barely recognizable as shoes. On his head was a Raiders cap, bill to the back, on his chin the quick sketch of a goatee. He nipped around the fence where it met the frontage road, approached the car from the driver's side, and dropped into the bucket seat, with his back to the boy. The boy said something, his voice rising at the end in a question. The man offered only a low monosyllable in reply. He reached one hand under his seat and felt around. A moment later his hand emerged, holding what looked to my not entirely innocent eye like a rolled zip-lock baggie. Then the man stood, and I heard the boy ask him another question that I couldn't make out.

"When I say so," the man replied. He walked back around the fence and disappeared into the bait shack. The boy in the Firebird turned and, as if he had felt me watching, looked over at me. We were perhaps twenty feet apart. There was no expression on his face at all. I suppressed an impulse to avert my gaze from his, though his blank stare unnerved me. Instead I nodded and smiled. He smiled back, instantly, a great big winning smile that involved every feature of his face.

"That your kid?" he said.

I nodded.

"He getting a pumpkin."

"Yep."

The boy glanced over at the bait shack. Then he threw his legs across the driver's seat and slid himself out of the car. He was a handsome kid, dark and slender, with a stubbly head and big, sleepy eyes. His clothes were neat and a little old-fashioned, stiff blue jeans rolled at the ankle, a sweater vest over a white-collared shirt, as if he had been dressed by an aunt. But he had the same non-Euclidean shoes as his father, or as the man I assumed was his father. He took another look toward the bait shack and then walked over to where I was standing.

"What he going to be for Halloween?"

"He's still trying to make up his mind," I said. "Maybe a cowboy."

"A cowboy?" He looked appalled. It was a hopelessly lame, outmoded, inexplicable thing for a little boy to want to be. I might as well have said that Nicky was planning to go trick-or-treating as a Scotsman, or as Johnny Appleseed.

"Or he was thinking maybe a cat," I said.

I felt something bump against my leg: it was Nicky, pressing his face to my thigh. I looked down and saw that he was carrying a remarkably tiny, rusty-red pumpkin, no bigger than a grapefruit. "Hey, Nick. What's up?"

There was, heavily, profoundly, no reply.

"What's the matter?"

The voice emerged from the fabric of my pant leg.

"Who is that guy you're talking to?"

"I don't know," I said. I smiled again at the kid from the Firebird. For some reason, I never feel whiter than when I am smiling at a black person. "What's your name?"

"Andre," he said. "Why he got such a little one?"

"I don't know."

"How he going to fit a candle in that midget?"

"That's a very good question," I said. "Nicky, why did you choose such a small one?"

Nicky shrugged.

"Did you already get yours?" I said to Andre.

He nodded. "Got me a big pumpkin."

"Go on, Nick," I said. "Go find yourself a nice big pumpkin. Andre's right—you won't be able to put a candle in this one."

"I don't want a big pumpkin. I don't want to put a candle in it. I don't want you to cut it open with a knife."

He looked up at me, his eyes shining. A tear sprang loose and arced like a diver down his cheek. You would have thought I was asking him to go into the henhouse and bring me a neck to wring for supper. He had never before shown such solicitude for the annual sacrificial squash. But lately you never knew what would make Nicky cry.

"I want to call Mommy," he said. "On the cell phone. She will tell you not to cut up my pumpkin."

"We can't bother Mommy," I said. "She's resting right now."

"Why is she resting?"

"You know why."

"I don't want her to rest anymore. I want to call her. Call her, Dad. She'll tell you not to cut it up."

"It ain't alive," Andre argued. He was taking such an interest in our family's pumpkin choice that I was certain his earlier boast had been a lie. Andre had no big pumpkin waiting for him at home. His father was a drug dealer who would not bother to take his son shopping for a pumpkin. This conversation was as close to the purchase of an actual pumpkin as Andre had any reason to expect. These may not in fact have been certainties so much as assumptions, and racist ones at that. I will grant you this. But what kind of father would leave his kid alone in a car, with the door open, at the side of a road that skirted the edge of a luckless and desolate place? What kind of man would do that? "It don't hurt them to be cut."

"I want this one," said Nicky. "And I'm going to name it Kate."

I shook my head.

"You can't do that," I said.

"Please?"

"No, honey," I said. "We don't name our pumpkins."

"We don't believe in it?"

"That's right." I did not want him telling all the people who set foot on our front porch the name that we had been tossing around the house over the past month or so, with an innocence that struck me now as wanton and foolish. My wife and I were given no real choice in the matter, and yet every time I look at Nicky's fuzzy knees poking out of his short pants, or smell peanut butter on his breath, or attend to his muttered nocturnal lectures through the monitor that we have never bothered to remove from his bedroom, I cannot shake the feeling that in letting ourselves be persuaded by mere facts and statistics, however damning, we made an unforgivable mistake. I had stood by once in an emergency room as doctors and nurses strapped my son, flailing, to a table to stitch up a gash in his forehead. I could picture, all too clearly, how your child looked at you as you betrayed him into the hands of strangers.

"Andre!"

The father was coming toward us, his gait at once lumbering and methodical. When I looked at him, I saw where Andre had learned to drain the expression from his face.

"What I tell you to do?" he said, softly but without gentleness. He did not acknowledge me, Nicky, the ten thousand pumpkins that lay all around us. "Boy, get back in that car."

Andre said something in a voice too low for me to hear.

"What?"

"Can I get a pumpkin?" he repeated.

The question was apparently so immoderate that it could not be answered. Andre's father pulled his cap down more firmly on his head, hitched up his pants, and spat into the straw at his feet. These appeared to be a suite of gestures intended to communicate the inevitable outcome if Andre did not return immediately to the car. Andre had reset his own face to zero. He turned, walked back to the Firebird, and got in. This time he went around to the big red door on his side of the car and heaved it open.

"Your son is a nice boy," I said.

The man looked at me, for the first and last time.

"Uh-huh," he said. "All right."

I was just another pumpkin to him—dumb and lolling amid the straw bales, in the middle of a place that was no place at all. He went to the car, got in, and slammed the door. The pinging of the alarm ceased. The engine came awake with a rumble, and the Firebird went scrabbling out of the lot and back onto the frontage road. Nicky and I watched them drive off. I saw Andre turn back, his eyes wide, his face alight and hollowed with an emotion that I could not help but interpret as reproach. I had abandoned him to a hard fate, one that I might at least have tried, somehow, to prevent. But there was nothing that I could have done. I didn't have any illusions about that. I dressed and fed my child, I washed his body, I saw that he got enough sleep. I had him inoculated, padded his knees and encased the twenty-eight bones of his skull in high-impact plastic when he got on his bicycle and pedaled down our street. But in the end, when the world we have created came to strap him to a table, I could only stand behind the doctors and watch.

I took Nicky's half-grown red runt and balanced it on my palm.

"Hey, Nick," I said. "Listen. You can name it Kate if you want to."

"I don't want it," Nicky said. "I want to get a bigger one."

"All right."

"Kate can have that one."

"All right."

"Because she didn't get to have a pumpkin, since she didn't get to ever be alive."

"Good thinking," I said.

"But I still don't want to cut it up," he said. Then he went back again into the world of pumpkins, looking for the one that would best suit his unknown purposes.

Sharon Olds
Visiting My Mother's College

This is where her body was
when it was sealed, her torso clear and whole,
she walked on these lawns. Curled as the Aesop
fox she sat in a window-seat, it
makes me sick with something like desire to think of her,
my first love—when I lay stunned
in her arms, I thought she was the whole world,
heat, smooth flesh, colostrum,
and that huge heartbeat. But here she had
no children, no husband, and her mother was dead,
no one was far weaker or far
stronger than she, she carried her rage
unknown, hidden, unknowable yet,
she moved, slowly, under the arches,
literally singing. Half of me

was deep in her body, dyed egg
with my name on it, in cursive script —
the most serene time of my life, as I
glided above the gravel paths
there near the center of her universe.
I have come here to walk on the stones she walked on,
to sit in the fragrant chapel with its pews
rubbed with the taken combs of bees, its
stained, glassy God, I want to
love her when she has not hurt anyone yet,
when all that had been done to her
she held, still, in her fresh body, as she
lay on her stomach, still a child, studying
diligently for finals, and before the dance
she washed her hair and rinsed it with lemon and
shook and shook her head so the interior of her
tiny room was flecked with sour bright citrus.

Dinty W. Moore

Son of Mr. Green Jeans:
An Essay on Fatherhood, Alphabetically Arranged

ALLEN, TIM

Best known as the father on ABC's *Home Improvement* (1991–99), the popular comedian was born Timothy Allen Dick on June 13, 1953. When Allen was eleven years old, his father, Gerald Dick, was killed by a drunk driver while driving home from a University of Colorado football game.

BEES

"A man, after impregnating the woman, could drop dead," critic Camille Paglia suggested to Tim Allen in a 1995 *Esquire* interview. "That is how peripheral he is to the whole thing."

"I'm a drone," Allen responded. "Like those bees."

"You are a drone," Paglia agreed. "That's exactly right."

CARP

After the female Japanese carp gives birth to hundreds of tiny babies, the father carp remains nearby. When he senses approaching danger, he sucks the helpless babies into his mouth, and holds them there until the coast is clear.

DIVORCE

University of Arizona psychologist Sanford Braver tells the story of a woman who felt threatened by her husband's close bond with their young son. The husband had a flexible work schedule but the wife did not, so the boy spent the bulk of his time with the father. The mother became so jealous of the tight father-son relationship that she filed for divorce, and successfully fought for sole custody. The result was that instead of being in the care of his father while the mother worked, the boy was now left in daycare.

EMPEROR PENGUINS

Once a male emperor penguin has completed mating, he remains by the female's side for the next month to determine if the act has been successful. When he sees a single greenish-white egg emerge from his mate's egg pouch, he begins to sing. Scientists have characterized his song as "ecstatic."

FATHER KNOWS BEST

In 1949, Robert Young began *Father Knows Best* as a radio show. Young played Jim Anderson, an average father in an average family. The show later moved to television, where it was a major hit, but Young's successful life was troubled by alcohol and depression.

In January 1991, at age 83, Young attempted suicide by running a hose from his car's exhaust pipe to the interior of the vehicle. The attempt failed because the battery was dead and the car wouldn't start.

GREEN GENES

In Dublin, Ireland, a team of geneticists is conducting a study to determine the origins of the Irish people. By analyzing segments of DNA from residents across different parts of the Irish countryside, then comparing this DNA with corresponding DNA segments from people elsewhere in Europe, the investigators hope to determine the derivation of Ireland's true forefathers.

HUGH BEAUMONT

The actor who portrayed the benevolent father on the popular TV show *Leave It to Beaver* was a Methodist minister. Tony Dow, who played older brother Wally, reports that Beaumont actually hated kids. "Hugh wanted out of the show after the second season," Dow told the *Toronto Sun*. "He thought he should be doing films and things."

INHERITANCE

My own Irish forefather was a newspaperman, owned a nightclub, ran for mayor, and smuggled rum in a speedboat during Prohibition. He smoked, drank, ate nothing but red meat, and died of a heart attack in 1938.

His one son, my father, was a teenager when my grandfather died. I never learned more than the barest details about my grandfather from my father, despite my persistent questions. Other relatives tell me that the relationship had been strained.

My father was a skinny, asthmatic, and eager-to-please little boy, not the tough guy his father had wanted. My dad lost his mother at age three, and later developed a severe stuttering problem, perhaps as a result of his father's disapproval. My father's adult vocabulary was outstanding, due to his need for alternate words when faltering over hard consonants like B or D.

The stuttering grew worse over the years, with one exception: after downing a few whiskeys, my father could sing like an angel. His Irish tenor became legend in local taverns, and by the time I entered the scene my father was spending every evening visiting the bars. Most nights he would stumble back drunk around midnight; some nights he was so drunk he would stumble through a neighbor's back door, thinking he was home.

As a boy, I coped with the family's embarrassment by staying glued to the television—shows like *Father Knows Best* and *Leave It to Beaver* were my favorites. I desperately wanted someone like Hugh Beaumont to be my father, or maybe Robert Young.

Hugh Brannum, though, would have been my first choice. Brannum played Mr. Green Jeans on *Captain Kangaroo*, and I remember him as being kind, funny, and extremely reliable.

JAWS

My other hobby, besides television, was an aquarium. I loved watching the tropical fish give birth. Unfortunately, guppy fathers, if not moved to a separate tank, will sometimes come along and eat their young.

KITTEN

Kitten, the youngest daughter on *Father Knows Best*, was played by Lauren Chapin.

LAUREN CHAPIN

Chapin's father molested her and her mother was a severe alcoholic. After *Father Knows Best* ended in 1960, Chapin's life came apart. At age sixteen, she married an auto mechanic. At age eighteen, she became addicted to heroin and began working as a prostitute.

MALE BREADWINNERS

Wolf fathers spend the daylight hours away from the home—hunting—but return every evening. The wolf cubs, five or six to a litter, rush out of the den when they hear their father approaching and fling themselves at their dad, leaping up to his face. The father backs up a few feet and disgorges food for them, in small, separate piles.

NATURAL SELECTION

When my wife Renita confessed to me her ambition to have children, the very first words out of my mouth were, "You must be crazy." Convinced that she had just proposed the worst imaginable idea, I stood from my chair, looked straight ahead, then marched out of the room.

OZZIE

Oswald Nelson, at thirteen, was the youngest person ever to become an Eagle Scout. Oswald went on to become Ozzie Nelson, the father in *Ozzie and Harriet*. Though the show aired years before the advent of reality television, Harriet was Ozzie's real wife, Ricky and David were his real sons, and eventually Ricky and David's wives were played by their actual spouses. The current requirements for Eagle Scout make it impossible for anyone to ever beat Ozzie's record.

PENGUINS, AGAIN

The female emperor penguin "catches the egg with her wings before it touches the ice," Jeffrey Moussaieff Masson writes in his book *The Emperor's Embrace*. She then places it on her feet, to keep it from contact with the frozen ground.

At this point, both penguins will sing in unison, staring at the egg. Eventually, the male penguin will use his beak to lift the egg onto the surface of his own feet, where it remains until hatching.

Not only does the male penguin endure the inconvenience of walking around with an egg balanced on his feet for months, but he also will not eat for the duration.

QUIZ

1. What is Camille Paglia's view on the need for fathers?
2. Why did Hugh Beaumont hate kids?
3. Who played Mr. Green Jeans on *Captain Kangaroo*?
4. Who would you rather have as your father: Hugh Beaumont, Hugh Brannum, a wolf, or an emperor penguin?

RELIGION

In 1979, Lauren Chapin, the troubled actress who played Kitty, had a religious conversion. She credits her belief in Jesus with saving her life. After *his* television career ended, Methodist Minister Hugh Beaumont became a Christmas tree farmer.

SPUTNIK

On October 4, 1957, *Leave It to Beaver* first aired. On that same day, the Soviet Union launched Sputnik I, the world's first artificial satellite. Sputnik I was about the size of a basketball, took roughly 98 minutes to orbit the Earth, and is credited with starting the US-Soviet space race.

Later, long after *Leave It to Beaver* ended its network run, a rumor that Jerry Mathers, the actor who played Beaver, had died at the hands of the communists in Vietnam, persisted for years. The rumor was false.

TOILETS

Leave It to Beaver was the first television program to show a toilet.

USE OF DRUGS

The National Center on Addiction and Substance Abuse at Columbia University claims that the presence of a supportive father is irreplaceable in helping children stay drug-free.

Lauren Chapin may be a prime example here, as would Tim Allen, who was arrested for dealing drugs in 1978 and spent two years in prison.

The author of this essay, though he avoided his father's drinking problems, battled his own drug habit as a young man. Happily, he was never jailed.

VASECTOMIES

I had a vasectomy in 1994.

WARD'S FATHER

In an episode titled "Beaver's Freckles," the Beaver says that Ward had "a hittin' father," but little else is ever revealed about Ward's fictional family. Despite Wally's constant warning—"Boy, Beav, when Dad finds out, he's gonna clobber ya!"—Ward does not follow his own father's example, and never hits his sons on the show. This is an excellent example of xenogenesis.

XENOGENESIS

(zen'*u*-jen'*u*-sis), n. *Biol.* 1. heterogenesis 2. the supposed generation of offspring completely and permanently different from the parent.

Believing in xenogenesis—though at the time I couldn't define it, spell it, *or* pronounce it—I changed my mind about having children about four years after my wife's first suggestion of the idea. Luckily, this was five years before my vasectomy.

Y-CHROMOSOMES

The Y-chromosome of the father determines a child's gender, and is unique, because its genetic code remains relatively unchanged as it passes from father to son. The DNA in other chromosomes, however, is more likely to get mixed between generations, in a process called recombination. What this means, apparently, is that boys have a higher likelihood of inheriting their ancestral traits.

My Y-chromosomes were looking the other way, so my only child is a daughter. So far Maria has inherited many of what people say are the Moore family's better traits—humor, a facility with words, a stubborn determination. It is yet to be seen what she will do with the many negative ones.

ZAPPA

Similar to the "Beaver died in Vietnam" rumor of the 1960s and '70s, during the late 1990s, Internet chatrooms and discussion lists repeatedly recycled the news that the actor who played Mr. Green Jeans was the father of musician Frank Zappa. But in fact, Hugh Brannum had only one son, and he was neither Frank Zappa nor this author.

Sometimes, though, he still wonders what it might have been like.

David Lehman
Abecedarius

Articles about the dismal state of poetry
Bemoan the absence of form and meter or,
Conversely, the products of "forms workshop":
Dream sonnets, sestinas based on childhood photographs,
Eclogues set in Third Avenue bars,
Forms contrived to suit an emergent occasion.
God knows it's easy enough to mock our enterprise,
Hard, though, to succeed at it, since
It sometimes seems predicated on failure.
Just when the vision appears, an importunate
Knock on the door banishes it, and you
Lethe-wards have sunk, or when a sweet
Melancholic fit should transport you to a
North Pole of absolute concentration,
Obligations intrude, putting an end to the day's
Poem. Poetry like luck is the residue of

Quirky design, and it
Refreshes like a soft drink full of bubbles
Sipped in a stadium on a lazy August afternoon
That was supposed to be spent at a boring job.
Ultimately poetry is
Virtue if it is our lot to choose, err, regret and
Wonder why in speech that would melt the stars.
X marks the spot of
Your latest attempt. Point at a map, blindfolded:
Zanzibar. Shall we go there, you and I?

Diane Wakoski

Sestina to the Common Glass of Beer: I Do Not Drink Beer

What calendar do you consult for an explosion of the sun?
And how does it affect our poor histories?
The event might be no different to our distant perspective
than a whole hillside of daffodils,
flashing
their own trumpet faces; or a cup of coffee, a glass of beer.

A familiar thing to common people: a beer,
when it is hot, and the sun
flashing
into your eyes. Makes you forget history's
only meaningful in retrospect. While flowers, like daffodils,
only have their meaning in the fleshy present. Perspective

cannot explain sexual feelings, though. Perspective-
ly, viewing a glass of beer,
we compare the color to daffodils
and perhaps a simple morning view of the sun.
The appetite is history's
fact. Common. Dull. Repetitious. Not flashing.

Suddenly, without explanation. The routine of bowels and lips. Flashing
past like a train, they come. No previews or perspective.
Sexual feelings are unexplained, as unexpected beauty. History's
no good at telling us about love either. Over beer

in a cafe, you might stay up till sun-
rise, but even that's routine for some, as every spring the returning daffodils,

waxy, yellow as caged canaries, spring daffodils
make me want to touch them. Is this the flashing
disappearing feeling of love and sex the sun
also brings to my body? With no object, no other body's perspective,
only the satisfaction of self wanting completion? I wdn't order beer,
I'd order a cognac or wine, instead. History's

full of exceptions, and I think I'm one. Yet, what history's
really about is how common, recurring, we all are. The daffodils,
once planted, really do come back each spring. And drinking beer
is a habit most ordinary men have. The flashing
gold liquid recurs in war, in factories and farms. The sun
has explosions that we do not know, record, or ever keep in perspective.

Thus, the sun embodies more of the unknown than most human histories.
We get little perspective outside ourselves. Daffodils
lift me above (to the sun), the faces flashing
each springtime when my friends, not I,
sit in some bar or outdoor cafe,
drinking beer.

John Yau
Chinese Villanelle

I have been with you, and I have thought of you
Once the air was dry and drenched with light
I was like a lute filling the room with description

We watched glum clouds reject their shape
We dawdled near a fountain, and listened
I have been with you, and I have thought of you

Like a river worthy of its gown
And like a mountain worthy of its insolence . . .
Why am I like a lute left with only description

How does one cut an axe handle with an axe
What shall I do to tell you all my thoughts
When I have been with you, and thought of you

A pelican sits on a dam, while a duck
Folds its wings again; the song does not melt
I remember you looking at me without description

Perhaps a king's business is never finished,
Though "perhaps" implies a different beginning
I have been with you, and I have thought of you
Now I am a lute filled with this wandering description

WRITING IN THE WORLD

PART THREE

The best way out is always through.
ROBERT FROST

*Writing ideally is recognizing your bad writing. I mean, people
ask if I write bad lines, and I say, Man, I write bad scenes!*
AUGUST WILSON

If I ignore my work, I start having anxiety attacks.
ROSEANNE CASH

CHAPTER TEN

REVISION

Revision is not separate from writing; the revision process involves moving deep inside the piece, working with the writer's tools, and then pulling back, working with the listener's tools: visualizing, experiencing, appreciating. Editing, which occurs at the very end of the process (presented at the end of this chapter), involves another kind of thinking altogether.

As you create, you work with energy, tension, insight, images, pattern, structure, working on one of these strategies, and then another, around and around. As you revise, you *do the same thing*. You work with those same strategies.

Once a piece of writing is up and running, the writer goes through each part, looking for places to increase energy, adjust tension, hone images, play with pattern. New writing students are often surprised to discover it's often easier to revise work in progress than it is to get that first draft completed.

> *If you think too much, you can't concentrate.*
> — YOGI BERRA

In revision, you assess. You try out options. You play with possibilities.

You are like a painter walking to the far side of his loft. How does the piece look from twenty feet away? Fifty feet? One foot? Writers take their pieces to a small group or a workshop, and get feedback.

As you worked with each tool in this book, you probably shared your writing and found ways to use the tools more adroitly. Revision and creating aren't separate—revising *is* writing. You've been revising all along.

The goal of revision: Intensify the work so it makes a moving picture inside the reader's mind. Your trick, what you are trying to pull off: The reader forgets she is reading at all—she has an *experience*. Work from the middle, out to the edges. Work on the opening and closing *after* you have your middle down. Skip around, and work in short sessions. This is intense concentration, redreaming your piece and catching where it falls out of the moment. Just do a little at a time.

CONQUERING YOUR FEAR OF REVISION

Revision is terrifying for some writers. The writer has to go into the dark, into the unknown. There are books like this one and classes to prepare you, but you can't really take anything with you—when you are writing, you are completely and utterly alone, without your weapons. There is no map. There is no clear route. To revise, you have to learn to deeply trust yourself, your gut, not your head. You can't think about what your teacher wants, what your parents will say, what your writing group wishes you would do. You have to deeply, deeply let the piece go where it has to go—and that *should* scare you. If you aren't a little nervous about it, there's a good chance the work isn't alive. Karen Armstrong writes in her memoir *The Spiral Staircase* of becoming a writer in these very terms.

> *The first draft of anything is shit.*
> — ERNEST HEMINGWAY

> [The writer] must fight his own monsters, not somebody else's, explore his own labyrinth, and endure his own ordeal before he can find what is missing in his life. Thus transfigured, he (or she) can bring something of value to the world that has been left behind. But if the knight finds himself riding along an already established track, he is simply following in somebody else's footsteps and will not have an adventure.

Revision, though, once you have enough experience with it to gain a little confidence, is usually the writer's favorite part of writing. It's easier than beginning a new piece, more rewarding to shape and grow a thing that is already alive.

One quality of the experienced writer is a kind of patience. Good writers are more kind to their first drafts—they are less shaken by the dreadful material they write. A beginner feels like giving up too early. Good writers know they have the tools and techniques to improve their writing; they know it's next to impossible to write a great first draft; good writing is a matter of time. Throw some·more time at a piece, and it *will* get better.

Revision can hurt. It can be painful to alter your words. Every writer feels this discomfort, at least some of the time. Good writers, like good athletes, get used to living with *some pain*. They ignore it, and move on. Remember, you have already developed revision skill—most writers revise as they go, not just at the end, right before a deadline. Revising is continuing to work on your writing.

> *Exaggerate in the direction of truth.*
> — HENRI MATISSE

You develop this skill—the ability to see more to do—as you write more pieces. You will learn how to feel less nervous about revision and you will feel energized when you see things you know how to fix or adjust. A dialogue exchange will be flat, and one day, you'll know why—you need three beats, not six. A passage of description, though you love it, has to go — you'll be able to accept the cut. These moments will come more frequently, and you will start to welcome them as part of your writing practice. Revision *is* writing. It's the confidence to go back to a piece, and simply do more of what you have been doing all along: fiddling with the dials, moving things around, adjusting the energy, the tension, the atmosphere.

> *Getting to good writing means writing every day, just like playing the piano. To miss a day or two of piano requires three or four more of practice to get to where you were.*
> — NICOLE LANTZ, STUDENT WRITER

PRINCIPLES OF REVISION

When you revise, follow the same principles of good writing you learned when you studied focus and concentration at the beginning of the course. The revision process *is* the writing process; the principles for revision are exactly the same as the principles of good writing.

Limit Your Time

Work in short sessions — you can get a lot of work done in twenty or thirty focused minutes. A week of twenty-minute daily revision sessions may be more useful to your piece than four hours on a Sunday night, where you end up frustrated, tired, hating your writing, too close to it to really *see* how it will play out in the reader's mind.

The successful reviser's secret: Stay a little in love with the piece, while willing to make changes (true in relationships, too, yes?). Don't get bogged down. Set out a small amount of the piece to focus on, see your way back in, and do what you can do to make that part of the piece come alive in the reader's head.

Revision is hard work because you have to concentrate intensely. For this reason, experienced writers keep their sessions short and focused. Work in bite-sized pieces. Revise a little bit at a time.

Read to Revise

If you aren't sure about revision, and you are procrastinating, read your favorite works. Drink in some books. Reading excellent writing infuses you with the power to see your own work with new eyes. With your favorite authors gathered around you, like muses, your work will often self-correct. You'll at the very least be able to tap into the reasons you are writing in the first place.

Everyone has to revise. Most published works you read go through dozens and dozens of drafts. James Dickey says that it takes him 50 drafts to get the poem and then another 150 to make it sound spontaneous. When you read something professional and polished, instead of feeling awkward and beleaguered and intimidated, let yourself feel inspired by what is possible.

Manage Distraction

Before you revise, you need to get ready for a writing session, just like any other kind of writing session. Remember, they aren't separate. Revision *is* writing. And a writer at work attracts criticism—internal voices that tell the working writer: *stop, why bother, the work is terrible, the work is perfect just as it is.* These voices are wholly unhelpful (tell them to go away and come back, you can use their picky nature when you are in the editing stage). Revision is all about going back into the work, into the scenes and images, and seeing *more.*

> *I've filled scrapbooks with rejection slips. I use them as coasters. Sometimes I have little rejection parties.*
> — LEE PENNINGTON

Before you sit down to revise, get calm, relaxed, and focused. Draw or sketch the scene or image, so you know exactly where you want your reader to be. Make notes about the scene—the time and place—that you are reentering.

You are trying to get caught back up in the piece, to let it deepen, redirect, or enrich the reader's experience. Have a strategy for dealing with the inner soundtrack—the distractions your mind creates every time you sit down to work. Everyone battles this; wanting to stop revision to go do laundry, check email, watch television, start a new piece of writing, just quit. Distraction is fear. Assure yourself repeatedly that you *can* do this, you know how to do this. You have strategies. Apply them to your writing and shut out the voices of doubt.

> *People ask for criticism, but they only want praise.*
> — W. SOMERSET MAUGHAM

REVISION TOOLS

Work with the Strategies

The simplest way to revise is to use the strategies you've learned about—energy, images, tension, pattern, and insight. Heighten the energy in every sentence. Add secondary layers. Increase the tension by studying the power relationships—between patterns of color in your poem, between the mother and daughter in your essay—and work to involve your characters in gestures and actions that reveal the fruits of this energy. Hone your insights and wisdom by studying other writers you like a lot—you can import wisdom without plagiarizing. Use your notebook or sketchbook to think on the page about why people act the way they do. Collect quotes, smart things people say, and layer perceptions into your pieces. Heighten pattern by paying close attention to sound. Tighten the structure of every beat. Nothing missing, nothing extra. And work at the image level, always—transporting yourself so that everything you write is the thing itself, and not removed from it, not *about* it.

The more you work in this way, picking up one tool and then another, the more pleasure you will find in the process. As writers, be more patient with, more inclusive of your bad writing. Your bad writing is the foundation on which your good writing stands. The bad writing is how you get to the good writing. You can't just write good writing all the time. You can't wait—it's too pinched, too uptight, too fearful a stance—and only tolerate good writing. The good, the bad, the ugly, the hilarious, the obscene, the upsetting—all the writing goes into the soup. Don't wait for just the good stuff. Write through. Use the "Workshop" questions at the end of Chapters 3 through 9 as you work on your piece. Refer to the checklists in Chapter 2 on pages 30 and 32 as well as the checklists that guide you through revision in specific genres, located on pages 33 through 39. In order to make sure your reader is absorbed and transported by your work, go over your piece many times.

Don't Start at the Beginning

Many beginners start revising by looking at their first sentence, and feeling two contradictory emotions: "It's fine," and, "It sucks." Which means: "I haven't got a clue what to do with this sentence." It's confusing to feel two opposite emotions at once, so is it any wonder that laundry suddenly seems like a great idea, rather than finishing your work on a sestina or a journey memoir? No. Laundry is easy. Doing laundry is not confusing. Feeling "great" and "awful" at the same time is confusing, but writers have to get used to that strange sensation. The truth is your piece *is* fine, and yes, it could be better, too.

> *I've spent my life making blunders.*
> — PIERRE-AUGUSTE RENOIR

So, don't start at the beginning. It's too likely you will get derailed. Instead, slice up the work in a different way. Resist the urge to start at the beginning, working straight through in a linear fashion. Choose a strategy, and focus your attention on honing the work on one front at a time.

For example, choose the strategy of energy and look for adverbs. They're usually flags that the writing has gotten weak—when you resort to a description to aid a verb, you know you're in trouble. Adverbs are like makeup. Experts can handle a lot of it, but beginners often end up looking, well, overly made-up and false. Not good. Take out your adverbs and replace them with gestures and actions and insights that make things happen for the reader to figure out on her own.

Focus on Images

Write from a place of focus, concentrating on the sensory image. Make sure *you* yourself are inside the scene, the moment, the physical space where your writing is taking place before you make any changes.

Don't write *about*; write from within, from inside. Don't add analysis, summary, explanation. Develop the details that create the dreamlike moving images that will play in your reader's mind on that screen in her head as she reads.

Before you change anything, fully anchor yourself physically and emotionally *inside the setting*, and experience what the character or speaker is experiencing. Take the time to get inside the physical body of the person from whose point of view you are writing. You have to be there. Skim through your piece, or have someone help you, and locate all the places where you report, summarize, explain, or discuss. Focus more tightly on actions and reactions. Replace filtering (thinking, knowing, realizing, staring, understanding) with action. Take out all the signals that direct a reader into his own thoughts, and out of the sensory experience your characters or speakers are engaged in.

Student writer Krista Mehari focused on images as her main revision strategy when she reworked the first two lines in her list poem, "Lies I've Been Told." The original opening lines in the list poem read:

> By my sister, that I didn't look like a swollen tomato in my prom dress.
> By my first grade art teacher, that she could tell it was an elephant.

In order to revise these lines, Krista used a technique introduced in Chapter 4. She set her timer for five minutes. Then, she did a quick sketch of exactly where she was, and what exactly she could see in each of the images—at home with her sister, and in the sunny first-grade classroom at East Elementary School. She made a list next to the sketch, on the same sheet of paper, of everything she heard, smelled, and noticed—focusing on tiny details.

Here's how the new version of "Lies I've Been Told" opens:

> By my sister in the fitting room, as I stood in front of the mirror, fidgeting and turning, smoothing the red satin of a prom dress down over my thighs. "You look great," she said. "That dress really slims you down."
> By Mrs. Manson, my first grade art teacher as she peered down at my lump of clay through plastic-framed glasses that hung around her neck on a beaded chain. "What a majestic elephant!" she said.

Krista worked through her whole poem, line by line, translating general into specific, thought into image. Notice how she worked on accuracy in her revision of the second-to-last line, which originally read:

By a hair stylist from a crazy-expensive salon that she worked with my type hair all the time.

To revise, Krista reimagined herself in that salon. She made notes on what day she was there, what she was wearing to the appointment, what the sounds and smells were like in the salon (she remembers Prince was playing). She did a brief floor plan of the salon, and anchored herself firmly in time and space. Using her eyes, as we learned in Chapter 3 of this book, she took stock of what actions she noticed. This is her revision of the original line:

By a hair stylist at an expensive, white-people salon, as I sat in the swirly chair in front of a big mirror. She pulled her fingers through my hair. "I know exactly what to do. I've worked with this texture before."

In the revision, Krista tells more of the truth. It's less a "crazy-expensive" salon than a "white-people salon." Krista goes deeper in her vision, risks more, and reveals more. It's just a small moment—a haircut—but Krista ends up making a statement about fear and prejudice, innocence and experience. The beautician is a complex person. So is the author. Revision helped Krista sharpen this focus. It's focusing on *images*—the live moving pictures that come from actual, firsthand observation—that gives the revisions their power and impact.

Side-by-Side Versions

As often as we say *writing is a process* and *drafting is nonlinear*, it's hard to stay patient if the piece isn't getting better in clear, measurable ways. We want the amount of time we spend worrying over a piece to be equal to its quality; we want to work and have the piece come out better. That's reasonable, but not realistic. Working on a piece of art is more like gardening than doing the dishes. Accidents happen. Cross-pollination. You ruin your bed of peas walking all over it to get to the lettuce. Suddenly, your eggplants turn pink. You didn't even know you had planted eggplants! Revision is messy and artists *have* to develop a tolerance for disorder in order to create order.

> *I've found that every time I've made a radical change, it's helped me feel buoyant as an artist.*
> — DAVID BOWIE

Free yourself from the tyranny of the straight line—the prevalent but false idea that drafts go neatly in order, from worst to best, that revision means simply *improving*. Try approaching the revision process in a different, more accurate way. Think of revisions as different *versions* of the original.

You have your first draft. Now, write three new versions. Does this sound like a lot of work to you? Most writers find this is much less work than worrying over a piece, line by line, night after night.

Student writer Chantelle Kramer tried the versions approach for a poem about her niece, entitled "A Girl with My Blue Eyes, with His Dark Hair." Here's the opening of her first version:

> I think of my niece—she'll eat anything, especially
> vegetables, especially little grape tomatoes. She's
> beautiful, daring, a pirate princess, running around with
> snarled curls, chasing skittish june bugs,

In this version, Chantelle is focusing on general thoughts and feelings. She has an image of her niece in mind—maybe they are in the garden? Playing together? As readers, we are asked to be in Chantelle's head with her, to see her thinking about her niece.

Compare to Chantelle's second version:

> Sissy, my three year old niece, loves vegetables
> Especially the warm little grape tomatoes, picked
> Right out of her mama's garden. She runs around with
> Snarled curls, telling the dogs to "Shoo! Shoo!"

Here, Chantelle grounds the poem in the garden and uses dialogue to point toward a specific occasion. We aren't in her head reflecting. For class, Chantelle was asked to do a third version of a poem, and she chose this one to work on, because she really likes it, but she didn't feel it had the right opening yet. Here's her third side-by-side version, titled "Identity Theft":

> When we are at the grocery store I pretend my niece is my daughter.
> Cradling her close on my hip, I call her sweetie and honey-pie,
> and open a box of graham crackers for her before we check out,
> leaving a trail of crumbs. I'm seventeen; I wave my bare ring finger,
> I force eye contact with strangers. I love the stares.

In this version, which Chantelle likes the best, she and the niece are clearly in a dramatic situation; like Sebastian Matthews in "Buying Wine," they're at a store, contending with other people. She's skipped out of her head, so there is more energy. The image is clear and controlled. There's tension—Chantelle *likes* people thinking she's a very, very young mother. "Cradling" and "trail of crumbs" create a pattern of images that makes us think of babies and fairy tales, maybe stolen children. The new title points toward interesting insights. When she looks over the complete poems (the original is forty-six lines long—a full page; the third version is half that long), she feels "Identity Theft" is the best

> ### WRITERS' TIPS: Writing Versions of a Piece
>
> 1. Focus your attention on one technique (energy, tension) at a time so each version "showcases" a technique.
> 2. Add a different new character or element to each version.
> 3. Reverse one piece of wisdom or insight in each version.
> 4. Title each version anew.
> 5. Change the ending in each version.
> 6. Change the genre of each version.

poem, but there are things in each version she likes. Chantelle feels the versions method helps her revise better than any other approach because she doesn't have to "kill off" any of her poems. She can simply try them in different ways.

Allow the piece to change significantly. Instead of nurturing the false hope that each new draft will be drastically better than the one before, this side-by-side approach to revision is perhaps a more honest way of learning how writers work on a piece. Keep trying new things until something perfect or almost perfect comes along. Hone your practice in this way. It's the process—learning how to work on a piece of writing in progress—that you are learning this semester. The outcome is somewhat less important. Train yourself to go back to a piece, reenter it, and heighten the experience the reader will have when she reads it. Side-by-side revising frees up, and introduces a sense of play helpful to revision. When it's not "engraved in stone" or "definitely improving," creative writing is more agile and alive. And that much more fun to read.

> *I don't want to discount talent and ability, but I still maintain that a lot of it is just sheer desire.*
> — DON HENLEY

Make More of the Good Parts

Maybe in high school you had late nights, rushing to finish a giant history paper. You were up at 1 a.m., six empty cans of diet soda on your floor, books all over the bed, your MP3 player, battery dead, still on your head. You were doing your revision draft. You had a sentence like this one: "An undeniably significant part of Dante's aim in writing the *Inferno* was to offer a large-scale commentary on the political nightmare of the fourteenth-century political condemnations in that century." For an hour, you bang your head on your desk. How to fix? How to fix? You can't get your head around the sentence, you can't get it "right."

One of the best ways to revise is this: Expand the good parts and cut the bad parts. Simple.

Write more good parts, then simply cut out the parts that don't work. Delete anything terrible. Instead of laboring over that sentence, cut it. Don't revise it. If you can't transport yourself into that sentence, if you can't *be there*, what hope does your reader have? If it's bad writing, you can spend hours trying to fix it. Or, you can conclude that because you weren't focused when you wrote that sentence, it's not worth it.

Some students approach revision using only this strategy; it works. Make more of the good parts and cut, instead of "revising" in that punishing, high-school way. Don't beat your sentences into submission. Let the bad ones move on to sentence heaven; kill them. They'll be out of their misery, and you will be free to reenter the sensory-alive places in your work, and make more of a good thing.

> *Always dream and shoot higher than you know how to. Don't bother just to be better than your contemporaries or predecessors. Try to be better than yourself.*
> — WILLIAM FAULKNER

Here's how student writer Katelyn Konyndyk utilized the "expand good/cut bad" revision technique to improve her nonfiction piece, "Flamingo Coffee." In the first version, below, notice how Katelyn uses summary, explanation, and reflection—she's a good writer. But summary, explanation, and reflection, while appropriate for essay writing, are not particularly helpful strategies in creative writing. In creative writing, we revise so that the *reader* can have the experience, and participate, not just hear about it secondhand. Here, Katelyn tells us all about her favorite beverage:

> I am a coffee addict. Coffee is my drug.
>
> The ritual of making my coffee is a part of what has me hooked. It is methodical and rarely changes. I begin by selecting my choice brew: Starbucks . . . and then carefully scoop four tablespoons into the filter. I pour six cups of water and anxiously await my drug's arrival. My heart reaches a sort of ecstasy as I hear the putter and drip of the machine at work. The rich, robust smell allows my mind to slip away into memories as I anxiously wait. Remembering—old conversations, loved ones lost, and joyous occasions—is the part of the methodical ritual I look forward to the most. . . .
>
> Flamingo Coffee with Grandma K is my first memory of coffee. Even back then it served the same purpose in my life that it does now. Flamingo Coffee was a way for me and my grandma to relax and simply enjoy each other's conversation. Through those miniature cups of coffee and conversations, a part of me was shaped and formed. Flamingo Coffee allowed me to hear the wisdom that only a grandmother can tell. Coffee is my drug because without it, Flamingo Coffee and so many other memories would have been forgotten.

What's the best part of the "Flamingo Coffee" piece? The part where Katelyn is making her cup of Starbucks. The writing has energy and images—Katelyn is into coffee! But there's not a lot of tension, or conflict. Can she add pattern, insight? Maybe. When she revised, Katelyn decided to make more of the part she liked the best—the part of the piece that inspired her to write about coffee. Her grandmother. Katelyn cut out the parts that didn't relate to her grandmother, and she made *more out of* that scene.

Decide for yourself—which do you like better? Here's Katelyn's revision:

> Snow blankets the backyard. My grandmother gets up from the table. The coffee maker has let out its last putter. It is ready. My grandmother opens the cabinet and takes out two coffee cups. Her mug is white and has a pink flamingo painted on the side. The words "Florida's Best" are inscribed underneath. My mug has a pink flamingo on the side too, but it is smaller than my grandma's. She walks to the table balancing the flamingo mugs in one hand and spoons in the other. Her heeled shoes click against the tile floor as she makes her way towards me. She sets flamingos one and two on the table. "Would you like a little sugar?" I shake my head, "I'll take it black today." My grandma smiles, "Black, huh? Are you sure you are ready for that?" She straightens the ribbon holding my left pigtail. I take a sip of the steaming liquid. The warmth flows down my throat, all the way to my toes. I shift in my seat. "Can I take off my tights? They're itchy." "I guess. Won't you be cold?" "Nope. I've got my coffee."

In creative writing, it takes time and space on the page to "do it right." Katelyn found she didn't have the time and space to fully expand both of the good parts of her piece—the Starbucks moment and the grandmother scene. She had to pick. A writer has to let go of favorite lines and passages in order to put all the focus on *the best part of the piece*.

The revision strategy of making more of what's juicy and rich and good, and simply deleting the rest *always* works.

Work by Hand

Sometimes the best way to work on a piece is to forget about your computer, and write by hand. Many writers, especially poets, find they have to have the feel of pencil on paper. Writing by hand slows you down, and lets you focus on physical images instead of the thoughts in your head. When you are stuck on a piece, try working on it by hand. If you never write by hand, this will feel awkward. That can be a good thing.

Great works have been written by hand for centuries. The computer lets you write too quickly, and sometimes you can miss tiny aspects of an image, the very details that make your piece come alive for the reader. It's also easy to erase huge blocks of text—forever. Good writers like to leave tracks and keep a record of the evolution of the piece. Examining your versions also teaches you not just about the piece at hand, but about your own writing process, your strengths and habits.

When you are really stuck on a piece, or can't get started on an assignment, or can't get yourself in the mood to revise, try working the old-fashioned way. It can be startlingly freeing.

Maxine Kumin, the prizewinning poet, describes her slow, steady revision process this way:

> "You are still using a typewriter?" people ask incredulously. I write my poems on my old IBM Selectric, running each revision through a new draft on a new page. Every time I retype a poem it magically shrinks or grows or rearranges itself in the actual physical process, not always for the best. But a poem is not a watercolor; it doesn't turn muddy and have to be abandoned after twenty minutes. The poet can always go back to an earlier version if she writes beyond the ending, as sometimes happens. All those typed drafts spread out on the desk suggest endless possibilities. I cannot imagine doing this on a computer. But there's no unanimity among poets.

EDITING

Editing and revision are opposite activities. But they have two things in common. Both require the writer to (1) deal with unhelpful judgmental thoughts while cultivating a *helpful* focused concentration, and (2) make the piece more interesting for a reader to experience.

Editing is how your eyes *clean* your piece. Editing is picking over the *surface* (as opposed to further illuminating the interior, as in writing and rewriting) of

---

QUESTIONS TO ASK: Editing for Flow

Is your writing as strong as it can be? Consider the following questions.

1. Is your writing clear? Is it easy to understand who is talking, who is in the piece, where we are, and what is happening?
2. Do you rely on weak verbs including *to be* verbs, *should, could, would, might,* and *may*? (See "Muscles," p. 79.)
3. Do you overuse filters, words that describe mental activity, such as *seemed, felt, realized,* and *thought*? (See the section on "Filters," p. 80.)
4. Do you explain too much?
5. Do you include too much description?
6. Do you use unnecessary adverbs?

QUESTIONS TO ASK: Editing for Common Grammar Errors

Use your grammar handbook to check for the following common mistakes.

1. Have you chosen the word you meant to use? Frequently confused word pairs include *lie* and *lay* and *less* and *fewer*.
2. Do your subjects and verbs agree?
3. Do you have any misplaced modifiers?
4. Are there unintentional sentence fragments?

your writing. Editing is the *opposite* of getting inside the piece and re-seeing all those alive moving images.

In editing you stay on the surface. You do not enter the visual world of the piece, you don't read like a reader: You read like a government official. You are cleaning house. You are the street sweeper.

The surface of writing is as important to its magical ability to take a reader to another place. It's like buying a house; the builder has a punch list, a detailed checklist of "little things" to finalize before you move in. If he doesn't do this stuff, living in the house will be incredibly annoying. The cupboard door that wasn't hung quite right doesn't close all the way. The unpainted area on the south wall of the garage, the missing garage door opener. The missing screw on the bathroom toilet paper roll holder. All little things. When they are correct, you don't notice them. When they are poorly done or undone, that's all you can think about.

Revision is an exercise in focus and concentration. Editing is a thinking process. It's vital to handle the two in separate work sessions. When you revise, you reenter the work, and visualize your scenes and stanzas, trying to get back into the full sensory moment. Revision may take place at any point—writing and revision go together. Editing is done at the very end, right before you turn the piece in or send it off for publication.

Lack of attention to editing can and will keep your work from serious consideration by your peers, your teacher, editors. Editing is *part* of what we do; it's your job as the writer to present your best version of your piece. Editing isn't an option. It's integral to the writing process. Perfecting each page is a vital part of your promise to your reader, who deserves an uninterrupted experience *in another world*. If you have typos, grammar mistakes, weird formatting, your reader will be yanked right back to the here and now. That's the opposite of what writers are supposed to be doing. Typos and grammar problems are distracting and annoying to readers. They puncture the dream.

QUESTIONS TO ASK: Editing for Presentation

Sometimes you'll receive specific guidelines for preparing your work. Even if you don't, you should always address the following conventions.

1. Do you need a title page, and if so, do you have one?
2. Are your pages numbered?
3. Are your margins at least one inch wide at the left, right, top, and bottom of every page?
4. Is the spacing between sentences, sections, and stanzas consistent?
5. Have you included any necessary headers and footers?
6. Have you followed dialogue and other punctuation conventions?
7. Have you checked your spelling?
8. Have you checked separately for typographical errors? For instance, you may have typed *from* instead of *form* or *then* instead of *than*. Spell-check won't catch these errors, since the words are spelled correctly. They just aren't the ones you intended to use.

Clean with your eyes. Read the piece forward and backward (literally, go from bottom to top at least twice, so you are more likely to snag on errors, less likely to be caught in the "dream" you have worked so hard to create, blind to errors). And, you'll want to have your writing group, or a partner, look at your work too. It's much harder to find your own typos than someone else's. Work with others.

Your instructor probably will have specific guidelines for turning in work to the class. Specific assignments and particular magazines and editors also have particular guidelines and format requirements. Always follow these to the letter.

Ask your instructor what errors she sees most often in your work, and concentrate on correcting those. Ask your instructor and your readers what mistakes you make most often, and consult your grammar handbook and vow to learn why you make those mistakes and how to fix them. To go on as a writer, now is the time to learn the rules of grammar and style. Editors and employers and publishers will not take your work seriously if it is plagued with serious grammar problems.

Your instructor may give you specific guidelines. See the checklists in this section for general guidelines to help you carefully edit your own work before turning it in.

REVISE YOUR WRITING LIFE

How are your habits? Do you write every day? Do you talk too much about writing without writing enough? Do you have writing fear? Do you have time, space, and materials? Are your friends controlling your work schedule, or are you? What else do you need to know about yourself as a writer, in order to do this work? What do you need to do to revise your writing life?

Cultivate good habits of mind: ignoring judgments, establishing writing rituals. Read widely, against your grain, extending your parameters of taste and knowledge. Read about writing. Read contemporary and classic authors. Show up, do the work, and practice concentration and focus.

You may want to consider "going public" with your work. The next chapter shows you how to get interested in revision by choosing a date, time, and place to share your work with a wider audience. Many writers find part of their writing life must include regular show dates. It's hard to revise in a vacuum.

CHAPTER ELEVEN

PUBLICATION

A vital part of improving creative writing is taking your work to an audience and trying it out. When are you ready to go public? After you have completed several pieces, working with your teacher and peers to improve them to the best of your ability.

When you turn your work over to a professor, you in a sense go public with it—you are finished working on it for the time being. The work is in the best form you can possibly get it into at this point. And you are saying, "Here it is." When you present or turn in or publish a piece of writing, you change your relationship to the work. It's not just yours anymore.

Piano students play for audiences at recitals. Football teams build all season to playoff and bowl games. Painters work on series of paintings to show to the public. Playwrights dream of opening night. Chefs open restaurants and invite other chefs to dine. Going public allows you to focus and shape your writing life as well as your writing. Keeping the audience in mind trains you to make good choices as you work. You think about your readers, and so you increase the tension in a piece, sharpening the images, intensifying the energy. Learning how to take work before an audience and come away with valuable information on your writing's strengths and weaknesses is the foundation for sustaining a lifelong writing habit.

You have a number of ways to take your work public. The big three are:

1. Give a reading of your own work (in class, at a coffee shop, etc.).
2. Publish in an online or print book or journal.
3. Create a chapbook or professional portfolio of your work (a compilation of your writing, bound and distributed to a limited number of people).

These are all forms of publication. Publication helps you stay in touch with the *reasons* you are revising your work. Publication gives you a deadline, and deadlines focus our energy. Publication celebrates your hard work, and lets others experience your view of the world.

Recitals, playoffs, performances, and publication are celebrations of *work in progress*. Artists, athletes, creators aren't usually ever truly *finished* with a piece—chefs perfect their béarnaise sauce over a lifetime, the backdoor pass always needs work. But there comes a time when showing, revealing, celebrating, saying "finished for now" is a necessary part of the process of evolving, of improving. You can *always* make your work better. At some point (usually toward the end of a course), it's a good idea to take stock of what you have done, hone one or more strong pieces, stand back, and see how they are received by the wider world.

PUBLIC READINGS

Many writers say there is nothing that lets them see their work more clearly than reading it aloud before an audience. All the flaws suddenly show up—if only to you—and new ways back into the piece become obvious. An upcoming public reading helps you revise with a clear, fresh eye and a sensitive ear.

Some writers feel they should wait until they are really, really good before they attempt some form of public presentation. However, presenting your work after writing intensively for a few months is a terrific way to educate yourself about your writing process—nothing else quite gives you this experience. Keep in mind the main mantra of this book—it's not about you, it's about your reader. You are not performing in order to have a cathartic emotional experience, to show off, to have everyone adore you. When you publish—whether in a live reading, a chapbook, or in a magazine your class decides to create—you present your work to get more information to help you with the piece, entertain and enlighten a reader or listener, and give you the confidence, ambition, and spark needed to continue on with this hard, lonely endeavor called Creative Writing.

Consider this situation. There's a sentence in your story you love, you adore it, it's your favorite. When your piece is discussed in class, everyone loves the line. It's not until reading the work aloud in front of a group of strangers that you realize the truth: The sentence has nothing to do with your story. Out it goes (maybe it's the first line of a new piece). Reading aloud, formally, lets you achieve another kind of completion with your work. You celebrate a nearly finished draft. You return to your work smarter, wiser.

It's one thing to sit at your desk late at night fussing with word order, last lines, titles, and tiny details. But when you present your work for others to see and hear—not just your group, your teacher, your friends, but a true *audience*—it does something to your ability to focus and revise: Both increase, sharply.

We complete our works many times.

Readings by accomplished writers usually last about one hour. Sometimes several well-known writers will share the stage. Beginning writers, like rock-and-roll fans, will drive hours to hear Lorrie Moore, Jorie Graham, A. Van Jordan, or Gish Jen. Sometimes the writer reads from published works or sometimes from a new piece, a work in progress, in order to try it out, to get information about what it's like to be inside the piece as a reader.

Writers interested in someday publicly reading their own work attend as many readings as they can. They watch and listen to what is interesting to read aloud, what bombs, what presentation techniques work, and how the talk in between the poems or pieces adds to or detracts from the poems themselves. Good writers take notes and learn from the example of others. Usually, writers read aloud the more accessible of their works. Dark, deeply disturbing, intricate, hard-to-follow pieces, or pieces that depend on your having the written page to look at as you read aren't going to be as successful. Some writers have a "read aloud" version of their work; the published or printed version is different. You may need to clarify your use and placement of speech tags (the "he said" and "she said"), placing them ahead of the dialogue lines and repeating character names more frequently.

Audiences have a hard time listening for more than one hour—listening to creative writing read aloud is harder work than viewing a popular film. If you aren't used to being read to, it may take a few experiences at live readings before you are comfortable sitting back and letting creative writing make a movie in your mind. We all know how to do it—our parents read or told us stories. And when we listened, we "saw" the story, we experienced it, we were *there*. But for many people, maybe even you, this is an experience we may not have kept up. We may have to remind the brain how much it loves this pleasure, this mix of relaxing and concentrating that constitutes all good play. At a live reading, you the writer must stick closely to your time limit: Going over is completely out of bounds. For new writers, quick readings—five-minute, three-minute, two-page, poem-and-a-paragraph readings work best. Practice extensively to work out your timing, and figure out the best piece to read.

Many coffeehouses around the country already have open mic nights; research the existing venues in your area. People aren't used to listening to poets and writers read out loud, so don't be alarmed if you don't feel entirely *listened to*. It takes effort and practice to concentrate on creative writing when you are out with friends.

However, you will likely be able to sense what parts do hold audience interest, and what parts may be too long, slow, or obscure. You may suddenly see how one or more of the tools—energy, images, tension, structure, pattern, insight— could be applied to a passage in your piece. After a live reading, you will more than likely be excited to work on your piece.

Take reading aloud for what it is: a chance to "publish" your work, give it an airing out, a good shake, to see what sticks. You will be able to tell immediately and intensely what falls flat and what is strongest in your work. No other experience with publishing your work gives you the kind of feedback—instant, laser-sharp, dead accurate—that reading aloud does. It's like stand-up comedy. The vibe in the room doesn't lie. It can't. You'll know. And you'll be able to make your best work even better—that's what every writer wants.

A class reading is a smart way to practice on friends who can't leave the room or order a beer! And you will gain confidence as you continue to give live readings. With practice you'll get better; you will probably even come to *love* the experience and the insight you gain into your work. Classes can decide on the format. Perhaps students who enjoy reading in front of groups will read excerpts or short works by students who are terrified of reading aloud. Short-shorts and narrative poems work very well for class readings, which can be held at the campus coffee shop—snacks and literature complement each other nicely!

WRITERS' TIPS: Giving a Public Reading of Your Work

Here are some important things to keep in mind before you read in front of an audience.

1. Plan out the order of your pieces carefully (if you are reading more than one short piece).

2. Plan out your comments (if there are brief things you need to say to explain the background of a poem, or the context of a story excerpt). Know what you will say when you take the stage. Do you need to thank anyone?

3. Practice reading the piece aloud several times. Practice in front of someone who can tell you if you're speaking too fast (this is the most common mistake—almost *everyone* reads too fast).

4. Absolutely stick to the designated time requirements.

5. Make sure you have water and a readable copy of what you will present.

6. Use your anxiety to infuse your reading with energy. If you are not nervous, you may read "flat."

7. Read more slowly than you think you should.

8. Have an exit strategy. Slow down, way down, as you read the last lines of your piece. Look at the audience directly. Say "thank you" and get off stage.

9. After the live reading, take a few minutes to make some notes on your text, marking places that you want to look at again more closely.

LITERARY MAGAZINES

Editors are constantly looking for new, undiscovered writers. Every magazine wants to be able to say it published the first story by Ernest Hemingway or Flannery O'Connor, the first poem by W. S. Merwin, the first essay by Sandra Cisneros. New writers should explore as many of the so-called little or literary magazines as time allows. Reading through the pieces published in small magazines gives you a terrific sense of what editors and readers are interested in. Look for the following in your library:

The CLMP (Council of Literary Magazines and Presses) Directory of Literary Magazines and Presses; www.clmp.org. This directory catalogs independent literary publishers. Like independent bookstores or independent record labels, these publishers focus on publishing poetry, fiction, and creative nonfiction, and they are mission-driven, meaning the concern isn't with ads, dollars, or fame, but on long-term, quality relationships with authors and small but devoted audiences. Contemporary literature is alive in these small magazines and literary journals. Emerging voices, and hybrid and experimental art forms that are overlooked by mainstream magazines are celebrated in the little magazines. The CLMP directory helps you find and purchase samples of these publications before sending work to them.

Writer's Digest "Market" series — for poets, writers, novelists, children's authors, playwrights; www.WritersMarket.com. Writer's Market is a much larger reference work, printed each year in several different volumes: one is devoted to the novel and short story markets, another to the children's literature market, another to poetry. It is updated annually, and also includes listings, as in the CLMP, of magazines looking for new writers and creative writing submissions. Both sources tell you how to order sample issues (many magazines will send you sample issues for free or for a few dollars). In addition, helpful articles on how to write attention-getting queries and effective cover letters precede the actual listings. Your library should have these volumes in the reference section.

Research a Wide Range of Publications

Magazines are like shops at the mall — each one has its own personality, its own look and feel. Reading literary magazines is empowering. You'll find some authors who knock you out. And you may also say, "Hey, I can write this well." Look up some of the following publications and see what you think of the work inside. You will find these literary magazines in your library, with the magazines, and in most bookstores with periodicals.

The Malahat Review	*Tin House*
The Gettysburg Review	*Calyx*
Zoetrope: All-Story	*The Southeast Review*
Swink	*Natural Bridge*
The Marlboro Review	*The Paris Review*
The Fourth Genre	*The Believer*
The Mississippi Review	*Callaloo*
Glimmer Train	*Image*

The Web site webdelsol.com offers a long list of links to literary magazine sites. Search for "literary magazines" to find other resources.

When you travel, you can find magazines with limited distribution—rare, local, and intriguing journals tucked away in unlikely places. Visit locally owned, independent bookstores, college bookstores, and art galleries, and keep an eye out for local authors in arts journals and literary magazines.

Do your research before publishing on Web sites; often you will not be able to publish the work in a print journal after publishing on a Web site. There are prestigious sites that you will be always proud to have given your work to; you don't want to simply give away your best works, though. Make sure you know the history of the Web site, and something of its standing—your instructor may be a good person to help you analyze the quality of the publication you are considering. This is important. You are permanently and irrevocably linked to a magazine that publishes you.

Submit Your Work to Literary Magazines

Before you submit your work for publication, take it through as many rounds of workshops, writing groups, and editing as you can. The manuscript must be without error—many editors simply won't read past the first line if they spot grammar mistakes, typos, lack of page numbering, or any failure to follow the magazine's submission requirements. Magazines get hundreds of manuscripts a week. Many of these are discarded quickly, without being read from beginning to end; experienced editors often know instantly whether the answer is "Maybe" or "No." It's common for an editor to glance at the first page of a story, the first lines of a poem, and decide, in an instant, that there is not enough energy, pattern, or tension to keep reading. Editors don't do your work for you. Editors edit *magazines*. You edit your work. Your piece must be absolutely perfect before you send it.

Never send money to anyone to read or publish your work. Unscrupulous organizations prey on young writers' desire to publish, and no one will take your publication seriously if you had to pay for it. You should be paid for your work (even if only in contributor copies; it's quite common for small magazines to send author's copies of the magazine instead of a check—budgets are tight at these nonprofits!). Don't pay to publish.

Decide Where to Send Your Work. Do your research before you submit. Read sample issues of the magazine so you don't end up sending your sexiest, rawest love poems to a magazine edited by clergy who are looking for uplifting stories about overcoming hardship. Be familiar with the submission guidelines, which you will find in the magazine (often in the first pages, in small print, or at the very back of the issue, and on the magazine's Web site).

Some writers suggest you have at least six pieces of submission quality before you start submitting your work. It's always a good idea to have a couple of pieces circulating so you aren't completely devastated when one comes back. Work on your writing (that's the whole point of this exercise—to keep you working, focused on improving your work). When a piece comes back, look at it. Can you improve it? Often, submitting work and having it come back changes your relationship to the piece. You read with a colder eye, more willing to cut weaker parts. You read like an editor, asking editor questions: *What's the experience of reading this like? Why would my subscribers be interested in this? Where's the energy, the tension, the insights?*

Once you are ready to move beyond your school's literary magazine, research local and then regional markets for creative writing. Check at locally owned bookstores. Two invaluable resources for creative writers who want to keep abreast of trends and discussions of the literary magazine world are:

> *Poets and Writers*; bimonthly magazine; www.pw.org
> *The Writer's Chronicle*; monthly information-packed periodical;
>   www.awpwriter.org

These magazines offer detailed information for new and publishing writers on grants, awards, graduate programs, writing techniques. They both feature interviews and essays by creative writers on topics of interest. Extensive listings in the back pages of each of these publications feature calls for work: Editors announce what they are looking for, and also publish their submission guidelines. As soon as you can afford to, subscribe to both.

Be realistic, stay creative, and have fun choosing where to submit your work. Most writers start small and close to home, building a resume of publications that way.

After you have written and revised (and perhaps read aloud in front of an audience) a body of work—three to five good poems or about ten pages of prose—

you are ready to prepare a submission packet, sending your work off to an editor. Remember that this process is lengthy and slow. Do not expect to get published the first time you try. Expect editors to take weeks, even months, to reply. Use the submission process as a way to learn the field of creative writing, to improve your work, and to discover exciting new authors in the literary magazines you encounter.

How to Send Your Work Out. First, obtain the magazine's submission guidelines from its Web site. Always research the submission guidelines, which vary for each publication, before submitting. Many publications have specific reading periods. Some do not accept unsolicited work at all. Magazine Web sites tell you exactly what to do; follow the directions carefully. Some magazines allow online submissions, but most still require hard copy submissions and a self-addressed stamped envelope (SASE). Magazine editors use the envelope to return your acceptance letter or rejection note. Plan on waiting two weeks to six months.

Most magazines are struggling to make ends meet, and because they receive so many submissions, they can't afford to subsidize the time and money it would cost to deal with extensive correspondence. You'll likely receive a form rejection, freeing you to resubmit the work to the next magazine on your list. Use a 9 × 12 inch envelope to mail the package and a business-size envelope for your SASE. Be professional, type addresses, and present your materials neatly.

Accept Rejection

Two words on rejection: Expect it.

All writers get rejected — it's part of what we do. We submit our work, and most of the time, editors can't use it. Perhaps they just published a short story featuring aliens, cathedrals, and a blind man, or a bunch of pantoums. Perhaps they like your work, but they see some rough edges.

Many editors want to see if you have two, three, or five stories, twenty decent poems, before they invest valuable pages in you and your writing. That's harsh, but fair. You have to have some *depth* as a writer in order to break into print.

Publication is a process that *includes* rejection. So, thinking through how you are going to feel when you get rejected (which you will) is useful if you plan to one day be a published author (you will).

Many nonwriters think they would never be able to handle rejection. But as all musicians, athletes, actors, and people who are trying to date know, rejection is part of the deal. It means you are at least in the game. You simply are not going to get every part you audition for. Acceptance — publication — is a process. Rejection is part of that process. Plan on being rejected. If you can't make *friends* with rejection right away, practice seeing rejection as unimportant — it really doesn't have anything to do with you, personally. Magazines publish a tiny percentage of what they receive (1 to 6 percent).

You don't need all editors to adore you, just one. Don't give editors, and rejection, more power than they really have. You'll resubmit your work (revising and improving along the way) many times before it finds a good home — that's how publication works. Notice how rejection means you are actually a *successful* writer: working, submitting, fine-tuning, paying attention, studying markets. The people who get published are the ones who keep on submitting, again and again and again. When a writer submits a piece of work, he usually plans on between ten and twenty rejections before he considers doing another revision. If you are going to give up after one, two, or three rejections, you do not yet have a realistic sense of how the marketplace works. Get friendly with rejection. Your path to publication is paved with dozens of rejections.

CHAPBOOKS AND PORTFOLIOS

In composition classes or other writing classes you have taken, you may have turned in a portfolio of your best work. In most art classes, the end of the semester provides an opportunity to show the body of work you have created, shaped, and polished, so that others can see what you do. Your teacher evaluates your growth by examining your portfolio, and you gain valuable insights into your strengths and weaknesses, and take stock of where you want to go next.

A portfolio is a sampling of your best work — your best poems, short-shorts, a terrific essay. Sometimes a portfolio requires an artist's statement, or other reflective writing where you discuss your process and your habits of mind as a writer. Portfolios can be copied for each class member, or simply discussed between you and your instructor. Portfolios present polished professional work — your best work, collected.

Many creative writing classes design their own literary magazine; a class literary magazine is the perfect introduction to publication. The entire class can serve as an editorial board, selecting a piece from each class member, working from portfolios of submitted works.

Or, small writing groups can form magazines, each with their own vision, mission, and personal predilections.

Creating a Chapbook

Another way to collect your best work is to create a chapbook. A chapbook is a small book, like a pamphlet, stapled and photocopied and sold or given away. The name derives from "cheap books," popular in Great Britain in the eighteenth and nineteenth centuries, where "chapmen" (peddlers) made up inexpensive publications—oftentimes just a single sheet of paper folded to make eight, sixteen, or twenty-four pages—to sell to the literate. Simplicity and economy are hallmarks of the chapbook. If you would like to look at some excellent examples, search for publishers who specialize in chapbooks. Main Street Rag is one example. Also examine Pecan Grove Press, Slapering Hol, Poetry Society of America, and Tupelo Press. All of these publishers have Web sites where you can order sample copies of chapbooks.

When the chapbook is made into a beautiful, expensive, well-illustrated book, it's called an artist's book; examine the Center for Book Arts (centerfor bookarts.org) for more information on how writers turn their work into art, taking the publishing process into their own hands.

The chapbook usually has a simple cover on regular paper or card stock, and may include illustrations by the author, clip art, or other graphic design elements. There's a table of contents, and often, in the back, a short biographical note about the author. Some creative writing classes ask each participant to create enough copies of their individual chapbooks so that all students have one. Chapbooks can be sold or given away at live readings. A chapbook can be printed on $8\frac{1}{2} \times 11$ inch paper with a landscape orientation, so that the creative writing can then be folded and saddle-stapled.

A class chapbook—essentially a joint portfolio where each student contributes one of her best pieces of writing—is a wonderful way to publish your work. The class decides on the guidelines. For example, each person might submit up to three pages of creative writing. Students decide who will put the selections in order, who will proofread, and who will prepare the table of contents. Depending on the budget, extra copies can be supplied so that each class member, the instructor, the department, and friends and family have a chance to read this work.

If you continue with creative writing, you could have chapbooks of your work (or your writing group's) to hand out at your live readings, just as musicians may offer CDs at their live performances.

Publishing your own work in a portfolio or chapbook helps you maintain high standards for revision and editing. While the process is time-consuming, it provides invaluable information to you as a writer. When you prepare work for public consumption, you suddenly are able to let go of things that were hard to cut during your earlier revision process. That long poem has to be fit to one page? Easy! The last four stanzas just aren't needed, you decide. You see how to start your story in the middle, that the beginning is preface. You discover links and connections in your work you never noticed before.

Lastly, some teachers ask students who assemble chapbooks to gather quotes from other classmates (or teachers or peers) to include on the back of the book, just as commercially published books have "blurbs" (blurbs are those quotes on the back that say things like "Luminous! Enchanting! The best new writer of this generation!"). You can gather quotes to place on the back cover of your chapbook, encouraging people to look inside. Simply pass around drafts of your work—the pieces you will include in the book—to a few friends, and ask them to write a few sentences about what they notice.

Writing an Artist's Statement

At the end of the semester, it's a good idea to take stock of what you have learned, how far you have come. Much literature of interest to creative writers— interviews, essays, biographies, letters, autobiographies such as Eudora Welty's *One Writer's Beginnings*, books on craft like Flannery O'Connor's *Mystery and Manners*—is in fact a kind of artist statement: an extended piece of nonfiction where the writer explores process, inspiration, and artistic progress. A written essay or statement of this kind is an important bookend to the semester.

When you reread your writing from a few months ago, take notes. Pay attention to what makes you cringe or wince. Were you trying to sound writerly? Confident? Intrepid? Teacher-pleasing? What does your four-months-ago voice sound like? How has it changed? Are there things you said back then that were false, but seemed true at the time? Things that make you laugh now? Myths you subscribed to, now debunked? What was true then, and is more true than ever now?

What were your preoccupations back then, and what are they now? Did the course end up like you thought it would? It's helpful to track your learning, and perhaps the first section of your artist's statement can be a reflection back on this earlier version of you. Write a reflective reaction to your earlier statement. What have you changed your mind about? Try to notice at least ten things.

Your instructor may ask you to create an artist's statement. Or, you may mull over these questions on your own. You may choose to use these questions to construct an artist's statement, to hand out at a live reading, post on a Web site, or include as an introduction or afterword in your portfolio or chapbook. You may wish to pull out just a few lines from your artist's statement to include in your class literary magazine or chapbook.

If you struggle with an artist's statement, or if you are someone who is very interested in what other writers have to say about the writing process, where great ideas come from, and creativity in general, the bibliography that follows will guide you to the best books on these topics.

Good luck. Keep writing. *Everyone* who wants to gets to "be" a creative writer. You don't need fancy tools. You do not need to be weird or artsy. Every human being on the planet is allowed to sing, to dance, to play, to draw, to make

QUESTIONS TO ASK: Writing an Artist's Statement

Consider the following questions when writing about your own work, whether for self-reflection or for someone else.

1. Will you take another writing class?
2. Have your goals as a writer changed?
3. What's the most important thing you have learned?
4. What do you wish you had learned that you didn't?
5. What do you want to say about your work?
6. What would you write if you had the time and talent to write anything? Will you?
7. What have you learned about your writing habits?
8. Do you see yourself as part of a writing community? Do you prefer to work in isolation, focusing on the work, and reading?
9. What's the most important thing you learned about getting and giving feedback about work in progress?
10. What techniques, authors, or exercises have been most useful to you?
11. What insights have you gained into the practice and art of creative writing?
12. Has your voice changed? Is your writing truer, deeper, better?
13. What authors do you want to read now (has that changed)? Do you have writer role models?
14. What's your best piece from the semester?

stuff, and to write. Making art is how we know we are alive. Making art is how we make sense of the world. Shaping experiences so we can look at them more closely, and laugh and cry and understand, and ultimately, see ourselves more clearly—that's creative writing. Creative writing is something you can do for the rest of your life. You have the tools—energy, tension, images, insight, pattern, structure. You have the equipment—cheap paper, a pencil, and ten minutes.

CHAPTER TWELVE

RESOURCES FOR WRITERS

Books on how to write, Web sites listing literary agents, magazines promising publication and lucrative possibilities in "Six Easy Little Steps"—information for writers is abundant. How do you sort through the pages and pages of material on *how to write* and come away with the good stuff? This chapter serves as a guide. Here are books, magazines, and Web sites that many writers find invaluable as they study creative writing further and begin to submit their work. You will certainly find additional resources of your own.

Your best resources as a writer are always your dedicated daily writing practice—the ten minutes or two hours you put in at the desk, along with your writing group. To supplement—not take the place of—those two resources, you may find yourself collecting writing books, surfing the Web looking for writing tips and connections, contests, and online instruction. Remember: Do not send money for any reason in order to publish your work, have it edited, or enter a contest unless your instructor has assured you it is a reputable and worthy venue.

Better to purchase a few good quality books on writing, ones you will turn to again and again. Below, you will find some of the most popular Web sites writers visit, a list of magazines you might consider subscribing to, and a thorough list of books that offer additional and specialized instruction, inspiration, ways to navigate the publishing world, and books to consider if you are going to someday teach creative writing to elementary, secondary, or college students.

Often, the best writing advice is hidden away in used or out-of-print books—you may have to search Abebooks.com or Powells.com for some of these titles, or consult your local independent booksellers; you will save money in the long run, and avoid making mistakes buying the new hotly marketed writing guide that, a few months later, seems tired and worn.

WEB SITES FOR WRITERS

www.poems.com. Poetry Daily. This Web site emails you a poem every day. The home pages are devoted to many topics of interest to writers (in any genre). Interviews with authors, background information on the featured poets and lively discussions of contemporary poetry.

www.wga.org. Writers Guild of America. A terrific introduction to the business side of creative writing, with links where you can "ask the expert," learn to write for television, and connect with other writers. Especially helpful is the guide to Internet developments of special interest to writers, updated monthly.

www.sfwa.org. The Science Fiction and Fantasy Writers of America features contests to enter, publications, writing instruction, and member discussion forums.

www.aldaily.com. Arts and Letters Daily is a news service collecting articles of interest to writers and artists from all over the world. It's like subscribing to 100 newspapers, but you only get the section you care about.

www.artsjournal.com. Arts Journal: the Daily Digest of Arts, Culture, and Ideas. Articles on art, dance, literature, music, and more, with well-written, interesting blogs in every area.

www.writersdigest.com. *Writer's Digest* magazine hosts this comprehensive site—slanted more toward popular writers rather than literary writers, but with good nuts-and-bolts information for everyone. Look for their annual feature, "One Hundred and One Best Sites for Writers." The sites are selected by reader-writers and are grouped into subsections: inspiration, fantasy writers, technique, finding a writing group, etc.

www.nanowrimo.org. National Novel Writing Month is November, and there is a thriving movement in this country made up of novel writers who push hard to get a full first "down" draft *done* in November of each year. The site offers instruction, guidance in forming the necessary support team, and excellent tips for completing a novel (and what to do next). One of the smartest features at Nanowrimo is how writers can connect with other writers at work.

www.dailywriting.net. Soul Food Café is a comprehensive, useful site devoted to those interested in setting up and maintaining a daily writing life. They send you reminders and inspiration to keep you focused.

WRITING MAGAZINES

The Writer's Chronicle. Association of Writers and Writing Programs. Mail Stop 1E3, George Mason University, Fairfax, VA 22030-4444. An annual subscription is included if you join the AWP association; otherwise, there is a student discount. Email them at services@awpwriter.org. Web site is www.awpwriter.org.

Poets and Writers. P.O. Box 543, Mount Morris, IL 61054. This magazine is a must-read for creative writers interested in literary publishing. News and trends, features on small presses, interviews with famous as well as up-and-coming writers, and articles on how to write and what to read—all of the very highest quality. www.pw.org/mag.

BOOKS

Creative Writers at Work

Images: Seeing More Closely. These books present different approaches to the "images" method presented in this textbook. In one, Elkins's philosophy of seeing, the art of looking more closely at the world and the people in it, is explained in great detail, with numerous visual examples to support his points. In another book, visual artist Frederick Franck teaches how to enter that focused state where you can see the aliveness in the image. While Franck is definitely talking to visual artists, his principles apply beautifully to the work creative writers do.

Cassou, Mitchell. *Point Zero: Creativity without Limits.* New York: Jeremy P. Tarcher/ Putnam, 2001.
Elkins, James. *How to Use Your Eyes.* New York: Routledge, 2000.
Franck, Frederick. *Zen Seeing, Zen Drawing: Meditation in Action.* New York: Bantam Books, 1993.

Teaching Creative Writing. If you are thinking about teaching after you leave college, you will absolutely enjoy these books on why art is necessary in schools, how students can be taught to make original, true art, and the role of the artist/ writer as teacher. The Flynn and both Koch books focus on teaching poetry, grades one through college.

Elkins, James. *Why Art Cannot Be Taught: A Handbook for Art Students.* Urbana: University of Illinois Press, 2001.
Flynn, Nick, and Shirley McPhillips. *A Note Slipped under the Door: Teaching from Poems We Love.* York, ME: Stenhouse Publishers, 2000.

Koch, Kenneth. *Making Your Own Days: The Pleasures of Reading and Writing Poetry.* New York: Scribner, 1998.

Koch, Kenneth, and Kate Farrell. *Sleeping on the Wing: An Anthology of Modern Poetry, with Essays on Reading and Writing.* New York: Random House, 1981.

London, Peter. *No More Secondhand Art: Awakening the Artist Within.* Boston: Shambhala, 1989.

Moxley, Joseph M., ed. *Creative Writing in America: Theory and Pedagogy.* Urbana, IL: National Council of Teachers of English, 1989.

Myers, David Gershom. *The Elephants Teach: Creative Writing since 1880.* Englewood Cliffs, NJ: Prentice Hall, 1996.

Schneider, Pat. *Writing Alone and with Others.* New York: Oxford University Press, 2003.

Stafford, William. *You Must Revise Your Life.* Ann Arbor: University of Michigan Press, 1986.

The Business of Writing: Agents, Freelancing, Book Proposals, Publishing.

There are dozens of books available on the business aspects of writing. I suggest you follow the 80/20 rule and spend 80 percent of your writing time working on your craft, and the remaining 20 percent on exploring markets, agents, and publishers. Here is a selection of the most useful books devoted to helping you seriously publish your work.

Banks, Michael A. *How to Become a Full-Time Freelance Writer: A Practical Guide to Setting Up a Successful Writing Business at Home.* Waukesha, WI: Writer Books, 2003.

Begley, Adam. *Literary Agents: A Writer's Guide.* 3rd rev. ed. New York: Penguin Books, 1993.

Council of Literary Magazines and Presses. *The CLMP Directory of Literary Magazines and Presses.* 21st ed. San Francisco: Manic D Press, 2004.

Herman, Jeff, and Deborah Levine Herman. *Write the Perfect Book Proposal: 10 That Sold and Why.* 1993. 2nd ed. New York: Wiley, 2001.

Higgins, George V. *On Writing: Advice for Those Who Write to Publish (Or Would Like To).* London: Bloomsbury, 1991.

Lerner, Betsy. *The Forest for the Tree: An Editor's Advice to Writers.* New York: Riverhead Books, 2000.

Lyon, Elizabeth. *Nonfiction Book Proposals Anybody Can Write: How to Get a Contract and Advance before Writing Your Book.* 1995. New York: Perigree Book, 2002.

Lyon, Elizabeth. *The Sell-Your-Novel Toolkit: Everything You Need to Know about Queries, Synopses, Marketing and Breaking In.* Hillsboro, OR: Blue Heron Publishing, 1997.

Maass, Donald. *The Career Novelist: A Literary Agent Offers Strategies for Success.* Portsmouth, NH: Heinemann, 1996.

Novel and Short Story Writer's Market. Annual serial publication since 1989. Cincinnati, OH: Writer's Digest Books.

Creativity and Inspiration

If you are interested in increasing your creative powers, or you just want to read about artists, writers, and how they work, there are many books available. Each book on this list is accessible, lively, fascinating, and packed with useful information on what it is to "be creative." If you are stuck, these books are extremely useful in helping you work through a block. Many of them have specific exercises for you to try in order to develop new creative muscles.

Ayan, Jordan E. *Aha! 10 Ways to Free Your Creative Spirit and Find Your Great Ideas.*
    Ed. Rick Benzel. New York: Crown Trade Paperbacks, 1997.
Bayles, David, and Ted Orland. *Art and Fear: Observations on the Perils (and Rewards)*
    of Artmaking. Santa Barbara, CA: Capra, 1993.
Brande, Dorothea. *Becoming a Writer.* 1934. Los Angeles: J. P. Tarcher; Boston:
    Houghton Mifflin, 1981.
Edgarian, Carol, and Tom Jenks, eds. *The Writer's Life: Intimate Thoughts on Work,*
    Love, Inspiration, and Fame from the Diaries of the World's Great Writers. New
    York: Vintage Books, 1997.
Maisel, Eric. *Fearless Creating: A Step-by-Step Guide to Starting and Completing Your*
    Work of Art. New York: Putnam, 1995.
Palumbo, Dennis. *Writing from the Inside Out: Transforming Your Psychological Blocks*
    to Release the Writer Within. New York: Wiley, 2000.
Perry, Susan K. *Writing in Flow: Keys to Enhanced Creativity.* Cincinnati, OH: Writer's
    Digest Books, 1999.
Rico, Gabriele L. *Writing the Natural Way: Using Right-Brain Techniques to Release*
    Your Expressive Powers. 1993. Rev. ed. New York: Tarcher/Putnam, 2000.
Tharp, Twyla, and Mark Reiter. *The Creative Habit: Learn It and Use It for Life:*
    A Practical Guide. New York: Simon & Schuster, 2003.
Ueland, Barbara. *If You Want to Write.* 1938. 2nd ed. St. Paul, MN: Graywolf Press, 1987.

Instruction in Specific Genres

This semester, you had a chance to practice in several different genres. If you want to go deeper in your study, these books will guide you in your pursuit of mastering a single genre—the short-short, the novel, the form poem, etc. Each of these books is a guidebook you can use yourself; some are textbooks, but most are designed for the individual writer working on his or her own.

Fiction

Bell, Madison Smartt. *Narrative Design: A Writer's Guide to Structure.* New York:
    W.W. Norton, 1997.
Bernays, Anne, and Pamela Painter. *What If? Writing Exercises for Fiction Writers.*
    1990. 2nd ed. New York: Pearson Longman, 2004.

Block, Lawrence. *Writing the Novel from Plot to Print*. Cincinnati, OH: Writer's Digest Books, 1979.

Browne, Renni, and Dave King. *Self-Editing for Fiction Writers: How to Edit Yourself into Print*. 1993. 2nd ed. New York: Harper Resource, 2004.

Burnett, Hallie Southgate. *On Writing the Short Story*. New York: Harper & Row, 1983.

Burroway, Janet, and Susan Weinberg. *Writing Fiction: A Guide to Narrative Craft*. 1982. 6th ed. New York: Longman, 2003.

Gardner, John. *On Becoming a Novelist*. New York: Harper & Row, 1983.

Koch, Stephen. *The Modern Library Writer's Workshop: A Guide to the Craft of Fiction*. New York: Modern Library, 2003.

Le Guin, Ursula K. *Steering the Craft: Exercises and Discussions on Story Writing for the Lone Navigator or the Mutinous Crew*. Portland, OR: Eighth Mountain Press, 1998.

Lukeman, Noah. *The Plot Thickens: 8 Ways to Bring Fiction to Life*. New York: St. Martin's Press, 2002.

Madden, David. *Revising Fiction: A Handbook for Writers*. New York: New American Library, 1988.

Stern, Jerome H. *Making Shapely Fiction*. New York: Norton, 1991.

Short-short Stories

Allen, Roberta. *Fast Fiction: Creating Fiction in Five Minutes*. Cincinnati, OH: Story Press, 1997.

Mills, Mark, ed. *Crafting the Very Short Story: An Anthology of 100 Masterpieces*. Upper Saddle River, NJ: Prentice Hall, 2003.

Poetry

Addonizio, Kim, and Dorianne Laux. *The Poet's Companion: A Guide to the Pleasures of Writing Poetry*. New York: W.W. Norton, 1997.

Behn, Robert, and Chase Twitchell, eds. *The Practice of Poetry: Writing Exercises from Poets Who Teach*. New York: HarperPerennial, 1992.

Drake, Barbara. *Writing Poetry*. 1983. 2nd ed. Fort Worth, TX: Harcourt Brace College Publishers, 1994.

Oliver, Mary. *A Poetry Handbook*. San Diego: Harcourt Brace & Co., 1994.

Wooldridge, Susan G. *Poemcrazy: Freeing Your Life with Words*. New York: Clarkson Potter, 1996.

Form Poetry

Dacey, Philip, and David Jauss. *Strong Measures: Contemporary American Poetry in Traditional Forms*. New York: Harper & Row, 1986.

Turco, Lewis. *The Book of Forms: A Handbook of Poetics*. 3rd ed. Hanover, NH: University Press of New England, 2000.

Nonfiction

Baker, Russell. *Inventing the Truth: The Art and Craft of Memoir.* 1987. Revised and expanded edition. Boston: Houghton Mifflin, 1998.

Bly, Carol. *Beyond the Writers' Workshop: New Ways to Write Creative Nonfiction.* New York: Anchor Books, 2001.

Gornick, Vivian. *The Situation and the Story: The Art of Personal Narrative.* 2001. New edition for writers, teachers, and students. New York: Farrar, Straus, and Giroux, 2002.

Ledoux, Denis. *Turning Memories into Memoirs: A Handbook for Writing Life Stories.* Lisbon Falls, ME: Soleil Press, 1993.

Plays and Screenplays

Downs, William Missouri, and Lou Anne Wright. *Playwriting: From Formula to Form.* Fort Worth, TX: Harcourt Brace, 1998.

Field, Syd. *Screenplay.* New York: MJF Books, 1998.

Hagen, Uta, and Haskel Frankel. *Respect for Acting.* New York: Macmillan, 1973.

Horton, Andrew. *Writing the Character-Centered Screenplay.* Berkeley: University of California Press, 1994.

McKee, Robert. *Story: Substance, Structure, Style, and the Principles of Screenwriting.* New York: ReganBooks, 1997.

Sossaman, Stephen. *Writing Your First Play.* Upper Saddle River, NJ: Prentice Hall, 2000.

Stanislavsky, Konstantin. *Building a Character.* 1949. Translated by Elizabeth Reynolds Hapgood. New York: Routledge/Theater Arts Books, 1989.

Vogler, Christopher. *The Writer's Journey: Mythic Structure for Writers.* 1992. 2nd ed. Studio City, CA: M. Wiese Productions, 1998.

Voytilla, Stuart. *Myth and the Movies: Discovering the Mythic Structure of 50 Unforgettable Films.* Studio City, CA: Michael Wiese Productions, 1999.

Children's Books

Lamb, Nancy. *The Writer's Guide to Crafting Stories for Children.* Cincinnati, OH: Writer's Digest Books, 2001.

Trotman, Felicity, and Treld Pelkey Bicknell, eds. *How to Write and Illustrate Children's Books and Get Them Published.* Cincinnati, OH: Writer's Digest Books, 2000.

Self-Expression and Personal Writing.
The assignments in this textbook are designed to help you write more effectively for others. Many creative writers enjoy writing for themselves, in a journal, blog, or informal daily practice. Here are some books that can help you go further with the writing you do just for yourself.

Adams, Kathleen. *Journal to the Self: Twenty-Two Paths to Personal Growth.* New York: Warner Books, 1990.

Aronie, Nancy Slonim. *Writing from the Heart: Tapping the Power of Your Inner Voice.*
New York: Hyperion, 1998.

Badonsky, Jill Baldwin. *The Nine Modern-Day Muses (and a Bodyguard): 10 Guides to
Creative Inspiration for Artists, Writers, Lovers, and Other Mortals Wanting to Live
a Dazzling Existence.* New York: Gotham Books, 2003.

Cameron, Julie. *The Right to Write: An Invitation and Initiation into the Writing Life.*
New York: Jeremy P. Tarcher/Putnam, 1998.

Cerwinske, Laura. *Writing as a Healing Art: The Transforming Power of Self-Expression.*
New York: Perigree Book, 1999.

Goldberg, Natalie. *Writing Down the Bones: Freeing the Writer Within.* Boston: Shambhala; New York: Random House, 1986.

Heard, Georgia. *Writing toward Home: Tales and Lessons to Find Your Way.*
Portsmouth, NH: Heinemann, 1995.

Hughes, Elaine Farris. *Writing from the Inner Self.* New York: HarperCollins College
Publishers, 1994.

Joselow, Beth Baruch. *Writing without the Muse: 50 Beginning Exercises for the Creative
Writer.* Brownsville, OR: Story Line Press, 1995.

Metzger, Deena. *Writing for Your Life: A Guide and Companion to the Inner Worlds.*
San Francisco: HarperSanFrancisco, 1992.

Sher, Gail. *The Intuitive Writer: Listening to Your Own Voice.* New York: Penguin
Compass, 2002.

Jamaica Kincaid. "Girl." From *At the Bottom of the River* by Jamaica Kincaid. Copyright © 1983 Jamaica Kincaid. Reprinted by permission of Farrar, Straus & Giroux, LLC. Reprinted with permission of Farrar, Straus & Giroux, LLC.

Carolyn Kizer. "Parents' Pantoum." From *Cool, Calm & Collected: Poems, 1960–2000* by Carolyn Kizer. Copyright © 1996, 2001 by Carolyn Kizer. Reprinted with the permission of Copper Canyon Press. www.coppercanyonpress.org.

David Lehman. "Abecedarius." From *When a Woman Loves a Man* by David Lehman (Scribner's, 2005). Copyright © 2005 by David Lehman. Reprinted with permission of Writer's Representatives, LLC. All rights reserved.

Dana Levin. "Techno." From *Wedding Day* by Dana Levin. Copyright © 2005 by Dana Levin. Originally published in *The Kenyon Review*, Winter 2004. Reprinted with the permission of Copper Canyon Press. www.coppercanyonpress.org.

Timothy Liu. "In Hot Pursuit." From *Of Thee I Sing: Poems* by Timothy Liu. Copyright © 2004 by Timothy Liu. Reprinted with permission of the University of Georgia Press.

Lorraine López. "The Night Aliens in a White Van Kidnapped My Teenage Son near the Baptist Church Parking Lot." Originally published in *Sudden Stories: The MAMMOTH Book of Miniscule Fiction*, edited by Dinty W. Moore, 2003. Reprinted by permission of the author.

Thomas Lux. "The Man into Whose Yard You Should Not Hit Your Ball." From *The Street of Clocks* by Thomas Lux. Copyright © 2001 by Thomas Lux. Reprinted with permission of Houghton Mifflin Company. All rights reserved.

James Manos Jr. and David Chase. "College." Episode 3 from *The Sopranos* by HBO Properties. Copyright © HBO, a division of Time Warner Entertainment, LP. By permission of Warner Books.

Sebastian Matthews. "Buying Wine." From *Buying Wine* by Sebastian Matthews. First appeared in the *Virginia Quarterly Review* and later in *From the Fishouse*. Copyright © 2005. Reprinted with permission of the author.

Lynne McMahon. "Carpe Diem." From *The Hudson Review*, Summer 2003. Copyright © 2003. Reprinted with permission of *The Hudson Review*.

Peter Meinke. "Atomic Pantoum." From *Liquid Paper: New and Selected Poems* by Peter Meinke. Copyright © 1991. Reprinted by permission of the University of Pittsburgh Press.

Rick Moody. "Boys." From *Demonology* by Rick Moody. Copyright © 2001 Rick Moody. By permission of Little, Brown and Company.

Dinty W. Moore. "Son of Mr. Green Jeans: An Essay on Fatherhood, Alphabetically Arranged." First appeared in *Crazyhorse*, Spring 2003. Reprinted with permission of the author.

Lorrie Moore. "How to Become a Writer." From *Self-Help* by Lorrie Moore. Copyright © 1985 by M. L. Moore. Used by permission of Alfred A. Knopf, a division of Random House, Inc.

Robert Morgan. "Squirt Gun." Originally published in *The Atlantic*, Vol. 239, No. 5, June 2004, p. 80. Reprinted with permission of the author.

Peter Morris. *Pancakes.* Reprinted with permission of the author. First premiered at the 8th Annual 15-Minute Play Festival, presented by the Turnip Theatre Company in association with the American Globe Theatre, New York, NY.

Kathleen Norris. "Rain." From *Dakota: A Spiritual Geography* by Kathleen Norris. Copyright © 1993 by Kathleen Norris. Reprinted by permission of Houghton Mifflin Company. All rights reserved.

Naomi Shihab Nye. "How to Get There." From *Mint Snowball* by Naomi Shihab Nye. Copyright © 2001 by Naomi Nye. Published by Anhinga Press. Reprinted with permission of the publisher.

Sharon Olds. "Visiting My Mother's College." From *The Wellspring* by Sharon Olds. Copyright © 1996 by Sharon Olds. Used by permission of Alfred A. Knopf, a division of Random House, Inc.

Anne Panning. "Candy Cigarettes." Originally published in *Brevity: Journal of Concise Nonfiction*, Spring 2007. Reprinted with permission of the author.

Aleida Rodríguez. "My Mother in Two Photographs, among Other Things." Originally published in *Prairie Schooner* (Winter 1994, Vol. 68, No. 4). Copyright © Aleida Rodríguez. *Garden of Exile.* Reprinted with permission of the author.

Richard Rodriguez. "Proofs." From *To the Promised Land* with photographs by Ken Light. Copyright © 1988 by Richard Rodriguez. Reprinted by permission of Georges Borchardt, Inc., on behalf of Richard Rodriguez.

Akhil Sharma. "Surrounded by Sleep." Originally published in *The New Yorker*, December 13, 2001. Reprinted with permission of the author.

Jessica Shattuck. "Bodies." Originally published in *The New Yorker*, September 30, 2002. Copyright © 2002 by Jessica Shattuck. Reprinted with permission of Janklow & Nesbit Associates.

Marisa Silver. "What I Saw from Where I Stood." From *Babe in Paradise* by Marisa Silver. Copyright © 2001 Marisa Silver. Used with permission of W. W. Norton & Company, Inc.

Anna Deavere Smith. "I Was Scared." Excerpted from *Twilight: Los Angeles 1992* by Anna Deavere Smith. Copyright © Anna Deavere Smith. Used by permission of Anna Deavere Smith and the Watkins/Loomis Agency.

Gary Soto. "Everything Twice." From *Junior College* by Gary Soto. Copyright © 1997 by Gary Soto. Reprinted with permission of Chronicle Books, LLC, San Francisco. Visit www.ChronicleBooks .com.

Art Spiegelman. From *Maus I: A Survivor's Tale/My Father Bleeds History* by Art Spiegelman. Copyright © 1973, 1980, 1982, 1984, 1985, 1986 by Art Spiegelman. Used by permission of Pantheon Books, a division of Random House, Inc.

James Tate. "Consolations after an Affair." First appeared in *The Massachusetts Review*, Summer 1989, Vol. 30, No. 2. Copyright © 1989. Reprinted with permission.

Dylan Thomas. "Do Not Go Gentle into That Good Night." From *The Poems of Dylan Thomas* by Dylan Thomas. Copyright © 1952 by Dylan Thomas. Reprinted with permission of New Directions Publishing Corp.

Ellen Bryant Voigt. "Winter Field." From *Shadow of Heaven* by Ellen Bryant Voigt. Copyright © 2002 by Ellen Bryant Voigt. Used by permission of W. W. Norton & Company, Inc.

Diane Wakoski. "Sestina to the Common Glass of Beer: I Do Not Drink Beer." From *Waiting for the King of Spain* by Diane Wakoski. Copyright © 1976 by Diane Wakoski. Reprinted by permission of the author.

Ellen Doré Watson. "Ghazal." From *Ravishing Dis-Unities: Real Ghazals in English*, edited by Agha Shadhid Ali. Copyright © 2000. Reprinted with permission of Wesleyan University Press.

White, Jack. Lines from "The Nurse." Featured on the album *Get Behind Me Satan* by Jack White. Released June 7, 2005, on V2 Records. Written by Jack White/Peppermint Stripe Music. Reprinted by permission of Stacy H. Fass, on behalf of Jack White.

John Yau. "Chinese Villanelle." From *Radiant Silhouette* by John Yau. Published by Black Sparrow Press, 1989. Reprinted with permission of the author.

Ofelia Zepeda. "Her Hair Is Her Dress." From *Ocean Power: Poems of the Desert* by Ofelia Zepeda. © 1995 by Ofelia Zepeda. Reprinted with the permission of the University of Arizona Press.

INDEX

QUESTIONS TO ASK: Reading as a Writer

Focus on these aspects when examining work by peers or published writers.

1. What creates the energy in this piece of writing?
2. Why is the piece interesting? What makes me read on?
3. If I want to stop reading, if I space out, why?
4. When am I fully transported, and how does that happen?
5. How does the writer hook me?
6. What are the patterns?
7. What am I learning?
8. What am I paying attention to?
9. What am I seeing differently?
10. Where does the writer start the piece, end the piece? Why there?

Index of QUESTIONS TO ASK

Use these additional checklists to respond to other writers' work and to help you revise your own.